LIBRARY OF RELIGIOUS BIOGRA

Edited by Mark A. Noll, Nathan O. Hatch, and Allen C. Guelzo

The LIBRARY OF RELIGIOUS BIOGRAPHY is a series of original biographies on important religious figures throughout American and British history.

The authors are well-known historians, each a recognized authority in the period of religious history in which his or her subject lived and worked. Grounded in solid research of both published and archival sources, these volumes link the lives of their subjects — not always thought of as "religious" persons — to the broader cultural contexts and religious issues that surrounded them. Each volume includes a bibliographical essay and an index to serve the needs of students, teachers, and researchers.

Marked by careful scholarship yet free of footnotes and academic jargon, the books in this series are well-written narratives meant to be *read* and *enjoyed* as well as studied.

LIBRARY OF RELIGIOUS BIOGRAPHY

Assist Me to Proclaim

The Life and Hymns of Charles Wesley

John R. Tyson

William B. Eerdmans Publishing Company
Grand Rapids, Michigan / Cambridge, U.K.

Published 2007 by
Wm. B. Eerdmans Publishing Co.
2140 Oak Industrial Drive N.E., Grand Rapids, Michigan 49505 /
P.O. Box 163, Cambridge CB3 9PU U.K.

Printed in the United States of America

12 11 10 09 08 07   7 6 5 4 3 2 1

Library of Congress Cataloging-in-Publication Data

Tyson, John R.
    Assist me to proclaim: the life and hymns of Charles Wesley / John Tyson.
       p.   cm.   — (Library of religious biography)
    Includes bibliographical references and index.
    ISBN 978-0-8028-2939-9 (pbk.: alk. paper)
    1. Wesley, Charles, 1707-1788.   2. Methodist Church — Clergy — Biography.
    3. Methodist Church — Hymns.   I. Title.

BX8495.W4T97   2007
287.092 — dc22
   [B]

                                 2007029899

www.eerdmans.com

Contents

Introduction

Charles Wesley (1707-88) was born three hundred years ago this year. I first met him in the yellow brick church on the corner of Center Avenue and Eleanor Street where, as a youngster, I learned to sing his hymns. Indeed, at that time I didn't even know they were *his* hymns. I simply learned to love "O for a Thousand Tongues to Sing" (from which the title of this book is taken), "Hark! the Herald Angels Sing," "Christ the Lord Has Risen Today," and many others like them.

My second and much more sustained encounter with Charles Wesley occurred in graduate school, at Drew University. I was looking for a topic for my Ph.D. dissertation, and had more or less decided upon "The Kingdom of God in the Theology of John Wesley." My advisor, James H. Pain, told me that he was tired of reading about John Wesley, and that I should consider doing something on the "other Wesley." And so it was that I began, in 1978, to make a concerted study of Charles Wesley. I did wind up writing my Ph.D. dissertation on "Charles Wesley's Theology of the Cross," and it seems I have been thinking and writing about him ever since.

Most people who are acquainted with the work of Charles Wesley rightly think of his hymns as his most enduring legacy and contribution to contemporary Christian life. He wrote between six thousand

and nine thousand hymns and sacred poems (depending upon what one is willing to call a hymn or poem), and more than four hundred of these continue in contemporary Christian hymnals. This was an incredible body of work for any one person — and all the more so for a busy evangelist who, at the height of his ministry, was preaching as often as four times a day in as many different towns and villages.

Wesley's hymns were born of his Christian understanding of life. They were the expression of his poetical muse and his remarkable ability to see all of life as an area of God's activity and an opportunity to respond in faith and praise. Written in the context of his busy ministry and in the face of sometimes conflicting demands of his public and private lives, Wesley's hymns reflected the emotional challenges of real life. Certainly this has been a part of their staying power and continuing relevancy.

Ironically, the Wesleyan leadership, upon recording the death of Charles Wesley in their "Minutes for 1788," remarked that "His *least* praise was his talent for poetry." Perhaps it is merely his most noticeable talent in retrospect, for certainly Charles made many other worthy contributions. He should be called the co-founder of the Wesleyan or Methodist tradition. To hear Charles Wesley tell the story, it was his acts of friendship that got the so-called Oxford "Holy Club" started, and the method of spirituality learned there became the foundation of the Methodist movement. Combining a poet's way with words with vibrant emotion and a musician's voice, Charles Wesley became an able evangelist. In fact, many of his hearers preferred the preaching of the younger Wesley to that of his more famous older brother; Charles's published sermon "Awake Thou That Sleepest" became the most purchased piece of Wesleyana during the brothers' lifetime.

Charles was the first Wesley to experience evangelical conversion, on May 21, 1738, a full three days before John Wesley felt his heart "strangely warmed." It was the out-flowing of this inner transformation that made Charles an effective evangelist and energetic hymn writer. Indeed, he provided the soundtrack for the eighteenth-century transatlantic revival that visited America first through the ministry of the Wesley brothers, and then in a more effective and sustained manner through the efforts of George Whitefield. Because they arose from this important historical context and savored some of the gospel power of conversion and new birth, Charles's hymns have been great shapers of the Protestant tradition, especially in the United States.

He had a unique ability to see God at work in everything. He wrote about biblical passages and great spiritual experiences, but there are also Charles Wesley hymns about everyday events and "regular" people: being caught up in the hurry of business, the death of a friend, and much more. A happily married man (something his brother was not), Charles wrote many hymns that celebrate the simple joys of family life; behind the joy and hopes of "Hymns for Young Men" and "Hymns for Young Women," one can detect the eye of a doting father. Able to see all of human life in the presence of God, Charles wrote "Hymns on the Death of a Child" when his son John died of smallpox. He also wrote about God's work in more mundane events: as he rocked a teething child in his arms, late into the night, Charles wrote a hymn on "A Child Cutting His Teeth." The teething pain, Charles mused, must be due to original sin, and so the event gave voice to a poetical prayer for his child's deliverance from all sin and pain.

How could one person write as many as nine thousand hymns? It seems like an extravagance of incredible dimensions. It is clear that Charles Wesley did not intend to become famous from his hymn writing, since he often published his hymns jointly with his brother John, refusing to attach his own name directly to any single composition. Further, he withheld many of his compositions from publication, fearing that they would attract too much attention — being either too private or too bombastic for popular consumption. Nor did Charles make much money from his hymns. When he became engaged to Sarah Gwynne in 1749, his future mother-in-law was so doubtful of Charles Wesley's financial wherewithal that she demanded that he have at least one hundred British pounds on hand before her permission for the marriage could be given. Charles's 1749 *Hymns and Sacred Poems* was his "bride price" hymnal. It was hastily constructed out of his notebooks, some of which had been in his saddlebags for over thirteen years. He sold the hymnbook while preaching his circuit across the English countryside, raised the requisite money, and never published the hymnbook again.

Yet his hymns endured, first as weapons forged for Wesleyan evangelism, then as enduring portraits of the Christian life and expressions of praise. Like the sermon of a traveling evangelist, many of

Charles Wesley's hymns tell the whole gospel in one setting (or singing). Many beloved Wesleyan hymns were written in poetical meditation upon Wesley's favorite sermon texts, and a close study of his sermon texts and his hymn references suggests that his hymn writing was a part of his devotional life and sermon preparation.

Why has Charles Wesley not been as well remembered as he deserves to be? There are likely several contributing factors. One is simply an accident of temperament: John Wesley was more comfortably a public person, an organizer, and an extrovert, and in this Charles was his brother's opposite. Charles was a shy and retiring person, humble to a fault. He shunned the limelight with the same vigor that his brother John seemed to crave it. Indeed, refusing to publish his journal, letters, and sermons, Charles left scant reliable record of his work; in fact, he told his family not to publish his journal even after his death. His many letters and papers remained uncollected, and only now are they being put together for publication. Soon after his death, his brother John began writing an account of Charles Wesley's life, but apparently that was never finished, and the manuscript — what of it may have been written — is not extant.

A second reason that Charles slipped into a secondary role with respect to John was his family life. After he was happily married in 1749, Charles gradually shrunk back from the incessant itinerant travels that characterized his first fifteen years of ministry. His frail health and the love bonds of his family gradually caused Charles to locate first in Bristol and then (after 1771) in London, and to chiefly serve the metropolitan centers of Methodism. As he ceased to itinerate from town to town, Charles did not seem to be carrying his "fair share" of the ministerial load. This made him seem to his contemporaries to be less industrious and less committed to the evangelistic cause than was his brother John.

Charles also had a rather stormy relationship with some of the lay preachers who eventually became the leaders of the Methodist movement. Many of them were his "sons" in the gospel, and they revered him as both a father in the faith and a co-founder of the movement. But more than his brother John, he was impatient with their many ineptitudes. He sometimes fired them as quickly as John hired them. An ardent Anglican, he was scandalized by the schismatic tendencies he often saw in the lay preachers; many of them wanted to assume full ministerial status, and to separate from the Church of England. He wrote many pointed poems challenging their pridefulness. John Wesley was their sponsor and frequent defender, and his memory they cherished, but Charles, their occasional critic and inquisitor, was not so fondly and faithfully remembered.

Both John and Charles Wesley were ardent Anglicans, but Charles's sentiments ran more strongly and consistently toward the Church of England — the "old ship," as he fondly called it. In addition to fighting the schismatic tendencies of the Methodist lay preachers, he also harshly criticized his brother whenever John took a step that seemed to signal a separation from the Church of England. For more than five decades Charles struggled against the Methodists' schismatic tendencies and tried to keep the movement firmly rooted in the Church of England. In this Charles remained true to the original vision of the movement, and he clung to it tenaciously even when most of the Methodists — including his brother John — gradually came to the conclusion that practical steps towards separation were both inevitable and necessary. As the Methodists moved precisely in the direction that Charles had warned against, it was more convenient to forget him than to deal with his persistent criticism.

In the biography that follows I have tried to present a faithful picture of Charles Wesley. I have tried to press behind the lengthening shadow of his more famous and more domineering elder brother. I have tried to point to those ways in which the younger Wesley made his own unique contributions to the Christian faith, to see him as significant in his own right. While I make no secret of the fact that I think Wesley was a remarkable man, and in some ways an exemplary practitioner of his faith, it is also clear that he was not without his faults. Certainly he was well aware of his faults, and frequently lamented at least some of them. He would probably want us to learn as much or more about the life of faith from his faults and failures as we might from his successes.

There are always quite a few people to thank at the outset of a work like this. I need to thank the effective staff at the Methodist Archives, U.K., and John Rylands University Library of Manchester. David Riley, John Tuck, and most recently Peter Nockles and Gareth Lloyd supplied me with copies of Charles Wesley's manuscripts. I must thank S. H. Mayor and his successors at the Cheshunt Foundation, Westminster College, Cambridge University, for copies of much of the correspondence between Charles Wesley and Lady Huntingdon. I thank Ken Rowe, formerly of the Methodist Archives, U.S., for use of their holdings at Drew University. Dick Heitzenrater and Randy Maddox were gracious dialogue partners with me about this project when I spent June 2006 with them at Duke University participating in their Wesley summer research seminar. I am grateful for the opportunity to use the important Frank Baker Collection of Wesleyana materials and the research facilities of the Duke Divinity School Library and Perkins Library at Duke University. I thank Mark Noll for his support and enthusiasm for this project and David Bratt for his editorial assistance in bringing it to fruition. Finally, I thank my wife, Jill, for her extraordinary care in preparing the index.

1 Beginnings

Charles Wesley, the eighteenth child of Samuel and Susanna Annesley Wesley, was born prematurely. John Whitehead, physician of his final years and first biographer, reported that "he appeared dead rather than alive when he was born. He did not cry, nor open his eyes, and was kept wrapt up in soft wool until the time when he should have been born according to usual course of nature, and then he opened his eyes and cried." It was an inauspicious beginning for a person who would subsequently give voice to so many people down through the centuries.

The England into which Charles Wesley was born was a tumultuous place, rife with recent religious, political, economic, and social upheavals. In the previous century the Puritans — Reformed Protestants who dissented against the high-church style and catholic structures of the Church of England — had taken over the government through a bloody civil war (1642-51) and executed the monarch, King Charles I. After a decade of dictatorship under Oliver Cromwell the Puritans were overthrown and the monarchy was reinstated under Charles II (1660). The Dissenters, who had controlled the government under the Puritan Protectorate, were now out of power and out of favor. As an obvious reaction against the Puritans and their theology, the tenor of

Anglicanism changed and the leading "divines" of the Restoration era (such as Thomas Ken and William Laud) were Arminians and high churchmen.

Samuel Wesley Sr., the father of Charles Wesley, was born early in the Restoration era. A man of action and integrity, Samuel Wesley resigned his place and his annual scholarship among the Dissenters and walked all the way to Oxford, where he enrolled at Exeter College as a "poor scholar." He functioned as a "servitor," which means he sustained himself financially by waiting upon wealthy students. He also published a small book of poems, entitled *Maggots: or Poems on Several Subjects never before Handled* (1685). The unusual title of the work is explained in a few lines on the first page of the work:

> In his own defense the author writes
> Because when this foul maggot bites
> He ne'er can rest in quiet:
> Which makes him make so sad a face
> He'd beg your worship or your grace
> Unsight, unseen, to buy it.

Since the Church of England was "established" by law as the state church, the monarch was deemed the "Head of the Church of Christ on earth." This meant that religion and politics, like church and state, were deeply interwoven. The religious preference of the English monarchs became a matter of extreme importance for their entire empire, and for the ecclesiastical structure that held it together from within. When "the Glorious Revolution" (1688-89) deposed King James II, a Stewart, from Scotland, for attempting to reinstate Roman Catholicism, William and Mary ruled England, because she was the Protestant daughter of James II. They were succeeded by Queen Anne, a Protestant sister of Mary. During her reign, when Charles Wesley and his brother John were born, Protestantism was even more firmly established as England's national religion. After the death of Queen Anne in 1714, England faced another crisis in the royal succession. Since Anne left no direct heir, the crown would go to one of her cousins. The question arose whether to turn to Scotland and the Roman Catholic Stewarts or to Germany and the Protestant Hanovers. Because the Anglican Church and English state were so deeply entwined, there could be no going back to Catholicism, and so — despite popular outcry to the contrary — the German-speaking Georges (I, II, III) would rule England in the eighteenth century. The supporters of the Stewart monarchy — called "Jacobites," from the Latin *Jacobus* for James — were left smoldering in the hinterlands, where they plotted rebellion. It was a feat they nearly accomplished in 1745 under the leadership of "Bonnie Prince Charlie" (Charles Edward Stewart, the Jacobite Prince of Wales), when 15,000 Scottish and French troops invaded England.

Because of the legal establishment of the Church of England, the clergy and their churches were supported by local levies and taxes as well as by parish funds. This meant that clergy were not directly dependent upon the good will of people they served, and this process fostered a certain mutual disdain in pulpit and pew. The clergy had to follow the lead of their bishops, who in turn were appointed by the crown. So it was that Samuel Wesley Sr. was appointed to the living at Epworth through the benevolence of Queen Mary. He may have come to her attention when in 1693 he dedicated his heroic poem on "The Life of Christ" to her.

The early eighteenth century into which Charles Wesley was born was a prosperous time for some. The population was growing slowly, but commerce was growing at a faster rate. Increased trade created greater demand for home-based industries like carding and spinning. Nascent manufacturing ventures began to emerge through "the domestic system" of commercial and manufacturing villages. But the industrial revolution was still half a century away; the power loom of the factory had not yet superseded the handloom of the cottage. With the population remaining fairly constant, cheap corn and grain prices kept food within the reach of artisans, cottagers, and laborers. But cheap grain prices were not good news for the small farmer. Those who owned significant tracts of land, or who had a skill and the means of production had ample opportunity for economic growth. But this prosperous picture fades significantly when one considers the large number of people who were not landholders or skilled artisans. Demographics produced by the economist Gregory King, based on statistics from the year 1688, suggest that more than half of the nation's population was becoming increasingly poorer in the midst of this period of economic expansion. When John and Charles would meet and minister to these people, they would describe them as "the working poor."

"I found some in their cells, others in their garretts," John wrote in 1753, "half starved with cold and hunger added to weakness and pain. But I found none of them unemployed who was able to crawl about the room. So wickedly, so devilishly false, is that common objection: 'they are poor because they are idle.'"

The religious climate of the early eighteenth century was quite diverse. Religious opinion ranged from the rational religion of Deism and the fashionable skepticism of the universities on the one hand to the traditional folk superstitions of the rural towns and villages on the other. Frequently it contained a combination of both extremes. Even John Wesley would be given to investigating the exploits of "old Jeffrey," the family ghost who reputedly haunted the Epworth manse, though his brother Charles would remain unconvinced.

John Locke's *Essay on Human Understanding* (1690) set the intellectual tone for most of the next century by dispatching the notion of innate ideas and replacing it with an emphasis upon what can be known reasonably, through a person's five senses. It was not long till John Toland applied reason directly to religion, debunking supernaturalism in his *Christianity Not Mysterious* (1696). Other popular works, like Matthew Tindal's *Christianity as Old as the Creation* (1730) — which was sometimes called "the Deists' Bible" — epitomized the naturalistic bent of academic religion. Latitudinarianism was common in the religious establishment, and it bred an indifferent kind of religious toleration among the intellectual elite; novelist Daniel Defoe reflected it well when he wrote, "Each man goes his own byway to heaven." The widely read sermons of Archbishop Tillotson (1630-94) epitomized the moderate and moralistic theological tone of the period.

The Anglican communion was favored by the landed gentry, and to a significant degree the church's policies and practices reflected the concerns of the ruling class. This posture bred apathy and disinterest among the commoners, many of whom felt as disenfranchised in the Church of England as they were in politics and Parliament. Merchants, artisans, and workers in the emerging industrial centers turned increasingly toward the Dissenting churches, which seemed to reflect more of their own interests. The proliferation of private devotional groups and religious societies, which began around 1678 through the efforts of men like Anthony Horneck, suggests that there were pockets of religious vitality throughout the land. Hence Voltaire, who visited from 1726-29, is said to have found England a land of a hundred sects — but only one sauce.

In the spring of 1697 Samuel and Susanna Wesley, along with their six children, moved from South Ormsby to the distant and more populous parish of Epworth. Epworth was a market town of roughly two thousand people on the Isle of Axholme. It was located in the marshy "fens" region, which was dotted with swamps and bogs. While many of the swamps had been drained, farming was not easy, and many people lived a hand-to-mouth existence that was often supplemented by smuggling and other clandestine ventures. Samuel Wesley's high-church liturgies, academic proclivities, and loyalist Tory politics were a complete mismatch for those of his illiterate parishioners. He was not warmly received, and his ministry was not widely appreciated. Furthermore, Wesley was soon deeply in debt because of the costs associated with relocating his family as well as furnishing the house and farm. Animosity against him continued to the degree that his cash crop of flax mysteriously burned one year. Then the chaplaincy of the military regiment — which had been another source of supplemental income — was suddenly withdrawn. In 1709 his parsonage was destroyed by fire. Charles Wesley, who was a babe in arms at the time, was carried to safety, and John Wesley, a small boy, was rescued from the flames, providentially saved — as his mother often reminded him — like a "brand plucked from the burning."

If the day-to-day struggle against grinding poverty was one of the constant realities of life in the Epworth manse, dealing with the ongoing needs of a burgeoning family was another. The family had the benefit of servants and wet nurses for the infants — utter necessities given the fact that Susanna was pregnant for twenty-one of the first twenty-four years of their marriage. Nineteen pregnancies resulted in ten living children being born to Samuel and Susanna; the sadness associated with infant mortality was another trying aspect of their family life. Three of their ten surviving children were boys, and seven were girls.

Life in the Epworth manse was regulated by Susanna Wesley's management and instruction. Her approach to parenting, as she described it, was simple: "the children were always put into a regular method of living, in such things as they were capable of, from their birth; as in dressing, undressing, changing their linen, &c." Her own Puritan rearing showed through in her determination to bend her children's will to her own, and in that process she prepared them to follow God's will: "I insist," she wrote, "upon conquering the will of children betimes because it is the only strong and rational foundation of a religious education. . . . Heaven or hell depends on this alone. So that the parent who studies to subdue it in his child works together with God in the renewing and saving of a soul." In tending to her children's religious instruction, Susanna was similarly firm: "The children of this family were taught, as soon as they could speak, the Lord's Prayer, which they were made to say at rising and at bed-time constantly; to which, as they grew bigger, were added a short prayer for their parents, and some collects, a short catechism, and some portion of Scripture, as their memories could bear." Her children were also raised to honor the Sabbath and participate in family devotions "before they could speak well or go [to church]. They were as soon taught to be still at family prayers, and to ask a blessing immediately after, which they used to do by signs, before they could kneel or speak."

Education for the Wesley children took place at home. Susanna was primary schoolteacher to her burgeoning brood. For most of them, school started at the age of five, at which time they were expected to learn their letters and begin reading. School hours in the Wesley home were nine in the morning until noon, and two until five in the afternoon. Mrs. Wesley's main textbook was the Bible, and all of her children learned to read it well. She also set aside part of her busy days to have searching, spiritual conversations with each child; Charles's special time with his mother came on Saturday nights. From their father the Wesley boys, and a few of the girls, learned classical literature and languages, logic, and theology. But most important of all, perhaps, they learned his dedication to scholarship in the midst of his busy parish work. Much of Samuel Sr.'s academic writing took the form of poetry. Indeed, the Wesleys were a family of poets; the father, all three sons, and at least one daughter wrote and published poems.

In personality and temperament, Charles Wesley was more his father's son than his mother's. He was impetuous, short-tempered, and given to outbursts of feeling. The unnamed editor of the 1816 edition of his sermons recalled, "Charles was full of sensibility and fire; his patience and meekness were neither the effect of temperament or reason, but of divine principles." Like his father, Charles Wesley was high-spirited and emotional; indeed, his hymns give ample witness to the fact that he could hit the whole scale of human emotions. Charles was also warm and personable, perhaps in ways his more measured brother was not. John Gambold, Charles's friend and associate from student days at Oxford, remembered him as "a man made for friendship; who, by his cheerfulness and vivacity, would refresh his friend's heart; with attentive consideration, would enter into and settle all his concerns; so far as he was able, would do anything for him, great or small; and by a habit of openness and freedom, leave no room for misunderstanding." But with Charles's personal warmth there occasionally also came some stronger heat, and when Charles was "all off the hooks," as John Wesley once wrote, one might as well "blow against the wind as try to reason with him."

Charles also had a meekness and unfeigned humility about him that was remarkable and attractive. His sermon editor observed, "His most striking excellence was humility; it extended to his talents as well as virtues; he not only acknowledged and pointed out but *delighted* in the superiority of another, and if there ever was a human being who disliked power, avoided pre-eminence, and shrunk from praise, it was Charles Wesley." He was possessed of the compliance and desire to please others that one often observes in a middle child in the family birth order; this coupled with his Christian humility frequently made Charles subject to others' (often his brothers') influence. And yet, as we shall also see, Charles could and did often follow his own course, whether with respect to marriage and the itinerant ministry, the doctrine of Christian perfection, managing the Methodist lay preachers, or the Methodists' relationship to the Church of England. In each of these, and many other instances, Charles Wesley could and did strike out in his own direction.

When he was eight years old Charles Wesley left the Epworth manse and went to live with his eldest brother, Samuel. In their high-church principles and ardent Anglicanism, as well as in their inclination toward scholarly activity and poetry, Samuel Sr. and Samuel Jr. were very similar. The two Samuels molded Charles's staunch Anglicanism, his love for the classics, and his poetical muse.

Samuel had gone to Westminster as a student in 1704, become a King's Scholar in 1707, and been elected to Oxford in 1711. After graduation he returned to Westminster as an usher. He provided a home and financial support for his youngest brother from the time Charles was eight until he was thirteen. These were formative years for Charles, and Samuel Jr.'s academic guidance paid big dividends, as Charles became captain of his school (over more than 400 boys) and a King's Scholar himself. The latter was an especially competitive and lucrative academic award, since it meant that Charles's subsequent educational costs would be covered by a scholarship. While Charles was at Westminster School he refused the offer of a distant and wealthy Irish relative, Garret Wesley, to become his ward and heir. Reflecting the Wesley family's contempt for wealth and power, John Wesley described Charles's decision as "a fair escape." Also while at Westminster, Charles defended and befriended a smaller boy, named William Murray, who was often bullied because of his thick Scottish brogue. In later life, Murray became Chief Justice of England and Earl of Mansfield. The two renewed their friendship in later years while living near each other in London.

In the fall of 1727, Charles left Westminster School for prestigious Christ Church College at Oxford University. Charles's letters from this period frequently mention his pressing financial needs. To his brother John, serving as their father's curate at Wroot, Charles wrote, "Tis in the power of a few Epworth or Wroot guineas and clothes to give things the favourable turn, and make a gentleman of me. Come money, then, and quickly, to rescue me from my melancholy maxim, *ex nihilo nihil fit* — I can't possibly 'save nothing, where there is nothing to save.'" In another letter to brother John he drew a line of connection between his poverty and the spiritual and academic lethargy he was feeling, calling his shortcomings in resources "great temptations to dullness."

In later reflections, Charles would consider his first year of college "lost in diversions." Indeed, freed from the structure and strictures of Epworth and Westminster, the youngest Wesley son went through a "moratorium" period, during which he seemed to throw off some of his earlier training. He relished breathing the "free though sharp air" of Christ Church, and he resisted what he termed "the gloomy and mechanical piety" of the place. He showed significant proclivities at the popular diversions, like cards, theater, music, and dancing. Charles's success at these things aroused significant concern back at Epworth, and his brother John was dispatched to make a lightning visit to Oxford for an on-site investigation. He described his brother's frame of mind in this way: "He pursued his studies diligently, and led a regular, harmless life; but if I spoke to him about religion he would warmly answer, 'What! Would you have me be a saint all at once?' and would hear no more." That a heated quarrel erupted between the brothers is suggested by Charles's subsequent resolve not to quarrel again: "I very think, dear brother," he wrote to John on January 22, 1729, "I shall never quarrel with *you* again till I do with my religion, and that I may never do *that* I am not ashamed to desire your prayers."

One of Charles's dalliances was with the stage, and there he met a number of actresses, including one named Molly, who saw in young Charles Wesley stability and propriety. One of Charles's letters to brother John confided that "but for my strange college dullness Molly *might* have made something of me." Others would not be, and perhaps were not, so slow to respond as he was to actresses' amorous advances, but "hints were *lost* upon so dull, stupid fellow as I was; and as such no doubt I have been since sufficiently laughed at." After resolving not to see Molly again, he showed a vicious wit in writing to his brother, "I can't imagine, by the by, why you should mistrust her abilities; she's never the less qualified for the stage for being a whore, sure!"

John's concerned visit to Charles was reinforced by a directive from the Vice Chancellor of the university, issued "with the consent of the Heads of Houses and Proctors," ordering "the several tutors of each college and hall in the university that they discharge their duty by a double diligence in informing their respective pupils in their Christian duty, as in explaining to them the *Articles of Religion* which they profess and are often called upon to scribe to, in recommending to them the frequent and careful reading of the Scriptures and such other books as may serve more effectually to promote Christianity, sound principles, and orthodox faith. " Charles enclosed a copy of this directive in one of his letters to John. Both brothers no doubt thought it a significant development, since it corresponded exactly with the Oxford Methodists' attempts to reform themselves and their fellow students. When Charles subsequently described his religious awakening during this period, he linked it to observing "the method of study prescribed by the University."

On January 5, 1729, Charles wrote to John describing how diffi-

9

cult it was for him to maintain his religious equilibrium while at college. "My standing *here* is so very slippery," he wrote, "no wonder I long to shift my ground. Christ Church is certainly the worst place in the world to begin a reformation in; a man stands a very fair chance of being laughed out of his religion at his first setting out, in a place where 'tis scandalous to have any [religion] at all." By the time he wrote John again, on January 22, Charles intimated that he hoped not to "relapse into my former state of insensibility." He was also beginning to doubt his ability as a student, especially as compared to his brothers' stunning success at the university. Charles did not think he was measuring up well: "I'm very *desirous* of knowledge, but can't *bear* the drudgery of coming at it near so well as you could. In reading anything difficult I'm bewildered in much shorter time than I believe you used to be at your first setting out. My head will by no means keep pace with my heart, and I'm afraid I shan't reconcile it in haste to the extraordinary business of thinking." This struggle in reconciling his "head" and his "heart" would be one of Charles Wesley's ongoing challenges.

Life at college was punctuated by pleasant visits to the home of the Wesleys' friend and colleague, Robert Kirkham, in Stanton. Kirkham's sisters, and their friends Mary Pendarves and Anne Granville, offered feminine fellowship, which the Wesleys enjoyed. Their activities ran the whole gamut of what was available to "proper" young people in that day: sprightly intellectual discussion, reading devotional books and partaking in spiritual conversation, parlor games, music, dancing, picnics, and long walks in the countryside. In the closeness of this little group, they adopted exotic sounding classical nicknames: Sally Kirkham was "Varanese," Mary Pendarves, "Aspasia," John Wesley, "Cyrus," Anne Granville, "Selima," and Charles Wesley was "Araspes." Both Wesley brothers seemed to be infatuated with "Varanese," but she was a particular favorite of John Wesley.

In a subsequent autobiographical letter Charles summarized the events of his second year at college: "The next [year] I set myself to study. Diligence led me into serious thinking. I went to the weekly sacrament, and persuaded two or three young scholars to accompany me, and to observe the method of study prescribed by the University. This gained me the harmless nickname of Methodist." This statement has led some biographers to argue that Charles Wesley was the "first

Methodist." But this is to miss the point of Wesley's statement, which was simply to explain the source of the term "Methodist." Still, something new was going on: Charles had begun a small group among his fellow students that met at Christ Church. "Providence," he wrote on May 5, 1729, "has at present put it in my power to do some good. I have a modest humble, well-disposed youth living next to me, and I have been (I thank God!) somewhat instrumental in keeping him so."

Robert Kirkham of Merton, and John Gambold, of Christ Church, were among the members of Charles's small group. Gambold, who described Charles Wesley as a "man made for friendship," seemed to be making steady progress in his spiritual growth in the midst of the persecution that rained down upon the "Methodists": "He is already content to live without any company but Bob [Kirkham]'s and mine. . . . he durst not receive the sacrament but at the usual times for fear of being laughed at. I have persuaded him to neglect censure on a religious account . . . by convincing him of the duty of frequent communicating I have prevailed on both of us to receive once a week." Kirkham's diligence was an utter contrast to Gambold's: "the less pains, he thinks, the better. I'm not uncharitable in my opinion; you can't imagine how wretchedly lazy he is, and how small a share either of learning or piety will content him: four hours a day he *will* spare for study out of his diversions, not so many hours for diversion out of his studies! What an excellent inverter!"

Describing his own spiritual state in this same letter, Charles complained of a spiritual "coldness," which he was willing to interpret as the "natural and just consequence of my past life." As he explained, "One who like myself has for almost thirteen years been utterly inattentive at public prayers can't expect to find there that warmth he has never known at his first seeking; he must knock oftener than once before 'tis opened to him; and this is (I think) in some measure answerable for a heartlessness of which he himself is the cause." Still, his little group began to grow.

Charles Wesley could be considered spiritually awakened at this point, and he was deeply committed to his own spiritual improvement, but his piety was still full of "duty." "I resolve," he wrote, "that my falling short of my duty in one particular shan't discourage me from vigorously prosecuting it in the rest." But he was utterly determined to succeed in the task of his own religious reformation. "I look upon this coldness as a trial," he wrote, "and that unless I sink under it t'will in the end greatly contribute to my advantage. I *must,* I *will,* in spite of nature and the devil, take pains. While my strength lasts I *will* put it to the utmost stretch." Charles even tried to deny himself the pleasant feminine fellowship of Stanton, fearing that it would impede his spiritual reformation. "I'm so far from expecting but small satisfaction at Stanton," he wrote to John, "all I fear is meeting too much. Indeed I durst on no account trust myself there without you, for as I take it strong pleasure would be dangerous to one in my unconfirmed condition."

It appears that John Wesley had recommended that his younger brother begin keeping a diary. Spiritual journals were a part of the practice of the Oxford Methodists, and we know quite a bit about their activities and inclinations because of the diaries of Oxford Methodists such as John Wesley, Benjamin Ingham, and George Whitefield. These diaries recorded, in minute detail, the prayers, practices, spiritual impressions, temptations, and feelings of the Oxford Methodists — often at fifteen-minute intervals. These diaries were composed in a "cipher" that had been invented by John Wesley, so that the diary entries could be quickly written in a standard form and yet remain confidential. In his letter of January 22, 1729, Charles told his brother, "I would willingly write a diary of my actions, but don't know how to go about it. What particulars am I to take notice of? Am I to give my thoughts and words besides? Must not I take account of my progress in learning as well as religion? What cipher can I make use of? If you would direct me to the same or a like method with your own, I would gladly follow it, for I'm fully convinced of the usefulness of such an undertaking." Benjamin Ingham subsequently reported in his diary that Charles Wesley had taught him how to keep a diary. Unfortunately, Charles's Oxford diary is not extant, but the diaries of several other Oxford Methodists have survived, and these give a fairly detailed picture of life in the "Holy Club."

In the autumn of 1729 John Wesley resumed his residence at Lincoln College and, as Charles put it, "came to our assistance." "We then proceeded regularly in our studies," he added, "and in doing what good we could to the bodies and souls of men." While Charles had the kind of winsome personality to be able to form a devotional group, he was willing to defer to John's leadership and organizational skills for its continuation and development.

Earlier that year Charles had received his B.A. degree at Christ Church and secured a position as a tutor. His father, the rector of Epworth, urged him to take advantage of this new opportunity to do good and to alleviate his financial struggles by taking on more students. Charles followed his father's advice, and tried with varying degrees of success to instill his newly acquired method of piety in his pupils. Charles's attempts at interesting his pupils in frequent communion were sometimes undone by other college officials: "Another of them [his students] may do me good, though I can do him little. Our Censor has put it past my power from the time that he dissuaded him from weekly communion, monthly, as he assured him, being sufficient. One step farther indeed the young man has taken, and receives it now but thrice a year. Instead of an Enthusiast (as it was feared I should make him) I have got a hopeful young heathen as my pupil." Charles subsequently added fasting to the religious duties that he practiced and sought to inculcate in his students. As he wrote to his brother Samuel in February 1733, "Since my last [letter] I met with a remarkable clause in our Statutes which not only justifies, but I think requires, my pressing the duty of fasting on my pupils."

The changes that the Holy Club had inspired in Charles were also apparent to the eldest Wesley brother. When Charles spent the summer of 1729 with Samuel and his family, he confided in a letter to John: "They wonder here I'm so strangely dull (as indeed mirth and I have shook hands and parted) and at the same time pay me the compliment of saying I grow extremely like you." This "compliment" was clearly not intended as such from brother Samuel, who had shaped young Charles Wesley in his own image. But at least Charles had become a model student. Indeed, John Wesley's Oxford diaries from this period describe Charles as a man who "merits emulation — in meekness, tenderness, and learning." Each of these qualities would become a hallmark of Charles Wesley.

The little company of Oxford Methodists garnered enough public notice to have earned themselves an interesting series of nicknames. They were called "the Sacramentarians," because they stressed the duty of frequent (they sometimes said "constant") communion. Others termed them "Enthusiasts," which carried connotations of religious fanaticism. Some of their student colleagues called the Oxford Methodists "Supererogation-men," which suggested they were doing

13

much more than moderate religion required of them, hoping to win divine approval. Indeed, the Oxford Methodists prayed often, fasted, gave alms to the poor out of their own meager incomes, and visited people in prison and in the work houses; to those for whom Christianity amounted to attending weekly church services prescribed by their colleges, the Methodists seemed to be going way overboard in their religious observances. They were viewed as being "righteous overmuch," which made them the frequent butt of ridicule and the source of suspicion for some. In fact, one of the early critics of the Methodist movement, Joseph Trapp, preached against them from the text "Be not righteous overmuch" (Ecclesiastes 7:16). He subsequently published a series of highly critical sermons against the Methodists under the title *The Nature, Folly, Sin and Danger of Being Righteous Overmuch* (1739). Their regular meeting for Bible study and their willingness to point to Bible passages as a basis for their actions and beliefs earned the Oxford Methodists the nickname "Bible-moths," which implied that they were literally devouring their Bibles, like moths feeding on wool. Perhaps it was their willingness to reprove more lax students from the standpoint of Scripture that earned them the epitaph of "Bible-bigots." By 1731 the collection of Oxford Methodists were frequently called "The Holy Club," and this title aptly summarized the central concern of the Methodist movement: to find that holiness "without which one shall not see God." A published critique of the Oxford Methodists, which appeared in *Fog's Weekly Journal* in 1732, described them as "the sons of sorrow," because their strict religious regiment, it was suggested, caused the illness and subsequent death of one of their members, young William Morgan.

To call this little company a "club," however, may imply a more formal organization and structure than the Oxford Methodists actually had. We think of clubs having qualifications for membership, elected officers, designated meeting days, meeting rooms, dues and so forth, and the Oxford Methodists had none of these. In fact, they were not even organized into one single, small group. The Oxford diary of Benjamin Ingham, for example, describes the function of at least four small groups, each of which could be called "the Holy Club." By 1731 there was a group of three to six young men meeting in John Wesley's rooms in Lincoln College; one was Charles Wesley, but the identity of the others varied significantly. Charles Wesley also led a similar group at Christ Church; several Christ Church students participated in that group, as did Benjamin Ingham, who was a student at Queens. Ingham also led a separate small group at Queens College. The Oxford diaries mention a fourth group, which met in town and was led by a certain "Miss Potts." These people received their spiritual direction either directly or indirectly from John and Charles Wesley, but the groups were more fluid and less formal than we might imagine. Nor did John and Charles Wesley invent this notion of using small student groups as an aid to Christian devotion. Henry Scougal, the author of the formative book *The Life of God in the Soul of Man*, had been president of a religious society during his student days in the 1660s. And Samuel Wesley Sr., their father, had been a member of a similar group at Oxford. He is said to have told John, "If you are the father of the Holy Club, then I am its grandfather."

The religious regimen of the Oxford Methodists was derived largely from their direct reading and literal application of the Bible — especially the Greek New Testament. Acts 2:42-45 was a passage that would continue to be significant as John and Charles Wesley subsequently developed the patterns and practices of the Methodist movement: "And they continued steadfastly in the apostles' doctrine and fellowship, and in breaking of bread, and in prayer. And fear came upon every soul: and many wonders and signs were done by the apostles. And all that believed were together, and had all things in common; and sold their possessions and goods, and parted them to all men, as every man had need." The Oxford Methodists intended to recapture the spiritual experience and vitality of the early church by emulating its beliefs and practices. Their scripture study was supplemented by reading the early Church Fathers — most especially the Eastern Church Fathers — whose understanding of sanctification as perfect love or Christian perfection would become attractive to the Wesleys.

Their "method" also included reading devotional classics. In June 1725 John and his mother Susanna corresponded about his reading *The Imitation of Christ* by Thomas à Kempis. He subsequently credited this book with teaching him the importance of inward religion: "the nature and extent of inward religion, the religion of the heart, now appeared to me in a stronger light than it ever had done before." The same work also stressed purity of heart, which would become one of the Methodists' main concerns. As John recalled, "I saw that giving even all my life to God (supposing it possible to do this and go no farther) would profit me nothing, unless I gave my heart, yea, all my heart to Him. I saw that 'simplicity of intention' and purity of affection, one design in all we speak or do, and one desire ruling all our tempers, and indeed the 'wings of the soul.' . . ." Bishop Jeremy Taylor was another favorite author among the Oxford Methodists. Taylor's influence upon John Wesley can be seen in Wesley's attempt to give a strict account of his time in his detailed diaries: "It was in pursuance of an advice given by Bp. Taylor, in his *Rules for Holy Living and Holy Dying,* about fifteen years ago, I began to take more exact account than I had before, on the manner wherein I spent my time, writing down how I had employed every hour."

William Law, a mystic and nonconformist with respect to the Anglican Establishment, was the contemporary writer who had the most impact upon the Oxford Methodists. His *Serious Call to a Devout and Holy Life* appeared in 1728, the same year that marked the inception of the Methodist "Holy Club." In his writing Law urged people who were interested in true and vital religion to "unite themselves into little societies professing voluntary poverty, virginity, retirement, and devotion, living upon bare necessities, that some might be relieved by their charities and all be blessed with their prayers and benefitted by their example." John Wesley reported that reading Law's *A Serious Call to a Devout and Holy Life* and his *Christian Perfection* (1726) convinced him, "more than ever, of the absolute impossibility of being half a Christian." Law became, as Charles later wrote in his journal, "like an Oracle to us." The Wesleys visited Law's home in nearby Putney, where they had searching conversations about holiness and Christian spirituality. Under William Law's tutelage the Wesleys caught a vision of Christian perfection and a desire for purity of heart that remained with them for the rest of their lives, but they eventually parted ways with their former mentor. Charles Wesley later explained, from the perspective of his post-conversion life in Christ, that he saw a fundamental error in Law's approach to salvation. "I told him," Charles remembered, "he was my school master to bring me to Christ; but the reason I did not come sooner to Him, was my seeking to be sanctified before I was justified." It was only in the context of Charles's "new birth" that he came to see that holiness could only truly come to a person who had first experienced justification by faith alone.

The informal meetings of the Oxford Methodists continued throughout this period, and a few new faces were added to the group. By 1732 George Whitefield had begun to meet with them as well. Like the Wesleys, Whitefield had been deeply affected by reading William Law's *Serious Call to a Devout and Holy Life* and *Christian Perfection.* These books began a period of heightened religious devotion in young Whitefield, and it was at this point that the Oxford Methodists came to his attention: "I now began to pray and sing psalms twice every day, besides morning and evening, and to fast every Friday and to receive the sacrament at a parish church near our College, and at the castle, where the despised Methodists used to receive once a month." It was to Charles Wesley that Whitefield sent word that a poor woman, in one of the work houses, had attempted suicide, offering that news to him as an opportunity for ministry. Wesley invited Whitefield to breakfast the next day, and they had, as Whitefield described it, "one of the most profitable visits I ever made in my life." Charles's conversation and demeanor in that visit caused Whitefield to describe him as "a wise winner of souls."

In a subsequent meeting, Charles loaned Whitefield a book that changed his life: Henry Scougal's *The Life of God in the Soul of Man.* As Whitefield later recalled, "though I had fasted, watched and prayed, and received the sacrament so long, yet I never knew what true religion was, till God sent me that excellent treatise by the hands of my never-to-be-forgotten friend." The "true religion" Whitefield discovered in this book was not the religion of duty and good works that was so prevalent in the church of his day. "At my first reading it," he reported, "I wondered what the author meant by saying, 'that some falsely placed religion in going to church, doing hurt to no one, being constant in the duties of the [prayer] closet, and now and then reaching out their hands to give alms to their poor neighbours.' Alas! thought I, if this be not religion, what is?" He did not have to wait long for his rhetorical question to be answered, for "God soon showed me: for in reading a few lines further, that 'true religion was an union of the soul with God, and Christ formed within us,' a ray of divine light was instantaneously darted in upon my soul; and from that moment, but not until then, did I know that I must be a new creature." Charles Wesley took the younger Whitefield under his care and helped him find the courage to attend church, despite the public derision he received for it: "Mr. Charles Wesley," George Whitefield wrote, "whom I must always mention with the greatest deference and respect, walked with me, in order to confirm me, from the church even to the College. I confess, to my shame, I would gladly have excused him; and the next day, going to his room, one of our Fellows passing by, I was ashamed to be seen to knock at his door." In this instance Whitefield likened himself to Nicodemus, who for fear of ridicule or harming his reputation came to visit Jesus by night. But eventually his courage grew. "I confessed the Methodists more and more publically every day. I walked openly with them, and chose rather to bear contempt with those people of God than to enjoy the applause of almost-Christians for a season."

In 1733 Charles Wesley completed his master's degree, and he seemed destined for an academic career at Oxford. But on April 25, 1735, his father died. Charles was on hand, along with most of the family, for his father's passing. Samuel Wesley Jr. was not able to be in attendance, and Charles wrote him a lengthy account of their father's last days. "The fear of death he had entirely conquered," Charles wrote, "and at last gave up his latest human desires, of finishing [his commentary on] Job, paying his debts, and seeing you." Charles also reported some prophetic words from the father to his youngest son. "He often laid his hand upon my head, and said, 'Be steady.' 'The Christian faith will surely revive in this kingdom. You shall see it, though I shall not.'"

2 An American Adventure

The death of Samuel Wesley Sr. in 1735 left his family in a state of utter turmoil. Not only were they racked by the grief that accompanied the passing of their revered spouse and father, but they were also riddled with uncertainty about the future care of Susanna Wesley and the disposition of the Epworth manse. Samuel Sr. had repeatedly pressed his son John to apply for the Epworth living, but John had resisted, arguing that he could do more good to himself and others by remaining at Oxford, and even providing his father with twenty-six specific reasons he should stay. John's brother Samuel also weighed in on his father's side, but to no lasting avail — though John did serve as his father's substitute during his final illness and a few months afterward. Charles Wesley seems to have escaped both his father's and eldest brother's pressure and pointed letters about the disposition of the Epworth living because he was not ordained and had no pastoral experience. It may have also been tacitly understood that Charles's emotional makeup and creative personality were not well suited to the rigors of rural parish life.

Samuel Sr., who was perennially in debt during his life, left debts of nearly £100 in death. His creditors seized the livestock from the Wesleys' farm and some of their better home furnishings to pay off his accounts. John Wesley remained fixed in his resolve not to take up his father's mantle, and the Epworth living was soon given to another. After the settling of the rector's estate, Susanna went to live with her daughter Emily in Gainsborough.

So with the disposal of the Epworth living and the settling of their father's estate, the future of John and Charles Wesley seemed to be linked to the lively academic life at Oxford. But such tranquility was short-lived. Within six months they found themselves on board a vessel named the *Simmonds* making the dangerous transatlantic crossing to undertake missionary work in Georgia.

Missionary zeal was a part of the Wesleys' family inheritance. Both grandfathers of John and Charles had intended to travel to America, and their father — who corresponded with James Oglethorpe, the first governor of the colony, about his publications and other religious matters — would have gone to Georgia had he been a younger man when the colony began. In a letter of November 7, 1734, he told Oglethorpe, "I had always so dear a love for your colony, that if it had but been ten years ago, I would gladly have devoted the remainder of my life and labors to that place." Samuel Jr. was also deeply enamored with the Georgia experiment. He not only donated a communion set for use in the colony, but also penned and published lyrical lines in support of it:

> See, where beyond the spacious ocean lies
> A wide waste land, beneath the southern skies;
> Where kindly suns for ages roll'd in vain;
> No e'er the vintage saw, or ripening grain;
> Where all things into luxuriance ran,
> And burden'd nature ask'd the aid of man:
> In this sweet climate and prolific soil
> He bids the eager swain indulge his toil;
> In free possession to the planter's hand
> Consigns the rich, uncultivated land.
> Go you, the monarch cries, go settle there,
> Whom Britain from her plentitude can spare:
> Go, your old wonted industry pursue,
> Nor envy Spain the treasures of Peru.

Samuel's tone of paternalism, which in this case viewed America as a "waste land" that needed the organization and cultivation of British colonialism, was very much in keeping with the tenor of the times.

It is not entirely clear how John and Charles Wesley first became interested in serving in Georgia. John Burton, who was a Fellow of Corpus Christi College, Oxford, was one of the trustees of the colony. He had been a friend and correspondent with John Wesley for more than a decade, and he was also one of Georgia's chief propagandists. By the autumn of 1735 (August 28, according to his diary), Dr. Burton had recruited John Wesley for the Georgia mission and was corresponding with him about the logistics of the adventure. John intended for Charles to come as well. Oglethorpe, Burton had intimated, intended to embark for America on October 5th. Expediency was necessary if the Wesleys were to sail with him.

Where John Wesley examined his conscience and agonized about his true motives for wanting to go to Georgia, Charles simply didn't want to go. His brother Samuel agreed with Charles and sought to buttress his resolve in the matter; both men seemed to know that Charles, who was thriving at the university, was unprepared and ill-suited for life on the American frontier. Also, Charles would need to be ordained into the ministry for the journey, which did not seem like an appealing prospect. But John's enthusiasm for the venture and reasons for going eventually won out. As Charles would later explain, "I took my Master's Degree, and only thought of spending all my days at Oxford. But my brother, who always had the ascendant over me, persuaded me to accompany him and Mr. Oglethorpe to Georgia. I exceedingly dreaded entering into holy orders; but he overruled me here also, and I was ordained Deacon by the Bishop of Oxford, Dr. Potter, and the next Sunday, Priest, by the Bishop of London, Dr. Gibson." The spacing of only one week between Charles's successive ordinations points to the pressure under which they were working as the Wesleys suddenly decided to go abroad. That his brother John's cool reason and adventurous enthusiasm was able to win Charles over to his own point of view also evidences something about their relationship. At Oxford the brothers had learned to work in concert with one another, and it was often (but not always) John's organizational talents and leadership traits that set the agenda and direction of their plans.

Prior to leaving Oxford the Wesleys met young James Hutton.

Like Charles, Hutton had been educated at Westminster. He went up to Oxford to visit old friends from his school days. At Oxford Hutton met Charles Wesley, who in turn introduced him to his brother John. Hutton, for his part, invited the Wesleys to visit at his father's home whenever they were in London. And indeed, they did wind up lodging with the Huttons as the brothers awaited their passage to the New World. John Wesley's published journal, which begins with his entry for October 14, 1735, indicates that Charles and John, along with two other Oxford Methodists, Benjamin Ingham and Charles Delamotte, left the city of London by boat and traveled to Gravesend, from which they would embark for Georgia.

Charles's first extant letter from his oceanic odyssey was directed to James Hutton, from Gravesend; it was dated October 19, 1735. It was full of care for Hutton's spiritual state. Whatever apprehension Wesley may have had about his impending journey was overshadowed, and perhaps masked, by his immediate concerns about Hutton's welfare. "The sadness you observed in me at our parting here," Charles wrote, "was not on my own account, but yours. I feared that as soon as I was gone you would fold your arms again, and sink down into your spiritual lethargy, that in nature would prevail over grace, and plunge you as deep as ever in that fatal lukewarmness which is more abominable with God than even sin itself." Charles's sadness at departing, which was understandable and genuine under those circumstances, became an avenue for expressing his pastoral concern for his new friend. Charles's spirits were buoyed by his excitement about the religious work that lay ahead. His "thanks" to the Huttons for their kindness and generosity during his visit in their home would be repaid, Charles hoped, by becoming the instrument of Hutton's salvation.

After lying in port for several days, the *Simmonds* embarked for America on October 21. As they headed to sea, the Oxford Methodists, under the guidance of the ever-methodical John Wesley, fell into a regular pattern of living, which they followed to greater or lesser degrees throughout the voyage. John left a full and vivid account of the way the Methodists intended to spend their shipboard days:

> Our common way of living was this: from four in the morning till five each of us used private prayer. From five to seven we read the bible together, carefully comparing it (that we might not lean to

our own understandings) with the writings of the earliest ages. At seven we breakfasted. At eight were the public prayers. From nine to twelve I usually learned German, and Mr. Delamotte, Greek. My brother writ sermons, and Mr. Ingham instructed the children. At twelve we met to give an account to one another what we had done since our last meeting, and what we designed to do before our next. About one we dined. The time from dinner to four we spent in reading to those of whom each of us had taken charge, or in speaking to them severally, as need required. At four were the evening prayers, when either the Second Lesson was explained (as it always was in the morning), or the children were catechized and instructed before the congregation. From five to six we again used private prayer. From six to seven I read in our cabin to two or three of the passengers (of whom there were about eighty English on board), and each of my brethren to a few more in theirs. At seven I joined the Germans in their public service, while Mr. Ingham was reading between the decks to as many as desired to hear. At eight we met again, to exhort and instruct one another. Between nine and ten we went to bed, where neither the roaring of the sea nor the motion of the ship could take away the refreshing sleep which God gave us.

These incessant religious reflections and activities had the intention of making the Methodists useful to God and their fellow travelers during the transatlantic crossing. The regiment was, more or less, a day in the life of an Oxford Methodist transplanted to a shipboard environment. The most obvious effect of this regiment was that they stayed busy and productive during the voyage. Their spiritual disciplines and devotional regimen also had a stabilizing effect. And they cultivated several talents that would stand them in good stead upon reaching America.

One such cultivation was signaled by John's terse comment, "My brother writ sermons." Charles, who had been ordained as priest on September 29, less than a month before their voyage, was busy building his sermon repertoire. He was to serve as administrative secretary to Oglethorpe as well as minister to the colonists, so he would need a backlog of sermons ready when he arrived. Several of these sermons by Charles Wesley have survived, and they evidence quite a bit about the shape of his mind and ministry from this early period. As many as seven of Charles's early written sermons were actually copies transcribed from John Wesley's manuscripts. Since they would be serving separate congregations, Charles in Frederica and John in Savannah, there was no danger of a duplication of homilies before the same audience.

Charles's manuscript sermon on Philippians 3:13-14, dated "21 October, 1735," was a three-point sermon, and Wesley delineated his points very clearly: "First to show that in this world, Christians are never absolutely certain of their crown of reward. Secondly, that it is never to be attained by resting contented with any pitch of piety short of the highest. Thirdly that a constant progress towards Christian perfection is therefore the indispensable duty of all Christians." While the sermon announced several themes that would become standard sermon fare among the Methodists, such as Christian perfection, virtue, and religious affections, it is also long on duty and moral obligation and short on the theology of grace and spiritual empowerment. Hence Charles urged, "He therefore that would be truly pious must be always exercised in piety; and he that would attain to real Christian charity must never cool in his labour of love. If we keep continually labouring in the task our great Master has given us to do, we must of consequence continually increase in our ability to perform it. But if we ever abate of our zeal, we must not wonder if our habit of virtue begins to fail us." "St. Paul's advice to the Hebrews," from Hebrews 6:1 and following, was affirmed as Wesley exhorted the reader to "leave the first principles of the doctrine of Christ, and go on to perfection." But the path to perfection was marked out only by an emphasis upon one's extraordinary endeavors and religious duties. Absent in this homily was Charles Wesley's characteristic post-conversion emphasis upon the liberating and transforming power of God's grace, which comes into a Christian's life by an invasion of Divine love and the power of the Holy Spirit.

Charles's spirits seemed to be quite high as he began the voyage, and his letter to James Hutton sounds bravely optimistic. But by November 28th a second letter to Hutton shows that the weariness, seasickness, and drudgery of the voyage were beginning to wear on Wesley. "I must add more," he wrote, "though I find no words to express myself. There is no writing down my sensations. I feel the weight and misery of my nature, and long to be freed from this body of corruption." This attitude was also evidenced in a hymn that he probably wrote during his crossing of "the Bosom of the Deep":

While Midnight Shades the Earth o'erspread,
    And veil the Bosom of the Deep,
Nature reclines her weary Head,
    And Care respires and Sorrow sleep:
My Soul still aims at Nobler Rest,
Aspiring to her Saviour's Breast.

Aid me, ye hov'ring Spirits near,
    Angels and Ministers of Grace;
Who ever, while you guard us here,
    Behold your Heav'nly Father's Face!
Gently my raptur'd Soul convey
To Regions of Eternal Day.

Fain would I leave this Earth below,
    Of Pain and Sin the dark Abode;
Where shadowy Joy, or solid Woe
    Allures, or tears me from my GOD:
Doubtful and Insecure of Bliss,
Since Death alone confirms me His. [NO!]

Till then, to Sorrow born, I sigh,
    And gasp, and languish after Home;
Upward I send my streaming Eye,
    Expecting till the Bridegroom come;
Come quickly, Lord! Thy own receive,
Now let me see thy Face, and live.

Absent from Thee, my exil'd Soul
    Deep in a Fleshly Dungeon groans;
Around me Clouds of Darkness roll,
    And lab'ring Silence speaks my Moans;
Come quickly, Lord! Thy Face display,
And look my Midnight into Day.

> Error and Sin, and Death are o'er
>> If Thou reverse the Creature's Doom;
> Sad, *Rachel* weeps her Loss no more,
>> If Thou the GOD, the Saviour come:
> Of Thee possest, in Thee we prove
> The Light, the Life, the Heav'n of Love.

Wesley entitled this hymn "Written for Midnight," and the title seems to suggest more than a time of day — it describes a dark night of the soul. The pre-conversion tone of the hymn is evidenced in the "doubtful and insecure" point of view that predominates the writer's perception of his present state. Only death and the welcoming presence of the Lord of Life seem to offer rest for this melancholy soul. John Wesley, who often edited Charles's hymns for publication, registered his disapproval of the line "Since Death alone confirms me His" by adding the emphatic "NO!" to Charles's manuscript. John also published this hymn several times, beginning with his *Hymns and Sacred Poems* in 1739, but he re-titled it "A Midnight Hymn for one convinced of Sin," bringing a theological basis to the melancholy tone.

One of the more positive events of the Atlantic crossing was the Wesleys' growing acquaintance with the Moravians, whose warmhearted, vibrant faith both encouraged and challenged John and Charles Wesley. While they already cherished hymns and hymnsinging, the example of the Moravians standing in song in the midst of a howling storm — a storm so severe that it caused the mainsail to split and brought waves breaking over the ship — showed the Wesleys the strength of congregational song. John's journal recounts the story: "A terrible screaming began among the English. The Germans calmly sang on. I asked one of them afterwards, 'was you not afraid?' He answered, 'I thank God, no.'" Wesley continued, "But were not your women and children afraid?' He replied mildly, 'No, our women and children are not afraid to die.'"

John and Charles translated several of the Moravian hymns and subsequently published them in their hymnbooks. One of these hymns, written by Paul Gerhardt and translated by John Wesley, seems to reflect upon the incident of the stout Moravians singing Christian hymns in the midst of a roaring storm:

Give to the winds thy fears;
Hope and be undismayed.
God hears thy sighs and counts thy tears,
God shall lift up thy head.

Through waves and clouds and storms,
God gently clears thy way;
Wait thou God's time, so shall this night
Soon end in joyous day.

This hymn, which continues in modern Methodist hymnbooks, not only evidences the Moravian emphasis on justification by faith; it also stresses a faith that one can *feel*. This kind of faith was uncharted territory to the Wesleys at the time. On February 7, 1736, for example, August Gottlieb Spannenberg, a Moravian missionary, asked John Wesley: "Does the Spirit of God bear witness with your spirit that you are a child of God?'" John reported, "I was surprised and knew not what to answer." They were more accustomed to thinking of faith as an assent to correct Christian doctrine and practice.

Charles Wesley's melancholy continued to deepen. Soon it spilled out in torrents through a long letter to his friends "Selima" and "Varanese." As the *Simmonds* lay off Tybee Island, Georgia, on February 5, 1736, Charles reported, "God has brought an unhappy, unthankful wretch hither, through a thousand dangers, to renew his complaints, and loathe the Life which has been preserved by a series of Miracles." Wesley knew he should be thanking God for his safe arrival off the American shore, but instead he wrote, "I still groan under the intolerable weight of inherent misery!" He urged his friends to pray for him, and he found himself refreshed in the literary conversation he was having with them: "Go where I will, I carry my Hell about me; nor have I the least ease in anything, unless in thinking of S[elima] and you! This very night conversing with, tho[ugh] but in a dream, I quite forgot that I was miserable but alas — 'I woke to all the woes I left behind.'" This kind of romantic melancholy was a part of the literary and poetical style of Charles Wesley's day, but in him it merged with the hardship of the voyage and a loneliness that was utterly distracting. Once again, Charles's head and heart were out of sync: "I cannot follow my own advice; but yet I advise you — Give God your hearts:

Love Him with all your souls; serve Him with all your strength. Forget those things that are behind; Riches, Pleasure, Honour, in a Word, whatever does not lead to God. From this hour let your eye be single. Whatever ye speak, or think, or do, let God be your Aim, and God only! Let your one end be to please and love God!" Charles gave his female friends profound Christian advice, but he could not find comfort in it for himself.

Charles's letter to Selima and Varanese closed, on February 5th, with a promise of sending them a transcription of "Cyrus's" (John Wesley's) journal, "which may possibly make you some amends for the Pain I put you to in reading this." The same letter reopened on February 14th, on a stouter note: "My Friends will rejoice with me in the Interval of ease I at present enjoy. I look with horror back on the Desperate spirit that dictated those Words above, but shall let them stand as the naked picture of a Soul which can never know reserve toward you." Charles's melancholy had turned to hope, and he described himself "a prisoner of hope." He continued: "God is able to save to the uttermost, to break my bonds in a sunder, and bring Deliverance to the Captive!" The reality of taking up "the care of 50 poor families" seemed to have an elevating effect upon Charles's mood; it diverted his attention away from his melancholy to the Christian good he hoped to do for this small community, "some of whom are not far from the Kingdom of God." Still, rarely free from self-analysis, Wesley reported: "Obstinate pride, Invincible Sensuality stand betwixt God and me. The whole Bent of my Soul is to be afflicted." But he resolved to rise above this, since "My Office calls for an ardent love of souls, a desire to spend and to be spent for them, and Earnestness to lay down my Life for the Brethren."

Charles Wesley's published journal begins with his entry for Tuesday, March 9th, 1736, and the event of his landing on St. Simon's Island, Georgia: "immediately my spirit revived. No sooner did I enter upon my ministry, than God gave me, like Saul, another heart." In the afternoon he conversed with "*my* parishioners. (With what trembling ought I call them mine!)." That evening Charles conducted his first worship service in the New World, evening prayers in the open air. Charles's journal happily noted that James Oglethorpe was present for the service. The pastor as well as the congregation found comfort and direction in the lesson's words: "Continue instant in prayer and watch in the same with thanksgiving; withal praying also for us, that God would open unto us a door of utterance, to speak the mystery of Christ; that I may make it manifest, as I ought to speak" (Colossians 4:2).

But it was not long before Charles Wesley began to be drawn into the malevolent maelstrom of Mrs. Hawkins and Mrs. Welch, two women who would become the chief adversaries of his ministry in Frederica. It all started innocently enough, as Wesley tried (unsuccessfully) to mediate a dispute between Mrs. Hawkins and her maid. "After prayers," he wrote, "I met Mrs. Hawkins's maid, in a great passion of tears, at being struck by her mistress. She seemed resolved to make away with herself, to escape her Egyptian bondage. With much difficulty I prevailed upon her to return, and carried her back to her mistress. Upon my asking Mrs. Hawkins to forgive her, she refused me with the utmost roughness, rage, and almost reviling." That evening Wesley "heard the first harsh word from Mr. Oglethorpe, when I asked for something for a poor woman. The next day I was surprised by a rougher answer, in a matter that deserved still greater encouragement. I know not how to account for his increasing coldness." But the governor's alienation was mild compared to that of Mrs. Welch, whom he "found all storm and tempest." The "meek, the teachable" Mrs. Welch had suddenly become "so wilful, so untractable, so fierce" that Wesley "could not bear to stay near her."

On Sunday, March 14, Charles's journal reports, "We had prayers under a great tree. . . . I preached with boldness, on singleness of intention to about twenty people, among whom was Mr. Oglethorpe." The text of Wesley's message has survived. It was originally published in the 1816 edition of Charles's sermons, and was probably one of the several sermons he copied from John's manuscripts during the transatlantic voyage. The sermon's text is Matthew 6:22, 23: "The light of the body is the eye: if therefore thine eye be single, thy whole body shall be full of light. But if thine eye be evil, thy whole body shall be full of darkness." Wesley described "singleness of eye" in this way: "The sum is this: as long as thou hast but one end in all thy thoughts, words, and actions, to please God, or which is the same thing, to improve in his ways of holiness, in the love of God, and of thy neighbor, so long shalt thou clearly perceive what is conducive to it. Thy God, whom thou servest, shall so tenderly watch over thee, that light, and love and peace, shall guide all thy ways, and shine on thy paths." Wesley averred, "I would not willingly believe that any of you need to be directed to have a single eye in your religious exercises." But an all-encompassing desire to please God should also undergird all worldly business. Hence, Charles urged his listeners, "Unless your single view be to please God, and to be upright before him, the most lawful business becomes unsanctified; for it is no more allowed a Christian to work, than it is to pray, with any other intention; and a mixture of impure motives does as much pollute our employments as it does our prayers." Indeed, consecrating all aspects of one's life to God for the service of Christ allows one "to preserve a single intention in all your business, which indeed converts it into religion, which ennobles every employment, renders the meanest offices of life a reasonable sacrifice, acceptable to God through Jesus Christ." Purity of intention is the key to living the whole of one's life with an attitude of Christian devotion. As he moved toward the conclusion, the sermon's urgency increased: "Behold all things about you are become new, be ye likewise new creatures. From this hour let your eye be single. Whatever ye speak, or think, or do, let God be your aim, and God alone. Let your great end be to please him, in all your business, your refreshments, your recreations, your converse, as well as in religious duties. — Let this be your one design."

The Wesleyan emphasis upon "singleness of eye" would become standard fare in the evangelistic preaching of John and Charles Wesley; it stressed the consecration of all of one's person and talents in entire sanctification. It is clear that the brothers were aware of and embraced this holiness emphasis several years before the Wesleyan revival erupted. Charles's early sermon on this topic is doctrinally correct and contains many of the distinctive emphases which would become hallmarks of the Wesleyan revival; they would be subsequently summarized as "holiness of heart and life." For all its theological propriety and characteristic Wesleyan emphasis, however, this sanctification sermon rings hollow at the point of experience and application. Charles's brief mention that the Holy Spirit dwells within and "shall purify your hearts by faith from every earthly thought and unholy affection," for example, has meager experiential reference. The "vivifying flame" of love, while mentioned, once again sounds more like a theoretical hope than a practical reality. And, in the final analysis, if one would ask the Wesley of this sermon *how* one was to achieve "the singleness of eye" or purity of intention, the answer would still come down simply to redoubling one's religious efforts.

Soon the drudgery of his administrative duties began to wear on Wesley. On March 16, his journal reported, "I was wholly spent in writing letters for Mr. Oglethorpe. I would not spend six days more in the same manner for all Georgia." Two days later, while Oglethorpe was away on a hunting expedition, Mrs. Welch visited Wesley to charge Oglethorpe with sexual impropriety. Astounded, Charles could do no more than to urge her to "trust in God and . . . seek satisfaction only in the means of grace."

The increasing hostility of his parishioners may have been reflected in what at the time seemed to be a near fatal accident while Charles was taking a meditative walk: "I went to my myrtle-walk," he wrote, "where, as I was repeating, 'I will thank thee, for thou has heard me, and art become my salvation,' a gun was fired from the other side of the bushes. Providence had that moment turned me from that end of the walk, which the shot flew through; but I heard them pass close by me."

Oglethorpe, reflecting current evangelical sensibilities about observing the "Sabbath," "had ordered, oftener than once, that no man should shoot on a Sunday." On Sunday, March 21, this order was tested several times, first by Mr. Germain, who was arrested by the constable and committed to the guard room for this breach of decorum. Later that same afternoon, the same crime was committed by the company's doctor, Mr. Hawkins. Upon being confronted by the constable, Hawkins retorted: "What, do you not know I am not to be looked upon as a common fellow?" After some debate, he too was escorted to the guard room. This event sent Mrs. Hawkins into a rage: she "charged and fired a gun; and then ran thither, like a mad woman, crying she had shot, and would be confined too. . . . She cursed and swore in the utmost transport of passion, threatening to kill the first man that should come near her." Since John Wesley thought he had led Mrs. Hawkins towards religious conversion, Charles added, parenthetically, "Alas, my brother! What has become of thy hopeful convert?" She reviled Wesley a second time that same day, charging, he wrote, "that I was the cause of her husband's confinement; but she would be revenged, and expose my d — — d hypocrisy, my prayers four times a day by the beat of a drum, and abundance more which I cannot write, and thought no woman, though taken from [the brothels of] Drury lane, could have spoken."

Charles Wesley's stock with his parishioners continued to fall throughout the month. When the pregnant Mrs. Lawley miscarried and lost her child, even Mr. Oglethorpe seemed to blame the tragedy upon Wesley for having the doctor imprisoned. Mr. Lawley, a sailor, defamed Charles to Oglethorpe as traitor and "stirrer-up of sedition." This charge was eventually dismissed when the governor confronted both the accused and the accuser. Mrs. Perkins reported to Charles that Mrs. Hawkins had joined Mrs. Welch in her false charges of seduction against Oglethorpe; little did Wesley know that these women were whispering the same lies to Governor Oglethorpe about him! By the end of March 1736, Charles wrote, "I could not be more trampled upon, was I a fallen Minister of State." Drawing upon his classical education, Wesley quoted several lines, in Latin, from the *Satires* of the ancient poet Juvenal to describe the people's apparent attitude toward him: "Let's run headlong, and while he lies upon the bank, let's trample the enemy of Caesar." Even his few remaining friends were apparently avoiding Charles on the only street in town: "My few well-wishers are afraid to speak to me. Some have turned out of the way to avoid me. Others desired I would not take it ill, if they seemed not to know me when we should meet." And to add discomfort to insult, even the "servant that used to wash my linen sent it back unwashed."

Wesley's main source of comfort during these trying days was his devotional and public reading of the scriptures. Often the words of the Bible seemed to directly address his own trials and tribulations. "This morning," he wrote in his journal on March 27, "we began our Lord's last discourses to his disciples: every word was providentially directed to my comfort, but particularly these: 'Let not your heart be troubled: ye believe in God, believe also in me.' 'I will not leave you comfortless: I will come to you.' 'Peace I leave with you, my peace I give unto you. Let not your heart be troubled, neither let it be afraid'" (John 14:1, 18, 27). At the beginning of another trying day Charles "was revived by those words of our Lord: '. . . In the world ye shall have tribulation: but be of good cheer; I have overcome the world'" (John 16:33). His letters to older brother Samuel, however, indicate that the situation was wearing Charles down, and he was beginning to doubt whether he ever had been a Christian: "That you had lived eighteen years without God," Samuel replied, "I either do not understand, or I absolutely deny."

Letters to John Wesley, who was serving in Savannah, indicate that their correspondence was being opened and read in transit, so the letters to and from the brothers were often written in a hodgepodge of English, Latin, New Testament Greek, and shorthand. Charles's epistle of March 27th reported: "I received your letter and box. My last to you was opened, the contents being publically proclaimed by those who were so ungenerous as to intercept it." Charles was beginning to see his ministry in Frederica as part of the refining process involved in Christian discipleship. Likening himself to St. Ignatius of Antioch, who traveled across the Mediterranean to a martyr's death in the Roman arena, the younger Wesley wrote to his brother: "God, you believe, has much work to do in America. I believe so, too, and begin to enter into the designs which he has over *me*. I see why he has brought me hither, and hope ere long to say with Ignatius, 'It is now that I *begin* to be a disciple of Christ.' God direct you to pray for me."

Charles also began writing poetry during these trying months in Frederica. A few verses from one extant example was referenced in a letter he wrote to Mrs. Oglethorpe, from Jekyll Island during the spring of 1736. The hymn was subsequently published in Charles's *Hymns and Sacred Poems* (1749 edition) under the title "An Hymn for Seriousness." The hymn aptly illustrates Wesley's spiritual state during his Georgia ministry:

> Thou God of glorious majesty,
> To Thee against myself, to Thee
>   A worm of earth I cry,
> An half-awaken'd child of man,
> An heir of endless bliss or pain,
>   A sinner born to die.
>
> Lo! on a narrow neck of land,
> 'Twixt two unbounded seas I stand
>   Secure, insensible:
> A point of life, a moment's space
> Removes me to that heavenly place,
>   Or shuts me up in hell.

O God, mine inmost soul convert,
And deeply on my thoughtful heart
   Eternal things impress,
Give me to feel their solemn weight,
And tremble on the brink of fate,
   And wake to righteousness.

Before me place in dread array
The pomp of that tremendous day,
   When Thou with clouds shalt come
To judge the nations at Thy bar:
And tell me, Lord, shall I be there
   To meet a *joyful* doom?

Be this my one great business here,
With serious industry, and fear,
   My future bliss to insure,
Thine utmost counsel to fulfill,
And suffer all Thy righteous will,
   And to the end endure.

Then, Saviour, then my soul receive,
Transported from the vale, to live,
   And reign with Thee above,
Where faith is sweetly lost in sight,
And hope in full supreme delight,
   And everlasting love.

The poetical voice of this poem, which seems to be autobiographical, depicts its author as a person in spiritual turmoil, as a "half-awakened" or half-saved person, longing for full salvation. His "great business here" on earth, or in Georgia, is to suffer and endure. Once again, however, it is death and not salvation that resolves the singer's spiritual turmoil. This clearly marks out this hymn as an early composition, though it remained substantially unaltered when Charles first published it in 1749.

Charles Wesley's living conditions in the primitive outpost were also a continued source of discomfort and ill health. Initially, his lodgings amounted to lying on the ground "in a corner of Mr. Reed's hut"; occasionally he slept upon a sea chest or in a rowboat. Upon hearing that a few boards were available, Wesley hoped to build a platform on which to sleep, but none were reserved for him. He had depended upon his position as Governor Olgethorpe's secretary to supply him with the basic necessities of life. On April 1, Charles was forced by "a friendly fever" to take to his makeshift bed. The fever was "friendly" only in that it took him out of the social obligations that were fueling the destruction of his ministry. A few days later an injured sailor died, and Wesley was given his bed. By April 6, Wesley's strength and his bed were both gone: "I found myself so faint and weak, that with the utmost difficulty I got through the prayers. . . . Today Mr. Oglethorpe gave away my bedstead from under me, and refused to spare one of the carpenters to mend me up another."

Benjamin Ingham, another of the Oxford Methodists, was working with Charles Wesley in Frederica. Ingham had come to the conclusion that they needed John Wesley's help in sorting out the mess Charles's ministry had become. Ingham left for Savannah on March 28 and returned with John Wesley on April 16. Good thing, too, as Charles's journal reports: "My brother brought off a resolution, which honor and indignation had formed, of starving rather than ask for necessaries." Upon going to Oglethorpe's tent to ask for something, the two men found opportunity to clear the air between them. Oglethorpe had suspected Charles of spreading rumors about his involvement with Mrs. Hawkins, but John Wesley's intervention had begun the process of reconciliation. Charles told Oglethorpe, "I absolutely deny the whole charge. I have neither raised nor spread this report, but wherever I heard it, checked it immediately. Some who themselves spoke it in my hearing have, I suppose gone and fathered their own words upon me."

On Easter eve, April 24, 1736, Govermor Oglethorpe sent for Charles Wesley. Oglethorpe was going on a mission in to Spanish territory. "I am now going to death," he declared. "You will see me no more." In a melodramatic flourish he gave Wesley a diamond ring to keep for him, and to present to Mr. Vernon of the colony's trustees in the event of Oglethorpe's death. It was a token of the governor's renewed trust in Charles. Five days later, Oglethorpe returned, and Charles returned his ring, saying, "I need not, Sir, and indeed cannot, tell you how joyfully and thankfully I return this." On May 1 Charles wrote to John Wesley: "The trial is at last over, but has left me as a man in whom is no strength. I am fully satisfied of Mr. O[glethorpe]'s innocency, and he of mine; nor can I say which has been traduced most." The balance of the spring was spent in Charles Wesley's two occupations, but that of secretary to the colonial governor began to predominate his time and his journal. There were several meetings with the Spanish and various Indian tribes, and there was a seemingly never-ending stream of letters, bonds, affidavits, and other official documents to be prepared by the colonial secretary.

By the end of April, Charles had begun considering leaving his post in America. Would this be an act of disobedience towards God? His brother Samuel did not think so: "'You repent not of obedience to divine providence.' I hope not; and I hope I never persuaded you to disobedience. I am sure coming back to England will not be looking back from the plough, while you can exercise your ministry here. Jack's passions, if I know anything of him, never were of the same kind as yours. I advised him to go — not you; nor will [I] ever consent to your staying." By early June Charles began to lay plans to resign his secretary's post and return to England. Six weeks later, Charles's plans were set; John had already arranged his passage back across the Atlantic.

On July 25th Charles gave Oglethorpe a formal letter of resignation, but the governor refused to accept it. Instead, Oglethorpe suggested that Charles should return to London as a courier for the colony. He gave Wesley a packet of documents for the colony trustees and the Board of Trade. The governor intended for Charles Wesley to reconsider his resignation, and at least postpone it till Oglethorpe could also return to London and pick a suitable replacement. Then the governor showed himself to be a shrewd judge of character when he offered some unrelated but sound advice for young Charles: "On many accounts I should recommend to you marriage, rather than celibacy. You are of a social temper, and would find in a married state the difficulties of working out your salvation exceedingly lessened, and your helps as much increased."

On Monday, July 26, 1736, Charles Wesley read morning prayers in Savannah and left Georgia. In his journal Charles wrote, "The words which concluded the lesson, and my stay in Georgia, were 'Arise, let us go hence.' Accordingly at twelve I took my final leave of Savannah.

When the boat put off I was surprised that I felt no more joy in leaving such a scene of sorrows."

Wesley's return trip to England was taken in several "legs." The first took him from Savannah to Charleston, South Carolina. In Charleston he saw first-hand the evils slavery brought to the American South. His journal preserves several pages of atrocities, which Wesley either heard about or witnessed, that slave owners perpetrated upon African slaves: "It were endless to recount all the shocking instances of diabolical cruelty which these men (as they themselves) daily practise upon their fellow-creatures; and that on the most trivial occasions."

A drunken captain, a leaky vessel, and a duplicitous traveling companion on the trip from Charleston to Boston made Charles's escape from Frederica seem less triumphant than it might have been. He did find time to transcribe at least four more of his brother's sermons, which were bound together in a small manuscript booklet with an annotation that indicates that they were copied on the *London Galley* in September 1736. The one based on Proverbs 11:30, "He shall give his angels charge over thee, to keep thee in all thy ways," was a particularly apt text for Wesley's tumultuous voyage. Upon arriving in Boston in October Charles wrote John to divulge the state of his soul: "Dear brother, I take advantage of the deepest seriousness and best temper I have known since the fatal hour I left Oxford to lay open my heart, as I call God to witness that what I now write comes from it. You know what has passed in Georgia. The spiritual man is himself discerned by none. " Wesley was roundly misunderstood, and perhaps most painfully so by his former associate Mr. Lawley: "The continual abuse about my embezzeling the public stores, my betraying secrets etc., etc., 'like drops of eating water on the marble' have left an impression which I am content should be indelible." Governor Oglethorpe's "tenderness for my reputation" was acknowledged and appreciated, but "it needed not." Charles had come to the conclusion that, as his reproach in Frederica was "the unavoidable persecution of all Christians, who must bear the reproach of Christ, and suffer this persecution," he would "willingly submit to it."

The youngest Wesley had also begun considering what to do with his life upon returning to England. "I can either live at Oxford," he wrote, "or with my brother [Samuel]; who before I left England had provided for me without my asking." Charles's mind was ringing with questions, several of which were passed on to John, for an unnamed companion (perhaps Benjamin Ingham or Charles Delamotte): "Pray ask Mr. ———, who knows me better than I do myself, two [questions] 1. Whether he thinks me fit to be trusted with the care of souls? 2. Whether I could have a small village remote from any town, where I may hide myself from all business and all company?" One of the leading clergy in Boston, Mr. Price, had also offered Wesley a living at Hopkinton — which he declined. A few days later, the same letter continued on again: "I am wearied with these hospitable people, they so pursue me and pull me about with their civilities. They won't let me be alone." The Bostonians seemed determined to give Charles a favorable impression of America, and it is clear that he liked New England far better than Georgia: "I am constrained," he wrote, "to view this England as more pleasant than the old, and cannot help but exclaim: 'O happy country, that sustains neither flies, nor crocodiles, nor informers!" Unfortunately, Charles's illnesses continued. As he confided to John, "All my friends urge me to see a physician, but 'I cannot afford so expensive a funeral.'" His illness had brought with it a sense of despair: "Though I am apt to think that I shall at length arrive in England to deliver what I am entrusted with [documents, etc.], yet do I not expect, or wish for, a long life. How strong must the principle of self-preservation be, which can make such a wretch as I am willing to live at all! Or rather unwilling to die; for I know greater pleasure in life, than in considering that it cannot last for ever." Yet despite his increasing illness, Charles Wesley was utterly determined to leave for England on the scheduled ship: "I am just now much worse than ever; but nothing less than death shall hinder me from embarking." In three days of waiting for good enough weather to embark, he later recalled, "I vomited, purged, bled, sweated, and took laudanum, which entirely drained me of the little strength I had left." When the ship was finally able to leave, he penned a short note to brother John: "The ship fell down as was expected, but a contrary wind prevented me from following till now. At present I am something better: on board the *Hannah*, Captain Corney: in the state-room, which they have forced upon me. I have not strength for more. Adieu."

Charles's Georgia adventure had taught him quite a lot about his own inadequacies, and certainly his apparent failure on the missionary field was part of the preparation that would lead him to the dramatic events of the spring of 1738 and the revival that came thereafter. The interpersonal intrigue that had emerged in Georgia had also taught him something about the differences between his brother John and himself. John, Charles decided, "was born for the knaves." His brother was too trusting and too easily took strangers into his confidence. Charles, still smarting from the duplicity he found among his colonial parishioners and various false friends, resolved to be more cautious in the future. "For my part," he wrote, "I will never imitate [him], I will ever beware of men, as He who best knows them advises. I will not think all men rogues till I find them otherwise . . . but I will insist upon a far different probation from what my brother requires before I take any one into my confidence." The pain of his experience in Georgia had convinced Charles to be more guarded and cautious about friendship and trust.

The transatlantic voyage was storm-tossed but uneventful. The *Hannah* arrived off Beachy-Head on December 2nd, and Charles Wesley was able to disembark at Deal the next day. "I knelt down," he wrote, "and blessed the Hand that had conducted me through such inextricable mazes; and desired I might give up my country again to God; when He should require."

3 Pentecost Becomes Personal

By early December 1736 Charles Wesley had arrived back in London. He spent the next few months visiting friends as well as the trustees of the Georgia Colony, for whom he had reports and dispatches. He renewed his friendship with James Hutton, visited his uncle Matthew Wesley (who lived in London), as well as his namesake, Charles Rivington, and John Hutchinson. Each of them offered Charles a place to live. His situation was already beginning to improve markedly. He also found time to visit his beloved "Varanese" and "Selima," as well as his brother Samuel.

On December 22, Charles received a letter from George Whitefield indicating that he was offering himself for missionary service in Georgia. This letter, along with his improved health and mental outlook, rekindled Wesley's resolve to return to America — but this time as a full-fledged missionary. He intended to resign his post as Oglethorpe's secretary. During this period Charles had several meetings with the bishop of London and then with the bishop of Oxford. The latter was particularly cordial: "He desired me to come as often as I could, without farther ceremony or invitation." He had several spiritually stimulating meetings with the Moravian bishop, Count Zinzendorf, and returned to Oxford on February 8, 1737. After a week at college, Wesley returned to London to take counsel with Zinzendorf about visiting the Moravian community in Germany.

The balance of the spring of 1737 Wesley spent visiting friends and renewing connections with his relatives, notably the home of his brother Samuel at Tiverton (which he termed "the Nunnery" because his mother and several sisters were also living there). During the first week of June he met with the Board of Trade several times, and subsequently returned to Oxford. Ever the reformer, Charles Wesley tried to have a positive influence upon several Oxford acquaintances: "I spied Robinson and Batley in the Long-walk," he wrote, "and crossed over to speak with them. They fell upon me unawares . . . charged the Methodists with intrusion, schism, and bringing neglect upon the ministry." Charles argued with them trying to change their point of view about the Methodists, and he left them with a prediction: "Remember, you will be of my mind when you come to die."

On Friday, August 26th, 1737, Charles Wesley was invited to Hampton Court to present the "Oxford Address" to King George II. The bishop of Oxford had recommended him. It was a "command performance" for the young Methodist preacher, in front of an elite and aristocratic audience. "The Archbishop told me he was glad to see me," he wrote. "We kissed their Majesties' hands, and were invited to dinner. I left that, and the company, and hastened back to town. The next day we waited upon His Royal Highness, and dined all together at St. James's [Palace.]"

Still stewing about his inner state and the direction his future should take, Charles Wesley visited William Law at Putney. He described Law as "our John the Baptist," the one who prepared the Wesley brothers for the coming of Christ into their lives. At this point, however, Law was deep into one of his more mystical moods: "The sum of his advice was, 'Renounce yourself; and be not impatient.'" But Charles *was* impatient, both by natural temperament and because of the momentous decisions he needed to make about the future course of his life. He visited his onetime spiritual mentor a second time, and Law more or less washed his hands of the young Wesley. Charles asked him several questions: "'with what comment[ary] should I read the Scriptures?' 'None.' 'What do you think of one who dies unrenewed, while endeavouring after it?' 'Shall I write once more to such a person?' 'No.' 'But I am persuaded it will do him good.'"

41

Law retorted, "Sir, I have told you my opinion." As Charles felt the door of Law's acceptance closing in front of him, he asked, "Shall I write to you?'" Again, William Law seemed to turn away from Wesley: "Nothing I can either speak or write will do you any good." It was a truly sobering session with a would-be spiritual counselor and former mentor. Yet if Charles was crushed by his interview with William Law, his journal gives no indication of it. He continued to read Law's books and even tried to follow his advice.

Charles was also preaching occasionally during this period of time, but even as he was preaching he was laying plans to return to the colonies. One of his letters from this period, written to Count Zinzendorf and dated November 26, indicates that Charles had given up on the idea of visiting Germany, but he still intended to return to Georgia. And he planned to take another former Oxford Methodist with him: "George Whitefield, a minister of fervent spirit — if I may say so, a second Timothy. God has wonderfully aroused by his means the twice-dead populace. The churches will not contain his hearers." Benjamin Ingham wrote to Charles and expressed his urgent desire to return to America: "My heart's desire is that the Indians may hear the gospel, for this I pray both day and night." Ingham was even learning one of the Indian dialects; Charles had requested a copy of his notes on the subject. Charles's family, however, was completely against his returning to America, and his mother told him so in no uncertain terms.

By now Charles's health had begun to fail him yet again. He was incapacitated by dysentery and perhaps also a recurrence of malaria. He was still willing to go to America, but he simply could not. He arrived in London on New Year's eve and was able to bid Whitefield farewell at Gravesend just before his ship set sail. But Wesley's illness forbade his return to Georgia.

As it turned out, John Wesley was leaving Georgia at roughly the same time that Charles was contemplating his return. John too had run afoul of his parishioners and was fleeing their wrath as well as the local authorities (on the minor charge of defamation of character). Charles had come to consider persecution as the badge of true Christian discipleship, and now John was receiving his fair share of it: "'All that will live godly in Christ Jesus *shall suffer persecution*,'" Charles told his brother. "'The disciple is not above his master'; — 'If they have persecuted Me, they *will also persecute you*;' — and a thousand other [scripture]s. Experience only can convince them that the sense of these Scriptures is literal and eternal. But this I need not tell you. You *know* the absolute impossibility of being inwardly conformed to Christ without this outward conformity, this badge of discipleship, these marks of Christ." Charles urged his brother to remember Athanasius, who stood against the world in the Arian debate: "The charge brought against *him* was worth bringing: treason, adultery, and murder, at once. I wonder no more is said against *you*. The devil himself could not wish for fitter instruments than those he actuates and inspires in Georgia." By early February 1738 John Wesley had returned to England.

Charles nevertheless longed to return to Georgia, but his illnesses continued throughout the spring of 1738. In March he wrote a short letter to his brother Samuel, in which he admitted what was already obvious to everyone else: he was not returning to Georgia. "Dear Brother, I borrow another's hand, as I cannot use my own. . . . [The doctors] bled me three times, and poured down draughts, oils, and apozems without end. For four days the balance was even. Then, as Spenser says, 'I over-wrestled my strong enemy.' Ever since I have been slowly gathering strength." The result of all this illness, however, would be received as good news to Samuel: "One consequence of my sickness you will not be sorry for, its stopping my sudden return to Georgia. For the doctor tells me to undertake a voyage now would be certain death." Charles's American interlude was over. He resigned his post as Secretary of Indian Affairs on April 3, 1738. But all was not lost; a new dimension of ministry was opening for Charles Wesley in England.

During the fall of 1737 and spring of 1738 Wesley had continued to search his soul and seek after a sense of forgiveness and cleansing from sin as well as an assurance of salvation. He was earnestly seeking these spiritual blessings, but they eluded him. He still did not have a sense that he was forgiven and was victorious over sin. Still, he found that his "desires of apprehending Christ increased."

Peter Böhler, a Moravian missionary, had been visiting Wesley and pressing him about matters like justification by faith and the inner witness of the Spirit. Wesley, for his part, had been teaching Böhler English. When Wesley again fell ill in late February, Böhler visited him. "I asked him," Charles wrote, "to pray for me. He seemed unwilling at first, but beginning faintly, he raised his voice by degrees, and prayed for my recovery with strange confidence. Then he took me by the hand and calmly said, 'You will not die now.' I thought within myself, I cannot hold out in this pain till morning — He said, 'Do you hope to be saved?'" Wesley said he did. Böhler pressed further: "For what reason do you hope to be saved?" Charles Wesley answered, "Because I have used my best endeavours to serve God." But Böhler simply "shook his head and said no more. I thought him very uncharitable," Wesley continued, "saying in my heart 'What! Are not my endeavours a sufficient ground of hope? Would you rob me of my endeavours? I have nothing else to trust to.'"

On May 11, 1738, the English Moravian John Bray called on Charles just as he was preparing to move to the home of John Hutton. Wesley's journal described the event in this way: "I was going to remove to old Mr. Hutton's, when God sent Mr. Bray to me, a poor ignorant mechanic, who knows nothing but Christ; yet knowing him, knows and discerns all things." This meeting with Bray seemed providential to Wesley, and after a moving prayer for faith in Christ, Charles was persuaded to move into Bray's house instead of Hutton's. Charles's journal reported, "Mr. Bray is now to supply Böhler's place. We prayed together for faith. I was quite overpowered and melted into tears, and hereby induced to think it was God's will that I should go to his house, and not Mr. Hutton's. He was of the same judgement."

Over the course of the next nine days Charles Wesley's illness returned, and he had a constant stream of visitors, each of whom brought him spiritual refreshment and encouragement. For Wesley, this period of illness in the house of John Bray was almost like being on a religious retreat. Charles's journal for these days is like a spiritual barometer, measuring his sense of forgiveness and nearness to "receiving the atonement." On May 12 he wrote, "I waked in the same blessed temper, hungry and thirsty after God. I began Isaiah, and seemed to see that to me were the promises made, and would be fulfilled, for that Christ loved me. I found myself more desirous, more assured I should believe." He spent the entire day reading scripture, praying and discoursing about faith. The next day, Charles reported, "I waked without Christ; yet still desirous of finding him." That same evening John Wesley visited his brother, and Charles wound up encouraging him: "At night my brother came, exceedingly heavy. I forced him (as he had often forced me) to sing a hymn to Christ, and almost thought He would come while we were singing: assured He would come quickly. At night I received much light and comfort from the Scriptures." The next day, Wesley awoke feeling "very heavy, weary and unable to pray; but the desire soon returned, and I found much comfort both in prayer and in the word, my eyes being opened more and more to discern and lay hold on the promises. I longed to find Christ, that I might show him to all mankind; that I might praise and, that I might love him."

Charles's soul-searching continued. On May 16 he "waked weary, faithless, and heartless. . . . In the afternoon I seemed deeply sensible of my misery, in being without Christ." The next day Mr. Holland brought Charles a copy of Luther's *Galatians*. Both Holland and Wesley were deeply moved by Luther's insights about justification by faith: they "found him nobly full of faith. My friend [Holland], in hearing him, was so affected, as to breathe out sighs and groans unutterable. I marveled that we were so soon and so entirely removed from him that called us to the grace of Christ, unto another Gospel. Who would believe our Church had been founded on this important article of justification by faith alone? I am astonished I should ever think this a new doctrine; especially while our Articles [of Religion] and [Standard] Homilies stand unrepealed; and the key of knowledge is not yet taken away."

The impact of this reading of Luther was foundational, since it provided a focal point for Wesley's spiritual longing and desires. It also provided him with a witness to pass on to those who visited him: "From this time," he wrote, "I endeavoured to ground as many of our friends as came [to visit] in this fundamental truth, salvation by faith alone, not an idle, dead faith, but a faith which works by love, and is necessarily productive of all good works and all holiness." Charles ended his day with Martin Luther, and after reading the second chapter of his *Galatians* commentary, Wesley recalled, "I laboured, waited, and prayed to feel 'who loved *me*.' When nature was near exhausted, forced me to bed, I opened the book upon 'For he will finish the work, and cut it short in righteousness, because a short work will the Lord make upon the earth.' After this comfortable assurance that [Christ] would come, and would not tarry, I slept in peace."

The pain in Charles's side increased the next day, May 19. His physical illness, which sounds like pneumonia or pleurisy, sapped Wesley's spiritual energy: "I received the sacrament," he wrote, "but not Christ." That evening, Mrs. Turner visited Charles Wesley and he had revived enough to ply her with searching questions: "Has God then bestowed faith upon you?" "Have you peace with God?" "And do you love Christ above all things?" Her answers being responsive and affirmative to these questions, Wesley ventured further: "Then are you willing to die?" Mrs. Turner answered patiently and fully: "I am; and would be glad to die this moment; for I know all my sins are blotted out; the hand writing that was against me is taken out of the way, and nailed to his cross. He has saved me by his death; he has washed me with his blood; he has hid me in his wounds. I have peace with Him and rejoice with joy unspeakable, and full of glory." Upon receiving this remarkable witness, Charles recorded his own reaction: "Her answers were so full to these and the most searching questions I could ask, that I had no doubt of her having received the atonement; and waited for it myself with a more assured hope."

The next day found Wesley once again without a sense of saving faith. "I waked," he wrote, "much disappointed, and continued all day in great dejection, which the sacrament did not in the least abate." Mr. Bray too was disappointed, but turned to the Bible for encouragement, and opening it he "read the first words that presented" — Matthew 9:1 — which included the phrase: "Jesus, seeing their faith, said unto the sick of the palsy, Son, be of good cheer; thy sins be forgiven thee." And when the scribes and Pharisees darkly doubted Jesus' ability to forgive sins and accused him (in their hearts) of blaspheme, Jesus said again: "For whether is easier, to say, Thy sins be forgiven thee, or to say, Arise and walk? But that ye may know that the Son of Man hath power on earth to forgive sins, (then saith he to the sick of the palsy), Arise, take up thy bed and go unto thine own house. And he arose, and departed to his house. And when the multitude saw it, they marveled, and glorified God." Bray was convinced that he had been directed to this scripture passage as a way of foretelling Charles Wesley's forgiveness by Christ as well his physical healing. Charles's journal recorded this emotional event in somber tones: "It was a long while before he [Bray] could read this through, for tears of joy, and I saw herein, and firmly believed, that his faith would be available for the healing of me."

The next day was Pentecost Sunday, and Charles was hoping for a Pentecost of his own. "O Jesus," he prayed, "thou hast said, 'I will come unto you'; thou hast said, 'I will send the Comforter unto you'; thou hast said, 'My Father and I will come unto you and make our abode with you.' Thou art God who canst not lie; I wholly rely upon thy most true promise: accomplish it in thy time and manner." After prayer, Wesley began to drift off into sleep, and as he did so Mrs. Musgrave, one of the women who had been nursing him, entered the room and said: "In the name of Jesus of Nazareth, arise, and believe, and thou shalt be healed of all thy infirmities." Wesley recalled, "I wondered how it should enter into her head to speak in that manner. The words struck me to the heart. I sighed and said to myself, 'O that Christ would but speak thus to me!'" At first, perhaps through embarrassment, she denied having made that pronouncement, and Charles Wesley felt "a strange palpitation of heart." In the midst of this quickening experience, Wesley ventured ahead: "I said, yet feared to say," he wrote, "'I believe! I believe!'" Mrs. Musgrave soon returned to his room and said, "It was I, a weak, sinful creature [that] spoke: but the words were Christ's: he commanded me to say them, and so constrained me that I could not forbear." Uncertain of what to make of these events, Wesley "sent for Mr. Bray, and asked him whether I believed. He answered, I ought not doubt of it: it was Christ spoke to me. He knew it; and willed us to pray together." Before prayer, however, Bray turned again to his Bible, which he opened upon the verse, "Blessed is the man whose unrighteousness is forgiven, and whose sin is covered: blessed is the man to whom the Lord imputeth no sin, and in whose spirit is not guilt." This text seemed to be scriptural confirmation of Wesley's redemption. "Still," he wrote, "I felt a violent opposition and reluctance to believe; yet still the Spirit of God strove with my own spirit and the evil spirit, till by degrees he chased away the darkness of my unbelief. I found myself convinced, I know not how, nor when. . . . I now found myself at peace with God, and rejoiced in hope of loving Christ."

The next morning, Monday, May 22, Wesley awoke with a sense of Christ's presence and protection. He found his own situation described in Psalm 107, "so nobly describing what God had done for my soul." "Today," Charles wrote, "I saw him [Christ] chiefly as my King, and found him in his power; but saw little of the love of Christ crucified, or of my sins past: though more, I humbly hope, of my own weakness and his strength." Later that same day, John Wesley visited;

"we joined in intercession for him," Charles recalled. "In the midst of prayer, I almost believed the Holy Ghost was coming upon him."

By Tuesday, May 23, waking with a sense of Christ's presence had become a familiar event for Charles Wesley. His journal reported, "I waked under the protection of Christ, and gave myself up, soul, body, to him." This act of faith and self-commitment took expression in what would become a familiar devotional act for Charles — the writing of a hymn. "At nine," he wrote, "I began an hymn upon my conversion but was persuaded to break off, for fear of pride. Mr. Bray coming, encouraged me to proceed in spite of Satan. I prayed Christ to stand by me, and finished the hymn." The next evening, "towards ten, my brother was brought in triumph by a troop of our friends, and declared, 'I believe.' We said the hymn with great joy, and parted with prayer."

Exactly *which* conversion hymn was written by Charles Wesley on May 23, 1738, and then sung in triumph the next night in celebration of John Wesley's evangelical conversion is a matter of some debate. "Where Shall My Wondering Soul Begin?" is the hymn favored by most scholars. The first two stanzas, which were based on the imagery of Zechariah 3:2 as well as John Wesley's own experience of being a "brand plucked from the burning" of the Epworth manse in February 1709, seem to suggest that verdict. The metaphor of being a "brand plucked from the burning" became, for both brothers, salvation language for being delivered from the fires of hell. The hymn is set in first person form, which gives it the feel of a testimony, and also places the conversion event on the lips — and perhaps in the heart — of the singer:

> 1. Where shall my wondering soul begin?
>   How shall I all to heaven aspire?
>   A slave redeem'd from death and sin,
>   A brand pluck'd from eternal fire,
>   How shall I equal triumphs raise,
>   And sing my great Deliverer's praise?
>
> 2. O, how shall I the goodness tell,
>   Father, which Thou to me hast show'd?
>   That I, a child of wrath and hell,
>   I should be call'd a child of God!

Should know, should feel my sins forgiven,
    Blest with this antepast of heaven!

The Wesleys' newly found doctrine, justification by faith alone, is asserted in the final verse of the same hymn.

8. For you the purple current flow'd
        In pardons from His wounded side;
    Languish'd for you th' eternal God,
        For you the Prince of Glory died.
    Believe, and all your guilt's forgiven;
        Only believe — and yours is heaven.

A second hymn that was probably written during these same days is the more familiar "And Can It Be," which the Wesleys published under the title "Free Grace." This hymn is also framed in first-person form, and hence has the feel of Charles Wesley's spiritual autobiography. The repeated emphasis upon the phrase "for me," reminds us of the impact that reading Luther's *Galatians* had upon Wesley. The first three verses of the hymn voice the singer's utter wonder at the lavish immensity of God's grace:

1. And can it be, that I should gain
        An interest in the Saviour's blood?
    Died He for me? — who caused His pain!
        For me? — who Him to death pursued.
    Amazing love! How can it be
        That Thou, my God, shouldst die for me?

2. 'Tis mystery all! Th' Immortal dies!
        Who can explore His strange design?
    In vain the first-born seraph tries
        To sound the depths of Love Divine.
    'Tis mercy all! Let earth adore;
        Let angel minds inquire no more.

3. He left His Father's throne above,
        (So free, so infinite His grace!)

> Emptied Himself of all but love,
>   And bled for Adam's helpless race:
> 'Tis mercy all, immense and free!
>   For, O my God! It found out me!

The bondage to sin and the darkness of doubt were broken and driven away when Christ came into the poet's life. Charles Wesley used images of manumission and liberation to communicate the freedom that he now felt because of his faith in Christ. Newfound freedom leads directly to Christian discipleship, as the singer now follows Christ:

> 4. Long my imprison'd spirit lay,
>   Fast bound in sin and nature's night:
> Thine eye diffused a quickening ray;
>   I woke; the dungeon flamed with light;
> My chains fell off, my heart was free,
>   I rose, went forth, and follow'd Thee.

The inner witness of the Holy Spirit and the feeling of an assurance of God's forgiveness, both of which Charles Wesley sought in the days prior to his conversion, are strongly voiced in this hymn as results of receiving Christ by faith:

> 5. Still the small inward voice I hear,
>   That whispers all my sins forgiven;
> Still the atoning blood is near,
>   That quench'd the wrath of hostile Heaven:
> I feel the life His wounds impart;
>   I feel my Saviour in my heart.

Upon reflecting upon the questions that Charles Wesley raised with Mrs. Turner, we can see that a sense of guiltlessness before God and a "willingness to die" were also important and concomitant emphases in his understanding of the experience of justification by faith alone. Both of these elements emerge in the last verse of the same hymn:

> 6. No condemnation now I dread,
>   Jesus, and all in Him, is mine:

Alive in Him, my Living Head,
  And clothed in righteousness Divine,
Bold I approach th'eternal throne,
  And claim the crown, through Christ, my own.

Charles Wesley's evangelical conversion began on Pentecost Sunday, often called "Whitsunday" in his day. The following hymn, which he wrote sometime immediately after his conversion, was sung during Charles's conversation with Mr. Ainsworth three days later. A line from verse eight of the hymn is quoted in Charles's journal entry for that day: "Now descend, and shake the earth"; upon singing that line, Ainsworth "fell down as in an agony." Three verses from this lengthy hymn evidence Charles Wesley's awareness of the role that the Holy Spirit plays in a person's conversion. Like the "dry bones" of Ezekiel 37, new life can come upon those who receive "the Comforter" — "the Promise of our parting Lord."

6. Come, Divine, and peaceful Guest,
     Enter our devoted breast;
   Holy Ghost, our hearts inspire,
     Kindle there the Gospel-fire.

7. Crown the agonizing strife,
     Principle, and Lord of life;
   Life Divine in us renew,
     Thou the Gift and Giver too!

8. Now descend and shake the earth,
     Wake us into second birth;
   Now Thy quickening influence give,
     Blow — and these dry bones shall live!

One of Charles Wesley's most familiar hymns is also a conversion hymn. "O for a Thousand Tongues to Sing" was written in 1739 and published in 1740 under the title "For the Anniversary of One's Conversion." The hymn's title and its contents link it with the events of May 1738. Spanning a full eighteen verses, Charles's hymn was soon pared down to a mere eight stanzas. The first six verses, which were jettisoned after 1740, set the theological and experiential context for the praise and celebration that not a "thousand tongues" could satisfy (originally verse seven). The reference to a "thousand tongues" is said to have come from Peter Böhler's joyous exclamation: "Had I a thousand tongues, I would praise Christ with them all!" The first six verses describe the conversion experience the subsequent verses celebrate. Once again, the hymn is written in first person, and is laden with personal language ("I," "my," "me," "mine") when it speaks of the experience of conversion:

1. Glory to God, and praise and love
   Be ever, ever given;
   By Saints below, and Saints above,
   The church in earth and Heaven.

2. On this glad day the glorious Sun
   Of Righteousness arose;
   On my benighted soul He shone,
   And fill'd it with repose.

3. Sudden expired the legal strife;
   'Twas then I ceased to grieve;
   My second, real, living life
   I then began to live.

4. Then with my *heart* I first believed,
   Believed with faith Divine;
   Power with the Holy Ghost received
   To call the Saviour *mine.*

5. I felt my Lord's atoning blood
   Close to *my* soul applied;
   Me, me He loved — the Son of God
   For *me,* for *me,* He died!

6. I found, and own'd His promise true,
   Ascertain'd for *my* part;
   My pardon pass'd in heaven I *knew,*
   When written on my heart.

Charles Wesley continued throughout his life to celebrate Whitsunday as the anniversary of his conversion.

Despite the spiritual high of late May, by June Charles once again found himself spiritually dull and uneasy. He felt averse to prayer, though he did manage to go to church. Instead of a blessing, however, the liturgy and the sacrament seemed painful to him. They were not a source of comfort; they simply magnified his sense of being apart from God. He searched his soul and demanded of himself to know whether there was a difference between his current dullness and the state he found himself in prior to his conversion. He concluded that his present darkness lacked the guilt of earlier times in his life. Even on this cloudy day in his soul, he was able to be confident of the love, mercy, and forgiveness of God to him in Jesus Christ. This caused Charles to see the current dullness as simply a "cloudy day" in the life of his soul, whereas he had previously lived in darkness and night.

This exercise in spiritual reflection was a very important one for Charles Wesley because it reminded him of his utter helplessness in the matter of his own salvation. He could not produce a sense of comfort or divine acceptance on his own, but when he turned his attention away from his feelings and towards the foundation of his forgiveness in Jesus Christ, he found it quite firm. From this experience Wesley also concluded that, since he could not produce a sense of comfort or divine acceptance in himself, he certainly could not produce it in anyone else. This realization would save him from a sense of pride in being able to convert others. He knew it would never be his own doing.

On Sunday, July 2, 1738, Charles Wesley finally had both strength and opportunity to preach — twice — for the first time since his conversion. Later that same evening, "we met," Charles wrote, "a troop of us, at Mr. Sims's. There was one Mrs. Harper there, who had this day in like manner received the Spirit, by the hearing of faith; but feared to confess it. We sung the hymn to Christ. At the words, *'Who for me, for me hath died,'* she burst into tears and outcried, 'I believe, I believe!' And sunk down. She continued, and increased in the assurance of faith; full of peace, and joy, and love." The hymn they sang "to Christ" is one that was subsequently published in the Wesleys' *Hymns and Sacred Poems* (1739) under the title "To the Son":

1. O Filial Deity,
     Accept my new-born cry!
   See the travail of Thy soul,
     Saviour, and be satisfied;
   Take me now, possess me whole,
     Who for me, for me hast died!

2. Of life Thou art the tree,
     My immortality!
   Feed this tender branch of Thine,
     Ceaseless influence derive,
   Thou the true, the heavenly Vine,
     Grafted into Thee I live.

3. Of life the Fountain Thou,
     I know — I feel it now!
   Faint and dead no more I droop;
     Thou art in me; Thy supplies,
   Every moment springing up,
     Into life eternal rise. . . .

The sermon that Charles preached on July 2 was probably John Wesley's sermon "Justification by Faith," which was based on Romans 4:5, "To him that worketh not, but believeth on him that justifieth the ungodly, his faith is counted to him for righteousness." Charles's practice of "borrowing" John's sermons during their ministry in Georgia likely continued in the first months of the Wesleyan revival. John had already preached this text twice, on May 14 and 28, 1738. It would, subsequently be published in John Wesley's *Standard Sermons*. One week later, on July 9, Charles's journal specifically reported that: "I preached my brother's sermon upon faith at ——— and a second time in St. Sepulchre's vestry."

Charles was beginning to write his own fresh stock of sermons during this same July. The first of these, which he called "The Three States," was begun on July 8 and not completed until July 15. He first preached it at St. George's Church, in Queen's Square, Blackfriars (London) on July 16. It is the first extant sermon he wrote after his evangelical conversion almost two months earlier. It is an important sermon for our understanding of Wesley's development as an evangelical preacher because in "The Three States" we see Charles undertaking the task of reconciling his newfound experience of the "new birth" or justification by faith with his Anglican theological heritage. It is thus as much a part of Charles's own faith pilgrimage as it is a public proclamation. It would become one of his favorite sermons; his sermon register indicates that he preached it, in one or two parts, as many as twenty-one times in 1738 and 1739.

The text for "The Three States" was 1 John 3:14, "We know that we have passed from death unto life." The notion of passing from death to life caused Charles to consider the three states through which all Christians pass. The first state is birth, which is suggested by "death" in the scripture passage; the third state is "second birth in Christ Jesus," New Birth, or "life," to use the phrasing of the same passage. But Wesley's main focus is on the state that looms between these two: "a middle state, which we are equally concerned to understand aright, lest we deceive ourselves by an ill-grounded hope, and forever stop short of the glory of God." These three states corresponded well to the threefold law laid out in the New Testament book of Romans: "The first is the law of sin, which is in the members (Rom. 7:23), the second is the law of the mind or conscience (Rom. 7:23), the third is the law of the Spirit of life (Rom. 8:2)." These three states of the "law" correspond exactly to the three states in which one finds human nature: "under the first law, the law of sin, are those who will and embrace sin purely and entirely; under the second law, the law of the mind, are those who refuse and stand averse to sin in some certain respects as evil, but yet do in effect will and choose it, by choosing it sometimes; under the third law, the law of the Spirit of life, are those who absolutely and thoroughly refuse to commit sin."

This "middle state" described Charles Wesley himself prior to his evangelical conversion. He believed he was sensitive to sin, but not always victorious over it; hence he lived a life of striving and doubt. He was one of those people who had been baptized as infants and who had thereby the seed of the life of faith planted in them, but they had not brought it to fruition. Charles described them as "those who, having renounced themselves, are striving to enter the straight gate; in whom the Divine principle received in baptism but buried ever since and seemingly extinct, begins to move and exhort the cry of the trembling gaoler [jailer] 'what must I do to be saved?' [Acts 16:30]." By combining the Anglican commitment to infant baptism with the evangelical conception of justification by faith as the new birth, Wesley had begun applying the Reformation doctrine to his own life and theological context.

He seemed to assume, perhaps rightly, that most of his hearers were also members of this "second state." They were people in whom "the work of repentance is begun and by it they endeavour to break off their sins. They use all the means of grace, do all good works, and labour after the renewal of their souls in all heavenly tempers, even the whole mind that was in Christ Jesus. In a word they are in 'earnest.'" These are people who even know what they lack: "They own and pursue 'the one thing needful,' even a participation of the Divine nature; the life of God in the soul of man." Yet knowing what they lack and having it are two different things. Wesley seems to have written autobiographically of his pre-conversion life when he described those stuck in the "second state": "Being dead to sin, he once served it willingly: it is now under the utmost reluctance; yet still he serves it, and so he must do till, being justified by faith, the law of the Spirit of life makes him free from the law of sin and death; but where the spirit of the Lord is, there is liberty, and whomsoever the Son makes free, that man is free indeed."

Wesley was beginning to find his own voice in writing sermons, but he was also beginning to move away from purely written sermons toward more extemporaneous preaching. His journal entry for October 15, 1738, shows that he "preached on 'the one thing needful'; and added much extempore." The sermon Wesley preached was an earlier sermon copied from John's manuscript while they were in Georgia. By October 20 Charles had begun experimenting with preaching with complete spontaneity. His journal for that date tells the story: "Seeing so few present at St. Antholin's, I thought of preaching extempore, afraid; yet ventured [forth] on the promise: 'Lo I am with you always'; and spake on justification from Rom. 1:15, for three quarters of an hour, without hesitation. Glory be to God, who keepeth his promise for ever." While some written sermons would still come from the pen of Charles Wesley, after the fall of 1738 he would increasingly preach without reading from a written sermon.

Just as Charles increasingly preached extemporaneously, so also he preached increasingly on salvation by faith alone. But he was not ready to abandon an emphasis on good works; indeed, he increasingly found himself concerned about the antinomianism that he thought he saw growing among his friends the Moravians during the so-called "Stillness Controversy." They thought they should be "still" and do nothing that God (through the Holy Spirit) did not directly lead them to do. The written law of God, they said, was being superseded by the rule of the Holy Spirit in their midst. The Church of England, however, taught that genuine faith always resulted in good works. Such good works were not to somehow replace faith in the process of justification; instead they were to complete faith and make it more vital. In a similar way, good works and spiritual disciplines became for the Methodists helps for a person's sanctification.

In his "personal Pentecost" Charles Wesley found a life-changing experience that moved him from that "middle state" to utter devotion to God through faith in Jesus Christ. He found forgiveness from sin and guilt, as well as power over sin and the presence of the Holy Spirit in his life. Hence in the fall of 1738 Wesley began to preach "full salvation," or holiness of heart and life. His evangelism was about being "born again," but it was also about more than that — it encompassed the transformation of the inner person through the creation of new habits of the heart ("religious affections") as well as outer obedience to the Word and commandments of God through holy living. He began to preach more spontaneously after his conversion experience, and often he preached without notes or a prepared message. Wesley's personal Pentecost supplied him with the message and the medium that he would apply throughout the Methodist revival.

His personal rebirth would lead to more prolific hymn-writing as well. His hymns were born in his own spiritual pilgrimage, life experiences, and personal study of the Bible. They were loaded with biblical phrases and doctrines, as well as vibrant emotion. Set in first-person form, they placed biblical words and experiences upon the singer's lips. In this way Wesley's hymns, like his sermons, were intended not simply to narrate evangelical doctrines and experience, but to induce them. By taking up the first-person language he had learned from the Moravians and Martin Luther, Wesley was able to make the singers of his hymns participants in the experiences they sang about. This was a relatively new development in hymnody, one that broke pattern with

Wesley's evangelical precursors like Isaac Watts and added a new vitality to singing in church. It brought his hymns their hallmark sense of immediacy that has helped them endure through the ages.

4 "Into the Streets and Highways"

In the fall of 1738 Charles Wesley was becoming an increasingly active evangelist. His terse journal entry for Sunday, September 3, for example, bears cryptic witness to his growing usefulness: "I preached salvation by faith at Westminster Abbey; gave the cup. In the afternoon I preached at St. Botolph's; and expounded Rom. 2, at Sims, to above two hundred people." That preaching three times a day was becoming standard fare for Wesley is indicated by his record for the next Sunday as well: "I preached faith in the morning at Sir George Wheler's chapel, and assisted in the sacrament. In the afternoon at St. Botolph's. In the evening at Sim's I was much strengthened to pray and expound to above three hundred attentive souls. Another lost sheep was brought home."

Wesley's friends continued to think he was ill-suited for the role of an evangelist. On November 28, 1738, George Whitefield "pressed" him to accept a college position. The following January, Charles wrote, "My brother, Mr. Seweard, Hall, Whitefield, Ingham, Kinchin, Hutchins, all set upon me; but I could not agree to settle at Oxford without farther direction from God." His Methodist friends wanted to be sure Charles had time to attend to his own spiritual growth.

The problem with stepping back now was that Wesley was becoming quite popular as a mass evangelist. This brought temptations of its own: he could sense the danger of feeling a large crowd responding to his oratory and emotion. He strove to keep his ego in check, and he urged his hearers not to confuse liking the preacher with embracing the message: "In explaining Isai. 50," he wrote, "I laid open the self-deceit of some who rested short of the promises, because they had a liking to the word, or me." Not even Deists were immune to Wesley and the gospel message he preached: "I preached with power and freedom in the Marshalsea. I prayed by Mrs. Cameron; who owned herself convinced. She had been a Deist, because it is so incredible [that] the Almighty God should condescend to die for his creatures."

Charles was more apt to be carried away by emotion than his more reasonable brother. As emotional outbursts became common during Charles's evangelism, he took steps to silence them — by completely ignoring them. He explained his approach in a letter to John Wesley about the outbursts in Bristol in 1740: "The noises and outcries here are over, I have not spoken one word against them, nor two about them. The Devil grows sullen and dumb, because we take no notice of him." Like his elder brother, however, Charles was "a reasonable enthusiast" who tried all supposed spiritual experiences by Scripture and common sense. People were permitted to testify, as many did with tears, after Wesley's preaching services, but the more vocal emotional outbursts were discouraged and in some instances forcibly halted.

As the fires of revival began to spread, controversies arose. When Charles Wesley and George Whitefield encountered "a dispute . . . about lay-preaching," which the Moravians supported, Wesley and Whitefield "declared against it." Lay preaching would be a continuing issue among the Methodists, one which threatened to separate them from the Church of England. While Charles Wesley and George Whitefield would subsequently support the innovation of lay preaching, in 1739 they reacted like typical Anglicans and opposed it. Charles's journal evidences ecclesiastical scruples over preaching in another Anglican clergyman's parish, without first asking his permission. On May 31, 1739, a Quaker sent Charles Wesley "a pressing invitation" to come to Thackstead to preach. Charles reported, "I scrupled preaching in another's parish, till I had been refused the church. Many Quakers, and near seven hundred others, attended, while I declared in the highways, 'The Scripture hath concluded all under sin.'" He preached there again, the next day: "My subject, to above one thousand attentive sinners, was, 'He shall save his people from their sins.' Many showed their emotion by their tears."

Such displays of emotion, along with other Methodist tendencies, meant that not everyone received Methodist evangelism with a favorable attitude. On July 27, 1738, for example, Charles Wesley reported, "In the coach to London I preached faith in Christ. A lady was extremely offended; avowed her own merits in plain terms; asked if I was not a Methodist; threatened to beat me."

Methodism was also beginning to provoke the ire of officials in the Church of England. Both brothers had to appear before the bishop of London to answer charges against them in October 1738. According to Charles's journal, they were charged with preaching "an absolute assurance of salvation." The Wesleys and the bishop quickly came to an agreement on the doctrine of assurance as an "inward persuasion, whereby a man is conscious in himself, after examining his life by the law of God, and weighing his own sincerity, that he is in a state of salvation, and acceptable to God." The bishop concluded, "I don't see how any good Christian can be without such an assurance." "This," Charles Wesley retorted, "is what we contend for: but we have been charged as Antinomians, for preaching justification by faith only." Again the bishop agreed — in principle — with the Wesleys' message; the brothers allowed, however, that "by preaching it strongly, and not inculcating good works, many have been made Antinomians in theory, though not in practice."

The Wesleys were also charged with re-baptizing an adult, which was against the laws of the church. Once again they agreed with the bishop, but they also stipulated that they felt free to re-baptize a person who was no longer satisfied with lay baptism or with baptism from a Dissenting clergyman (considering that to be no baptism at all) and sought episcopal baptism from them. Here the bishop disagreed with their interpretation of church law.

The bishop absolved the Wesleys of another charge: violation of the Conventicle Acts (1662, 1664, and 1670), which stipulated against reading prayers or preaching in "conventicles" — assemblies for worship in houses, barns, or fields — and offered prison and financial penalties for those who did. These laws were designed to force people to attend the Church of England, and by enforcing "uniformity" to put an end to seditious worship. Those who sought to stand apart from the Church of England could do so, under the Toleration Act of 1689, if they formally registered with the government as Dissenters. The Methodists, because they saw themselves as loyal members of the Church of England, did not see themselves as guilty of sedition, and they did not want to register their preaching houses as Dissenting houses of worship under the Toleration Act, because that would be tantamount to admitting that the Methodists were not loyal to the Church of England. This dilemma forced the bishop to decide whether the Methodist societies should be considered "conventicles" or not. For the time being at least, he was not prepared to acknowledge them as such. The Wesleys were free to go.

The next meeting with the bishop, on November 14, 1738, did not go nearly as well. Charles appeared before the bishop to give notice that he intended to baptize a Dissenter. According to Wesley's journal, the bishop "immediately took fire, and interrupted me: 'I wholly disapprove of it: it is irregular.'" Wesley retorted that he did not expect the bishop's approval; "I only came, in obedience, to give you notice of my intention." Though the bishop did not inhibit or charge Charles Wesley, he did deliver a homiletical rant: "He railed at Lawrence on lay-baptism; blamed my brother's sermon, as inclining to Antinomianism." Though it did not directly impede the Wesleys' actions, the Anglican establishment clearly disapproved of their irregular efforts and actions.

This disapproval soon began to manifest itself in local parishes. On Sunday, November 12, 1738, for example, Charles's journal reports that "Mr. Piers refused me his pulpit, through fear of man, pretending tenderness to his flock. I plainly told him, if he so rejected my testimony, I would come to him no more." On December 31, Charles had to answer to the clerk of session prior to preaching at St. Antholin's Church: "the clerk asked my name, and said 'Dr. Venn has forbidden any Methodist to preach. Do you call yourself a Methodist?'" Charles replied: "I do not: the world may call me what they please." "Well," the clerk replied, "it is a pity the people should go away without preaching. You may preach."

In this changing ecclesiastical climate, Charles Wesley began to encounter sharp questions at St. Mary's Church in the Islington section of London, where he often preached. On Sunday, April 15, 1739, for example, Charles's journal reports, "At Islington in the vestry, the churchwardens demanded my licence." Two weeks later, he met a closed door there: "At Islington vestry the churchwardens forbad my preaching: demanded my local licence. I said nothing but that 'I heard them.' Scions was very abusive; bidding me shake off the dust from my feet, &c.; and said, 'You have all the spirit of the devil,' mentioning Mr. Whitefield, Stonehouse, and me by name." After the reading of prayers, Mr. Stonehouse offered to clear the way for Charles Wesley to ascend to the pulpit, but several of the church officers physically barred the way. Wesley wrote that "I thought of, 'the servant of the Lord must not strive,' and yielded" to them. After a meeting of the vestry, Charles recalled, "Mr. Streat advised to ask Mr. Stonehouse to discharge me from ever preaching again."

That same afternoon George Whitefield preached to more than ten thousand people outdoors, but Charles Wesley's liturgical conservatism and his allegiance to the Church of England made it very difficult for him to consider preaching outside the walls of a church. His personal shyness and his high sense of ecclesiastical propriety made this innovation seem utterly distasteful to him. Slowly, though, the positive example of Whitefield's success, along with continued opposition from local churches, gradually wore down Wesley's reservations about open-air evangelism. And when he continued to encounter physical opposition to climbing the pulpit stairs at Islington, Wesley started to look for alternative venues. By the end of May 1739 he had preached — without great reluctance — in a farmer's field. "Franklyn," he explained, "a farmer, invited me to preach in his field. I did so, to about five hundred, on 'Repent, for the kingdom of heaven is at hand.' I returned to the house rejoicing." By the middle of June it was clear that his welcome at the Islington church had run out. Rev. Stonehouse told the Wesleys that the bishop of London had vindicated and upheld the churchwardens in their forcible expulsion of Charles Wesley from his pulpit.

Pressure soon began to come from the highest seat in the Church of England. On June 19, 1739, Charles Wesley went with Mr. Piers, another evangelical clergyman, to visit the Archbishop of Canterbury at Lambeth Palace, his residence in London. It was clear that the agenda of the meeting concerned the Methodists and their irregularity. Wesley's journal reports, "His Grace [the archbishop] expressly forbade him [Rev. Piers] to allow any of us to preach in his church: charged me with breach of the canon [ecclesiastical law]. I mentioned the Bishop of London's authorizing my forcible exclusion. He would not hear me; said he did not dispute." The archbishop pointed out the irregularity of Wesley's preaching in other pastors' parishes without a proper ecclesiastical call to that parish or proper assignment to it. Wesley replied by pointing to the general call that all Christians and ministers have to witness to the gospel of Christ. Charles's journal entry records this conversation in a terse and truncated fashion: "He asked me what call I had. I answered, 'A dispensation of the gospel is committed to me.' 'That is, to St. Paul [the archbishop replied,] but I do not dispute; and will not proceed to excommunication YET.'"

Since the issue of field preaching also loomed in the background of this confrontation, Charles Wesley addressed the question directly: "I asked him, if Mr. Whitefield's success was not a spiritual sign, and sufficient proof of his call: recommended Gamaliel's advice." "Gamaliel's advice" was an allusion to Acts 5:34-40, a New Testament account of the apostles being dragged before the Sanhedrin in Jerusalem to be placed on trial for preaching Jesus as the Christ. Gamaliel was identified as "a Pharisee," and "a teacher of the law, held in honor by all the people" (Acts 5:34, RSV). He rose up and gave the Sanhedrin this advice about the apostles: "Keep away from these men and let them alone; for if this plan or this undertaking is of men, it will fail, but if it is of God, you will not be able to overthrow them. You might even be found opposing God" (Acts 5:38-39, RSV). That Charles Wesley felt as though he were standing before his own "Sanhedrin" facing charges for preaching the gospel of Christ was clear to the Anglican archbishop: "He dismissed us," Wesley wrote, "Piers with kind professions; me, with all the marks of his displeasure." More than fifty years later Charles penned a hymn that preserves his understanding of the relevancy of "Gamaliel's advice" to the situation of the early Methodists:

1. Ye sages of the world, be wise,
   Take the judicious scribe's advice,
       And let these men alone:
   Their work if plann'd by human thought
   Shall soon decay and come to nought,
       And prove itself their own.

2. But if this counsel is Divine,
   In vain the powers of earth combine
       To hinder or o'erthrow:
   Your utmost skill and strength employ,
   Man never can the work destroy,
       Which God revives below.

3. Wisely ye may consult, contrive,
   Earth's potsherds with your Maker strive,
       Your God withstand, defy:
   But O! 'tis quite impossible
   Against the Almighty to prevail
       Or conquer the Most-High!

Five days after his visit with the archbishop, on the feast day of St. John the Baptist, Charles Wesley preached outdoors without hesitation to a multitude at Moorfields in suburban London. Charles's journal records the event: "The first Scripture I cast my eye upon was 'Then came the servant unto Him, and said Master, what shall we do?' I prayed with [Mr.] West, and went forth in the name of Jesus Christ. I found near ten thousand helpless sinners waiting for the Word in Moorfield. I invited them in my Master's words, as well as name: 'Come unto Me, all ye that travail, and are heavy laden, and I will give you rest.' The Lord was with me, even me, His meanest messenger, according to His promise."

Wesley's new approach was sometimes received coldly in his old haunts, though he always tried to tailor his message to his audience. When he traveled to Oxford to visit his college and to fulfill his obligation to preach in the cathedral there, the dean did not give him a warm welcome: "I waited upon the Dean, who spoke with unusual severity against field-preaching, and Mr. Whitefield: explained away all inward religion, and union with God." On July 1, Wesley preached at Oxford on Romans 3:23-25: "For all have sinned, and come short of the glory of God; being justified freely by his grace through the redemption that is in Christ Jesus: whom God hath set forth to be a propitiation through faith in his blood, to declare his righteousness for the remission of sins that are past, through the forbearance of God" (KJV). He began with a prayer for the "catholick Church" and the British Sovereign, King George, and since he was addressing an educated, Anglican audience, Charles abandoned the extemporaneous preaching style that he was using among the multitudes. This was a carefully crafted homily that repeatedly quoted from the standard Homilies and Articles of "Our Church" to prove that Wesley's exposition of justification by faith alone was precisely the position of the Church of England. He carefully laid out the outline for the sermon at its beginning: "In discoursing upon each word I shall first show that all have sinned and come short of the glory of God. Secondly, that we are justified freely by His grace through the redemption that is in Jesus Christ. Thirdly, I shall show what that faith is through which we are receive the atonement applied to our soul in particular; and fourthly, I shall conclude with a particular application."

The last two points betray Wesley's distinctive approach to the topic. We hear echoes of the particularity of God's grace being applied to each individual person by agency of personal faith and repentance. The "for me" emphasis of Charles Wesley's conversion experience and conversion hymns is clearly sounded throughout this sermon. He stressed both the freedom and privileges justification by faith brings. Among these privileges are (1) peace with God ("attested by that peace which passes all understanding"); (2) "The love of God . . . shed abroad in all believers' hearts by the Holy Ghost which is given unto them. This love they show by keeping His commandments. . . . Sin shall not have dominion over them for they are not under the law but under grace"; (3) the victory of God over the world: "And this is the victory that overcometh the world, even our faith. . . . The spirit of this world continually oppresses the spirit of holiness, and he is more than conqueror through Christ that loveth him and dwelleth in his heart by faith"; and (4) a transforming union with Christ, which is the "greatest and most glorious privilege of the true believer." Wesley married the classical Reformation emphasis upon justification by faith alone to (using a Wesleyan euphemism) "holiness of heart and life."

One of Charles Wesley's early hymns, entitled "The Just Shall Live by Faith," was written during this period, and it illustrates many of the same themes that emerge in his Oxford sermon on justification:

> 5. For ten long, legal years I lay
>   An helpless, though reluctant, prey

To pride, and lust, and earth, and hell:
Oft to repentance vain renew'd,
Self-confident for hours I stood,
    And fell, and grieved and rose, and fell.

6. I fasted, read, and work'd and pray'd,
Call'd holy friendship to my aid,
    And constant to the altar drew;
'Tis there, I cried, He *must* be found!
By vows, and new engagements bound,
    All His commands I now shall do.

7. Soon as the trying hour return'd,
I sunk before the foes I scorn'd,
    My firm resolves did all expire:
Why hath the law of sin prevail'd?
Why have the bonds of duty fail'd?
    Alas! The tow hath touch'd the fire.

But the soul that despairs of self-salvation is one that is prepared for the righteousness of Christ:

9. 'Twas then my soul beheld from far
The glimmering of an orient Star,
    That pierced and cheered my nature's night
Sweetly it dawn'd, and promised day;
Sorrow and sin it chased away,
    And open'd into glorious light.

10. With other eyes I now could see
The Father reconciled to me;
    Jesus the Just had satisfied:
Jesus had made my sufferings His,
Jesus was now *my* righteousness;
    Jesus for *me* had lived and died.

The singer now looks for Christ and for love within as the fruit of justification. Satan's tyranny is over, and the saved is as a "brand pluck'd from the fire." Hence, the ransomed soul cries: "O Saviour help me to proclaim/Help me to show forth all Thy praise." This life lived in total reliance upon Christ is how "The Just shall live by Faith":

18. Fain would I spread through earth abroad
    The goodness of my loving God,
        And teach the world Thy grace to prove.
    Unutterably good Thou art!
    Read, Jesu, read my panting heart;
        Thou seest it pants to break with love.

19. I only live to find Thee there:
    The mansion for Thyself prepare,
        In love anew my heart create:
    The mighty change I long to feel:
    For this my vehement soul stands still,
        Restless — resign'd — for this I wait. . . .

Wesley the Methodist was beginning to develop a method for evangelism. Just as St. Paul went first to the synagogue to preach among believers and then directly to the general populace during his missionary journeys, Charles asked first to borrow the pulpit of the local parish church. "Before I went into the streets and highways," he wrote from Gloucester in 1739, "I sent according to my custom, to borrow the use of the church. The minister, being one of the better disposed, sent back a civil message that he would drink a glass of wine with me, but durst not lend me his pulpit for fifty guineas. Mr. Whitefield, however, durst lend me his field, which did just as well." Indeed, the field probably served Charles's purposes better, because there he was able to "exhort about two thousand sinners to repent and believe the Gospel." It was a crowd larger than the church would hold, and very likely many in that audience would not have darkened the door of a church. In Runwick, in August of the same year,

The minister . . . lent me his pulpit. I stood at the window (which was taken down), and turned to the larger congregation of above two thousand in the church yard. They appeared greedy to hear, while I testified "God so loved the world, that He gave His only begotten-Son." . . . In the afternoon . . . the church was full as it could crowd. Thousands stood in the churchyard. It was the most beautiful sight I ever beheld. The people filled the gradually rising area, which was shut up on three sides by a vast perpendicular hill. On the top and bottom of this hill was a circular row of trees. In this amphitheatre they stood, deeply attentive, while I called upon them in Christ's words, "Come unto Me, all that are weary." The tears of many testified that they were ready to enter into rest. God enabled me to lift up my voice like a trumpet, so that all distinctly heard me. I concluded with singing an invitation to sinners.

This combination of gospel preaching, vibrant emotion, and hymn singing would become hallmarks of Charles Wesley's preaching style. In the latter two aspects Charles's evangelism seemed to differ from that of his brother John. Charles had a fine musical voice and a poet's way with words. He combined sermon and song to form a blended form of spontaneous worship. One of Charles's hymns, entitled "The Invitation," suggests how he sang his congregation into a readiness to receive the gospel:

1. Weary souls, who wander wide
   From the central point of bliss,
   Turn to Jesus crucified,
   Fly to those dear wounds of His,
   Sink into the purple flood,
   Rise into the life of God!

2. Find in Christ the way of peace,
   Peace unspeakable, unknown:
   By His pain He gives you ease,
   Life by His expiring groan;
   Rise exalted by His fall,
   Find in Christ your all in all.

3. O believe the record true,
   God to you His Son hath given,
   Ye may now be happy too,

> Live on earth the life of heaven;
> Live the life of heaven above,
>   All the life of glorious love.

4. This is the universal bliss,
>   Bliss for every soul design'd,
> God's original promise this,
>   God's greatest gift to all mankind:
> Blest in Christ this moment be,
>   Blest to all eternity!

Another account of Charles Wesley's early open-air preaching comes to us from Joseph Williams, a Congregationalist, and no friend of the Methodist movement:

> I found him standing upon a table, in an erect posture, with hands and eyes lifted up to heaven in prayer, surrounded with (I guess) more than a thousand people; some few of them persons of fashion, both men and women, but most of them of the lower rank of mankind. I know not how long he had been engaged in the duty before I came, but he continued therein, after my coming, scarce a quarter of an hour; during which time he prayed with uncommon fervency, fluency, and variety of proper expression. He then preached about an hour from the five last verses of the fifth chapter of the second Epistle to the Corinthians, in such a manner as I have seldom, if ever, heard any minister preach: i.e. though I have heard many a finer sermon, according to common taste, or acceptation of sermons, yet I scarce ever heard any minister discover such evident signs of a most vehement desire, or labour so earnestly, to convince his hearers that they were all by nature in a state of enmity against God, consequently in a damnable state, and needed reconciliation to God. . . . These points he backed all along as he went on with a great many texts of scripture, which he explained, and illustrated; and then freely invited all, even the chief of sinners, and used a great variety of the most moving arguments, and expositions, in order to persuade, allure, instigate and if possible, compel them to come to Christ, and believe in him for pardon and salvation.

As relationships with the "mother church" were becoming strained, the Methodists began taking steps that would gradually create an ad hoc, alternative establishment that would turn the Wesleys' outdoor evangelism into an organized religious movement. One of the first steps in this direction was John Wesley's purchase of land in the Horse Fair, in Bristol, in May 1739. There he subsequently built the "New Room" — a Methodist preaching house and society room that became the hub of Wesleyan activities in that region. It had several meeting rooms and a preaching room (the sacraments were not offered there until the Methodist separation from the Church of England, after the Wesleys' death). It also held rooms for lay preachers and apartments that were utilized by John and Charles Wesley, as well as Susanna Wesley during her widowhood. Charles Wesley began his ministry in Bristol in October 1739, and it continued to be the hub of his activities until he and his family relocated to London in 1771.

As Charles Wesley took his evangelistic ministry into the streets and highways, he found himself preaching to multitudes that most churches would not hold. While this approach seemed to be forced upon him by the Anglican religious establishment, as the churches closed their doors to him, the way towards it was paved by the previous example of George Whitefield and the effectiveness he enjoyed with open-air evangelism. Charles found himself occasionally buffeted by scruples and uncertainties about the propriety of what he was doing, but the message bore such fruit that gradually his ecclesiastical scruples and personal shyness melted away. If Charles Wesley found his gospel message on Pentecost 1738, in the ensuing year and a half he found his evangelistic medium. His open-air, spontaneous evangelism and his gospel hymns were married together to form an effective tool for challenging people to live holy lives. He was taking the church's message to people who had not the time, opportunity, or inclination to attend church; he met multitudes on common ground, and won over many. The dramatic fruits of his labors gradually wore down Wesley's concerns about the innovation of field preaching even as it exposed him to increased opposition and persecution.

5 "He Offers Christ to All"

Open-air evangelism, which the Wesleys stumbled upon more or less by accident as they were barred from preaching in Anglican churches, had the notable benefit of allowing them to take the gospel message to where the largest and hungriest crowds could be found. Given that the majority of the common people were uneducated, unchurched, and even unable to attend church, this approach was a stroke of genius. It meant, however, that the reader of Charles Wesley's journal frequently finds him preaching in unusual places at unusual times. Wesley scrupulously avoided preaching during stated hours of Anglican worship, so that he could not be accused of diverting people from attending church. He often attended Anglican worship and received the Lord's Supper — along with a troop of Methodists — and then spent the afternoon or evening preaching outdoors. This practice reinforced the point that the Wesleys (and especially Charles Wesley) wanted to make obvious to all: Methodism was to be understood as a renewal movement that existed within and for the benefit of the Church of England. While he sought to bring the multitudes to saving faith in Jesus Christ, Wesley wanted them to express their faith through association with the Church of England.

His open-air evangelism took Wesley to where the people were.

He preached in fields, town markets or town squares, and village greens, places that were near the traffic patterns of normal village life. These evangelism events were well planned, and an advance team — generally made up of local Methodists — advertised the time and place of his proclamation so that many people could attend. Hence Charles often preached to crowds that numbered into the thousands. Near Bristol he preached in "the Weaver's Hall." At Kingswood and St. Ives he preached at mine entrances in the morning and evenings, so that he could address the miners as they came to and went from their work. At Portsmouth and Plymouth he preached at the docks, standing on bales of cotton or crates of merchandise waiting to be loaded on ships. He could as readily be found preaching from the local courthouse steps or in a churchyard — often the yard of a church that had forbade him the use of its building. In the latter instance Wesley often stood on the steps or upon a convenient monument, while his listeners stood among or sat upon the gravestones. Still, Charles was more at home preaching at Westminster Abbey, or St. Mary's Church, Oxford. He was equally at home at Lady Huntingdon's London houses, witnessing to the aristocratic dinner guests she hosted in "the salon" she held there. Preaching outside was an affront to Charles Wesley's sense of ecclesiastical propriety, as well as his retiring personality. It was also an offense to the proper people of his day. Many proper Anglicans were scandalized to see this diminutive Oxford don address the unwashed masses while wearing his pulpit gown and clerical collar. But it symbolized the ironic combination of ecclesiastical propriety and pragmatic ingenuity that lay at the heart of the Methodist experiment.

To whom did Charles Wesley preach? Mrs. Seward, the wife of one of Charles's friends, put it best: "he offers Christ to all." The Wesleyan gospel was for everyone. In fact, when Charles Wesley came to summarize "the two great truths of the everlasting gospel," the ones that distinguished the Wesleyan perspective, he enumerated them as "universal redemption and Christian Perfection."

A message that applied to everyone had to be taken to everyone. This was the theological basis of Wesleyan evangelism, the innovation of open-air preaching, and the establishment of an itinerant, mobile ministry. Taken together with open-air evangelism, their traveling approach to ministry meant that the Methodists were able to reach and preach to multitudes. Often these were people whose lives had been devoid of the comforts of Christianity because of social, economic, and ecclesiastical restrictions. Occasionally Charles Wesley's practiced eye noticed the fashionable or aristocratic people that stood at the fringes of his audiences, and his journal often reports seeing them. On September 13, 1741, he reported, "I preached at night to a numerous congregation of gentry and others. God gives me favour in their sight. O that I could make them displeased with themselves." But "the gentry" were the exception rather than the rule for the audiences of Methodist evangelism. Aristocratic and wealthy people like Robert Jones of Fonmon Castle, Selina Hastings — the Countess of Huntingdon — and Ebenezer Blackwell also associated themselves with the Methodist movement, but they were clearly in the minority.

Although Charles Wesley did not share his brother John's antipathy for the rich and famous — "genteel Methodists," he called them — neither was Charles overly concerned about people of rank and station. Indeed, his satirical hymn "A Man of Fashion" illustrates Wesley's impatience with transient values and a fopish, fashionable lifestyle:

> A man of taste and dissipation . . .
> In sleep, in dress, and sport and play
> He throws his worthless life away . . .
> With a disdainful smile or frown
> He on the riff-raff crowd looks down;
> The world polite his friends and he;
> And all the rest are — nobody! . . .
> Custom pursues, his only rule,
> And lives an Ape, and dies a Fool.

When Charles Wesley was found in the company of "genteel Methodists" it was because of his appreciation of their Christian character, not because of his awe or awareness of their worldly status. He was more often found preaching to the Colliers of Kingswood, the Keelmen who worked the barges in Newcastle, or the "Tinners" of St. Ives or St. Just in Wales.

In 1740 Charles Wesley began his itinerant ministry in earnest. He and John Wesley planned their evangelism travels and strategies together, but because of his administrative gifts John took the lead. While their partnership in ministry lasted more than fifty years, it was also true that over the years Charles became less amenable to his older brother's requests and demands for evangelistic assistance. After his marriage in 1749, the obligations of home and children caused Charles to travel less. As the century wore on he was apt to annotate his brother's demanding letters "Trying to bring me under his yoke," and file them unanswered. At times their partnership became strained, but it was never broken.

Itinerant, open-air evangelism was also an attack upon Charles's frail health. Exposed to the wind, rain, and weather by his incessant travels, Charles was frequently ill. Born prematurely, Charles's health was never as robust as John's. The deprivation of his years at Oxford and his rough work in Georgia seemed to leave Charles's respiratory system permanently compromised. In an undated letter, written home to his wife Sally at Bristol, Charles lamented, "Next Monday my brother sets out for Bristol by Oxford and etc. I dare not accept his offer and venture with him. His way of traveling would kill a younger man. Now I know not when I shall see Bristol, or at all."

Bristol would ultimately become Charles Wesley's base of operations for several decades. The Methodist "New Room," located in the Horsefair section of town, provided him with a preaching post, strong Methodist society, and living quarters. It also offered a convenient jumping-off point for his ministerial labors in nearby Kingswood, Bath, Wales, and Cornwall. After his marriage, Charles continued to live and work out of Bristol, taking a house on Charles Street (which still stands), about a ten-minute walk from the New Room.

Charles Wesley's journal for 1742 has not been published, but a manuscript journal letter places him in Newcastle and its vicinity for most of September of that year. The Methodist society increased in membership from 70 to 250 during his tenure there. He preached to multitudes that rivaled or exceeded those he more typically met at London's Kennington Common. Wesley was drawn out in love and compassion for his Newcastle congregation, and they reciprocated his love: "I told them sincerely that I would rather be the Keelmen's chaplain than the King's. There is no expressing their love for me; they would even pluck out their eyes [Matthew 5:29] and give them to me; I am so canny a creature! The tiller of the colliers! Preacher in the square on the grand promise of the Father [Luke 24:49]." The early Methodist preacher John Nelson remembered hearing Wesley preaching upon his return from one of his evangelistic crusades in Newcastle:

> When Mr. Charles Wesley came back from Newcastle, the Lord was with him in such a manner, that the pillars of hell seemed to tremble: many that were famous for supporting the devil's kingdom, fell to the ground, while he was preaching, as if they had been thunder-struck. One day he had preached four times; and one that had been amongst the people all day, said at night, twenty-two had received forgiveness of their sins that day.

In 1742 at Oxford Charles preached what would become perhaps his most famous sermon: "Awake Thou That Sleepest," based on Ephesians 5:14. "Sleeping" became a metaphor for the life of sin, and awakening from it symbolized justification by faith and the new birth. The sermon was hugely popular and became the most frequently published and purchased Methodist pamphlet. Thomas Salmon, a popular historian who claimed to have been in Wesley's congregation on that day, subsequently published a very negative report of the event in his *A Foreigner's Companion through the Universities of Cambridge and Oxford* (1748): "when I happened to be in Oxford, in 1742, Mr. Wesley, the Methodist, of Christ Church, entertained his audience two hours, having insulted and abused all degrees from the highest to the lowest, was in a manner hissed out of the pulpit by the lads." Charles, who apparently read Salmon's report, quoted it verbatim in his journal entry for April 15, 1750, and refuted it in unequivocal terms: "And high time for them to do so, if the historian said true; but, unfortunately for him, I measured the time by my watch, and it was within the hour: I abused neither high nor low, as my sermon, in print, will prove; neither was I hissed out of the pulpit, or treated with the least incivility, either by young or old." This event did mark a watershed, however; it signaled the last time that Charles Wesley "preached before the University."

By 1743 Charles Wesley had established the pattern that would mark out his itinerant ministry, more or less, for the next decade and beyond. Beginning in London, after the worst of winter and spring thaw was over, he would preach his way north — generally by way of Oxford — to Newcastle upon Tyne, where the Methodists subsequently established an orphanage and third base of operations. With the subsequent forays into the north the so-called "Methodist triangle" was established, with bases of operation in London (the Foundery, an old factory the Methodists had set up as a meeting place in 1740) in the southeast, Bristol (the New Room) in the west, and Newcastle (the orphanage) in the north. In this way the Wesleys established logistical coverage that allowed them to minister to most of the population of Britain. John made his principal base in London, and Charles worked out of Bristol; both brothers itinerated to the other's location and each took a swing northward at least once (and usually more) each year.

Charles moved around relentlessly in 1743, preaching to growing (and not always receptive) crowds. His hymn "Before Preaching in Cornwall" gives a strong sense of the calling and expectancy with which he met these audiences:

1. True witness of the Father's love,
    Celestial Messenger Divine,
  Come in Thy Spirit from above,
    The hearts which Thou hast made incline
  Thy faithful record to receive;
    That all may hear Thy voice and live. . . .

5. Fisher of men ordain'd by Thee,
    O might I catch them by Thy love!
  Thy love be first bestow'd on me,
    And while the pleasing power I prove,
  My tongue shall echo to my heart,
    And tell the world how good Thou art.

6. Teach me to cast my net aright,
    The gospel net of general grace,
  So shall I all to Thee invite,
    And draw them to their Lord's embrace,
  Within Thine arms of love include,
    And catch a willing multitude.

7. O might I every mourner cheer,
    And trouble every heart of stone,

> Save, under Thee, the souls that hear,
>   Nor lose, in seeking them, my own,
> Nor basely from my calling fly,
>   But for Thy gospel live, and die.

The hymn Wesley entitled "Written at the Land's End" was probably written during this period of Charles's ministry. It speaks eloquently of Wesley's passion for saving "every soul" through the agency of God's grace:

> 2. Carry on Thy victory,
>   Spread Thy rule from sea to sea,
>   Reconvert the ransom'd race,
>   Save us, save us, Lord, by grace.

> 3. Take the purchase of Thy blood,
>   Bring us to a pardoning God;
>   Give us eyes to see our day,
>   Hearts the glorious truth to obey.

> 4. Ears to hear the gospel sound;
>   Grace doth more than sin abound,
>   God appeased, and man forgiven,
>   Peace on earth, and joy in heaven.

> 5. O that every soul might be
>   Suddenly subdued to Thee!
>   O that all in Thee might know
>   Everlasting life below. . . .

Behind the almost frenetic energy of their itinerant ministry lay the Wesleys' substructure of societies, classes, and bands. It was this infrastructure that gave eighteenth-century Methodism its staying power. The presence of a traveling evangelist in a congregation three or four times a year, even someone as talented as John or Charles Wesley, was not enough to keep the Methodist movement vital and growing. Indeed, the Wesleys did not even consider those multitudes who attended their evangelistic services to be bona fide Methodists. Only the organizational structure of Methodism could sustain it, and one had to join that structure to be considered fully Methodist. For the Wesleys, Methodists were those who, having been motivated and raised up by earnest evangelism, committed themselves to the "General Rules" of the Methodist societies and were willing to join a Methodist "class." Each class was made up of ten to twelve people who lived in the same vicinity. They met together weekly for prayer, Bible study, and pastoral care. Each class was led by a "class leader," a mature lay person who had been trained by the Wesleys for that role. Each class took up a penny per person (if possible) to aid the poor in their midst. It became the pastoral care agency of the movement, thanks in part to the way the class leader became a sort of lay pastor and spiritual director to those in his or her class. In December 1738 the Wesleys had drawn up a set of four questions, preserved in their "Rules for the Band-Societies," which were to be asked of each person at each meeting:

1. What known sins have you committed since our last meeting?
2. What temptations have you met with?
3. How were you delivered?
4. What have you thought, said, or done, of which you doubt whether it be sin or not?

Every Methodist had to be a member of a class, and every member of a class was examined periodically and issued a "class ticket" signed by either Wesley brother to certify that he or she was in good standing with God and their fellows. The combined meeting of all the Wesleyan classes in a particular town constituted the Methodist society. A typical town could have a Methodist society of eighty to a hundred members, divided into five or six classes.

The societies had lifestyle expectations that included challenging the bad habits of some of the members — such as taking snuff. Charles diagnosed this problem as the spiritual failing of the formerly stalwart society at St. Ives. His manuscript journal for July 21, 1746, reports:

> Returned to St. Ives and immediately found *their* burden. J[ohn] Tremblath informed me that almost the whole Society are slaves to snuff or tobacco. Those that stood like a rock in time of persecution are well-nigh subverted now by so base a lust. Their pipes they

could not so conveniently use, but as to their snuff, they take it continually in the midst of singing, preaching, and praying. Yet such deceitfulness of the heart, they could see no harm in it. They would not acknowledge it to be an idol, but said "Why if God convince us it is contrary to His will, we will leave it off." I was too much weighed down this evening to speak, but on Tuesday night I declared and disburdened my whole mind. I laid down the Christian's rule, "whether ye eat or drink or whatsoever ye do do all to the glory of God" [1 Cor. 10:31], then asked, "do ye take snuff or smoke to the glory of God? If not tis contrary to the written Word and therefore Sin." Again, "Do you take snuff to please God or yourselves? If to please yourselves tis contrary to Christ's example, for Christ pleased not Himself; [tis] contrary to His command, 'if any man will come after me let him *deny* himself' [Matt. 16:24]. To do anything merely to please yourself is to deny Christ." . . . I gave notice of my design to talk with each of the Bands again, and put out of the Society [all] who could not say either "I take snuff to the glory of God, to please God by preserving my health," or "I promise through His grace to take it no longer." Several of them threw away their [snuff] boxes before they left the room.

Soon a second type of small group called the "band" (referred to in the passage above) was added for mature Christians that were seeking a deeper dimension of Christian living. These bands were segregated by gender, since some of the challenges people faced in living a holy life revolved around issues associated with gender and sex. This meant that, almost from the outset, the Methodist movement employed mature Christian women as leaders of women's bands. From this reservoir of mature, well-trained Christian lay women would eventually spring an occasional female Methodist lay preacher.

Methodist societies met several times a week, generally Sunday afternoon and evening, Wednesday night, and Saturday night, for preaching, teaching, and fellowship occasions. A point was made to have Methodist meetings follow, but not compete with, the scheduled worship opportunities of local Anglican churches. The Methodists were expected to attend worship and sacrament at their parish church and then attend the functions of the society and class meetings as a way of enhancing and supplementing their Anglican experience. As the societies grew they also took up social services, adopting benevolent works like establishing a traveler's aid society and interest-free loans for society members. It was not uncommon for the societies to take an interest in teaching people to read and organizing Bible societies to make inexpensive copies of the scriptures available to their members. The Wesleys recognized that their organizational structure was the genius of the Methodist movement, and they spent considerable time and efforts making the connection of classes, bands, and societies function well. John Wesley, in fact, is said to have quipped that George Whitefield's people were "a rope of sand" because they lacked the solid infrastructure that characterized the Wesleyans.

In his early years of itinerant ministry Charles Wesley spent much of his time organizing, visiting, and preaching and teaching in the Methodist societies. He met with bands and classes to examine the spiritual state of their members. He met with leaders to train them and equip them for their various ministries.

The Wesleys also employed lay assistants, who traveled with them to help them in their work. Gradually, these lay assistants were apprenticed to become lay preachers. Thomas Maxfield, who traveled with Charles Wesley in 1740, was one of the first lay preachers in the movement. After traveling with Charles as an assistant, Maxfield was made a kind of pastoral supervisor at the Foundery. While the Wesleys were traveling on their itinerant circuits he was pressed into preaching in their stead, which he did with great effectiveness. While the Wesley brothers were initially angry at Maxfield for apparently usurping the office of preaching, their mother, Susanna Wesley, and Selina Hastings, the Countess of Huntingdon, both testified that he had been used by God and should not be hindered. Commenting on the contrast between Thomas Maxfield's humble beginnings and his powerful preaching, Lady Huntingdon wrote, "He is one of the greatest instances of God's peculiar favour that I know. He has raised from the stones one to set among the princes of his people. He is my astonishment. How is God's power shown in weakness!"

The Wesley brothers eventually found that lay preachers were a necessary and helpful supplement to their own evangelistic and pastoral efforts. Of course, the more pragmatic John was more accepting of the lay preachers' deficiencies than was the more ecclesiastically proper Charles. John often added to their ranks, and Charles frequently fired them as quickly as John hired them. As Charles confided to John Bennet, in a manuscript letter dated August 11, 1751, "A friend of ours [John Wesley] (without God's counsel) made a preacher of a tailor. I with God's help shall make a tailor of him again." Over the years, as the lay preachers clamored for more and more rights and authority in the Methodist movement (such as the authority to administer the Lord's Supper), Charles Wesley assumed the role of reproving them and striving to keep them in the proper role for unordained laymen.

As more preachers became associated with the Methodist movement, both lay preachers and ordained Anglican priests, the Wesleys began holding annual conferences for the Methodist preachers. They often lasted several days, during which time searching conversations were held on doctrinal and practical matters associated with Methodism. The formal minutes of these conversations were voted on and approved as doctrinal standards for the Methodist movement. The first recorded annual conference was held at the Foundery in London in 1744, attended by John and Charles Wesley and four others. The group grew exponentially, such that by the end of the eighteenth century John Wesley had bequeathed his leadership role to the Methodist annual conference and the "legal one hundred" preachers that comprised it.

There was at the heart of early Methodism an egalitarian mood. It extended to the diversity found in the congregations who heard the Wesleys preach, as well as to the makeup of their societies, classes, and bands. The belief that the gospel was for all people, not just the elect, was a bedrock Wesleyan assumption that worked itself out in Charles Wesley's theology of ministry. It gave both Wesley brothers a passion for preaching the gospel of salvation and holiness to all people, in every place possible. It was the motivating force for the thousands of miles the Wesleys logged. It even propelled them to consider the innovation of lay preachers — in yet another break with the law of the Church of England — and to countenance the gifts of an occasional female evangelist who professed and evidenced "extraordinary" call to preach the gospel. Offering the gospel to "all" would shape the band of messengers as well as the message.

6 "The Snare of Stillness"

The Wesley brothers read and studied various sources of Christian mysticism, and their writings indicate how formative these works were for their faith and thought. From the ancient church writers they also learned the value of spiritual disciplines such as prayer and fasting, and they began to practice them regularly. John Wesley read William Law's *Christian Perfection* in 1726 and soon began recommending it to his colleagues. Law's *A Serious Call to a Devout and Holy Life* appeared in 1728, and it too was devoured by the Oxford Methodists.

But by 1739 the Wesleys were beginning to break with the practical mysticism of William Law and others. This departure was first signaled in their "Preface" to *Hymns and Sacred Poems* of that year, which the brothers published jointly. Some of the hymns in this collection (which stem from the earliest years of their hymn writing) "were built upon the scheme of the Mystic divines." The mystical writers now seemed to savor too much of the first foundation which the Wesleys themselves laid — good works. Hence their "Preface" warns, "Neither our own inward nor outward righteousness is the ground of our justification. Holiness of heart, as well as of life, is not the cause of, but the effect of it." The Wesleys sought to square their early appreciation of the mystical writers with what they had learned on Whitsunday and at Aldersgate Street — justification by faith alone. "The sole cause of our acceptance with God," they wrote, ". . . is the righteousness and death of Christ, who fulfilled God's law, and died in our stead." The 1739 "Preface" had no patience for solitary, self-centered, spirituality: "Directly opposite to this is the Gospel of Christ. Solitary religion is not to be found there. 'Holy solitaries' is a phrase no more consistent with the Gospel than holy adulterers. The Gospel of Christ knows of no religion, but social; no holiness, but social holiness." The "holiness" the gospel of Christ demands, said the Wesleys, is Christian perfection, which they defined in this manner: "Faith working by love in us is the length and breadth and depth and height of Christian perfection. This commandment have we from Christ, that he who loves God, love his neighbor also; and that we manifest our love by doing good unto all men, especially to them that are of the household of faith."

In late 1739 a controversy emerged among the early Methodists over the issue of "stillness." This emphasis, which stemmed from the Moravian wing of the movement, stressed Christian liberty with respect to outward things such as attending public worship, studying the scriptures, or receiving the Lord's Supper. In fact, these "outward" means were seen by some as a hindrance to inner piety — if one depended upon them for their salvation. Since most of the people who came to this emphasis were associated with the Moravians, "stillness" doctrine soon became a line of demarcation that was drawn between the Wesleyan Methodists and the English Moravians. In a letter to an unnamed colleague in Bristol, which Charles Wesley wrote from London on April 25, 1740, he described the issues between the Methodists and the Moravians as he saw them:

> My brother came most critically. The snare, we trust will now be broken and many simple souls delivered. Many here insist that a part of their Christian calling is liberty *from* obeying, not liberty *to* obey. The justified, say they, are to be still; that is, not to search the scriptures, not to pray, not to communicate [take the Lord's Supper], not to do good, not to endeavour, not to desire; for it is impossible to use the means without trusting in them. Their practice is agreeable to their principles. Lazy and proud themselves, bitter

and censorious towards others, they trample upon the ordinances and despise the commands of Christ. I see no middle ground whereupon we can meet.

Several important issues emerge in this description. One is that "Christian liberty," properly understood, is a freedom to obey God from the heart. Another is that good works, while not earning salvation, are the fruit of justification by faith and are therefore a part of the process of sanctification. The "means" or "ordinances" mentioned here are the "means of grace" or spiritual disciplines that the Methodists (drawing upon their Anglican heritage) insisted were useful ways of encountering Jesus Christ. Since they were ordinances whereby a person could meet Christ by faith, spiritual disciplines like the Lord's Supper, prayer, fasting, scripture reading, and Christian conference (fellowship) were esteemed as "means of grace"; that is to say, they were viewed as faith-based opportunities to meet God's forgiveness and grace in a transforming way. Both John and Charles Wesley understood passages like "Do this in remembrance of me" (1 Corinthians 11:24), with respect to the Lord's Supper, and "when you pray" (Matthew 6:5) or "when you fast" (Matthew 6:16) as being commandments from Jesus Christ enjoining Christians to participate in these spiritual disciplines. Hence, failure to use these "ordinances," for the Wesleys, was a very serious matter. It not only barred a person from opportunities to receive God's sanctifying grace; it also constituted a willful disobedience of important injunctions given to Christians by Jesus Christ.

An anonymous letter from London, dated December 14, 1739, included in John Wesley's published journal, reports schismatic activities in the Methodist bands. It represents the opening salvo in the battle over "stillness":

This day I was told, by one that does not belong to the bands, that the society would be divided. . . . I believe Brother Hutton, Clark, Edmonds, and Bray are determined to go on, according to Mr. Molther's directions, and to "raise up a church," as they term it; and I supposed above half our brethren are on their side. But they are so very confused they don't know how to go on; yet are unwilling to be taught, except by the Moravians. . . .

85

The fact that James Hutton and John Bray, who had long been friends and close associates of Charles Wesley, were counted among the "still brethren" made this a very painful matter for him. Charles's journal seems to foreshadow the coming of this controversy, as he recorded on June 5, 1739, that Mr. Bray and Bowers were "drunk with the spirit of delusion." George Whitefield, Charles reported approvingly, "honestly said, 'they were two grand enthusiasts.'"

Most of Charles's controversies, however, were with John Simpson, who endeavored to convert the London Methodist Society over to "stillness" doctrine. Simpson was a "fringe" figure in the early Methodist movement. He had graduated from Lincoln College, Oxford (John Wesley's old school), in 1725, and may have had some contact with the Oxford Methodists. He served a pastorate in Leicestershire, and was considered by the Countess of Huntingdon as one of the two "awakened" pastors in that region. Simpson then became a major player in the Fetter Lane Society of London and eventually joined the Moravian Church.

In an attempt to quell the controversy, John Wesley went to London in April 1740 "with a heavy heart." He found the society in disarray and full of contention and controversy; the disputes were so widespread that they were diverting the Methodists' attention from their focus on Christ ("their first love"): "Here I found every day the dreadful effects of our [still] brethren's reasonings, and disputing with each other. Scarce one in ten retained his first love, and most of the rest were in the utmost confusion, biting and devouring one another." There were six points wherein John disagreed with the Moravians, but most important was the sixth point:

> [6] As to *the way to faith*, you believe: that the way to attain it is to *wait* for Christ and be *still*. i.e. Not to use (what we term) "the means of grace"; Not to go to church; Not to communicate; Not to fast; Not to use *so much* private prayer; Not to read the Scriptures; . . . Not to do temporal good; Nor to attempt doing spiritual good. . . .

Charles Wesley took note of the controversy in his journal. "I talked with poor perverted Mr. Simpson," Charles wrote. "The still ones have carried their point. He said some were prejudiced against the Moravian brethren . . . but that he had received great benefit from them." With a touch of irony, Wesley asked "whether he was *still in* the means of grace, or *out* of them." "Means of grace!" Simpson retorted, "There are none. Neither is there any good to be got by those you call such, or any obligation upon us to use them. Sometimes I go to church and Sacrament," he continued, "for example's sake: but it is a thing of mere indifference. Most of us have cast them off. You must not speak a word in recommendation of them; that is setting the people upon working [out their own salvation]." Charles was pained to find out that many London friends, including his old friend Charles Delamotte, had been drawn to stillness. "The Philistines have been upon him," Wesley wrote of Delamotte, "and prevailed. He has given up the ordinances, as to their being a matter of duty. Only his practice lies a little behind his faith. He uses them *still*." Delamotte urged Charles Wesley not to make an issue of the "stillness" theology and its attack upon the spiritual disciplines the Methodists held dear. "They are mere outward things," Delamotte opined. "Our brethren have left them off. It would only cause divisions to bring them up again. Let them drop," he urged, "and speak of the weightier matters of the law." Wesley opted for a different course of action: "I would hear them of their own mouth, who talked against the ordinances; first have my full evidence, and then speak and not spare."

During this same period Charles penned his hymn entitled "The Means of Grace." It was probably written in 1739 and published in 1740. In this hymn, Wesley sought to steer a middle course between trusting Methodist practices, the means of grace, as an end in themselves, and the extreme of avoiding the means of grace entirely on the other. The hymn begins by urging the singer not to trust the ordinances as a means of salvation, which is to make them into "an idol." This may be Charles Wesley speaking autobiographically of his pre-conversion life, when he sought to please God by doing "his duty" and striving to keep God's laws:

> 5. But I of *means* have made my boast,
>   Of *means* an idol made;
>   The spirit in the letter lost,
>   The substance in the shade.

6. I rested in the outward law,
    Nor knew its deep design;
The length and breadth I never saw,
    The height of love Divine.

The person who looks at "the means of grace" in this way sees nothing of the inner work of God that can come to a person through them. The singer is tempted to leave off practicing spiritual disciplines because of the dangers of trusting in them for salvation; this was the argument of the "still brethren." Yet in this hymn Charles succeeded in expounding his own theology of "the means of grace" while using some of his opponent's "stillness" terminology. Addressing the question of whether a person should leave off using the "means of grace," Wesley intones:

8. Thine is the work, and Thine alone —
    But shall I idly stand?
Shall I the written Rule disown,
    And slight my God's command?

9. Wildly shall I from Thine turn back,
    A better path to find;
Thy holy ordinance forsake,
    And cast Thy words behind?

10. Forbid it, gracious Lord, that I
    Should ever learn Thee so!
No — let *me* with Thy word comply,
    If I Thy love would know.

Hence the Christian liberty that Wesley cherished was the liberty to obey Christ's commands. Freed from bondage to sin, self, and the flesh, a Christian can live a life that follows Christ. In this case that means following Jesus' specific injunctions about spiritual disciplines:

11. Suffice for me, that Thou, my Lord,
    Hast bid me fast and pray:
Thy will be done, Thy name adored;
    'Tis only mine t'obey.

12. Thou bidd'st me search the Sacred Leaves,
     And taste the hallow'd Bread:
    The kind commands my soul receives,
     And longs on Thee to feed.

13. Still for Thy loving kindness, Lord,
     I in Thy temple wait;
    I look to find Thee in Thy word,
     Or at Thy table meet.

As we have seen from his journal, Wesley enjoyed an ironic play of words (especially upon the word "still") inherent in this debate. Working from the phrase "Be still and know that I am God," Charles sought to give the singer a proper understanding of pious "stillness" — as waiting in God's "appointed ways" — which allows a person to encounter the living God and feel the saving power of Jesus' blood. Hence, a person could be renewed inwardly by faith-filled participation in the outward signs of God's grace:

14. Here, *in Thine own appointed ways,*
     I wait to learn Thy will:
    Silent I stand before Thy face,
     And hear Thee say, "Be still!"

15. "Be still — and know that I am God!"
     'Tis all I live to know;
    To feel the virtue of Thy blood,
     And spread its praise below.

16. I wait my vigour to renew,
     Thine image to retrieve,
    The veil of outward things pass through,
     And grasp in Thee to live.

Charles Wesley enjoined a Christ-centered understanding of God's ordinances, whereby a person trusts God's provision in Jesus Christ and thereby can use "the means of grace" without trusting in them. One's trust, rather, is in Christ (the "great eternal 'Mean'") and not in the "means" or in good works:

19. I do the thing Thy laws enjoin,
    And *then* the strife gives o'er:
    To Thee I *then* the whole resign:
    I *trust* in means no more.

20. I trust in Him who stands between
    The Father's wrath and me:
    JESU! Thou great eternal Mean,
    I look for all from Thee. . . .

By April, Charles Wesley had already begun to despair of a reconciliation with the "still brethren." He confided in his journal on April 5, 1740, "A separation I foresee unavoidable. All means have been taken to wean our friends of their esteem for us. God never used us, say they, as instruments to convert one soul." The next day was Easter, and Charles was scheduled to preach at the Foundery, which he did — from Philemon 3:9, 10 — "I strongly preached Christ, and the power of his resurrection," he wrote. "My intention," he recalled, "was not to mention one word of the controverted points, till I had spoke with each of the seducers." But in the course of the sermon Wesley felt God leading him "into the very line of battle and struggle. My mouth was opened to ask, 'Who hath bewitched you, that you should let go of your Saviour? That you should cast away your shield and your confidence, and deny you ever knew him?'" The impact of this direct assault was made evident by the tears of Wesley's listeners: "The whole congregation was in tears. I called them back to their Saviour, even *theirs,* in words which were not mine; pressed obedience to the divine ordinances." Later, as he sat at dinner at Hiland's house, the church bell rang, signaling it was time for public worship. The Moravians present offered not to go to the church for services, saying "It is good for us to be *here.*" "Well, then," Charles Wesley retorted, "'I will go myself [to church], and leave you to your antichristian liberty.' Upon this," he reported, "they started up and bore me company." While they were at church, Charles heard one of them tell a poor man, "that comfort you received at the sacrament was given you by the Devil." "I should have less blasphemously have called it, the drawing of the Father, or preventing grace," he added.

Later that same day Charles Wesley had a strained conversation with John Bray, his friend who had played such an instrumental role in Wesley's evangelical conversion. As Charles asked him pointed questions, Bray equivocated. "I asked Bray," Wesley recalled, "whether he denied the ordinances to be commands. He answered indirectly, 'I grant them to be great privileges.' (Edmonds confessed more honestly, that he had cast them off). Whether he had not denied George Whitefield to have faith? This question he answered by begging to be excused it." At the end of this conference Charles told Bray, "whosoever cast off the ordinances, I would cast him off, although it was my own brother."

Two days later, Charles Wesley met with Simpson, who told him, "if I recommended the ordinances, he must preach against me." Wesley in turn avowed his "resolution never to give them up, as he and our poor deluded brethren had done." That same evening Wesley preached at the Foundery and met with the "women bands." He found them in "the wilderness state," with a sense of lostness and feeling forsaken by God. Wesley recalled, "I told them that their forsaking the ordinances sufficiently accounted for their being forsaken by Christ." The meeting of the Fetter Lane Society that same evening was full of tension and disputes. Among the charges that Simpson and the "still ones" brought against Charles Wesley was the fact of his "preaching up the ordinances." Wesley reported that he went home "weary, wounded, and bruised, and faint, through the contradiction of sinners; *poor* sinners as they called themselves, these heady, violent, fierce contenders for stillness. I could not bear the thought of meeting them again." Returning to the Foundery, once again Charles found himself preaching on the ordinances. "I finished Isaiah 1, at the Foundery," he wrote, "which led me to speak explicitly on the ordinances. God gave me great power . . . sealing my words on many hearts."

Simpson and others continued spreading division among the London Methodists. Charles's journal reports, "Simpson and the rest have dissuaded them, and indeed all our friends, from ever hearing my brother or me, or using any of the means. They condemn all doing good, whether to soul or body. 'For, unless you *trust* in them,' say they, 'you would not do good works, so called.'" Their refusal to do good to people's souls or bodies was a sore point for Charles Wesley because the "Rules of the United Societies," which he had probably helped draft in 1739, explicitly urged the Methodists to "do no harm"; "to do good," that being "in every kind, merciful after their power as they have opportunity, doing good of every possible sort, and as is possible to all men — to their bodies, of the ability which God giveth, by giving food to the hungry, by clothing the naked, by visiting or helping them that are sick, or in prison — to their souls, by instructing, reproving, or exhorting all. . . ." And "by attending upon the ordinances of God. Such are public worship of God; the ministry of the word, either read or expounded; the supper of the Lord; family and private prayer; searching the Scriptures, and fasting or abstinence." These three obligations — of doing no harm, doing good, and attending upon the ordinances of God — had been fundamental obligations of members of the Methodist societies since their inception.

John Simpson's extravagances continued to increase on almost a daily basis, and Charles Wesley's journal continued to record them in detail. One day, Charles learned that Simpson urged that "No soul can be washed in the blood of Christ, unless it be first brought to a true believer, or one in whom Christ is fully formed." Simpson knew of only two such ministers in London: Philip Molther and George Bell. This Wesley viewed as being a blasphemous notion relative to the redemption offered by Jesus Christ. He wrote in his journal, "First perish Molther, Bell, and all mankind, and sink into nothing, that Christ may be all in all." Charles continued, writing angrily but also with gratitude for God's guiding hand in these difficult circumstances: "I am astonished at the divine goodness. How seasonably did it bring us hither, and lead us since! The adversary roared in the midst of the congregation, and set up his banners for tokens. A new commandment, called 'stillness,' had repealed all God's commandments, and given a full indulgence to lazy, corrupt nature."

Now the "still ones" sought to divide his authority from that of his brother John. "The still ones rage above measure against *me*," Charles wrote, "for my brother, they *say*, had consented to their pulling down the ordinances, and here come I, and build them up again." The "divide and conquer" theme emerged again on April 11, 1740. "The still brethren confront me with my brother's authority," Charles wrote, "pretending that he consented not to speak of the ordinances, that is, in effect to give them up, but leave it to every one's choice, whether they would use them or not. That necessity is laid upon us to walk in them, that 'Do this in remembrance of me' has the nature of a command, they absolutely deny." Later that same day Simpson called upon Charles Wesley again, this time laying down "two postulatums, that 1. The ordinances are no commands. 2. It is impossible to doubt after justification." Charles reported, "I maintained the contrary . . . they were fighting against God, robbing him of his glory, offending his little ones, and were under a strong delusion." By the end of April, the breach between the Wesleys and the "still brethren" seemed irreparable, and on both sides there was talk of the "division which must soon ensue."

In early June, when John again returned to London from Bristol, it seemed the time for formal division had finally come. "My brother," he recalled, "proposed new-modeling the bands, and setting by themselves those few who were still for the ordinances." The "noisy still ones" clamored against this plan, because they sought to win over the entire lot. As Wesley reported, "they grudged us even this remnant, which would soon be all their own, unless immediately rescued out of their hands. Benjamin Ingham seconded us; and obtained that the names should be called over, and as many as were aggrieved put into new bands." Charles was shocked at the results of this "new-modeling." "We gathered up our wreck," he wrote, moaning that "nine out of ten are swallowed up in the dead sea of stillness." Full of self-recrimination, Wesley asked, "O why was this not done six months ago? How fatal was our delay and false moderation!" One person, perhaps John Wesley himself, said, "Let them along, and they will soon be weary, and come to themselves of course." Charles reported, "I tremble at the consequence." Looking at the new stillness bands, Charles Wesley "told them plainly I should only continue with them so long as they continued in the Church of England." "My every word was grievous to them," he recalled; "I am a thorn in their flesh and they cannot bear me."

During this time Charles wrote a hymn entitled "Acts 2:41 and etc." The biblical passage's emphasis upon "the Gospel-word" and the Lord's Supper, the attendance upon Christian fellowship, as well as the community of faith being free from strife and contentions are aspects of this hymn which seem to fit well the context of the controversy over "stillness":

1. The word pronounced, the Gospel-word,
       The crowd with various hearts received:
   In many a soul the Saviour stirr'd,
       Three thousand yielded, and believed.

2. These by the apostles' counsels led,
       With them in mighty prayer combined,
   Broke the commemorative bread,
       Nor from the fellowship declined.

3. God from above, with ready grace
       And deeds of wonder, guards His flock;
   Trembles the world before their face,
       By Jesus crush'd, their Conquering Rock.

4. The happy band whom Christ redeems,
       One only will, one judgment know:
   None of this contentious earth esteems,
       Distinctions or delights below. . . .

Throughout June and July of 1740, John Wesley continued to do battle against the "still brethren" and their doctrine. On July 20 he went one last time to the Fetter Lane Society, where he read the following paper:

> About nine months ago, certain of you began to speak contrary to the doctrine we had till then received. The sum of what you asserted is this:
>
> 1. That there is no such thing as *weak faith;* that there is no justifying faith where there is any doubt or fear, or where there is not, in the full, proper sense, a new, clean heart.
>
> 2. That a man ought not to use those *ordinances* of God which our Church terms "the means of grace," before he has such a faith as excludes all doubt and fear, and implies a new, a clean heart.
>
> 3. You have often affirmed that "to search the Sciptures," *to pray,* or *to communicate,* before we have this faith, is *to seek salvation by works,* and that till these works are laid aside no man can received faith.

I believe these assertions to be flatly contrary to the Word of God. I have warned you hereof again and again, and besought you to turn back to the law and the testimony. I have borne with you long, hoping you would return. But as I find you more and more confirmed in the error of your ways, nothing now remains but that I should give you to God. You that are of the same judgment, follow me.

John's journal reports, "I then, without saying anything more, withdrew, as did eighteen or nineteen of the society."

Meanwhile, Charles Wesley was back in Bristol ministering to the Methodist societies and bands in that vicinity. On June 28, 1740, he wryly wrote John for an update on how things fared in London: "Has the numb-fish touched you?" Charles asked, "Are you *still*, that I have no account how things are carried on in L[ondon]?" In the same letter Charles told John that they needed at least two new rules for their United Societies: "Two rules are wanting," he wrote. "(1) that every person before he can be admitted into the United Society, *be in business* [that is employed]; (2) allow of, and use, the means of grace."

At the end of the summer of 1740, Charles Wesley fell seriously ill. His letter to George Whitefield, dated September 1, 1740, reports: "For this month past [God] has visited me with a violent fever. There was no possibility of my surviving it; but I knew in my self I should not die. I had not finished my course, and scarce begun it. The prayer of faith prevailed. Jesus touched my hand and immediately the fever departed from me." In the same letter Charles described how the "stillness controversy" had divided the Fetter Lane Society to the point it was no more. "The most violent opposers of all are our own brethren of Fetter Lane, that were, for we have gathered up between twenty and thirty from the wreck, and transplanted them to the Foundery. The remnant has taken root downward, and bore fruit upwards. A little one is become a thousand. They grow in grace, particularly humility, and in the knowledge of our Lord Jesus Christ."

In early 1741 Charles met with Peter Böhler, who did so much to win back the younger Wesley's esteem for the Moravians that he professed to contemplate returning to Germany with him. Wesley became convinced that a union with the Moravians was both possible and desirable. Toying with the idea of leaving the scene of conflict was attractive to the younger Wesley, though it is hard to believe he seriously considered going to Germany with Peter Böhler. But he was utterly weary of the months of controversy with old friends, and he still earnestly desired union with them.

Charles's letter of March 10, 1741, to his brother John suggests his growing sympathy with the Moravians. Surprisingly, in his letter Charles plied his brother with searching questions about his own motives in the controversy: "My dear Brother, I fear all is not right in your own breast, otherwise you would not think so hardly of them [the Moravians]. Is not there envy, self love, emulation, jealousy? Are you not afraid lest they should eclipse your own glory, or lessen your own praise? Do you not give too much credit to all that you only hear of them?" Charles had been having productive meetings and conversations with the principals of the Moravians and had softened his own opinion of them. "I am sure," he conceded, "they are a true people of God. There is life and power amongst them." He had also discovered a genuine preference for the Lord's Supper among them, which had been missing in the earlier rhetoric of the controversy. "This I know," Charles wrote, "the Brethren have the greatest respect for the ordinances of the Lord. Four times I received the Lord's Supper with them, and I never saw that sacred mystery so solemnly celebrated any where else. Neither did I ever feel so great power and grace." The issue of the ordinances had been Charles's chief bone of contention with the "still brethren," and now as that matter was being resolved his attitude towards the Moravians began to soften.

John Wesley, who had met with Peter Böhler, on April 4th, felt conflicted about the Moravians. "I had a long conversation with Peter Böhler," he wrote in his journal. "I marvel how I refrain from joining these men. I scarce ever see any of them but my heart burns within me. I long to be with them. And yet I am kept from them." In his reply to Charles, written on April 21, 1741, John Wesley reported, "As yet I dare no wise join with the Moravians." He gave his brother six reasons for maintaining the separation from the "still ones":

1. Because their whole scheme is mystical, not scriptural, refined in every point above what is written, immeasurably beyond the plain doctrines of the gospel;
2. Because there is darkness and closeness in all their behaviour, and guile in almost all their words;

3. Because they not only do not practice, but utterly despise and decry, self denial and the daily cross;
4. Because they upon principle conform to the world in wearing gold and gay or costly apparel;
5. Because they extend Christian liberty, in this and many other respects, beyond what is warranted by Holy Writ; and
6. Because they are by no means zealous of good works, or at least only to their own people; and lastly because they make inward religion swallow up outward in general.

John worried about the change of attitude that seemed to have come over his younger brother: "O my brother," he wrote, "my soul is grieved for you. The poison is in you. Fair words have stole away your heart." John continued meeting with the principal leaders of the Moravian movement in London, but their disagreements could not be papered over. The separation between the Methodists and the Moravians, between the Wesleys and so many of their early friends in the faith, would become complete. And even though it involved breaking with old friends, Charles went along.

The "stillness controversy" taught the Methodist movement the value of its Anglican roots. It would have been easy enough to go with "the still ones" down the road that led to a more private and more radical evangelical faith. But this controversy showed how deeply the Methodists were tied to the Anglican "means of grace," and how deep their desire was for a "social holiness" that made a difference in the world around them. The controversy refined the Methodists' commitment to spiritual disciplines, the Lord's Supper, and the importance of good works as fruits of their justification. In part as a result of this controversy the "means of grace" became enshrined in all the formative documents of the Methodist societies, classes, and bands. And the Methodists continued to be committed to an Anglican understanding of the Lord's Supper. Their practical theology about "the means of grace" was hammered out and set in place in the context of their emphasis upon sanctification and Christian perfection.

Charles Wesley learned many painful lessons through his intimate involvement in the controversy. He learned, for example, that friendship can be a painful hindrance to doctrinal clarity. He cherished his friendships with John Bray, John Gambold, James Hutton, John

Simpson, and the Delamottes and bore with them for a very long time, even though it was clear that they would divide from one another — as Charles himself admitted several times. Having his head and his heart sometimes out of sync was not an uncommon experience for Charles Wesley. But friendship meant quite a lot to Charles Wesley, and he bore with his friends longer than may have been safe for the Wesleyan movement, and even for himself.

Charles's efforts in the stillness controversy reaffirmed his commitment to the Church of England and her sacraments. In fact, after "new-modeling" the Methodist bands in London, he forcefully warned them that he "should continue with them only so long as they continued with the Church of England." His alliance to the mother church meant even more to him than his friendship to those on the other side of the controversy. It was a painful choice for a "man made for friendship" — as John Gambold had once described him — to make. Charles's struggle to keep the "still brethren" within the practices and beliefs of the Church of England would prove to be good practice for the similar and subsequent struggle he would face.

7 "The Poison of Calvin"

The Wesleys had already been Arminians for at least two generations prior to the beginning of the Methodist revival. The Anglican establishment, under the leadership of James I, began to veer away from the strict Calvinism of the sixteenth-century Reformation. In reaction to the Calvinistic Puritan theology of the "Protectorate," Anglican Archbishop William Laud (1573-1645) began a process of theological readjustment that continued through the "Caroline Divines" of the Restoration era. After the fall of the Puritan government, the Anglican establishment worked out its revenge against them by repressing the Puritans and their theology. The thoroughgoing Calvinism of the Puritans was moderated and persecuted during the Restoration era. By the time of John and Charles Wesley, many Anglicans were not strict Calvinists, and most "Dissenters" who stood outside the Church of England were.

Charles Wesley seems to have come by his Arminian perspective on salvation through the Anglican tradition and his own forays into the Scriptures, as well as his parents' influence. The same could be said of John Wesley, but Charles also had his elder brother Samuel's influence, and he too was a staunch Anglican and Arminian. When John was preparing to receive "holy orders" in the Church of England, his father rec-

99

ommended that he study the Dutch Arminian Hugo Grotius's commentary on the Old Testament. Their mother, Susanna Wesley, took an Arminian point of view, as is made clear in her publication of a pamphlet entitled *Some Remarks on a Letter From the Reverend Mr. Whitefield to the Reverend Mr. Wesley, In a Letter from a Gentlewoman to her Friend* (1741). In it she defended John Wesley's treatise entitled *Free Grace* and opposed George Whitefield's strict Calvinism. Susanna Wesley even sought to defend her sons against the label of "Arminian." In the popular mind, "Arminianism" was associated with a "free will" approach to salvation, which did not take seriously enough either God's grace or human sin. Thus, the Wesleys were (and are) sometimes mistakenly called "Semi-Pelagians," to associate them with the heretical views of Pelagius, which were condemned at the Council of Ephesus in 431.

The Wesleys saw themselves as standing in the heritage of the Protestant Reformation. As if to reinforce this point, the Wesleys and the preachers in connection with them explored this question in their "late conversations" at the Methodist Conference of 1744:

Question: 23. Where in may we come to the very edge of Calvinism?

Answer: (1) In ascribing all good to the free grace of God. (2) In denying all natural free-will, and all power [in humans] antecedent to grace. And (3) In excluding all merit from man; even for what he has or does by the grace of God.

The Wesley brothers, subsequently, came to accept the title "Arminian" more or less by default. It was what people called them because they were not predestinarian Calvinists. Just as Charles had taken "Methodist," the earlier title of derision, and turned it into a badge of honor during their Oxford days, so also did the Wesleys accept the title "Arminian" and work to redeem the epitaph from popular misunderstanding and reproach. Hence in 1770 John Wesley published his treatise *What is an Arminian?* and in 1778 began publishing his bimonthly journal *The Arminian Magazine.*

John Wesley's tract *What is an Arminian?* explained the Wesleyan position on salvation with a calmness that certainly belies nearly forty years of debate and dispute. He hung his distinction between Calvinists and Arminians on what he termed the "undeniable difference" between absolute and conditional predestination: "The Arminians hold," he wrote, "God has decreed, from all eternity, touching all that have the written word, 'He that believeth shall be saved'; he that believeth not, shall be condemned." Thus, Wesley stressed "conditional election," the idea that God has eternally decreed to save all those who profess faith in Jesus Christ. In the Wesleys' view, God's decree had to do with the "means" and conditions whereby all people could be saved. This was a very different perspective from that of the strict Calvinists, who opined that God chose (elected) some specific individuals for salvation, and some for damnation — before the foundations of the earth were laid. The Wesleys' doctrine of conditional election was foundational for their corollary belief in unlimited atonement (that Christ died for all people), resistible grace (that God's offer of saving grace can be refused by sinful people), and conditional perseverance (that a people can lose their salvation if they willfully and intentionally turn away from Jesus Christ). These would become standard Wesleyan doctrines, but they were hammered out on the anvil of controversy, and in the face of persecution so fierce that John Wesley could wryly write: "To say, 'This man is an Arminian,' has the same effect on many hearers, as to say, 'This is a mad dog.' They run away from him with all diligence; and will hardly stop, unless it be to throw a stone at the dreadful and mischievous animal." Charles encountered similar sentiments when he preached his standard evangelistic message of an unlimited atonement ("Christ died for all") and the universality of God's love and grace.

The controversy between Calvinistic and Arminian approaches to the doctrines of salvation emerged almost at the inception of the Methodist movement. It was symptomatic of a larger conversation that had been going on within Anglicanism for nearly a century, and which had begun to emerge again in the eighteenth century among Anglican evangelicals. A mere five months after his "personal Pentecost," Charles Wesley found himself disputing over predestination in the little religious society that met in the home of his friend John Bray. On September 22, 1738, Charles tersely wrote, "At Bray's I expounded Eph. 1:4. A dispute arising about absolute predestination, I entered my protest against that doctrine."

Nearly a year later, on June 22, 1739, Charles Wesley's journal reports that disputes about the doctrines relating to predestination were becoming more frequent among the Methodists. "The sower of tares is beginning to trouble us with disputes about predestination," Charles wrote. "My brother was wonderfully owned at Wapping last week, while asserting the contrary truth. To-night I asked in prayer, that if God would have *all* men to be saved, he would show some token for good upon us. Three were justified in immediate answer to that prayer. We prayed again; several fell down under the power of God, present to witness his universal love."

Wesley's distaste for the Calvinistic option on salvation, though it was certainly founded in his scriptural and ecclesiastical convictions, went beyond sterile doctrinal debate. He had a revulsion towards "the poison of Calvin" that was based in his practical experience. Just as he reveled in the "universal love" of God that was willing and able to save all people who turned to him, Wesley was repulsed by the haughty pride he saw in some of those who had come to consider themselves "the elect." Soon after the coming of "the sower of tares" Charles's journal reports his counseling one such woman: "In the afternoon I spoke a word of caution to one who seems strong in the faith, and begins to be lifted up [prideful]; the sure effect of her growing acquaintance with some of Calvin's followers." In a similar way, in 1747, Charles wrote his wife Sally bewailing the practical effects of a friend pressing the doctrine of predestination among unawakened souls: "To urge that doctrine on unawakened souls, is to stop them at the very threshold and to infuse it into those who are a little convinced, is, to drive them either into presumption or despair."

In 1739 the Wesleys published John's sermon in a pamphlet entitled *Free Grace* as an antidote to predestination and to countermand the claims that they were preaching "free will"; in fact John's sermon demonstrates that he preached that God's grace was offered to all people but could be refused. Charles supplemented John's sermon with a thirty-six-verse hymn entitled "Universal Redemption." The title communicates the emphasis of the hymn clearly enough; God wills that all people would be saved, God's redemption is for all:

> 13. For as *in Adam all have died,*
>   So *all in* Christ *may live,*
>   May (for the world is justified)
>   His righteousness *receive.*

14. Who'er to God for pardon fly,
    In Christ may be forgiven,
    He speaks to all, "why *will* ye die,
    And not accept my heaven?"

When attempting to integrate universal redemption with eternal election, Charles seemed to consider God's prevenient grace as giving fallen people "a power to choose," and God's foreknowledge as the basis of his ability to elect those who would respond to God's grace:

9. A power to choose, a will to obey,
   Freely his grace *restores;*
   We all *may* find the Living Way,
   And call the Saviour ours.

10. Whom his eternal mind *foreknew,*
    That they the power would use,
    Ascribe to God the glory due,
    And not his grace refuse;

11. Them, only them, his will *decreed,*
    Them did he *choose* alone,
    Ordain'd in Jesus' steps to tread,
    And be like his Son.

Like his brother John, Charles considered the notion of a eternal decree of "reprobation" to be unworthy of the God of the Bible, whom they viewed as a God of love:

23. Horror to think that God is hate!
    Fury in God can dwell!
    God could an helpless world create,
    To thrust them into hell!

24. Doom them an endless death to die,
    From which they could not flee —
    No, Lord! Thine inmost bowels cry
    Against the dire decree!

25. Believe who will that human pain,
      Pleasing to god can prove:
    Let *Moloch* feast him with the slain
      Our God, we know, is love.

26. Lord, if indeed, without a bound,
      Infinite Love Thou art,
    The *horrible decree* confound,
      Enlarge thy people's heart! . . .

By November 1740 Kingswood was becoming the storm center of a controversy over predestination that threatened to divide the fledgling Methodist movement once again (even as the "stillness" controversy was raging in London). On November 30, Charles expounded the Scripture lesson from Hebrews 6, a passage that seems to teach that a person committing apostasy can lose salvation. As Charles spoke, however, several of the pillars (formerly faithful members) of his congregation began to rail against him. Wesley wrote of them, "The poison of Calvin has drunk up their spirit of love." It turned out that the person John Wesley had sent to be their assistant in Kingswood and master of the Kingswood School, John Cennick, was a closet Calvinist who had been preaching against the Wesleys' doctrine. "Alas!" Charles lamented, "we have set the wolf to keep the sheep! God gave me great moderation toward him, who, for many months, has been undermining our doctrine and authority." On December 2, 1740, Wesley met with Cennick, hoping to reach some sort of resolution. Wesley's journal records the event very tersely: "I had a conference in Kingswood with Mr. Cennick and his friends, but could come to no agreement, though I offered entirely to drop the controversy if he would."

Around that time Wesley wrote Cennick a lengthy letter. Interestingly, Wesley never touched upon the controverted points of doctrine that separated them, but he gave a pointed evaluation of Cennick's handling of the situation:

My dearest Brother, John Cennick, — In much love and tenderness I speak. You came to Kingswood upon my brother's sending for you. You served under him in the Gospel as a son. I need not say how well he loved you. You used the authority he gave you to overthrow his doctrine. You everywhere contradicted it. Whether true or false, is not the question: but you ought first to have fairly told him, "I preach contrary to you. Are you willing notwithstanding, that I should continue in your house gainsaying you? If you are not, I have no place in these regions. You have a right to this open dealing. I now give you fair warning. Shall I stay here opposing you, or shall I depart?"

My brother, have you dealt thus honestly and openly with him? No; but you have stolen away the people's heart from him. . . .

Where we might have expected Wesley to enter into a doctrinal debate over predestination and its associated beliefs, Charles remonstrated with Cennick about his pastoral ethics. He wrote to Cennick in a tone of paternal love and utter disappointment. And at their conference over the matter, when Wesley could have used his authority to silence Cennick, he offered instead a truce based on mutual silence on the controversial topics. Once again, Wesley emphasized the importance of friendship and practical concern for Christian unity over strict doctrinal agreement.

By December 6, however, Charles felt he had to warn his brother John, who was in London dealing with the "still ones," about the trouble that was brewing in Kingswood. Charles's journal reports, "I wrote my brother a full account of the predestinarian party, their practices and designs, particularly 'to have a church within themselves, and to give themselves the sacrament [of the Lord's Supper] in bread and water.'" "Things are come to a crisis at Kingswood," Charles wrote. "They tell me plainly they will separate from me if I speak one word against final perseverance, or hint at the possibility of a justified person's falling from grace. . . . All the bands, they say, are of their opinion; and no one who is not can love Christ." He added, of his dispute with Cennick, "I condescended to say that I would not speak *against* final perseverance, if he would not speak for it. But he would not agree even to this." Charles urged his brother to set out for Bristol "as soon as this reaches you." John Wesley arrived in Bristol on Friday, December 12. He began preaching in Kingswood and trying to heal the breach with John Cennick. The latter's efforts, combined with his popularity, meant that Wesley found himself before tiny gatherings when he preached there. Eventually the Methodist societies in Bristol and Kingswood would need to be split into Arminian and Calvinist bands.

This division of the Bristol and Kingswood Methodist societies into Wesleyan-Arminian and Calvinistic bands might have been the end of the controversy had it not already spread to involve the Wesleys in confrontations and controversies with several of their closest friends and allies in the revival, including "the grand itinerant" George Whitefield. Cennick enlisted Whitefield for battle. He wrote to Whitefield, "With universal redemption Bro. Charles pleases the world. . . . Bro. John follows him in everything. I believe no atheist can more preach against predestination than they. And all who believe election are counted enemies of God, and called so." He pleaded with Whitefield to come to his aid: "Fly, dear brother. I am as alone. . . . I am in the midst of the plague."

For his part, Charles Wesley wrote to his old friend Whitefield, "Many, I know, desire nothing so much as to see George Whitefield and John Wesley at the head of different parties, as is plain from their truly devilish pains to effect it, but be assured, my dearest brother, our heart is as your heart. O may we always thus continue to think and speak the same things!" Charles expected God to teach them "mutual forbearance, long-suffering, and love through this controversy." Wesley opined, "I do not think the difference [between us] considerable." He vowed, "I shall never dispute with you touching election, and if you know not yet to reconcile that doctrine with God's universal love, I will cry unto him, 'Lord what we know not, show thou us'; but never, offend you by my different sentiment." Wesley concluded, "My soul is set upon peace, and drawn out after you by love stronger than death." He annotated the letter, "labouring for peace," and mailed it.

Throughout 1740 George Whitefield had written John Wesley indicating his awareness of their divergent views on Christian perfection, election, and "final perseverance" (whether or not a person in Christ could lose his/her salvation). But more emphatically, Whitefield wrote urging Wesley to avoid stirring up a public controversy between them: "for Christ's sake, if possible dear Sir, never speak against election in your sermons; no one can say that I ever mentioned it in my public discourses, whatever my private sentiments may be. For Christ's sake, let us not be divided amongst ourselves; nothing will so much prevent a division as you being silent on that head." To a mutual friend, Whitefield wrote in a similar vein, "for Christ's sake desire dear Brother Wesley to avoid disputing with me. I think I would rather die than see a division between us; and yet how can we walk together if we oppose each other?" On September 25, 1740, Whitefield wrote John Wesley from Boston, defending his understanding of predestination, election, and reprobation. He attacked the senselessness of Wesley's doctrine of unlimited atonement: "I see no blasphemy in holding the doctrine, if rightly explained. If God might pass by *all*, he might pass by *some*. Judge you if it is not a greater blasphemy to say that Christ died for souls now in hell."

Neither of the Wesleys saw any connection between their publication of *Free Grace*, containing John's sermon and Charles's hymn, and the ensuing debate about election and predestination among the Methodists. But George Whitefield certainly did. In a letter he wrote to John Wesley during his return trip to England from America in February 1741, he pointedly asked the Wesleys: "My dear brethren, why did you throw out the bone of contention? Why did you print that sermon against predestination? Why did you in particular, my dear brother Charles, affix your hymn, and join in putting out your late hymn book? How can you say you will not dispute with me about election, and yet print such hymns, and your brother send his sermon over against election to . . . America? Do you not think, my dear brethren, I must be as much concerned for truth, or what I think truth, as you?"

By mid-March Whitefield was back in England and in the middle of the controversy about predestination. While Charles Wesley's journal for this period is missing, one of his letters reports that Whitefield preached predestination — in Charles's presence — from the Wesleyan pulpit at the Foundery in London. Charles reported that "G.W. came into the desk [pulpit] while I was showing the believer's privilege, i.e. power over sin. After speaking some time I desired him to preach. He did — predestination, perseverance, and the necessity of sinning. Afterwards I mildly expostulated with him, asking if he would commend me for preaching the opposite doctrines in his orphan-house." Whitefield had just finished drawing up a reply to *Free Grace*, and he offered Charles a chance to read it prior to its publication. "The title is rough," Charles wrote to John; "I endorsed it 'Put up again thy sword into its place,' and deferred reading till it is in print." The title of the treatise was *A Letter to the Rev. Mr. John Wesley in Answer to his Sermon entitled "Free Grace."*

In a letter written late in 1741, Whitefield complained to John that "dear brother Charles is more and more rash. He has lately printed some very bad hymns." These "rash" and "bad" hymns were Charles's *Hymns on God's Everlasting Love.* They were explicitly constructed to contradict the Calvinist conception of predestination and its various corollary beliefs. These hymns were so popular and useful that they were released in two successive collections, both of which shared the same title. The first collection was published by Felix Farley in 1741. The hymnbook contains fourteen long poems, which were written in a great variety of meters and poetic feet. The first hymn in the collection explained the focus of the hymnal — "God's everlasting Love":

> 1.   Father, whose *Everlasting Love*
> Thy only Son for sinners gave,
>   Whose grace to *all* did *freely* move,
> And sent Him down a *world to save.*

> 2.   Help us Thy mercy to extol,
> Immense, unfathom'd, unconfined;
>   To praise the Lamb who *died for all*
> The *general Saviour of all mankind.*

> 3.   Thy *undistinguishing regard*
> Was cast on *Adam's* fallen race;
>   *For all* Thou hast in Christ prepared
> *Sufficient, sovereign, saving* grace.

> 4.   Jesus hath said, we *all* shall hope,
> Preventing grace for *all* is free:
>   "And I, if I be lifted up,
> I will *draw all men* unto *Me. . . ."*

The basic thrust of both collections is illustrated in this opening hymn. "Everlasting love" became the Wesleyan euphemism for unlimited atonement and unlimited, prevenient grace. This first hymn affirmed unlimited atonement (generally using the word "all") more than twenty-three times in seventeen verses. It concluded on the same note upon which the hymn began: "And praise, and worship, evermore,/ The Lamb that died for all." Throughout these hymns and subsequent collections, the Wesleyan "all" became a hammer with which Charles tried to demolish particular election and limited atonement. The little word "all" allowed him to insist, incessantly, that there are no limits on God's saving love — that Christ died for "all."

Charles Wesley's emphasis on God's everlasting love had important theological corollaries. One of these was conditional election. Since the Wesleys held that Christ died for all people, they did not believe that God had chosen certain individuals from the entire human race for salvation, thereby "passing by" or damning those who were not chosen. Hence, in Charles Wesley's poetical presentation of the doctrine of salvation, the distinction between those who were "saved" and those who were "lost" lay not with the "Lamb" but rather within the will of those who must respond to Christ's call to redemption:

> Behold the Lamb of God, who takes
>   The sins of all the world away!
> His pity no exception makes,
>   But all that *will* receive Him may.

A second important Wesleyan theological constant that emerged in Charles's emphasis on everlasting love was the corollary of "free grace." "Free grace" is the universal offer of the gospel of God's love and acceptance; it is "undistinguished" in that God's grace is not for some people and withheld from others. Grace is "free" in that it is not earned or deserved. Since it is "grace" it comes to people with God's power; it breaks through their sin and allows them to decide whether to accept salvation:

> Free as air Thy mercy streams,
>   Thy universal grace
> Shines with undistinguish'd beams
>   On all the fallen race;
> All from Thee a power receive
>   To reject, or hear, Thy call;

> *All may* choose to die, or live;
> Thy grace is free for all.

Hence "free grace" is an empowering grace, which Charles Wesley also termed "preventing grace" or "assisting grace." He described how prevenient grace opened the way to God and salvation, using an analogy based on Psalm 5:7 ("But as for me, I will come into Thy house in the multitude of Thy mercy: and in Thy fear will I worship toward Thy holy temple"). Charles wrote:

> ASSISTED by preventing grace,
> I bow me toward the holy place,
> Faintly begin my God to fear,
> His weak, external worshipper:
> But if my Lord His blood apply,
> Entering into the holiest I
> Boldly approach my Father's throne,
> And claim Him all in Christ my own.

Because the Wesleys accepted the doctrine of original sin, they did not believe that sinful people, apart from God's grace, could or would turn to God. Hence, the assistance of God's prevenient grace was a necessary precondition to salvation, since, as Charles wrote, "unassisted by Thy grace/We can only evil do;/Wretched is the human race/Wretched more than words can show,/Till thy blessing from above,/Tells our hearts that God is love." Prevenient grace comes into human lives by the agency of God's Word and Spirit. The younger Wesley described this process using the metaphor of the star that foretold Jesus' birth (Matthew 2:21), "which by its sure unerring light/Conduct me to my Lord." In a similar way, grace is "proffer'd" — or offered before our choice. Using the imagery of the Parable of the Prodigal Son (Luke 15:11), he depicted God as our Father, waiting for lost sinners to come home with his arms spread open wide: "Open are Thy arms to embrace/Me, the worst of rebels me:/*All in me the hindrance lies,*/Call'd, I still refuse to rise."

Charles's first edition of *Hymns on God's Everlasting Love* carried two highly polemical poems that surpassed the other hymns in that collection in controversy. They not only sang in favor of God's universal love, but they also mounted a decisive offensive against particular Calvinist doctrines. The first of these polemical pieces was called "Cry of a Reprobate." The spokesperson of this hymn presents his or her own spiritual biography: "By my own sin betray'd and bound,/A sheep I to the slaughter go." The singer of the hymn, having heard the account of the reprobate's self-destruction and damnation, and having examined the prospect of hell — which Wesley vividly paints in the hymn — should be moved to repent and turn to God in order to receive salvation. In this way the "Cry of a Reprobate" was a tool of Wesleyan evangelism. It continues Charles's themes of conditional election and free grace, applying them in more dramatic form. The hymn concludes with the reprobate resolutely accepting responsibility for his or her own plight:

25. By my own hands, not His, I fall;
    The hellish doctrine I disprove;
    Sinner, His grace is free for all:
    Though I am damn'd yet God is love!

The "hellish doctrine" disproved by the reprobate's self-damnation is, of course, the Calvinistic doctrine of absolute predestination. Charles Wesley's solution to the dilemma of affirming the justice of God in condemning the guilty and yet affirming that God is love was found in the sinner's willful rejection of God's "free grace."

The second polemical hymn in this same collection was titled "The Horrible Decree." It is a thoroughgoing attack upon the Calvinist notion of predestination unto damnation; the idea that some people are chosen, before the foundation of the earth, to go to hell. In this heated hymn the writer established a dialogue between his spokesperson and Christ, or between his spokesperson and adherents of the Calvinist perspective. Wesley showed his familiarity with his opponents' theological language and used several Calvinistic catch-phrases to attack their point of view:

1. Ah! gentle, gracious Dove;
    And art Thou grieved in me,
    That sinners should restrain Thy love,
    And say, "It is not free;

It is not free for *all*";
   The *most* Thou *passt by,*
And mockest with a fruitless call
   Whom Thou hast doom'd to die.

2. They think Thee *not sincere*
   In giving each his day:
"Thou only draws'st the sinner near.
   To cast him quite away.
To aggravate his sin.
   His sure damnation seal,
Thou Show'st him Heaven, and say'st go in —
   And thrusts him into Hell."

3. *O horrible decree,*
   Worthy of whence it came!
Forgive their hellish blasphemy
   Who charge it on the Lamb,
Those pity Him inclined
   To leave His throne above,
The Friend and Saviour of mankind,
   The God of grace and love. . . .

Charles's second series of *Hymns on God's Everlasting Love* continued the leading emphases established in the first collection, including the disparaging depiction of predestination in "The Horrible Decree." In hymn number thirteen in the second series, the predestination controversy has become "The Lord's Controversy," in which the ministers of true religion struggle against the heretical "Priests of Moloch" whose views are attacked, once again using Calvinistic theological language and catchphrases. In hymn number three in this collection, "the enemy" or "tempter" (Satan) preaches classical Calvinist doctrines to unsettle and confuse a seeker's heart:

5. Arm'd with this fiery dart,
   The enemy drew nigh,
And preach'd to my unsettled heart
   His bold presumptuous lie;

> "You are secure of heaven,"
>   (The tempter softly says,)
> *"You are elect,* and once forgiven
>   Can never fall from grace.

6. "You never can receive
     The grace of God in vain;
   The gift, be sure, He did not give,
     To take it back again;
   He cannot take it back,
     Whether you use or no
   His grace; you cannot shipwreck make
     Of faith, or let it go.

7. "You never can forget
     Your God, or leave Him now,
   Or once look back if you have set
     Your hand unto the plough;
   You never can deny
     The Lord who you hath bought,
   Nor can your God His own *pass by,*
     Though you receive Him not. . . ."

Small wonder that George Whitefield considered these hymns "bad" and "rash!"

Hymn number eleven in the "Second Series" of *Hymns on God's Everlasting Love* ends on an autobiographical note, which explains something of Charles Wesley's motive in opposing the predestinarians and in publishing these hymns:

7. O unexampled Love,
     O all-redeeming Grace!
   How freely didst Thou move
     To save a fallen race!
   What shall I do to make it known
   What Thou for all mankind hast done?

8. For this alone I breathe,
     To spread the gospel sound,

113

> Glad tidings of Thy death
>> To all the nations round;
> Who all *may* feel Thy blood applied,
> Since all are freely justified.

9. O for a trumpet voice
>> On all the world to call,
> To bid their hearts rejoice
>> In Him who died for all!
> For all my Lord was crucified;
> For all, for all my Saviour died.

10. To serve Thy blessed will,
>> Thy dying love to praise,
> Thy counsel to fulfil,
>> And minister Thy grace;
> Freely what I receive to give,
> The life of heaven on earth I live.

The Wesleys and Whitefield eventually reached a kind of truce regarding the doctrines associated with predestination. John Wesley and George Whitefield corresponded to effect a reconciliation in the fall of 1741. Whitefield's letter of October 11 reports: "I had your letter dated Oct. 5. In answer to the first part of it. I say, 'Let old things [like the recent controversy] pass away, and all things become new.' I can heartily say, 'Amen.' To the latter part of it, 'Let the King live forever, and let controversy die.' It has died with me long ago." They agreed to disagree. They agreed not to preach or publish against each other with respect to this controversial doctrine. After preaching in Cornwall in June 1746, Charles wrote in his manuscript journal, "Our hearts were strongly opened and warmed. For my part I found no manner of difference betwixt them and our colliers or tinners or children at the Foundery, and they embraced me as a younger brother of G[eorge] Whitefield. Satan's accusations were turned to good and the doctrine of Free Grace was doubly welcome to them from so strong an Arminian."

That this public truce did not entirely put an end to the controversy is clear from a letter Charles wrote to John Bennett, dated September 3, 1750: "our dear friend G. Whitefield has not *preached* predestination, but he has *talked* it among our children when he came and made converts of two or three of our preachers. He has not brought *you* over to his opinion, I hope." Yet Charles Wesley did not think differences over the doctrines of election and predestination was sufficient grounds to divide a Methodist society. This is evident from a reconciliation he engineered in Cornwall on June 15, 1746. His journal entry reports,

> They complained to me a brother who had made a division and carried away 15 of the flock into a separate Society. I went and talked with him and each of his company. They told me they were convinced (by reading my brother's books) of universal redemption and *therefore* met by themselves to avoid dispute, and hearing such books read as they did agree to, and to confirm one another in what they thought the truth. I told them that was not sufficient reason for separating. They were not so many but one Society might hold them all, that our common enemies would triumph in our dissensions; that charity was more than true opinions, and that they ought to go back to their brethren, and continue with them to the end. They yielded to my persuasions, and I carried them with me to the Society, who received them with open arms and hearts. I exhorted them all to love and unity and mutual forbearance. . . .

Still, the predestination controversy marked another painful schism and separation within the early Methodist movement. Henceforth there would be Calvinist Methodists and Wesleyan Methodists. It also caused strained relationships between Charles Wesley and a few of his favorite friends — most notably George Whitefield. Like the carver's steel sharpens metal, however, this controversy also sharpened Charles Wesley's theology. Where he had formerly advocated for universal salvation as one of the "grand truths of the everlasting gospel," now he insisted upon it. To that extent, the Calvinistic controversy found a resounding echo in almost every hymn Charles Wesley wrote after it; the Wesleyan "all" became standard parlance in his hymns and preaching. The notion of "reprobation" continued to be a sensitive topic with Charles Wesley because he considered it blasphemous to say that God would lovingly create people and select particular individuals for damnation. As he moved throughout the busy circuits and duties of his ministry, he also saw what he considered the negative results of predestinarian theology. He counseled with people who had become convinced that they were reprobate because they had fallen into sin after receiving Christ. He met people who became haughty and full of pride, possessing "a narrow spirit" because they had become convinced that they were elect. And he met shocking examples of antinomianism in which people were so convinced they could not lose their salvation that they lived in willful disregard of God's will and laws.

The effect of the Wesleys' campaign against popular Calvinism was dramatic. Despite the controversy they faced from friends and former friends, John and Charles Wesley continued this campaign throughout their ministry. And while Dissenters, prominent theologians, and members of the aristocratic elite would do battle with them across the eighteenth century, the Wesleys' preaching and hymns became powerful weapons against the strict Calvinistic interpretation of salvation for years to come.

8 "A Man Made for Friendship"

Friendship was a fundamental aspect of Charles Wesley's life and personality. He was, as his college friend, John Gambold, described him, "a man made for friendship." Charles worked to establish his friendships and keep them vital despite the frenetic activities of his ministerial work and travels. It is much more difficult to think of John Wesley having close friends; the older Wesley brother was more aloof and autocratic. Charles was more vivacious and outgoing, with a winsome personality. He valued friendship so much that he often called his wife, Sally, "my dearest friend"; this was not to demean matrimony, but rather to show what an elevated understanding of friendship he had.

Over the course of more than a decade Charles Wesley wrote fifty-five "Hymns for Christian Friends." This significant corpus of poetical work spans more than 420 verses, which were hurriedly brought together in 1749 and published in Charles's *Hymns and Sacred Poems.* These hymns give voice to Wesley's understanding of friendship. He saw it as a good gift of God, given to persons to teach them about God's love and to help them become partakers of the divine nature through love. Friendship, then, was an instrument of refreshment and spiritual improvement. For Wesley, the goal of Christian friendship was sanctification and heaven, in that order. Friends were supposed to "provoke one another to good works" and "draw each other out" in love. The hymn "At Meeting of Friends" is an apt representative of Wesley's writing on the matter of friendship:

1. ALL praise to our redeeming Lord,
    Who joins us by His grace,
    And bids us, each to each restored,
    Together seek His face.
    He bids us build each other up,
    And gather'd into one,
    To our high calling's glorious hope
    We hand in hand go on.

2. The gift which He on one bestows,
    We all delight to prove,
    The grace through every vessel flows
    In purest streams of love.
    Even now we speak, and think the same,
    And cordially agree,
    Concentered all through Jesu's name
    In perfect harmony.

3. We all partake the joy of one,
    The common peace we feel,
    A peace to sensual minds unknown,
    A joy unspeakable.
    And if our fellowship below
    In Jesus be so sweet,
    What height of rapture shall we know
    When round His throne we meet!

But friends, even Christian friends, do not always "speak and think the same" or "cordially agree," especially when theological distinctions like predestination and Christian perfection are introduced into the mix of friendship. Rivalry in building up societies, establishing circuits, and preaching posts would also wear hard on the relationships between Charles Wesley and other Methodist leaders like

George Whitefield and Selina Hastings, the Countess of Huntingdon. By looking at Charles Wesley's life in the context of these two friendships — friendships which were among the most precious to him — we can discover an important side of his story.

George Whitefield was the son of a tavern operator, and he spent his early years living above his parents' tavern. His father died when George was two years old. In the absence of her spouse, George felt that his mother depended upon him; "even when I was an infant," he wrote, "she expected more comfort from me than any other of her children." Whitefield saw his humble origins and his mother's high expectations as being of significant benefit to his spiritual development and maturation: "the circumstance of my being born in an inn," he wrote, "has been often of service to me in exciting my endeavours to make good my mother's expectation, and so follow the example of my dear Saviour, who was born in a manger belonging to an inn."

Charles Wesley first met Whitefield after his arrival at Oxford in 1732, when the latter was a "servitor." This meant Whitefield had a demeaning status in the all-important university hierarchy of things, and loneliness and isolation drew him towards Charles Wesley. During his Oxford years Charles had loaned him several devotional books, through which he experienced an evangelical conversion. Soon Charles Wesley became a spiritual mentor to the nineteen-year-old Whitefield, and Wesley began integrating him into his Oxford "Holy Club."

Part of the "hardness" the Oxford Methodists had to endure was public ridicule so stiff that Whitefield found it impossible to walk alone to the Lord's Supper at St. Mary's Church. Realizing this development, Charles Wesley made it his practice to go by George Whitefield's college room to walk with him. Whitefield's journal described his own initial hesitancy and Wesley's early support: "Mr. Charles Wesley, whom I must always mention with the greatest deference and respect, walked with me, in order to confirm me, from the church even to the college. I confess, to my shame, I would gladly have excused him; and the next day going to his room, one of our Fellows passing by, I was ashamed to be seen to knock at his door. But blessed be God! This fear of man gradually wore off. As I had imitated Nichodemus [John 3:2] in his cowardice, so by Divine assistance I followed him in courage." That Charles Wesley sometimes functioned as young Whitefield's spiritual director is evident from another journal entry: "One morning in particular, rising from my bed," Whitefield wrote, "I felt an unusual impression and weight upon my breast, attended with inward darkness. I applied to my friend, Mr. Charles Wesley. He advised me to keep my [prayer] watch, and referred me to a chapter in Kempis."

That a deep and mutual affection and admiration had developed between Whitefield and Charles Wesley is evident in the frankness with which George questioned Charles about his willingness to go to Georgia as General Oglethorpe's secretary. "My friend will not take it amiss," Whitefield wrote, "if I enquire why he chooses to be secretary to Mr. Oglethorpe, and not go where labourers are wanted, in the character of a missionary. Did the Bishop ordain us, my dear friend, to write bonds, receipts, and etc. or to preach the Gospel? Or dare we not trust God to provide for our relations without endangering or at least retarding, our spiritual improvement? But I go too far. *Habe me excusatum* [Please excuse me]. You know I was always heady and self-willed." That Whitefield described himself as "heady" and "self-willed" is also apt; the controversy with the Wesleys over predestination illustrated that he had a stubborn streak that rivaled, if not exceeded, their own.

George Whitefield received his sense of divine call to missionary work in Georgia through the instrumentality of correspondence with Charles and John Wesley. First came a letter from Charles Wesley, who had returned from Georgia in late 1736. Whitefield's journal reports, "About the middle of December came a letter from Mr. Broughton, informing me that Mr. Charles Wesley was arrived at London. Soon after came a letter from Mr. Charles himself, wherein he informed me that he had come over to procure labourers; but added he 'I dare not prevent God's nomination.'" John Wesley's letter arrived a few days later, and it was even more pointedly direct: "Only Mr. Delamotte is with me, till God shall stir up the hearts of some of His servants, who putting their lives in His hands, shall come over and help us, where the harvest is so great, and the labourers so few. What if Thou art the man, Mr. Whitefield?"

In December 1736 Charles Wesley's journal reports that he had "received a letter from Mr. Whitefield, offering himself to go to Georgia." Charles himself still contemplated returning to Georgia — this time as a full-fledged missionary — and he intended to take George

Whitefield with him. He called Whitefield "a minister of fervent spirit — if I may say so, a second Timothy. God has wonderfully aroused by his means the twice-dead populace. The churches will not contain his hearers."

Charles Wesley had intended to accompany George Whitefield on his mission to America during the autumn of 1736, but Charles's illness barred his way, and he was able to arrive in Bristol only in time to see his friend depart for his transatlantic voyage. During this period of time Charles was so enamored with Whitefield and his mission that he penned several poems about his evangelistic journey. These were subsequently published in the Wesleys' *Hymns and Sacred Poems* (1740). Wesley's "To the Rev. Mr. Whitefield" celebrates his friend's call to ministry and evangelistic talents:

> 1. Brother in Christ, and well-beloved,
>   Attend, and add thy prayer to mine,
>   As *Aaron* call'd and *inly moved*,
>   To minister in things Divine!
>
> 2. Faithful, and often own'd of God,
>   Vessel of grace, by Jesus used;
>   Stir up the gift on thee bestow'd,
>   *The gift* through hallow'd hands transfused.
>
> 3. Fully thy heavenly mission prove,
>   And make thy own election sure;
>   Rooted in faith, and hope, and love
>   Active to work, and firm to endure. . . .

A second hymn in this same series and collection was entitled "To the Same [Whitefield], Before His Voyage." It amounts to a commissioning prayer for a friend and minister about to brave the dangers of a long voyage and a ministry in a strange and wild new world:

> 1. SERVANT of God, the summons hear;
>   Thy Master calls, arise, obey!
>   The tokens of His will appear,
>   His providence points out the way.

2. Lo! We commend thee to His grace:
   In confidence go forth! be strong!
   Thy meat His will, thy boast His praise,
   His righteousness be all thy song.

3. Strong in the Lord's almighty power,
   And arm'd in panoply Divine,
   Firm mayst thou stand in danger's hour,
   And prove the strength of Jesus thine. . . .

A third hymn, "In a Storm," pleads for Whitefield's protection and asks for a God-given calm to descend upon the traveler when his ship is beset by storms. The poem is clearly written by a person who has experienced firsthand the fearful dangers of riding out an ocean storm in the fragile ships of that day:

3. What though the floods lift up their voice,
   Thou hearest Lord, our louder cry;
   They cannot damp Thy children's joys,
   Or shake the soul, when God is nigh.

4. Headlong we cleave the yawning deep,
   And back to highest heaven are borne,
   Unmoved, though rapid whirlwinds sweep,
   And all the watery world upturn.

5. Roar on, ye waves! Our souls defy
   Your roaring to disturb our rest:
   In vain to impair the calm ye try,
   The calm in a believer's breast.

6. Rage, while our faith the Saviour tries,
   Thou sea, the servant of His will:
   Rise, while our God permits thee, rise;
   But fall, when He shall say, 'Be still!'

Whitefield rapidly began to eclipse the Wesleys in ministry and in popularity during his first American adventure. His experiences in

London during the summer of 1736 had turned the younger man into an effective and innovative mass evangelist. Where Charles Wesley had been a failure as a colonial missionary and John had been only marginally successful, Whitefield was well on his way to becoming a superstar among the preachers of the age. When he returned from his first American mission Whitefield was no longer a younger and somewhat subordinate colleague; his popularity and status among the Anglican evangelicals had eclipsed that of the Wesleys.

In 1739 with the rise of his popularity also came a growing disaffection towards Whitefield from the Anglican establishment. Whitefield was mentioned "mildly" in the Wesleys' conference with the archbishop of Canterbury on February 21, 1739. The bishop of London was less mild. He considered Whitefield's published journal to be "tainted with enthusiasm, though he was himself a pious, well-meaning youth." That same spring Charles Wesley continued to meet Whitefield at the Fetter Lane Society, and in April Charles found himself approving of Whitefield's preaching outdoors. "I heard G. Whitefield in Islington church-yard," Charles wrote. "The numerous congregation would not have been more affected within the walls." Two days later, Whitefield was preaching "abroad" again — to multitudes — and Charles reported: "I heard that George had had above ten thousand hearers."

While the Wesleys preceded him to Georgia in 1735, Whitefield preceded them in becoming a mass evangelist. By early June 1739 George Whitefield had begun pressing Charles to follow him into the innovation of field preaching. By June 23, under Whitefield's urging and patient example, Charles's hesitancy about field preaching was gradually breaking down. "My inward conflict continued," Charles wrote, "I perceived it was fear of man, and that by preaching, in the field next Sunday, as George Whitefield urges me, I shall break down the bridge and become desperate." The next day, Wesley became "desperate" and found "near ten thousand helpless sinners waiting for the Word, in Moorfields. . . . The Lord was with me, even me, his meanest messenger, according to his promise." While Whitefield took the Methodist revival on the road by traveling to Bristol and continuing his preaching ministry there, Charles Wesley supplied his place in London well. When Whitefield returned to London in September 1739, his journal reports, "Blessed be God for what has been done here since

I left London, by my honoured friend and fellow-labourer, Mr. Charles Wesley. Surely we can see the fruits of our labours. All love, all glory be to God, for giving so great an increase."

At the end of June Charles Wesley had "waited upon the Dean [of Oxford] who spoke with unusual severity against field preaching, and Mr. Whitefield; explained away all inward religion and union with God." The dean's censure against field preaching implicated Wesley as well, but Charles's report that he also "explained away all inward religion" was tantamount to Wesley saying that he discounted the dean's criticism. Clearly Charles Wesley's admiration for Whitefield was undimmed by this (and other) criticisms by notable people in the Anglican establishment; Whitefield was still his friend, and was, as Charles viewed things, still mightily used by God despite his ecclesiastical irregularities.

Siding with Whitefield and against the ecclesiastical establishment had a galvanizing effect upon Charles's relationship with Whitefield. They became co-conspirators in a common cause, and Whitefield became and remained a person to whom Charles Wesley trusted his inner longings and conflicts. On August 10, 1739, for example, Wesley wrote in his journal, "I gave George Whitefield some account of my labours and my conflicts." Charles went on to confide to Whitefield, "I am continually tempted to leave off preaching and hide myself. . . . I should be freer from temptation, and at leisure to attend my own improvement. God continues to work *by* me, but not *in me,* that I can preceive." Whitefield could write to Charles Wesley, as he did on August 17, 1739, with equal frankness: "Are you yet the Lord's prisoner?" Such frankness rarely came from or to Charles Wesley; it was a sign of deep and unusual friendship.

Meanwhile, another important friendship had entered Charles's life: that of Selina Hastings, the Countess of Huntingdon. She was a landed aristocrat who could trace family roots all the way back to a distant relative of King Edward the Confessor. She began hearing Methodist preachers like Benjamin Ingham and George Whitefield in 1738, largely through the influence of her sister, who subsequently married Ingham. She experienced evangelical conversion the following year and soon thereafter became a fixture in London Methodism. She came to know the Wesleys through the Fetter Lane Society, and she sided with them in the stillness controversy. When her husband died in 1746, Lady Huntingdon threw herself entirely into the Methodist movement and spent the balance of her years constructing a far-flung network of chapels, societies, and preaching posts. Her insistence on always getting her way made friendship more difficult with John, who could not bear the thought of taking orders from her, but her relationship with Charles grew and remained strong for many years. Only her attack on his brother John would prove to be strong enough eventually to wean Charles from her friendship.

Lady Huntingdon and Charles Wesley seemed to be soul mates in that their spirituality occasionally took a melancholy or morbid cast. Like the Moravians, they saw the inner struggles of the human soul as being part of the process of salvation. Both were prone to periods of spiritual "darkness" or "heaviness," and they both had a tendency to judge their spiritual state by reflecting upon their feelings. Yet they were also able to comfort and encourage each other during these periods of "darkness." Charles visited her during one such "dark night of the soul," and she wrote to thank him in July 1743: "You visited me in the time of my distress but you nor no soul *can* conceive the darkness, perplexity, [and] misery I have constantly surrounding me. It is what I have never felt since I was known of God. I have the world and the things of it, but I am so ruffled by outward things, so confounded by a variety of events, that to tell you one quarter of what I feel would fill sheets. Upon the whole I am and have been this five days so ill in body I am scarcely able [to] move about and my mind so distracted that I know not what to do — all owing to the justice and love of our Lord." Later that same month, she wrote, "I have just time to tell you I am what I was at one time: a dark unbeliever, and then gleams of Divine Light break into my soul. I am distressed, perplexed, but not in despair."

Charles, like Lady Huntingdon, had a tendency to doubt God's previous blessings when in a current state of "darkness" or despair. She wrote, "I must beg you to consider what you say of yourself. I trust neither a false notion of being humble (and which I charge you often with) can bring you to these declarations nor any impatience of temper to disown the works of God, or if this is particularly the case you cannot but think the testimony of believers and the promises of God, you cannot assent to facts of your own experience, but [more] of this when we meet." He subsequently replied, in shorthand, "Then would you bless and love Him whom your soul loveth for the great love and goodness which he shows forth in you. [The] Lord hath done great things for you already, but you shall see greater things [would you] only give yourself into His gracious hands that He may do what He will by you and with you." In mid-1744 she wrote Charles, "Your packet this morning revived my fainting spirits." It contained portions from his journal, which she was reading — presumably for publication. On February 25, 1752, she told him, "Your letter was full of spiritual comfort and instruction. I trust God will abundantly reward those prayers you offer for me, I value them more than thousands of worlds."

Initially Lady Huntingdon sided with the Wesleys against Whitefield and the predestination party, but eventually, and certainly by 1748, she embraced the Reformed doctrines of election and predestination. This caused some distance between her and the Wesleys. She appointed George Whitefield as her personal chaplain and became one of his chief benefactors; she was now effectively the administrative head of the Calvinistic wing of Methodism. In his unpublished hymn "Written for Lady Huntingdon" during the stillness controversy, Charles Wesley depicted her as being seduced by "the Serpent" into giving up good works and the means of grace:

> 7. "Foolish child," he [the Serpent] suavely cried,
>   "Spare thyself this needless pain,
> Cast thy zealous works aside,
>   Harry not thyself in vain;
> Do not bend so much and strive,
>   Do not labour up the hill,
> I a new commandment give,
>   Spare thyself, I say, be still.
>
> 8. "Run not after means of grace,
>   Fancying them by God enjoin'd,
> Leave the consecrated place,
>   Look at him and ye shall find:
> Ordinances profit not,
>   Ordinances cannot save,
> Cast them by, be all forgot,
>   Word and church and altar leave. . . ."

As the controversy over predestination was beginning in Bristol, Charles wanted peace and unanimity with Whitefield more than he wanted theological clarity: "My soul is set upon peace," Charles wrote, "and drawn out after you by love stronger than death." It is small wonder, then, that Whitefield was shocked and dismayed that Charles wrote "Universal Redemption" and allowed it to be appended to John Wesley's pamphlet *Free Grace,* and then subsequently published two volumes of *Hymns on God's Everlasting Love* (1741), which were pointedly critical of predestination and its adherents. About this same time Whitefield wrote to a mutual friend, "for Christ's sake desire dear Brother Wesley to avoid disputing with me. I think I would rather die than see a division between us; and yet how can we walk together if we oppose each other?" While the Countess of Huntingdon eventually sided doctrinally with Whitefield, she did take the opportunity to remonstrate him for his treatment of the Wesleys: "I charged him with some severity about his conduct to you," she wrote to Charles on February 19, 1742. "He seemed ashamed and was much provoked by your brother's calling them [the predestinarians] priests of Molock [1 Kings 11:7]."

That Charles Wesley's affection for George Whitefield remained undimmed despite the acrimony and controversy that erupted between the Wesleys and Whitefield over the doctrine of predestination is evident in one of his unpublished poems. In July 1743 Charles wrote "An Epistle to a Friend." In 630 rambling lines, Wesley unburdened his heart about the enmity between himself and his friends. Whitefield is named and lamented in several lines:

> Whitefield begins his course, and rises fair,
> And shoots and glitters like a Blazing Star.
> He lets his light on all impartial shine,
> And strenuously asserts the Birth divine,
> While Thousands listen to th'alarming song,
> And catch Conviction darted from his Tongue.
> Parties and sects their ancient Feuds forget,
> And fall, and tremble at the Preacher's feet,
> With horror in the wise Inquiry join,
> "What must we do to escape the Wrath divine?"

Meek, patient, humble, wise above his years,
Unbrib'd by Pleasures, and unmoved by Fears,
From Strength to Strength the young apostle goes,
Pours like a Torrent, the Land o'erflows:
To distant Climes his healing Doctrine brings,
And joins the morning's with the Eagle's Wings,
Resistless wins his way with rapid Zeal,
Turns the World upside down, and shakes the Gates of Hell.

Even as he lauded the many gifts and talents of his friend, however, Charles Wesley could not refrain from voicing his opinion that
George Whitefield had not "kept the post by heaven assigned": the
role of an evangelist who invited all people to come to Christ. Wesley
still lamented his friend's willingness to embrace and proclaim "the
horrible decree, the foulest tale" of predestination:

O had he kept to the Post by Heaven assign'd,
Sent to invite, and waken all Mankind!
O had he 'scap'd that Plague, that deadly draught,
Which rigid *Calvin* from old *Dominick* caught!
Unless to Heathen *Zeno* we ascribe
What *Mahomet* taught his wild *Elected* tribe.
Shall Whitefield too misspend his noble might
To wash the Ethiop Reprobation white?
Shall Whitefield too to prop the Doctrine try
The hellish blasphemous, exploded Lie,
The horrible Decree, the foulest Tale,
The deadliest, that was ever hatch'd in Hell!
And shall I spare the Doctrine? Spare the Fiend?
Th'old Fatalist? The Murderer of my Friend?
No: while the Breath of GOD these Limbs sustains,
Or flows one Drop of Blood within these veins,
War, endless War, with Satan's Scheme I make,
Full vengeance on the hellish Doctrine take,
Its sworn, eternal Foe, for my own Whitefield's sake!

Wesley, in the final analysis, saw Whitefield as a good and godly person "innocent of thought," who has been beguiled and enflamed into

128

controversy by false teachers and evildoers. After poetically examining the plight of Delamotte, Simpson, Harris, and the rest of his friends
who have separated from the Wesleys, Charles's poetical "Epistle"
ends with a prayer:

> Father, regard the faithful fervent Prayer,
> And me, and all my scatter'd Brethren spare;
> Recall the Shepherds, and the Sheep bring back.
> And save the Remnant for thy Jesus' sake.
> See the great Advocate of Sinners stand,
> To ward thy vengeance from a guilty Land.
> Turn not away the presence of thy Son,
> But save us, save us, by thy Grace alone,
> Thy Jesus cries, Forgive, and seal them for thine own.

The Wesleyans and Whitefieldites established separate organizational structures in 1743, but the principal players in the Wesleyan and
Calvinistic wings of the Methodist movement continued to be close
friends, and they tried to cooperate with one another in ministry. In
September 1747, when someone had written George Whitefield spreading unfavorable gossip about Charles Wesley, Whitefield responded by
writing his friend to assure him of the constancy of his love and support: "Some have wrote me things to your disadvantage. I would not
believe them. Love thinks no evil of a friend. Such are you to me. I love
you most dearly." In July 1748, George wrote Charles to inform him of
his impending arrival in London: "I came last from the *Bermudas*,"
Whitefield wrote, "where the Friend of sinners has been pleased to own
my poor labours abundantly. I hope, I come in the spirit of love, desiring to study and pursue those things which make for peace. This is the
language of my heart:

> O let us find the ancient way,
>   Our wond'ring foes to move;
> And force the heathen world to say,
>   See how these Christians love."

On March 3, 1749, Charles Wesley kept the promise he made during his years in the Oxford Holy Club to consult with Whitefield (as

129

well as his brother John) should he intend to marry. Charles's journal reports: "I met with George Whitefield, and made him quite happy by acquainting him with my design [to marry]." In that same autumn, however, at a conference at which they sought to overcome their differences and establish a cooperative union, it was difficult for the principals to keep from losing their tempers: "Our conference this week with Mr. Whitefield and Mr. Harris came to naught, I think, through their flying off." Two months later Charles Wesley was writing his friend Ebenezer Blackwell, from Sheffield, to praise George Whitefield for the work he was doing among the Wesleyans:

> My dear Friend — I snatch a few moments before the people come, to tell you what you will rejoice to know, — that the Lord is reviving his work as at the beginning; that multitudes are daily added to his church; and that G[eorge] W[hitefield] my brother and I are one. "A threefold cord which shall not be broken."
>
> The week before last, I waited on our friend George to our house in Newcastle, and gave him full possession of our pulpit, and people's hearts; as full as was in my power to give. I attended his successful ministry for some days. He was never more blessed or better satisfied. While troops of Dissenters he mowed down. They also are so reconciled to us, as you cannot conceive. At Leeds we met my brother, who gave honest George the right hand of fellowship, and attended him everywhere to our Societies. Some in London will be alarmed at the news; but it is the Lord's doing, as they, I doubt not, will by and by acknowledge. . . .

In this passage and others like it, the phraseology of Ecclesiastes 4:12, "a threefold cord is not quickly broken," became a metaphor for describing the fraternal unity that the Wesleys and George Whitefield achieved. They had "agreed to disagree" about the doctrinal issues surrounding predestination and allowed their longstanding friendship and mutual concerns for ministry to win out over the things that divided them. Whitefield's impact in Sheffield had been so profound that, two years later, Charles Wesley still referred to it: "The door has continued open ever since Mr. Whitefield preached here and quite removed the prejudices of our first opposers. Some of them were convinced by him, some converted, and added to the church. 'He that escapeth the sword of Jehu [Wesley] shall Elisha [Whitefield] slay.'" On October 8, 1749, Charles confided to his wife that "G[eorge] W[hitefield], and my brother and I are one, a three fold cord which shall no more be broken."

As others, including a few of their lay associates, seemed intent upon creating distance between John and Charles Wesley, George Whitefield wrote to Charles on December 22, 1752, to assure him that this sort of separation was not his goal. Whitefield's letter also revealed that he sensed a bit of a rivalry between John Wesley and himself. "The connection between you and your brother, hath been so close and continued, and your attachment to him so necessary to keep up his interest, that I would not willingly for the world do or say any thing that may separate such friends. I cannot help thinking, but he is still jealous of me and my proceedings; but, I thank God, I am quite easy about it. Having the testimony of a good conscience, that I have a disinterested view to promote the common salvation only."

If some of their associates sought to pull them apart, others worked to keep them together despite their differences. Lady Huntingdon, for example, wrote to Charles in December 1755 a letter about — and delivered by — Whitefield. "I am sure he will act the *honest* part in whatever he is entrusted with," she wrote of Whitefield; "all the mischief arises from these *sweet and* wise *lay preachers* whose interest it is to keep you [Charles, John, and George] from *being all friends,* but I trust the Lord will brake [sic] the snare." Later that month, she wrote again: "I wish you would *see* Mr. Whitefield and *talk matters over with him* as he has done with your brother. His heart is honest, and he has a truly brotherly love for you and I think I know when he proved it. I think if your brother *found you in friendship* then it *would keep him in order* more than any thing. I know he would not like you both to unite against those preachers he espouses." Her intercession must have met with some success; near the end of the month, Charles confided to his wife, "I have talked largely with George Whitefield who is (what I wish all our preachers and children to be) a right honest man." The following fall, Charles wrote more exuberantly to his wife, "Here [at Manchester] I rejoiced to hear of the good Mr. Whitefield has done in our Societies. He preached as universally as my brother. . . . He beat down the separating spirit, highly commended the prayers and services of our Church, charged our people to meet their bands, and classes constantly,

131

and never to leave the Methodists, or God would leave them. In a word: he did his utmost to strengthen our hands, and deserves the thanks of all the churches, for his abundant labour of love."

Worn out by his labors, George Whitefield died in 1770, during his seventh missionary journey to America. The "threefold cord" which could not permanently be broken through doctrinal differences or petty rivalries was broken by death. Charles eulogized his friend in a poetic "Epistle to the Reverend Mr. Whitefield," which had been written earlier (perhaps in 1755) but was only published after Whitefield's death. The "Epistle" of 120 lines begins by reporting "the strife is past," celebrating the friendship and "mutual league" which has existed between the author and Whitefield:

> COME on, my Whitefield! (since the strife is past,
> And friends at first are friends again at last,)
> Our hands, and hearts, and counsels let us join
> In mutual league, to advance the work Divine,
> Our one contention now, our single aim,
> To pluck poor souls as brands out of the flame;
> To spread the victory of that bloody Cross,
> And gasp our latest breath in the Redeemer's cause.

Soon after Whitefield's death, Charles Wesley reminisced with Lady Huntingdon about Whitefield's utter honesty and freedom from deception. "I wish I could say *any thing to add* to the best *impressions of my* late, dear friend, Mr. Whitefield," he wrote. "One part of his character ever the most to be admired by me, was the most *artless mind* — 'an Israelite indeed in whom there was no guile'" [John 1:47].

The next year, however, Charles's friendship with Lady Huntingdon would be strained to the breaking point. On June 8, 1771, a letter from Lady Huntingdon apprised Charles of her response to the Methodist Minutes of Conference from the year before. She had become convinced that the Wesleyans, as represented by those theological minutes, had forsaken justification by faith and were teaching salvation by works. The Countess wrote, "Enclosed you have your brother's minutes sent with those resolutions taken in consequence of their appearing in the world and that under the proper explanation of them — (viz.) 'Popery Unmasked.' They have long affected my mind

with deep concern and thinking all ought deservedly to be deemed papists who did not disown them, I readily complied with the proposal
of an open disavowal of them." Charles did not attend the conference
that drafted the minutes, and Lady Huntingdon was willing to absolve
him of complicity in what she saw as doctrinal error: "As you had no
part in this," she wrote, "I find it difficult to blame your brother to you,
while as an honest man I must pity and not less regard you, as you
must suffer equal disgrace and universal distrust from the supposed
union with him."

The Wesleyans answered Lady Huntingdon's charges about the
1770 minutes in public documents and private correspondence. John
Wesley wrote, " the Minutes lay no other foundation than that which is
laid in Scripture, and which I have been laying, and teaching others to
lay, for between thirty and forty years. Indeed, it would be amazing,
that God should at this day prosper my labours as much as if not more
than ever, by convincing as well as converting sinners, if I was 'establishing another foundation, repugnant to the whole plan of man's salvation under the covenant of grace, as well as the clear meaning of our
Established Church, and all other Protestant churches.' This is a charge
indeed! But I plead, Not guilty."

Lady Huntingdon, for her part, refused to believe that John Wesley was not teaching heresy in the 1770 minutes, and she persisted in
trying to force Charles Wesley to choose between denying the minutes
or denying his brother. She seemed intent upon coming between the
Wesley brothers in trying to convince Charles to denounce John's actions. Put in those terms it was not, ultimately, a hard choice for
Charles to make. The Countess's complaining letter to Charles Wesley
was filed away with his annotation: "Lady Huntingdon's LAST. June
8, 1771. Unanswered by John Wesley's *brother.*"

The younger Wesley saw Christian friendship as a part of the
process of sanctification and heartily embraced it. He risked himself in
relationships and gave himself freely in friendships to a degree that
John seemed incapable of doing. For example, Charles's relationship
with George Whitefield was more mutual and genuine than John's
seemed to be. And Charles's friendship with Lady Huntingdon was
something John could have never had, because John could not withstand the Countess's penchant for giving orders and having her own
way in matters great or small.

Charles Wesley's friendship with George Whitefield was one of his life's constants, and it proved to be more powerful even than Wesley's own doctrinal certainty. Their friendship weathered the storms of controversy and grew stronger as the century wore on. When Whitefield emerged as the "grand itinerant," eclipsing the Wesleys in fame and notoriety, the resulting tension and even rivalry made it more difficult for John Wesley and Whitefield to be close friends. But Charles, who so relied on friendship, clung to his relationship with Whitefield even after the challenges of rivalry and doctrinal differences. And only when Lady Huntingdon tried to get Charles to denounce his brother and his brother's policies did Charles forfeit his relationship with her. Friendship was crucial to Charles Wesley. Only his relationship to his brother mattered more.

9 "The Lions' Den"

Charles Wesley was a courageous and tenacious man. Even as a child at Westminster School, he became "captain" of the school — in part because of his courage and tenacity, and in part because he was willing to use his fists to defend another child who had become the brunt of a bully's attacks. The other child grew up to become Lord Mansfield, Chief Justice of England. In their old age, after Charles Wesley had relocated to London, he and the chief justice exchanged visits and were frequently seen walking and talking in city parks and gardens.

One of the challenges of the Wesleys' open-air approach to evangelism is that it exposed them to the whim and ridicule of the mob. Sometimes it seemed that as many people turned out to oppose their preaching as came to hear it. Why did the crowds sometimes react so negatively to Wesleyan evangelism? It is a difficult question to answer, because the reasons were as varied as the locations in which the Wesleys preached. Often the ignorant, who were full of superstitions about religion, were turned against the Wesleys by the local gentry or Anglican ministers (who often preached against the Methodists). The Methodists were roundly accused of being against the Church of England, and those who were loyal to the state church thought they were doing her a service by silencing the Methodist detractors. In Cornwall, for example, they sang a ditty to welcome Charles: "Charles Wesley is come to town, To try if he can, to pull the Churches down." In staunchly Protestant regions Charles Wesley and his associates were rumored to be "Papists," or closet Roman Catholics, and this turned crowds against them. In Roman Catholic areas, like Dublin, Ireland, they were persecuted for being Protestants. In the volatile political climate, with Bonnie Prince Charlie of Scotland attempting to wrestle the throne from the English Hanovers, it was dangerous to be seen as disloyal to King George II and his government. On at least one occasion, at Wakefield, Wesley was brought before local justices on the charge of treason.

Wesley often faced mob violence and hostility with no hope of protection from the law or local authorities. Occasionally a local mayor or constable — "one of the better sort," as Charles would describe them — would use the Anti-Riot Act of 1713 (which had been developed to protect the Dissenters and their places of worship) to protect the Methodists. But often it seemed as though the mob would have its way with Charles Wesley and that the Methodists were without civil rights. In response, Wesley advocated non-violence and passive resistance. By example and by exhortation Charles urged the Methodists to follow Jesus' injunction to "turn the other cheek" and to "resist not evil." Wesley's behavior in these challenging situations, and because of him the behavior of the Methodists as well, often won the admiration of local authorities and many of their attackers. It was not unusual for Charles Wesley to endure savage persecution, only to find former rioters among the Methodist society the next time he visited town. Local persecution was sometimes met by the tenacity of the Methodists in that same vicinity. In Newcastle, for example, the "Keelmen," boatmen who guided barges of coal up and down the river Tyne, were among the defenders of Charles Wesley. These rough people were prone to violence in defense of their preachers. An unpublished segment of Charles's journal describes how the wives of the Keelmen attacked a vocal detractor who sought to make a disturbance while Wesley preached:

> I live by the gospel, and renewed my strength to preach it this morning. . . . Breakfasted at a constant hearer of the Word, and several of the poor Keelmen (Keel-women I should say) flocked to us.

They related some instances of their zeal which pleased them more than me. At that [instance] a gentleman happening to say, while I was preaching, that I should be sent to Bedlam [a mental hospital], a stout woman collared and kicked him down the hill. More of her fellows joined in the pursuit so that he was forced to fly for his life. Another poor scoffer they put into the pond. I do indeed believe that were any to offer me violence, the people would stone them; but by and by, I trust they will learn to suffer wrong and to turn the other cheek. . . .

Sometimes Methodism caused serious divisions in families, as in the case of the Seward family of Gloucester. William Seward was a devout Methodist, a friend and follower of the Wesleys and Whitefield, but his brother, Henry Seward, was staunchly anti-Methodist. Indeed, he blamed the Methodists for making his brother "mad," and he opposed them with all his might. Henry incited a mob against Charles Wesley in March 1740 that stopped just short of throwing him off a bridge into the river. Later that year William Seward died from a head injury he received during a violent anti-Methodist riot in Wales.

Yet Charles Wesley's rough treatment by some, and his patient witness in the face of it, had positive results for the course of his ministry. The day after his encounter with Henry Seward, he wrote in his journal, "My yesterday's treatment provoked many to love. They received me the more gladly into their houses, *because* Mr. Seward's is shut against me." Seward, by continuing his opposition, had the opposite effect of what he intended: "Mr. Henry Seward," Charles wrote, "mad with passion at my stay, spreads the news of it everywhere, and much increases my audience." That evening, while Charles was preaching his way through the beatitudes, a mob poured out of a neighboring alehouse to mock and drown out his sermon. Ironically, they appeared just as Wesley preached, "Blessed are they which are persecuted," as if they intended to fulfill the gospel message completely unawares. The mob set their "champion," a school master, upon a bench directly across from Wesley, and he railed and mocked Wesley for nearly an hour as Charles preached. The next evening, news reached Charles Wesley's ears about the source of the most recent persecution: "Last night's disturbance, we now hear, was contrived at the alehouse by the "Squire and Rector" of the local Anglican church.

The further into 1743 Charles Wesley's ministry went, the more severe the persecution came that accompanied it. In Walsal on May 21, he was met by a mob when he arrived in town, and he walked through the streets of town "to the noisy greetings of our enemies." They railed, blasphemed, and mocked as Wesley made his way to the steps in front of the market house, which was to be his "pulpit" in this location. The disturbance raised by the mob was so severe that it sounded to Wesley like waves on the ocean: "The floods lifted up their voice and raged horribly. I opened the Book on the first presented words, Acts 20:24, 'But none of these things move me; neither count I my life dear unto myself, so that I have received of the Lord Jesus, to testify the Gospel of the grace of God.'" Charles preached on through the roar of the crowd and a hail of stones, unharmed: "The street was full of Ephesian beasts," he wrote, "the principal man setting them on, who roared, and shouted, and threw stones incessantly. Many struck, without hurting me. I besought them in calm love to be reconciled to God in Christ." After he had finished and as he was leaving, a group of ruffians grabbed him and pulled him down from the steps. He tried to stand up and ascend them again, but was beaten to the ground — twice. The third time Charles was able to stagger to his feet and ascend back up the steps, from whence he gave a benediction and urged them to depart in peace. He then walked away, through the midst of the mob, untouched. "They reviled us," he wrote, "but had no commission to touch an hair on our heads."

May 25, 1743, found Charles Wesley in Sheffield, where once again he found that the local ministers had been preaching and speaking against the Methodists. Charles had given notice that he intended to preach at the Methodist Society room that evening at 6:00. A torrent of stones and blasphemies met him as he began to speak. A mob had gathered outside and was attacking the building: "Hell from beneath was moved to oppose us. As soon as I was in the desk with David Taylor, the flood began to lift up their voice. An officer (Ensign Garden) contradicted and blasphemed. I took no notice of him, and sung on. The stones flew thick, hitting the desk and people. To save them and the house, I gave notice [that] I should preach out[side], and look the enemy in the face."

As he went outside and walked to an appropriate place from which to speak, "the whole army of aliens" followed Wesley. Their leader, Ensign Garden, took hold of Charles and began to abuse him verbally. For his answer, Charles Wesley handed the ensign a Wesleyan tract, *A Word In Season, or Advice to a Soldier.* He then tried to lead the people in prayer for His Majesty King George, so that no one would mistakenly charge him with treasonous actions or opinions, and preached "with much contention." As he ended the service with solemn prayer for repentant sinners and those who persecuted the Methodists, the ensign forced his way through the crowd and the cadre of Methodists who stood around Wesley to protect him. As he came the ensign drew his sword and threatened revenge for Wesley's abuse of him and the king. When he approached Charles, he aimed his sword at his breast. "My breast was immediately steeled," Wesley wrote. "I threw it open, and fixing mine eye on his, smiled in his face and calmly said, 'I fear God, and honour the King.' His countenance fell in a moment, he fetched a deep sigh, put up his sword, and quietly left the place." One member of the local Methodist society had heard the officer say, "You shall see, if I do but hold my sword to his breast he will faint away." Charles had passed the officer's test, but he believed that it was not by his own strength and courage that he had prevailed; Wesley assumed supernatural power had intervened. After the preaching service Charles Wesley walked to the home of his friend and fellow preacher John Bennet. "The rioters followed, and exceeded in their outrage all I have seen before," he later recalled. "Those of Moorfields, Cardiff, and Walsal were lambs [compared] to these." Since there was no magistrate in Sheffield, or at least none that would keep law and order, the rioters were free to do as they pleased. While the Methodists conducted a prayer meeting at Bennet's house, the mob devised another sort of entertainment: "Satan now put it into their heads to pull down the Society house, and they set to their work, while we were praying and praising God. It was a glorious time with us," Wesley wrote. "Every word of exhortation sunk deep, every prayer was sealed, and many found the Spirit of glory resting on them."

Someone went for the constable, and when he arrived his solution to the disturbance was to urge Charles Wesley to leave town, since Wesley was, as he put it, "the occasion of all this disturbance." Charles thanked the constable for his advice, and then told him, "I should not go a moment sooner for this uproar; was sorry for *their* sakes that they had no law or justice among them; as for myself, I had my protection, and knew my business, as I supposed he did his." In response to Wesley's report, the constable "went from us and encouraged the mob."

While the Methodists continued on in John Bennet's house the mob began pressing hard against the door, trying to force their way in. Charles Wesley offered to go out to the rioters and "look them in the face," but those within the house forbade him, fearing for his life. Unable to break in the door, they began tearing the house down around Wesley and his associates. He later wrote, "They laboured all night for their master, and by morning had pulled down one end of the house. I could compare them to nothing but the men of Sodom, or those coming out of the tombs exceeding fierce. Their outcries often waked me in the night; yet I believe I got more sleep than any of my neighbors."

It was in reflection upon situations like this one that Charles Wesley wrote his hymn titled, "After Deliverance from Death by the Fall of an House." On several occasions, like the one above, he faced mobs so fierce and lawless that they literally tried to tear the house down to get at Wesley. As Charles Wesley meditated on his own safety and that of the others, the riotous actions of the mob caused him to think of the Judgment Day, when the righteous ones now persecuted and oppressed would be vindicated:

1. Glory and thanks to God we give!
   Our sacred hairs are number'd all,
   Not one, we find, without His leave,
   Not one unto the ground can fall.

2. How blest whom Jesus calls His own,
   How quiet, and secure from harms!
   The adversary cast us down,
   The Saviour caught us in His arms.

3. 'Twas Jesus check'd his straighten'd chain,
   And curb'd the malice of our foe,
   Allow'd to touch our flesh and pain,
   No farther could the murderer go.

4. 'Twas Jesus raised our bodies up,
   And stronger by our fall we stand;

Our life is hid with Christ our Hope,
Hid in the hollow of His hand.

5. We rest in His protection here;
But languish for the final day,
When Christ shall in the clouds appear,
And heaven and earth shall pass away. . . .

The next day Charles Wesley preached twice more in Sheffield and met with the society as well as with representatives from societies in neighboring towns. In the evening, since it had already been agreed that Wesley would preach "in the heart of the town," he walked there to preach, not doubting God's protection. Charles's journal reports: "We heard our enemies shouting from afar. I stood up in the midst of them, and read the first words that offered. 'If God be for us, who can be against us? He that spared not his own Son,' and etc. God made bare his arm in the sight of the Heathen, and so restrained the fierceness of men, so that not one lifted up [his] hand or voice against us." As Wesley and his assistant, David Taylor, walked through the mob to John Bennet's house, they passed the wreck of the Methodist society house. Wesley observed, "they had not left one stone upon another." But he took symbolic meaning from the fact that the foundation of the house stood firm: "Nevertheless, the foundation standeth sure, as I told one of them, and our house not made with hands, eternal in the heavens."

The mob followed Wesley to his lodgings "with great civility," but as soon as he entered the house they began to stone it and try to tear it down. "The windows were smashed in an instant," he wrote, "and my poor host so frightened, that he was ready to give up his shield [faith]." The fears and distress of the family within the house seemed to call upon Wesley to go out and face the mob. He spied a familiar face in the crowd, and noticed that he had brought a copy of "The Riot Act" (of 1713) with him. The act had been passed to protect the Dissenters from persecution, and their property from destruction, but it could be as easily applied to the Methodists as well. "At their desire, I took it and read it, and made a suitable exhortation. One of the sturdiest rebels our Constable seized, and carried away captive into the house. I marveled at the patience of his companions; but the Lord overawed them." Wesley's journal reports that he returned to his

141

room, which was now partially dismantled, and went sound asleep in about five minutes. He subsequently heard that within an hour of his speech the rioters had quit their destructive work and left them in peace.

By May 27, 1743, Charles Wesley and David Taylor were on the road again, making their way toward Barley-Hall by way of Thorpe, where it had been reported that "the people were exceeding mad against us." As the riders approached the town they were ambushed by a mob that pelted them with stones, eggs, and clods of dirt. Wesley nearly lost control of his horse during the melee, as it bounded from side to side, eventually making its way through the crowded lane. David Taylor was wounded in the forehead by a stone; he lost his hat and a considerable amount of blood. At that point Charles Wesley turned to the rioters and asked what was wrong with them that a clergyman could not pass through their town without such rough treatment. Initially, the rioters were cowered, but their leader rallied his troops and they showered the travelers with so many threats and stones that Wesley thought they would have been killed but for divine intervention. Once again Charles's horse bolted, this time wildly carrying him away from the danger. His journal rejoiced, "Blessed be God, I got no hurt, but only eggs and dirt. My clothes indeed abhorred me, and my arm pained me a little by a blow I received at Sheffield."

With all this danger, then, small wonder that Wesley's *Hymns and Sacred Poems* (1749 edition) contained an entire section of "Hymns for the Persecuted." One of these, entitled "The Trial of Faith," was based on the Scripture passage "Christ also suffered, leaving us an example" (1 Peter 2:21), and explained the spiritual principles behind Wesley's willingness to endure such severe persecution unflinchingly:

> 1. Come, O my soul, the call obey,
>   Take up the burden of thy Lord!
> His practice is thy living way,
>   Thy guide His pure unerring word,
> The lovely perfect pattern read,
> And haste in all His steps to tread.
>
> 2. What did my Lord from sinners bear?
>   His patience is the rule for me:

Walking in Him I cannot err:
    And lo! The Man of Griefs I see,
Whose life one scene of sufferings was,
Quite from the manger to the cross.

3. Here then my calling I discern
    ('Tis written in affliction's book),
My first, and latest lesson learn,
    For nothing here but sufferings look,
I bow me to the will Divine,
To suffer *with* my Lord be mine.

4. To suffer *as* my Lord I come:
    How did the Lamb His wrongs endure?
Clamorous, and warm? or meek, and dumb?
    Did He by force His life secure?
He injured innocence defend;
Or bear His burden to the end?

5. Did He evade the pain, and shame,
    Impatient of unjust disgrace?
Did He throw off the imputed blame?
    Did He from spitting hide His face?
Did He to man for succour fly;
Or offer up Himself, and die? . . .

The rhetorical question, raised in verse five, is answered throughout the remaining five stanzas of the hymn; Jesus did not evade pain, shame, or suffering, and for righteousness' sake neither should those who follow him and seek to live by his example. Hence Charles's concluding verse prays,

10. O that I might like Him *withstand*,
    Like Him mine innocence *clear*,
Like Him *resist* the ruffian band,
    Like Him *refuse* the cross to bear,
Like Him the persecutor *fly*;
Like Him submit to live, and die?

143

Wesley used much irony in this verse; he was determined to follow Jesus' example, not resisting the ruffians, not refusing to bear his own cross, and not flying from persecution — because Jesus, the Christian's example in this situation, did none of those things. Indeed, when he preached among the Methodists, during times of persecution, he challenged the spirit of vengeance and resistance to the violence of persecution. His journal entry for February 3, 1744, for example, reports, "I preached and prayed with the Society, and beat down the fiery, self-avenging spirit of resistance, which was rising in some, to disgrace, if not destroy the work of God." Wesley's hymn "Written After a Deliverance" indicates that having a sense of God's grace and love in God's deliverance from persecution was far better than life itself; it was a foretaste of heaven: "Tis pure delight, and perfect bliss,/ And everlasting joy." In solidarity with the ancient church of the martyrs, he sang:

4. Saved by a miracle of grace,
    Lord, I with thankful heart embrace
       The token of Thy love:
    This, this the comfortable sign,
    That I the first born church shall join,
       And bless Thy name above.

In July of 1743 Wesley was preaching in Cornwall. On July 22nd, as he preached at St. Ives, an "army of rebels" broke in upon the meeting: "They began in a most outrageous manner, threatening to murder the people, if they did not [leave] that moment. They broke the sconces, dashed the windows in pieces, tore away the shutters, benches, poor-box, and all but the stone walls." "Several times," Wesley wrote, "they lifted up their hands and clubs to strike me; but a stronger arm restrained them." As rioters beat the Methodists without mercy, "particularly one of great age," Wesley urged his congregation "to stand still and see the salvation of God"; he resolved to stay with them to the bitter end. In about an hour the rabble stopped as Charles Wesley preached from the text, "Hitherto shalt thou come, and no farther." At which "the ruffians fell into quarreling among themselves, [and] broke the Town-clerk's (their captain's) head, and drove one another out of the room." Wesley concluded: "Having kept the field, we gave thanks for the victory; and in prayer the Spirit of glory rested upon us."

The next day, Saturday, July 23, 1743, a mob attacked the Methodists again. This time they were led by the mayor's son. "The gentlemen," Wesley wrote, "had resolved to destroy all within doors. They came upon us like roaring lions, headed by the Mayor's son. He struck out the candles with his cane, and began courageously beating the women. I laid my hand upon him, and said, 'Sir, you appear like a gentleman: I desire you would show it, by restraining these of the baser sort. Let them strike the men, or me, if they please, but not hurt the poor helpless women and children.'" Almost immediately the man Charles Wesley confronted seemed to come to his senses, and he did as Wesley asked; soon the room was emptied of attackers. Since the rioters were determined that Wesley should not preach in St. Ives, he did so again, that same evening. "I proved the devil a liar, by preaching in the room at five. The words I first met were Isa. 54: 'For thou shalt break forth on the right hand and on the left. Fear not; for thou shalt not be ashamed: neither be thou confounded; for thou shalt not be put to shame. Behold, I have created the smith, and the waster to destroy. No weapon that is formed against thee shall prosper.'" The mayor of the town subsequently told Charles Wesley that "the Ministers were the principal authors of all this evil, by continually representing us in their sermons as Popish emissaries, and urging the enraged multitude to take all manner of ways to stop us. Their whole preaching is cursings and lies; yet they modestly say, my fellow-labourer and I are the cause of all the disturbance. It is always the lamb that troubles the water." An unpublished journal letter continues Wesley's statement, which was cut short for publication: "However they have gained their point, by making the rabble of St. Ives (including the gentry) likeminded with themselves, and all the cry, both of the great and vulgar, and the small is *Ad Leones!* ['To the Lions!'] It is not that I begin to be a minister of God! O that we may approve ourselves such in all things!" Charles Wesley found both direction and vindication in the Bible text of 2 Corinthians 6:4-10, which he transcribed directly into his letter to explain his role in the midst of this persecution: "In much patience, in afflictions in necessities, in distress, in stripes, in imprisonments, in tumults, in labours, in watchings, in fastings, by pureness, in knowledge, by long-suffering, by kindness, by the Holy Ghost, by love unfeigned, by the word of truth, by the power of God, by the armour of righteousness on the right and on the left, by honour and dishonour, by evil report and good report, as deceivers and yet true, as unknown and yet well known, as dying and behold we live, as chastened and not killed, as sorrowful yet always rejoicing, as poor yet making many rich, as having nothing, yet possessing all things." His published journal (along with the unpublished record) concludes, "Yesterday we were stoned as Popish incendiaries; today, it is our turn to have favour with the people."

By October of 1743 the Methodists had clearly begun to make headway against their strongest opposition. Preaching in Wednesbury on October 25th, Charles Wesley discovered that the leader of the rioters, a man named Munchin, petitioned to join the Methodist society. Wesley wrote, "I took several new members into the Society; and among them, the young man whose arm was broke [during the riot], and (upon trial) Munchin, the late captain of the mob. He has been constantly under the Word since he rescued my brother. I asked him what he thought of him. 'Think of him!' said he, 'That he is a man of God; and God was on his side, when so mony of us could not kill one mon [sic]." The minister of strife-torn Darlston was also won over by the Methodist's patient witness. He sent John Wesley word that he would join him in any efforts to suppress and punish the rioters there; "the meek behaviour of our people," wrote Charles, "and their constancy in suffering, convinced him the counsel was of God; and he wished all his parish [were] Methodists."

Working in the area around Birmingham in the spring of 1744, Charles Wesley was utterly frustrated by the failure of local constables and magistrates to provide the Methodists with the sort of protection they deserved according to their basic civil rights under the law. As he reported in his journal entry for February 3, 1744, "the magistrates do not themselves tear off [the Methodists'] clothes, and beat them; they only stand by, and see others do it. One of them told Mr. Jones, it was the best thing the mob ever did, so to treat the Methodists; and he would himself give 5£ to drive them out of the country. Another, when our brother Ward begged his protection, himself delivered him up to the mercy of the mob (who half murdered him before), threw his hat around his head, and cried, 'Huzza, boys! Well done! Stand up for the Church!'" With this sort of example set for the common people by their leaders and the representatives of justice, it was small wonder that they felt they could do as they pleased to the Methodists.

The Methodists in Darlston (near Walsall) Wesley identified as "the greatest sufferers." In that location the rioters of town summoned the Methodists to the local pub and addressed them with a public proclamation which demanded that they swear an oath that they would not go near the Methodist preachers or societies. Those who failed to "set their hand" to the agreement they compelled with blows. They watched and listened against the Methodists and violently intervened when they heard them singing, praying, or reading the Scriptures. They also watched their houses so that none could go to Wednesbury and give aid to the persecuted society there. Wesley observed that those who encouraged the rioters were creating a monster that not even they could control. He reported that the Methodists' "enemies are the basest of the people, who will not work themselves, but live more to their inclination, on the labours of others." "I wonder," he wrote, that "the gentlemen who set them on [us], are so shortsighted as not to see that the little all of our poor colliers will soon be devoured; and then these sons of rapine will turn upon their foolish masters, who have raised a devil they cannot lay."

In this dangerous climate, Charles Wesley continued to preach and pursue his plan of nonviolent resistance. On February 4 he preached from Isaiah 54:17, "'No weapon that is formed against thee shall prosper.' This promise shall be fulfilled in our day," he wrote. "I spoke with those of our brethren who have this world's goods, and found them entirely resigned to the will of God. All thoughts of resistance are over, blessed be the Lord; and the chief of them said to me, 'Naked came I into the world, and I can but go naked out of it.' They are resolved by the grace of God to follow my advice, and suffer all things." Wesley did have the people report their imminent danger to the justices and constables, but once again they reproved the Methodists rather than protecting them.

The next day Wesley was on the road again, this time riding west to Wednesbury, another place of severe persecution. So impressed was Charles Wesley with the Christian courage of the Methodists of Wednesbury that he composed a hymn "For the Persecuted," which was published under the subtitle "For the Brethren at Wednesbury."

1. Dear dying Lamb, for whom alone
    We suffer pain, and shame and loss,
   Hear Thine afflicted people groan,
    Crush'd by the burden of Thy cross,
   And bear our fainting spirits up,
   And bless the bitter, sacred cup.

2. Drunkards, and slaves of lewd excess,
    Bad, lawless men, Thou know'st we lived;
   The world and we were then at peace,
    No devil his own servants grieved,
   Evil we did, but suffer'd none;
   The world will always love its own.

3. But now we would Thy word obey,
    And strive to escape the wrath Divine,
   Exposed to all, an helpless prey,
    Bruised by our enemies and Thine,
   As sheep 'midst ravening wolves we lie,
   And daily grieve, and daily die.

4. Smitten, we turn the other cheek,
    Our ease, and name, and goods forego;
   Help, or redress no longer seek
    In any child of man below;
   The powers Thou didst for us ordain,
   For us they bear the sword in vain. . . .

On February 20, 1744, while preaching in the Newcastle area, Charles Wesley received news that the French had invaded England in support of the claims of the "Pretender," Scottish Bonnie Prince Charlie, upon the British throne. His journal reports, "I heard, without any surprise, the news of the French invasion; which only quickened us in our prayers, especially for His Majesty, King George." It was in this politically charged situation of the French-Scottish attempt upon the throne of England that Charles Wesley was charged with treason in Yorkshire, West-riding, and forced to appear at Wakefield to answer the charges.

Charles Wesley was preaching his way through Yorkshire when he was presented with the news that the constable of Birstal had a warrant against him on the charge of "speaking any treasonable words or exhortations [such] as praying for the banished, or for the Pretender." Mary Castle, upon whose testimony the warrant was issued, was also to appear at the hearing to give evidence. Wesley believed that he was innocent of the charges brought against him, and he looked forward to the hearing as an opportunity to vindicate himself and the Methodists against the false charges that the populace brought against them.

When Charles Wesley arrived at Wakefield on March 15, he found the justice who would hear the case along with two other justices at the White Hart tavern. Appearing before them, Wesley was told that he could depart. Wesley replied, "that was not sufficient, without clearing my character, and that of many innocent people, who their enemies were pleased to call Methodists." "Vindicate them!" Rev. Zouch retorted. "That you will find a very hard task." Wesley answered, "As hard as you may think it, I will engage to prove that they all, to a man, are true members of the Church of England, and loyal subjects of His Majesty King George." Charles then requested that the justices administer an oath of loyalty to him, adding: "If it was not too much trouble, I could wish, gentlemen, you would send for every Methodist in England, and give them the same opportunity you do me, of declaring their loyalty upon oath."

In his defense Charles Wesley gave the justices a copy of his Oxford sermon, hymnbooks, and their most recent book — John Wesley's *Appeals to Men of Reason and Religion* — all of which specifically petitioned for God's blessing upon the Church of England and King George. After giving the justices a moment to examine the books, Charles told them: "I am as true a Church-of-England man, and as loyal a subject as any man in the kingdom." "That is impossible!" the three justices cried together. Since, as he confided in his journal, Wesley came to testify, not to dispute with them, he made no reply. When those witnesses who were subpoenaed to testify against him did not appear, Charles withdrew to a neighboring house to await them.

As Wesley waited, the constable of Birstal visited him. He reported that the principal witness, Mary Castle, had set out for the trial on horseback, but upon being informed that Charles had not gone on to London — as he had announced — but intended to appear at the hearing instead, she turned back to Birstal, saying that she had not heard Charles Wesley speak treason herself, but had heard someone *say* that he had spoke treason and prayed for the Pretender. Hearsay evidence would not be admissible at the hearing, so she was excused. Three other witnesses who were to support Mary Castle's testimony likewise retracted their report. The fifth witness, one Joseph Woods, an ale-house keeper, was still scheduled to appear that same afternoon.

"Honest Mr. Woods," as Wesley's journal sarcastically styled him, arrived between two and three o'clock. Wesley waited at the door while they examined him and conduced other business — till seven o'clock that evening. At seven o'clock they asked: "What would Mr. Wesley desire?" "I desire nothing, but to know what is alleged against me," Charles replied. Justice Burton told Charles Wesley that he could depart, since they had nothing against him. But Wesley insisted: "Sir, that is not sufficient: I cannot depart till my character is fully cleared. It is no trifling matter. Even my life is concerned in the charge." Joseph Woods had come, and Wesley demanded to hear his accusations. The justices reported that Woods had nothing to say. "Had I not been here," Wesley retorted, "he would have had enough to say." Woods finally said, "I have nothing to speak against this gentleman; I only heard him pray that the Lord would call home his banished." Wesley then explained what those words of prayer had meant: "I had no thoughts of praying for the Pretender, but for those that confess themselves strangers and pilgrims upon earth, who seek a country, knowing this is not their place. . . . We are not at home till we are in heaven." Wesley pressed the justices again and again to give him the chance to swear an oath of loyalty to the king, until they finally satisfied him by stating in explicit terms that his loyalty was "unquestionable."

Within half an hour Charles Wesley was on the road again, heading south to Birstal, "and a joyful journey we had," he wrote. Wesley was met along the way by the Methodists from Birstal. They "sang praises lustily, with good courage." Charles wrote a hymn inspired by the proceedings at Wakefield, entitled "Afterwards," that offers a window into his state of mind at this turn of events:

1. Who that trusted in the Lord
     Was ever put to shame?
   Live, by heaven and earth adored,

Thou all-victorious Lamb;
Thou hast magnified Thy power,
    Thou in my defense hast stood,
Kept my soul in danger's hour,
    And arm'd with Thy blood.

2. Satan's slaves against me rose,
    And sought my life to slay;
Thou hast baffled all my foes,
    And spoil'd them of their prey;
Thou hast cast the accuser down,
    Hast maintain'd Thy servant's right,
Made mine innocence known,
    And clear as noonday light.

3. Evil to my charge they laid,
    And crimes I never knew;
But my Lord the snare display'd,
    And dragged the fiend to view;
Glared his bold malicious lie!
    Satan, show thine art again,
Hunt the precious life, and try,
    To take my soul in vain.

4. Thou, my great redeeming God,
    My Jesus still art near,
Kept by Thee, nor secret fraud,
    No open force I fear;
Safe amidst the snares of death,
    Guarded by the King of kings,
Glad to live, and die beneath
    The shadow of Thy wings.

Wesley came to see the victory at Wakefield as an important stroke against the persecution the Methodists faced elsewhere. "Now I see," he wrote in his journal, "if I had not gone to confront my enemies, or had been evil entreated at Wakefield, it might have occasioned a general persecution here, which the Lord hath now crusted in the birth. No weapon that is forged against us in judgment we shall condemn."

Persecution of Charles Wesley and the Methodists continued throughout the 1740s. In some instances the opposition used ever more inventive approaches to silence them. In Devizes (in Wiltshire), for example, their enemies commandeered a fire engine and turned its hoses upon the Methodists. But gradually persecution lessened as Wesley's demeanor and witness, as well as that of his followers, vindicated them against most of the popular charges. Charles's nonviolent resistance wore down the opposition. The Methodists' willingness to "turn the other cheek" gradually won over local authorities and many of those who were former persecutors of the movement. For their part, the Methodists seemed to thrive under persecution, as religious movements so often do. Their ability cheerfully to bear persecution became a badge of courage among the early Methodists even as it helped continue to swell their ranks.

10 "My Dearest Sally"

Although celibacy was the norm for the members of the Oxford Holy Club, Charles Wesley's commitment to singleness gradually waned over the years. The loneliness and depression he experienced during his American adventure had taught Charles that he was not well suited for the single life. General Olegthorpe, the governor of the Georgia colony, made the same assessment. As Charles Wesley prepared to leave for England, Oglethorpe urged him: "On many accounts I should recommend to you marriage, rather than celibacy. You are of a social temper and would find in a married state the difficulties of working out your salvation exceedingly lessened and your helps as much increased." At the height of the stillness controversy, James Hutton offered a similar assessment — though for a very different reason. In a gossipy letter to the Moravian bishop Count Zinzendorf, Hutton wrote, "J.W. and C. Wesley are dangerous snares to many young women; several are in love with them. I wish they were married to some good [Christian] sisters, but I would not give them of my sisters, if I had any." Hutton's letter raises some interesting questions about the tacit connection between religious love and romantic love that might have occurred in the throes of the Methodist revival; no doubt these two were frequently linked and occasionally confused.

And his satirical pun about not wanting either Wesley to marry his sister — if he had one — evidences Hutton's disillusionment with the Wesley brothers because of the way they took sides against him in the stillness controversy.

Charles Wesley's relationship with Sarah ("Sally") Gwynne began innocently enough. He met Sally through his friendship with her father, Marmaduke Gwynne. On Friday, August 28, 1747, he saw her for the first time. While Wesley was staying at the house of a Rev. Phillips, the rector of Maesmynis, Wales, he had three visitors from the Gwynne family. It was a case of love at first sight that grew into an ever-deepening relationship despite the fact that she was almost half his age (she was twenty-one and he was forty) and from an aristocratic family. As Charles confided to Sally in a letter of February 1749: "You have heard me acknowledge that at first sight [of you], 'My soul seemed pleased to take acquaintance with thee.' And never have I found such a nearness to any fellow-creature as to you. O that it may bring us nearer and nearer to God, till we are both swallowed up in the immensity of His love!" Sarah's sister, Becky, was probably the third person at that first meeting. She would become Sally's confidant during her courtship and the Wesleys' faithful friend for fifty years during their marriage.

At the time, Charles was on his way to Ireland for a six-month evangelistic stint. It would not be an easy six months. Sometimes it was only the intervention of British soldiers, who were among his most faithful converts, that preserved his life. When his Irish tour was over he stopped at the Gwynne home, in Garth, Wales, as worn out as his clothing. He had been battling a toothache and heavy rains for five days on his journey to Wales. After spending five more painful days in bed, Charles's health began to return. In a shorthand section of his manuscript journal for April 3, 1748, Charles lovingly intimated that Sally had nursed him "like a guardian angel." He was so overcome by emotion in his fragile state that Wesley impulsively asked Sarah whether she could "trust herself with me for life" — a move he deeply regretted the next day. After two days of limited exercise, Wesley was well enough to be on his way back to London, accompanied by Sally and her father for the first hour of the journey. His short intervals of good health at Garth had been filled up with "conference, prayer, and singing." During these periods of time he and Sally had begun getting to know one another.

Charles's journal entry of April 19, 1748, records that he had already begun thinking about marrying Sarah Gwynne after their first brief meeting while he was still in Ireland in that same spring. He rode over to Shoreham, on that same day, to confer with Rev. Vincent Perronet, who had been like a father to him. Perronet encouraged Wesley to pray and wait for a "providential opening" to broach the topic with Sally and the Gwynnes.

At this point Wesley was in a quandary as to whether he should marry at all. He was falling in love with Sally, and he feared such love might crowd out his highest and first affection for Jesus Christ. Hence he prayed to "Christ, my Life, my Only Treasure" to be set free from "all Earthly Expectation" and "Strength of Passion":

1. Christ, my Life, my Only Treasure,
    Thou alone
    Mould Thine own,
  After thy Good Pleasure.

2. Thou, who paidst my Price shalt have me!
    Thine I am,
    Holy Lamb,
  Save, and always save me.

3. Order Thou my whole Condition,
    Chuse my State,
    Fix my Fate
  By thy wise Decision.

4. From all Earthly Expectation
    Set me free,
    Seize for thee
  All my Strength of Passion.

5. Into absolute Subjection
    Be it brought,
    Be Every Thought,
  Every fond Affection.

6. That which most my Soul requires
      For thy sake
      Hold it back,
   Purge my Best Desires.

7. Keep from me thy loveliest Creature,
      Till I prove
      Jesus' Love
   Infinitely sweeter;

8. Till with purest Passion panting
      Cries my Heart,
      "Where Thou art
   Nothing more is wanting."

9. Blest with thy Abiding Spirit,
      Fully blest
      Now I rest,
   All in Thee inherit.

10. Heaven is now with Jesus given;
      Christ in me,
      Thou shalt be
   My Eternal Heaven.

Charles turned to his hymns to work out his thoughts and feelings about this important decision. He wrote more than fifty hymns about his courtship and marriage, scattered through four different manuscripts. They had as a common theme his uncertainties and quandaries about marriage. He feared substituting human love for the "Perfect Love" which had become his life's goal:

1. Lord, if Thou know'st it good for me
      Friendless, and alone to be,
         While in the Vale I live,
   Do Thou supply me every Want,
   And still unto thy Servant grant
         Thy saying to receive.

2. Far from the cheerful Ways of Men
    Lead me in a Path unseen,
        To all but Thee unknown;
Fast by the Silent Waters lead;
And let me find whate'er I need,
        In thy pure Love *alone.*

3. Thy only Love sufficient is,
    Perfect Love is perfect Bliss;
        And All, to whom 'tis given,
Thy Love to taste, thy Face to see,
They want no Other Good but Thee,
        They want no other Heaven!

4. Yet if thy wise Eternal Will
    Foreordain'd me to fulfil
        The Social Character,
A Ray of Heavenly Light impart,
And speak thy Counsel to my Heart,
        And all thy Mind declare.

Typically, Wesley asked God for grace and direction in this crisis so that he was confident that he was following God's will for his life and not merely his own feeble judgment. In these melodramatic lines Charles wishes to die rather than choose wrongly in the matter of his marriage:

5. O for thy Truth & Mercy sake
    Do not leave me to mistake
        My own weak Will for Thine,
Thou all my Thoughts direct, control
Or let me now give back my Soul
        Into the Hands Divine!

6. In jealous self-mistrusting Fear
    Lest my heart should settle here,
        And cleave to Things below,
I pray Thee end the doubtful Strife,

> And kindly cut the Knot of Life,
> And let my Spirit go. . . .

On June 20, 1748, Mr. Gwynne and "Miss Sally" met Charles Wesley in Bristol. By June 28 "Miss Sally," had become "Sally" in Charles's writings. Two days later, the Gwynnes set out with Charles for his swing to London; after preaching in Bath, they arrived at the Foundery on July 2. After spending two weeks in London, Charles, Marmaduke, and Sally set out again, at four in the morning, for an evangelistic tour of the west country. At Windsor, Charles's horse stumbled and fell — unseating both him and Sally. "My companion fell upon me," he wrote; "the guardian angels bore us in their hands, so that neither was hurt." At the beginning of August Charles set out with the Gwynnes for their home in Garth, where he spent another week with the family. When he left, Sally, Betsy, and Marmaduke Gwynne rode with Wesley as far as Llanidoles. Charles and Sally had spent another three weeks of chaperoned, uninterrupted time together; Sally saw what it would be like being married to a traveling evangelist, and they seemed to draw strength and joy from each other's presence. On Thursday, August 11, 1748, Charles's journal located him in "my Prophet's chamber, or closet among the rocks" at Holy Head, waiting for his passage to Ireland. The next day he penned an important letter to Sally from that location.

The letter was full of Christian piety and concern for Sally's spiritual welfare, but behind the language of piety, romance throbbed. Charles began his letter by describing her as his "best beloved friend" and implying that the bond between them was so deep that they could feel each other's thoughts and emotions: "I write this from the prophet's chamber where I am still detained a willing prisoner to *converse* with my best, beloved Friend. I ask you, 'is your heart cheerful?' and answer for you, that it surely is or mine would be in greater heaviness. Who is it that so strangely bears our burdens? The Creator of all the ends of the earth. He who fainteth not, neither is weary. He who loved us and gave Himself for us." The same letter not only implied that they were now "a couple," but using the Wesleyan theology of love and the language of Christian eschatology ("the marriage supper of the Lamb"), Charles seemed to hint that he and Sally had reached an understanding about their own marriage as well:

Both you and I have a baptism to be baptized with, and how should we be straightened till it is accomplished! This, this is the One Thing Needful — not a Friend, not Health — not Life itself, but — the pure perfect Love of Christ Jesus. — O give me Love or else I die! — O give me Love and *let* me die! I am weary of my [lack] of Love — weary to Death; and would fain throw off this Body; that I may Love Him who so loved me. . . . O, eternal Spirit of Love come down into my Heart and into my Friend's [Sally's] Heart, and knit us together in the bond of Perfectness. Lead us by the waters of comfort, swallow up our will in Thine. Make ready the Bride, and then call us up to the marriage supper of the Lamb.

On September 17, 1748, Charles wrote Sally from Dublin. His heart and mind were focused upon her and the potential of their life together: "Why did Eternal Wisdom bring us together here, but that we might meet hereafter at His right hand, and sing salvation unto God who sitteth upon the throne, and to the Lamb for ever. Surely the will of God is our sanctification. . . . My heart is deeply engaged for you." He also enclosed a hymn. In it he begins to celebrate the mutual advantages of their being a couple. In verse 4, Charles mentions the "Flood" or Irish ocean separating them; the same verse depicts them singing salvation around the throne of God, a theme also mentioned in his letter:

1. Two are Better far than one
     For Counsel, and for Fight;
   How can One be warm alone,
     Or serve his GOD aright?
   Join we then our Hearts and Hands,
     Each to Love provoke his Friend,
   Run the Way of His Commands,
     And keep them to the End.

2. Woe to Him, whose Spirits droop,
     To Him, who falls alone!
   He has none to lift him up,
     And help his Weakness on;
   Happier We Each other keep,

We Each other's Burden bear;
   Never *need* our Footsteps slip,
   Upheld by Mutual Prayer.

3. Who of Twain hath made us One
      Maintains our Unity,
   JESUS is the Corner-stone,
      In whom we ALL agree;
   Servants of our Common LORD,
      Sweetly of one Heart and Mind,
   Who can break a Threefold Cord,
      Or part whom GOD hath join'd?

4. Breathes as in us Both One Soul,
      When most distinct in Place,
   Interposing Oceans roll,
      Nor hinder our Embrace;
   Each as on *his* Mountain stands,
      Reaching Hearts across the Flood,
   Join our Hearts, if not our Hands,
      And sing the Pardoning GOD. . . .

Wesley spent August and September and half of October 1748 in Ireland, preaching to large crowds of Roman Catholics and Protestants. After another perilous voyage across the Irish sea, Wesley returned to Wales and the Gwynnes. After spending several days in that vicinity, Charles took leave of "our family" and headed for Bristol. While Charles's journal makes no mention of Sally and the time they spent together or the conversations they had, the couple likely finalized their plans to marry on this visit.

In November Charles began to share his plan to marry Sally with friends and family. His published journal explained why his brother John's support in this matter was so important to Charles: "My brother and I having promised each other . . . that we would neither of us marry, or take any step towards it, without the other's knowledge and consent, today I fairly and fully communicated every thought of my heart. He had proposed three persons to me, S.P., M.W. and S.G.; and entirely approved of my choice of the last. We consulted together about every particular, and were of one heart and mind in all things." By early December Charles was back at the Gwynne home to make the proposal of marriage. He sought Sally's counsel on the matter, who suggested he write to her mother. Two days later, Charles "took farther counsel with Sally, quite above all guile and reserve. I was afraid of making the proposal. The door of prayer was always open." On December 5 the couple enlisted the help of Sally's sister, "Miss Becky," who "heartily engaged in the cause, and at night communicated it to her mother." The word came back from their go-between that Mrs. Gwynne would "rather give her child to Mr. Wesley than to any man in England."

This was a remarkable reply from a person of the Gwynnes' rank and station. One of her aristocratic contemporaries, Lady Mary Wartley Montagu, reported the huge amount of gossip occasioned by the news that the daughter of the Earl of Huntingdon — the Countess of Huntingdon's sister-in-law, Lady Margaret Hastings — was to marry former Oxford Methodist Benjamin Ingham. Mrs. Gwynne, who was a friend and supporter of the Wesleyan revival, was not concerned about the social stigma associated with Methodism, but she was concerned about Charles's financial means. She wanted some sort of guarantee that he could support her daughter in the manner to which she had become accustomed. To assuage her concerns, Charles proposed that an annual income of £100 be placed at Sally's disposal. Mrs. Gwynne answered, "her daughter could expect no more." His journal reports that "Mr. Gwynne leaving the whole matter to his wife, I talked the matter fully over, and left it wholly with her to determine. She behaved in the most obliging manner and *promised her consent*, if I could answer for £100 a year."

By mid-December Charles was back in London. He met with his brother and "rejoiced his heart with the account of my prosperous journey." He sought the advice and support of London banker Ebenezer Blackwell, who promised to assist Charles in the subscription of £100 per year; other moneyed friends, including the Countess of Huntingdon, made similar commitments.

Not wanting to rely only on his wealthy friends for the money needed to support his future wife, Charles rushed into print a large, two-volume version of *Hymns and Sacred Poems*. It was a hastily constructed offering comprised of hymns Charles already had on hand, some of which had been in his saddle bags for more than a decade. So quickly was this hymnbook put together that it escaped John Wesley's editorial pen and organizational skills. In a subsequent letter, John admitted that there were some things in the *Hymns and Sacred Poems* of 1749 that he did not approve of. But Charles was not looking for his brother's approval; he was looking for income to show his future mother-in-law. He put together a list of subscribers who would promise in advance to buy the hymnal when it was printed. He put Sally's name at the top of the list. "The enclosed shows my first subscriber," he wrote, "whom I set at the head of my list as a good omen. Many have followed the copy already, being readier to part with their money than I am to take it."

As a leading figure in the Methodist movement Charles could not simply make all his own financial decisions. At the end of December, Charles and John Wesley met with Ebenezer Blackwell. John suggested, and his fellow Methodists agreed, that the primary source of Charles's annual income should be the Wesleyan hymnals and other books. On January 3, John Wesley put this financial arrangement in writing and sent it to Mrs. Gwynne; Charles also wrote Mrs. Gwynne describing the financial provision he intended to make for Sally. In the same letter Charles made it clear that he had no interest in Sally's inheritance, and suggested that it should be secured independently of his own interest in the event of her death: "If after the strictest scrutiny you are satisfied as to a Provision, and Mr. G[wynne] and you see cause to give your consent, I would desire Miss S[ally] might secure her Fortune in case of her own mortality, that it may return to her own family. I seek not her's but her; and if the Lord should give and take away I shall want nothing upon earth. I abhor the thought of being a gainer by her in temporals and could not rest, unless secured from this danger."

His heartfelt plea met with a cold response: Mrs. Gwynne was not satisfied with the financial arrangement John had proposed. Distraught, Charles solicited Vincent Perronet's advice. Perronet "acted the part of a father" in the whole matter; he wrote Mrs. Gwynne on Charles Wesley's behalf. Not only did Rev. Perronet stress the intangible benefits that would come to Sally through marriage to Charles Wesley, but he also stressed the value of the Wesleys' literary works — perhaps as much as £5,000 — to indicate that the proposed income was by no means uncertain. Charles's long letter to Sally, dated January 15, was bravely optimistic: "Your mother's *consenting so far* is plainly miraculous and what I never expected, although my friends insisted on it, as my duty, to make the proposal. I cannot think Providence would suffer the matter to proceed so far, were it to stop here. The hinge on which all turns, is not fortune, not even the consent of friends (which will *follow* and fall in the Will of Providence) but the glory of God, and the good of souls, (yours especially)." Still, Charles was intent upon steeling himself and Sally against the possible disappointment of her mother's eventual refusal: "In case of a disappointment (as the world calls it)," he wrote, "*I know you* shall rejoice, if not immediately, yet in this life, seeing it a *blessing* superior to our meeting here, and O! How thankful will you be in the life to come! When the whole scheme of Providence will be unraveled and explained; and we shall both confess in the Spirit of Praise and Rapture, that the Gracious God *deferred* our Union for our own infinite Eternal Advantage."

On January 19, Sally wrote to Charles to report that her mother's objections were beginning to melt away. "O what a good God do the Christians serve!" she wrote. "What a mercy is it that such a poor, weak worm as I am enabled to say 'thy gifts if call'd for, I resign, pleased to receive, pleased to restore.' Hitherto, hath God helped me! This was your language of my heart in perusing your sweet letters last night; and my prayers were almost swallow'd up in praise for the unspeakable blessings which the Lord had made me a partaker of already through your ministry." The good news was that Mrs. Gwynne had put the decision entirely in her husband's hands, and that she would agree entirely with whatever he decided. The next day, Sally found that her mother had decided to write to Charles herself, inviting him and John to visit them as soon as she returned from a brief journey. Sally took this as an indication of her mother's approval of their marriage. "Far was it from me, yesterday morn, to expect the least token of my M[other's] willingness and consent to go with my F[riend], but GOD has surely touched her heart, yet I still dare not be sure of its coming to pass. The happiness seems too great for me to presume so. On Thee, O Lord will I wait; 'I cannot choose, Thou can'st not err.' And if we are permitted to join hands as well as hearts, (the latter we have done already) I shall (I'm fully persuaded) receive you as the greatest blessing heaven could bestow this side of the grave."

Sally was right. Marmaduke Gwynne, Sally's father, wrote Charles Wesley telling him that the Gwynnes had accepted Charles's proposal and the financial arrangement drawn up by John Wesley for the couple's annual support. He specifically mentioned Mr. Perronet's letter as being instrumental in closing the deal. Charles's terse journal entry for January 23rd certainly belies the exhilaration he must have felt as he penned these words: "I received letters from Garth, consenting to our proposals." His letter to Sally, dated January 28th, was a bit more exuberant: "Are the consolations of GOD small with thee? I hope they increase and multiply upon you exceedingly. I pray the Lord to extend unto you peace like a river, to fill you with all joy in believing and make you abound in hope and love through the power of the Holy Ghost!"

During their courtship, Charles Wesley wrote a hymn which expressed the unity and love he and Sally felt for one another; they had become "kindred Spirits." The hymn voices Wesley's Christian faith as well as his love for the woman who would become his wife:

1.   Thou GOD of Truth and Love,
           We seek thy Perfect Way,
       Ready they Choice t'approve,
           Thy Providence t'obey,
       Enter into thy wise Design,
       And sweetly lose our Will in Thine.

2.   Why hast Thou cast our Lot
           In the same Age and Place,
       Or why together brought
           To see Each other's Face,
       To join with softest Sympathy,
       And mix our friendly Souls in Theee?

3.   Didst Thou not make us One,
           That Both might One remain,
       Together travel one,
           And bear each other's Pain
       Till Both Thine utmost Goodness prove,
       And rise renew'd in perfect Love.

4.   Surely Thou didst unite
        Our kindred Spirits here,
     That Both hereafter might
        Before thy Throne appear,
     Meet at the Marriage of the Lamb,
     And all thy Glorious Love proclaim.

5.   Then let us ever bear
        The blessed End in view,
     And join with mutual Care
        To fight our Passage thro',
     And kindly help Each other on,
     Till Both receive the Starry Crown. . . .

By April 1, with the marriage fast approaching, John Wesley was
having second thoughts; "full of scruples," Charles wrote, "he refused
to go to Garth [for the wedding]." Charles's journal reports that he restrained his temper and told John "if he could not be satisfied there, to
desist," but Charles was moving steadily ahead. They arrived at Garth
on April 7, where they "talked over matters with Mrs. Gwynne; and all
[John's] fears were scattered." Charles added, "We crowded as much
prayer as we could into the day."

The next day dawned bright and sunny, and Charles took it as a
good omen. His journal reports, "At eight I led MY SALLY to
church. . . . Mr. Gwynne gave her to me (under God): my brother
joined our hands. It was a most solemn season of love! Never had I
more of the divine presence at the sacrament. My brother gave out the
following hymn:

Come, thou everlasting Lord,
By our trembling hearts adored;
Come, thou heaven-descended Guest,
Bidden to the marriage-feast!

Sweetly in the midst appear,
With thy chosen followers here;
Grant us the peculiar grace,
Show to all thy glorious face.

Now the veil of sin withdraw,
Fill our souls with sacred awe, —
Awe that dare not speak or move,
Reverence of humble love. . . ."

The group must have been overtaken by the solemnity of the situation and sacred awe bidden by this hymn, for, as Charles's journal reports, a stranger to the proceedings thought it looked "more like a funeral than a wedding," adding, "My brother seemed the happiest person among us." That same day, Charles wrote to Ebenezer Blackwell, "Pray for me. I want [need] your prayers rather than you congratulations; yet I believe God has lent me a great blessing this day; and that I *ought* to be thankful and employ every blessing and every moment to His glory."

Charles wrote a "Wedding Song" around this time, probably with his own wedding in mind:

> 1. O Thou, who didst an Help ordain
>   To bless the pure primaeval Man,
>   And crown the Joys of Paradise,
>   See at thy Feet a Simple Pair,
>   Bound in the Closest Bond to bear
>   Each other's Burthen to the Skies.
>   Met in the mighty Jesus's Name
>   We come, great GOD, the Grace to claim
>   For All design'd by thy Decree,
>   For Us, whose prostrate Souls adore
>   Thy Wisdom, Truth & Love, & Power
>   And gasp to find their All in Thee.
>
> 2. Throughout our Lives to vindicate
>   The reverend, pure, & high Estate,
>   For this our Hearts & Hands we join,
>   Resolv'd, if Thou thy Blessing give,
>   Its sacred Honour to retrieve,
>   And prove its Dignity Divine:
>   So worthy of Thyself t'ordain,
>   So suited to the State of Man,

So *like* the Fellowship above,
Type of that Awful Mystery
   That Union of thy Church with Thee,
      The glorious League of Nuptial Love.

3. But who sufficient is to *shew*
   Thy Marriage with thy Church below,
      So dearly Each to Each allied?
   Who shall the spotless Pattern give,
   And represent the Second Eve,
      That issued from her Husband's Side?
   Jesu, to Thee we humbly pray,
   Thou only canst thy Grace convey,
      The mystic Power of Love unknown,
   Pure heavenly Love that flows from Thee,
   From all the Dross of Nature free,
      And perfects both our Souls in One.

Charles had extracted two prenuptial promises from Sally; one was that he be permitted to continue with his "vegetable diet," and the second was that he would not preach one less sermon or travel one less mile now that he was married. So far as we can ascertain, the first promise was fulfilled, but the second would prove impossible for both partners on several accounts. Putting up a brave front, however, he wrote, "I *cheerfully* left my partner for the Master's work, and rode on with Harry for Bristol. We made so much haste," he continued, "that I left all my strength behind me." April 28 brought "some letters from Garth" and some "life" with them. He concluded, "I prayed and wept over the beloved writers." In his first (extant) letter to Sally since their separation, he wrote, "What shall I say in this solemn moment to my most beloved Friend! — I am setting out again, to seek his Face; to know his pleasure and prove his will concerning me, and one infinitely dearer to me than myself. — My heart (I own) recoils and trembles."

Thus would begin the pull and push of the next decade of Charles Wesley's life, as he felt simultaneously pushed into incessant ministerial travels and sermons and at the same time pulled back into the bosom of his wife and family. During one of his early absences from Sally, Charles wrote this hymn entitled "For a Friend," which his daughter Sally later edited, on the manuscript, to read "His Wife":

1. In Body remov'd from a Friend
      But nearer in Heart than before,
   My infinite Wishes I send,
      My Prayers to the Heavenly Shore:
   Our Souls are in Jesus's Hand;
      And let us in Jesus abide,
   Till both are admitted to Land,
      And seated aloft by his side. . . .

4. So mingled her Soul is with Mine,
      With mine so united her Heart,
   So link'd in Affection Divine,
      No Creature is able to part:
   Still closer in Death we shall cleave
      Recover our Native Abode,
   Our Fullness of Rapture receive,
      And bath[e] in an Ocean of GOD. . . .

Although Charles had intended to live as an itinerant, traveling from place to place and taking Sally with him as he could, this plan soon proved unworkable, and he rented a small house in Bristol. It lay within easy walking distance of the New Room. The Wesleys moved into their new home on September 1, 1749. They lived in the small house, described by Charles as "one suited for a stranger and pilgrim on earth," for twenty-two years. Gradually Sally stopped traveling with Charles; her first miscarriage, on February 3, 1750 — which occurred after she had been traveling with her husband — loomed large in that decision. Charles too began traveling less and less.

The Wesleys had eight children over the course of those early years, but only three survived childhood: Charles (1757), Sally (1759), and Samuel (1766). Their first child, John, died of smallpox at the age of sixteen months. His death left an indelible mark upon the young couple. Sally clipped a lock of his golden hair, tied it with a ribbon, and folded it into a sheet of paper upon which she had written, "A lock of my dear Jacky's hair. I shall go to him but he shall not return to me"

(2 Samuel 12:23). Turning to his familiar medium for expressing his innermost feelings, Charles tried to make sense of his son's death by writing an anguished hymn entitled "On the Death of a Child":

1. Dead! dead! the child I love so well!
    Transported to the world above!
 I need no more my heart conceal:
    I never dared indulge my love:
 But may I not indulge my grief,
 And seek in tears a sad relief?

2. Mine earthly happiness is fled,
    His mother's joy, his father's hope;
 O had I died in *Isaac's* stead!
    He *should* have lived, my age's prop,
 He should have closed his father's eyes,
 And follow'd me to paradise.

3. But hath not Heaven, who first bestow'd,
    A right to take His gifts away?
 I bow me to the sovereign God,
    Who snatch'd him from the evil day!
 Yet nature *will* repeat her moan,
 And fondly cry, "My son, my son!"

4. Turn from him, turn officious thought!
    Officious thought presents again
 The thousand little acts he wrought,
    Which wound my heart with soothing pain;
 His looks, his winning gestures rise,
 His waving hands, and laughing eyes!

5. Those waving hands no more shall move,
    Those laughing eyes shall smile no more:
 He cannot now engage our love
    With sweet insinuating power,
 Our weak unguarded hearts ensnare,
 And rival his Creator here.

6. From us, as we from him, secure,
   Caught to his heavenly Father's breast,
He waits, till we the bliss ensure,
   From all these stormy sorrows rest,
And see him with our angel stand
To waft, and welcome us to land.

Their daughter Martha Maria Wesley (1755) died after only one month. Susanna (1761), named for her paternal grandmother, lived eleven months; Selina (1764), named for Lady Huntingdon, lived only five weeks; and John James (1768) died after seven months.

This pattern of joyous births and mournful young deaths, while not uncommon at that time, was a severe trial for the Wesleys. It increased Charles's unwillingness to be apart from his wife and children. Sally, who had buried several of her children without him, tried not to exert pressure on Charles to stop traveling circuits to spend more time at home, but such circumstances certainly had that effect. On at least one occasion she wrote Charles, asking him whether she and his family were a hindrance to his ministry. Charles's reply came back: "the next time you hinder me in my work will be *the first* time." Charles tried to make the best of the situation by arguing that his incessant ministerial work extended his health and life: "The more heartily I labour in the vineyard, the longer I shall continue with you. Let us join with greater earnestness . . . even to seek the Kingdom together."

11 A Partnership Strained

John and Charles Wesley enjoyed a partnership in ministry that lasted more than fifty years. Their partnership — like their friendship — was complicated by the fact that they were brothers as well as men of nearly opposite emotional makeup. John described himself as being in "some sense, the head" while Charles was "the heart" of the Methodist movement; while this description exaggerated their differences, there was some truth to it.

In temperament Charles seemed to be his father's son: impetuous, short-tempered, and given to emotional outbursts. He was capable of hitting the full scale of human emotions, vacillating between energetic highs and melancholy lows. John's measured, rational reserve and quiet persistence, on the other hand, seemed more closely tied to his mother. The rector of Epworth once quipped that John could not attend to the most pressing needs of nature without giving a reason for it. Charles was a shrewder judge of character than his brother, who he said was "born for the benefit of knaves." In a letter written to Charles on June 2, 1785, John admitted, "Many times you see farther into men than I do." Their differing personalities took expression in divergent preaching styles as well as in distinctive theological emphases. "In connexion I beat you," John told Charles, "but in strong pointed sentences, you beat me. Go on, in your own way, what God has peculiarly called you to. Press the instantaneous blessings; then I shall have more time for my peculiar calling, enforcing the gradual work."

John accepted and sometimes claimed the leadership role in the Methodist movement, and things went along more smoothly when Charles allowed him to have it. An obvious case in point was the way in which Charles had been swept up into his brother's plans to serve as a missionary in the New World. As Charles explained in a retrospective letter to Dr. Chandler in 1785, "I took my Master's Degree, and only thought of spending all my days at Oxford. But my brother, who always had the ascendant over me, persuaded me to accompany him and Mr. Oglethorpe to Georgia." This event, as we saw in their early correspondence, amounted to a tug-of-war over Charles's will; John wanted him to go, and their elder brother Samuel Wesley Jr. wanted him to stay in England.

What was it about Charles that made him so pliable to his brother John's will? We could point to birth order. John, being almost five years older, was well used to receiving the deference, and to some degree also the homage, of his younger brother. While they were separated during their early schooling, with Charles going to Westminster and living with elder brother Samuel and John attending Charterhouse, they were reunited at Oxford. John Gambold, a college friend to both Wesley brothers, recorded — with some surprise — Charles's similarity to and deference towards his brother John: "I never observed any person have a more real deference for another, than [Charles] had for his brother. . . . He followed his brother entirely. Could I describe one of them, I should describe them both."

Their rather opposite emotional makeup was also a factor in Charles's deference to his brother John. Charles recognized that he was a compliant person who hated confrontation, and he confessed as much in a letter to Sally, dated December 24, 1755. "You know my principle. I sacrifice all, even *my own* brother, to peace and quietness. Rather than hazzard a quarrel I would run away from every human creature, excepting *you*."

Where Charles shunned the limelight, John seemed to crave it. One witness to Charles's deference comes from the inner circle of his own family. The unsigned editor of the 1816 edition of his published sermons, who was either his daughter or wife — or perhaps both working in concert — described Charles's humility at some length. "His most striking excellence was humility; it extended to his talents as well as virtues; he not only acknowledged and pointed out but *delighted* in the superiority of another, and if there ever was a human being who disliked power, avoided preeminence and shrunk from praise, it was Charles Wesley." There was, deep in Charles's personality, something that made him willing to be led by his brother, just as there was something in John that made him prone to lead. Things went along smoothly with their shared ministry when each man settled into his unspoken but well established role.

Charles's temper sometimes intervened, and when it did, all bets were off with respect to what he might do. One of John's letters to his brother, written at the height of a perfectionist schism that was dividing their London society (July 9, 1766), evidences this aspect of their sometimes volatile relationship. "How apt you are," John lamented, "to take the colour of your company! When you and I [talked] together you seemed at least to be of the same mind with me, and now you are all off the hooks again! . . . unless you only talk [so] because you are in the humour of contradiction; if so, I may as well blow against the wind as talk with you." Clearly Charles had it within himself to disagree stubbornly "in the humour of contradiction," arguing simply for the sake of arguing — or at least it seemed that way to John.

Charles's deference to and cooperation with his brother John apparently started at home when they were children and, after a hiatus when he was within the influence and orbit of elder brother Samuel, resumed to a significant degree when they were reunited at Oxford. Their deep friendship and cooperation lasted well into the first decade of their ministry, when — after both men experienced evangelical conversions during May 1738 — they began evangelizing England, Wales, and Ireland. Charles's marriage to Sally Gwynne in 1749 altered the Wesley brothers' earlier relationship; now Charles found himself frequently torn between the love that tied him to his wife and growing family and his long-standing relationship with his brother. He simply could not comply with John's many demands upon his time and continue to be an effective husband and father. Caught in the push and pull of these conflicting loyalties, Charles gradually learned to refuse John's directives and began to resent his brother's all-too-frequent demands upon him and his time. At least one of John's epistles of this period was angrily inscribed by Charles with the words "Trying to bring me under HIS yoke."

A second disruptive watershed in the Wesley brothers' relationship occurred because of Charles's impetuous intervention in John's courtship of and engagement to Grace Murray. And while the "Grace Murray affair" seems more germane to John Wesley's biography than Charles's, a clear understanding of the events surrounding it can help explain the growing distance between the Wesley brothers and Charles's increasing willingness to strike out in his own direction in various matters.

During the 1748 Methodist conference in London, John Wesley had introduced a manuscript entitled "Thoughts upon Marriage," which took a negative opinion about the suitability of the married state for a minister of the gospel. After what John Wesley described as "a full and friendly debate" among the conferees, they convinced him "that a believer might marry, without suffering loss in his soul." In August of that same year, while John had taken ill at Newcastle, he was nursed to health by Grace Murray. Her patient care for him and the pastoral skills she had shown while working at the Newcastle orphan house brought the widowed Mrs. Murray to John Wesley's attention. As he described it: "Grace Murray attended me continually. I observed her more narrowly than ever before, both as to her temper, sense, and behavior. I esteemed and loved her more and more. And, when I was a little recovered, I told her, sliding into it I know not how, 'If ever I marry, I think you will be the person.'" John Wesley was often unclear when confiding his heart to women, and this was a typically oblique proposal — or at least John thought it was a marriage proposal. Then, "After some time," he wrote, "I spoke to her more directly. She seemed utterly amazed and said, 'This is too great a blessing for me: I can't tell how to believe it. This is all I could have wished for under heaven, if I had dared to wish for it.'"

John Wesley believed that he had made his feelings and plans clear to Grace Murray and that she had embraced them, a feeling she seemed to confirm when she begged Wesley not to leave her when he left Newcastle. She accompanied him on a tour throughout Yorkshire and Derbyshire, finally leaving him in Cheshire to work alongside Wesley's helper, John Bennet. John was shocked, then, when he received letters not long after from both Bennet and Murray announcing their intention to marry. Wesley recalled, "I was utterly amazed: but wrote a mild answer to both, supposing they were married already. She replied in so affectionate a manner, that I thought the whole design [of Bennet's marriage to her] was at an end." The vacillation of Grace Murray's affections between the two men dragged on, however, and it would prove to be a vexation for all three of them and a source of scandal among the Methodists. When she received a letter from John Wesley "she resolved to live and die with me and wrote to me just what she felt." When she received a letter from John Bennet her affection tilted towards him, and she wrote him in "the tenderest manner." At one point she even seemed to be engaged to both men.

In September 1749 rumors began swirling among the Methodists about the love triangle that had developed between John Wesley, John Bennet, and Grace Murray, and they quickly reached the ears of Charles Wesley. Another person, one Jane Keith, told him that "(1) Mr. [John] W. was in love with G[race] M[urray] beyond all sense and reason; (2) That he had shown this in the most publick [sic] manner, and had avowed it to all the Society, and (3) that all the town was in an uproar, and all the Societies ready to fly to pieces." Upon hearing and believing all this information Charles rushed to Whitehaven, where he expected to find his brother and Grace Murray together. Upon arriving, Charles remonstrated with his brother, "All our preachers would leave us, all our Societies disperse, if [John Wesley] married so mean ["low"] a woman." Charles further objected that Grace Murray was already engaged to John Bennet. John Wesley reasoned, "As I knew she was pre-engaged to me, as I regarded not her birth, but her qualifications, and as I believed those consequences might be prevented, I could see no valid objection yet." Charles left Whitehaven in a rage, telling John, "I renounce all intercourse with you but what I would have with a heathen man or a publican." John then wrote Charles a lengthy letter in which he recounted the events surrounding his decision to marry Grace Murray and his reasons for doing so.

But John's letter was not as convincing as he had hoped it would be. Charles still believed that Grace Murray belonged with John Bennet, and urged her to marry him as a way of clearing her conscience and also preventing the dire consequences that he thought would accompany her marriage to John Wesley. On October 3, Charles Wesley took Grace Murray with him to Newcastle, where she was wed to John Bennet, with Charles and George Whitefield serving as witnesses.

There was still more to the Wesley family intrigue. Grace later told John Wesley that, as he put it, "when my brother took her thence [to Newcastle], she thought he was carrying her to me; that when she knew more of his design [to marry her to John Bennet], she told him, 'I will do nothing, till I have seen Mr. W.' But that when it was told her at Newcastle, among a thousand other things, 'that Mr. W. will have nothing to say to you'; then she said, 'Well, I will have Mr. B. if he will have me.'" At this point John Wesley realized the depth of his own brother's complicity in the ruin of his betrothal to Grace Murray. John poured his heart out to God in 31 verses of a manuscript poem, one of the last poems he wrote. It concluded,

> 30. What thou has done I know not now!
>   Suffice I shall hereafter know!
> Beneath thy chastening Hand I bow:
>   That still I live to Thee I owe.
> O teach thy deeply-minded Son
> To say, "Father, thy Will be done!"
>
> 31. Teach me, from every pleasing Snare
>   To keep the Issues of my Heart:
> Be thou my Love, my Joy, my Fear!
>   Thou my eternal Portion art.
> Be thou my never-failing Friend,
> And love, O love me to the End!

We have no record of Charles Wesley's own description of his motives in the Grace Murray affair. He undoubtedly thought he was preserving his brother and the Methodist movement from scandal and an unseemly action. Grace Murray's "low birth" and role as a servant may have been a problem for Charles's sense of propriety, as was his genuine desire for his brother to have a good and suitable "match." But most troubling, perhaps, was Mrs. Murray's engagement to John Bennet and the repeated vacillation of her affections between the two men. Charles truly believed that John had acted wrongly and dishonorably in proposing marriage to an engaged woman. When John found out about her relationship with John Bennet, which reached back to 1745, Charles was convinced that John should have completely removed himself from the picture instead of pressing his own case. With the gossip swirling throughout the Methodist movement about this love triangle, Charles took action that was guaranteed to squelch it. In a letter he wrote to Murray during this period, Charles seemed to blame her for the whole misunderstanding, and he viewed his own impetuous action as delivering them all from "the brink of ruin" and "the snare":

> Fain would I hope that you can say something in your defense (when I come to talk with you) which now I know not. But the case appears thus to me:
> You promised J[ohn] B[ennet] to marry him — since which you engaged yourself to another. How is this possible? And who is that other? One of such importance that his doing so dishonest an action would destroy himself and me and the whole work of God. It was on the very brink of ruin; but the snare is broken, and we are delivered.

Charles also seemed to believe that John was called to the celibate life, as John's earlier writings suggested. Charles may have also feared for the stability of his own marriage should his brother marry; he was beginning to allow John to carry the greater burden of the travel and itinerant work, and this would increase significantly over the years.

But whatever his reasons, Charles acted impetuously and with utter disregard for his brother's deep feelings for Grace Murray. John Wesley, for his part, felt utterly betrayed and abandoned, as though Charles and his friends had conspired against him to rip the love of his life from his bleeding heart. John never trusted Charles as fully after the Grace Murray affair as he had before it, and a coldness descended upon their brotherly relationship that lasted for several years.

A shorthand section of Charles's manuscript journal indicates that he had hoped to have an extended conversation with his brother regarding this matter in late October 1749. Charles went to the meeting, as he described himself, "troubled and burdened." John, for his part, did not want to talk with his brother on any terms. Charles bewailed the state of their relationship: "No confidence on either side," he wrote. He seemed resolved to the eventuality of an utter separation from his brother and the Christian work they had undertaken together. Charles told his brother that he would "honor him before the people," and "would retreat gradually, and hide it from the world." He thought that John "seemed pleased at the thought of parting." Charles hung on to his self-righteous attitude about his handling of the Grace Murray affair: "God knows, as I told him, that I had saved him from a thousand false steps." Still, despite the estrangement between the brothers, Charles confided to Vincent Perronet, "I am persuaded we shall stand or fall together."

Charles was determined to stand in John Wesley's place and carry on his ministry "till his spirit should revive and his strength and reason return," as he told Perronet. But Charles had also been extraordinarily tried by the conflict caused by his brother's proposed marriage to Grace Murray. He told Perronet he was depleted of strength and "next to useless." "For when I preach," he wrote, "my word is without power or life. My spirit is that of the whole people. All are faint and weary. All seem on the brink of desperation." Charles found himself thoroughly excluded from his brother's counsel and sorely pained by that exclusion.

In a letter he wrote to John Bennet, dated December 15, 1750, Charles depicted himself as trying to save "the whole work of God," but he also acknowledged that he had lost his brother's love in the process:

> If the Lord Himself had not been on our side, well may we both and all Israel say, "They had swallowed us up quick, and *by us ourselves* destroyed the whole work of God." . . . It is all over with our friend [John Wesley]. Only me he cannot love as before. But I must have patience and suffer all things that the gospel be not hindered.

Charles was reaching out to Bennet, but the strain caused by the conflict was too much. John Wesley's former rival in courtship emerged as one of his chief critics among the Methodists, and Bennet left the Methodist movement by 1752.

Even after the debacle of the Grace Murray affair, John Wesley was still determined to marry. By February 1751 he had found a new bride named Molly Vazeille. She was the daughter of a successful London merchant and the widow of another London merchant, Mr. Anthony Vazeille. He was a naturalized French Huguenot (Protestant) refugee, and acquaintance of Vincent Perronet; Perronet, who was himself of Huguenot extraction, became the point of contact between John Wesley and Mrs. Vazeille. Charles Wesley had first met Molly Vazeille in July of 1749, at the home of Edward Perronet, and had summarized the encounter by describing her as "a woman of a sorrowful spirit."

Charles Wesley's journal entry for February 2 reveals his state of shock: "My brother, returned from Oxford, sent for and told me *he was resolved to marry!* I was thunderstruck, and could only answer, he had given me the first blow, and his marriage would come like the *coup de grace.* Trusty Ned Perronet followed, and told me the person was Mrs. Vazeille! One of whom I had never had the least suspicion." Charles's shock at his brother's decision to marry, and perhaps more emphatically his disappointment at the person John had chosen, made it impossible for him to keep his sorrow to himself. Once again, as his journal indicates, Charles reacted badly: "I refused his company to the chapel, and retired to mourn with my faithful Sally. I groaned all the day, and several following ones, under my own and the people's burden. I could eat no pleasant food, nor preach, nor rest, either by night or by day." Charles was not accustomed to bearing his disappointments quietly, and it is easy to imagine that Charles's frustration with John's marriage was well known throughout the inner circle of the Methodist movement.

On February 17, 1751, at the Foundery society, Charles heard John Wesley's "apology" for his impending marriage. But in both cases, with his brother and with the society, John had announced his marriage plans rather than consulting about them. On February 27, Charles was able to bear hearing John preach, but he could not stand to hear his apology again: "My brother came to the chapel-house with his wife. I was glad to see him; saluted her; stayed long enough to hear him preach, *but, ran away when he begun his apology.*"

The marriage between John Wesley and Molly Vazeille, as it was reported by *The Gentleman's Magazine,* occurred on February 18, 1751; the *London Magazine,* however, reports that it occurred on February 19. Ironically, the entire matter passed without a single word of notice in John Wesley's scrupulously detailed journal. On February 17 Charles's journal reports, "At the Foundery I heard my brother's apology. Several days afterwards I was one of the last that heard of his unhappy marriage."

Charles's journal and letters offer ample indications of the problems he and his wife had with the new Mrs. John Wesley. Unfortunately, however, the specific subject matter of their disagreement is never mentioned. Whatever the issue was, it seems to have predated John Wesley's marriage. On Friday, March 15, Charles "called on my sister; kissed and assured her I was perfectly reconciled to her, and to my brother." Three days later, after reading a treatise by Marcus Antonius, Charles was resolved to learn "some useful lessons" from him, particularly "not to resent, not to revenge myself, not to let my peace lie at the mercy of every injurious person." Since this admission occurred in the midst of his dispute with Mrs. Vazeille, it may be reasonable to conclude that she was the "injurious person" mentioned.

Exactly what had transpired between Molly and Charles prior to or immediately after John's marriage to her is not completely clear. It seems entirely likely that she knew of Charles's disapproval of John's selection of her as a spouse. Also, both Molly and Charles were plainspoken to a fault; neither was accustomed to practicing tact or reserve. One of John Wesley's earliest biographers, Luke Tyerman, posited a powerful factor in their mutual estrangement: he intimated that, at some point, Molly had "accused Charles of idleness, and declared that, for years, his dearest Sally had been John's mistress. Charles danced with rage at this imputation, but Sally calmly smiled, and said, 'Who will believe my sister now?'" This is borne out to some degree by a later letter written by Samuel Wesley Jr., the son of Charles and Sally. In 1792, long after his father's death, Samuel wrote to his mother defending the character of Charlotte Louisa Martin, the woman he loved. He admitted that "she has been called a Coquette, nay more; a Wanton." But Samuel concluded, " She is as guilty of the charges against her, as you were of those laid to you by the wicked wife of John Wesley."

Over the years Charles and Sally continued to try to stay in Molly's good graces, but given the amount of time and effort they seemed to have put into their reconciliation, it all availed very little. In April 29, 1755, for example, Charles wrote Sally to express his frustration, "What shall you and I do to love her better?" he mused. "'Love your enemies' is with man impossible: but is anything too hard for

God? I fear you do not *constantly* pray for her. I *must* pray for her or sink into the spirit of revenge." Lady Huntingdon became Charles Wesley's confidant regarding his strife with his brother and his brother's wife. On May 30, 1755, he told her, "You will shame me out of the thought that my brother has injured me. But I have adopted your maxim, that ministers (like Kings) can do no wrong." On June 11, perhaps of the same year, Charles confided to the Countess that he was thinking of separating from the Methodists: "My way is plain — to preach every where as a supernumerary if not Independent. My brother, I foresee, will treat me as a Deserter, but he has cured me of my implicit regard to him! Many mouths will be opened against me on another account, my Implacableness, I mean. Neither do I fear what man can do unto me here." In another letter, dated July 12, 1755, Charles seemed more philosophical about the strife between himself and his brother. He seemed to be trying to make some sense of it all in terms of God's great eternal plan: "My brother's weakness," he wrote, "is permitted (like his wife's perverseness) for some Providential end unknown as yet to us, but which will appear in due time. He is sadly at a loss what to do with me now that I will neither lead nor drive."

Lady Huntingdon tried to be a peacemaker between the Wesley brothers. Charles's letter of June 9, 1755, indicates that John was going to visit her: "You will shortly see my Brother, for what end I know not, neither want to know. I have no favour to ask of one who denies me Justice and uses all his authority to oppress an innocent man." Charles protested his own innocence: "He desired me, in his dangerous sickness to bear with his wife's injuries for his sake; and if she should relapse into what he called her Jaundice of Jealousy, to suffer whatever she said or did against me. I have done as he desired and turned the other cheek again and again; neither shall I ever make her any other return (God being my Helper) than good for evil. What he can justly require of me, I see not." But an additional letter, dated July 28, indicates that John was still trying to get Charles to travel on evangelistic circuits for him. Once again Charles refused, this time because his wife, Sally, was pregnant and about to deliver a child. Charles wrote Lady Huntingdon, "My brother has gathered much displeasure against me. 1. Because I was not pleased with his Conference, neither can I yet see [it] with his eyes. 2. Because I am not in Cornwall. He cannot *feel* my Reasons for staying with my wife. I sent him more as soon as she was delivered." When the child subsequently died, Charles's grief turned into further resentment against his brother and Molly. He had withheld the news of the birth of the child so as not to cause the childless couple added pain; now he also withheld news of her death because he wrongly imagined they would take pleasure in his loss.

John, for his part, expressed frustration with his brother's unwillingness to carry his equal portion of the itinerant ministry they had formerly shared. On October 30, 1753, an ill and angry elder brother wrote: "What I have desired any time these ten years is, either you would *really* act in connexion [with me] or that you would never *say* you do. Either leave off *professing*, or begin *performing*. . . . O brother, *pretend* no longer to the thing that is not. You do not, will not act in concert with me. Not since I was married only (the putting it on that is a mere finesse), but for ten years last past, and upwards, you have no more acted in connexion with me than Mr. Whitefield has done. I would to God you would begin to do it now; or else, talk no more *as if* you did." Again, on July 16, 1755, John wrote Charles sarcastically: "I should wonder if Wales or Margate or something did not hinder you [from] taking any step which I desire, or which might save my time or strength. Then I will go to Cornwall myself, that is all." Then in shorthand, John added: "For a wife and a partner I may challenge the world! But love is rot!"

While the rift between the brothers would gradually heal, the tension between Molly and Charles and Sally continued. For example, Charles reported to Sally he was showing Molly public respect despite the distrust and disapproval he felt towards her: "Last Saturday afternoon, after my brother and I had settled everything in the four preceding days, on my way to Wakefield, I met my good angel and sister. I have done her much honour before the people, and behaved (though I say it) very much like a gentleman; only that I took a French leave this morning, that is, left Leeds without telling either her or her husband." The following September, Charles laughingly celebrated the fact that he was able to spend a full two minutes with Molly without having a quarrel. In September 1757, Molly Wesley was in Bristol, while Charles was on the road, and he wrote home to fortify Sally: "I hope Mrs. W[esley] keeps her distance. If malice is stronger in her than pride she will pay you a mischievous visit." Since Molly had the nasty habit of opening and reading other people's mail, in July 1759 Charles warned

Sally, "You may safely direct to me at the Foundery, only not omitting Charles [in the address], nor mentioning my best friend." Molly also seems to have had the habit of spreading rumors about her husband as well as her brother and sister-in-law. Two weeks later Charles was running down the source of some unpleasant gossip, and the trail led directly to Molly Wesley, whom he wryly called "my best friend." "Yesterday morning," he wrote to his wife Sally, "I traced Mrs. G.'s intelligence, through Miss Bradshaw and Mrs. Allen to the fountainhead, *my best friend.* I do not wonder that my poor brother trembles and quakes at the thought of coming [home] to London." In 1766 Charles wrote to fortify Sally before her sister-in-law visited: "My brother and sister will call on you, I presume, next Wednesday. She continues quite placid and tame. You can be courteous without trusting her."

The ongoing distrust, not to mention the occasional animosity and open warfare, that existed between Molly Wesley and Charles Wesley had deep and lasting effects upon the brothers' relationship for almost two decades. By 1777 John Wesley eventually separated from Molly and lived apart from her, and only her absence made her cease to be a disruptive force at the center of early Methodism. But the brothers were able to overcome what Charles described as her "perverseness." Hence, in an undated letter to Sally, written in the late 1750s or early 1760s, Charles concluded, "I should tell you, my brother preached and won all our hearts. I never liked him better and was never more united to him since his unhappy marriage."

Charles's frequent ill health and frail physical constitution along with his family obligations made him increasingly unwilling to continue to follow John equally into itinerant ministry. The early Methodist preacher John Pickard remembered that Charles told him, "Young and healthy Christians are generally called to glorify God by being active in doing his will; but old and sick Christians in suffering it." Charles was gradually resigning himself to a less active role in the brothers' shared ministry. And he resented John Wesley's attempts to engage him in frequent travel and relentless preaching assignments.

This shift away from the balanced tasks of the earlier shared ministry reached its pinnacle in December 1753 when John's life-threatening illness threatened to throw the full weight of the Methodist movement upon Charles's shoulders. In a letter to Sally written on December 1, Charles intimated that his brother was "far gone, and very suddenly, in a consumption." After making hasty arrangements through Sally for someone to fill in for him, Charles wanted to be sure to get to John before he died. But as John Wesley lingered between life and death, Charles made it clear to the early Methodists that he had no intention of being his brother's successor. "I told the Society on Saturday night," he wrote, "that I neither could nor would stand in my brother's place (if God took him to himself), for I had neither a body, nor a mind, nor talents, nor grace for it." This declaration of Charles's independence seemed to come at a particularly inopportune time. It also evidences Charles's own awareness that his body was wearing out, and that he did not have the leadership and organizational talents that his brother used so well in guiding the Methodist movement.

On December 3, Charles's journal reports that the brothers availed themselves of an opportunity to reconcile one with another, and the three of them (Molly included) resolved to put their rancorous past behind them: "My brother entreated me, yesterday, and his wife, to forget all that is past on both sides. I sincerely told him I would, for his as well as Christ's sake." John did survive his illness of December 1753, and he would subsequently outlive Charles, but the developments of this period had the effect of solidifying the general feeling among the Methodists that Charles Wesley was not as committed to the movement as his brother was. They raised further doubts, perhaps even on the part of his brother, whether Charles could be counted on to fill John's sizable shoes in the event of his brother's absence or incapacity.

During the mid-1750s Charles began also began to feel the financial pinch of the £100 per annum guaranteed by his marriage settlement. This must have seemed like a huge sum of money to John, who continued to live on the same £30 a year he had been allotted by Lincoln College almost twenty years before. As the years rolled by and more children were born to Charles and Sally, and costly music lessons and other necessities needed to be paid for, there is some indication that John Wesley came to resent the amount of money that Charles's family drained from the Methodist movement. A letter to Sally, dated December 3, indicates that Charles had lost the document recording his settlement with the Methodists; the loss of this income was such a pressing matter that he felt the need to take a bond against its loss. By 1755 Charles had come to view the settlement as a kind of wage slavery. In a manuscript letter to Samuel Lloyd, dated July 5, 1755, Charles lamented, "L[ady] H[untingdon] thinks the time of my redemption draws nigh. I am heartily tired of the yoke, and if once I get it off my neck, [I] shall never more call any man Master. That £100 *a year*, will not buy my liberty. I seem very easy if it be paid me no longer."

By the end of the same month, however, Charles was complaining to Lady Huntingdon that John Wesley's book agent refused to pay his quarterly financial draft. Charles had come to see the financial arrangement that the brothers had engineered to make Charles's marriage possible as part of the control and manipulation that his brother tried to exercise over him and his movements. The truth of the matter was that Charles had come to resent the implications of the settlement almost as much as he needed the income that it generated for him and his family. As he told Lady Huntingdon, in a letter of July 28, 1755, "Mr. Lloyd tells me my b[rother]'s agent has refused my draft for the last quarter. Surely he cannot hope to *starve* me into compliance with his will. He must know me better. He can *cancel* his *covenant* at pleasure only by saying, 'He made it, before he had considered.'" In an interesting aside Charles concluded, "If he *should* do so I do not apprehend it would give me an hour's uneasiness. But I do not lay the *whole* blame on him." Perhaps Charles had come to recognize that he too shared a portion of the blame for the bumpy state of the brothers' relationship.

The Wesley brothers would once again find themselves able to work together as partners. But they would find their love for each other sorely tested as John gradually took pragmatic steps that Charles believed signaled a growing separation from the Church of England. And they would find themselves teaching and preaching different doctrines of Christian perfection at precisely the same time when a misguided presentation of that doctrine brought schism and public ridicule down upon the Methodists. Before that, however, they would need to come together to examine just what was being preached in their fledgling movement.

12 Reforming the Preachers

The Methodist movement grew significantly through the 1740s, and with it grew the infrastructure of societies, classes, and bands that welded the movement together. By May 1, 1743, the "General Rules of the United Societies," which provided the goals for the Methodist meetings, were published over the names of John and Charles Wesley. There was only one condition for "admission into these societies — a desire 'to flee from the wrath to come.'" This desire, however, was to take expression by "first, doing no harm, by avoiding evil in every kind; especially that which is most generally practiced." And it was "expected of all who continue in these societies, that they should continue to evidence their desire for salvation. Secondly, by doing good, by being, in every kind merciful after their power; as they have opportunity, doing good of every possible sort, and as far as is possible, to all men." The societies were organized into "circuits" or "rounds," and these were staffed by lay preachers who traveled from town to town preaching, exhorting, and examining the members of the societies. These men — and all the assigned preachers were men, although several women like Sarah Crosby (1729-1804), and Mary Bosanquet Fletcher (1739-1815) were acknowledged to have an "extraordinary call" to preach among the Methodists — were for the most part very ardent and faithful people who had served apprenticeships by traveling as an assistant to either John or Charles Wesley. But they often lacked theological education and had no ministerial standing in the Church of England; as a consequence of the latter aspect, they were forbidden to administer the Lord's Supper or baptism even among the Methodists.

The "Minutes of Several Conversations Between the Rev. Mr. [John] Wesley and Others from the year 1744 to the year 1789," which amounted to an ongoing collection of the minutes from the annual conferences held by the Wesleys and their preachers, describe the emergence of the lay preachers in this way: "After a time [in 1738] a young man, named Thomas Maxfield, came and desired to help me as a son in the gospel. Soon after came a second, Thomas Richards; and then a third, Thomas Westell. These severally desired to serve me as sons, and to labour when and where I should direct." Sensitive to the gibe of becoming "Pope John," Wesley replied, "This carries no face of truth. The Pope affirms that every Christian must do all he bids, and believe all he says, under pain of damnation. I never affirmed anything that bears any the most distant resemblance to this. All I affirm is, the Preachers who choose to labour with me, choose to serve me as sons in the gospel. And the people who choose to be under my care, choose to be so on the same terms they were at first." The explicit allusion to John Wesley's authority over the preachers, which is hidden behind the phrase "at first," signals that the lay preachers were as thoroughly under Wesley's authority as an eighteenth-century son was under the authority of his father. Despite his disclaimer, the gibe naming him "Pope John" continued, as the preachers often chafed under the pressure of being unequal partners in the Wesleys' ministry. Forsaking both wealth and temporal comfort by working with the Wesleys, they desired at least the status of ordained ministers and a greater degree of authority in determining the direction of the Methodist movement. When these benefits were not forthcoming many of the preachers left the movement for other opportunities, while others remained with the movement to clamor for a less ambiguous status and greater ministerial rights.

In 1744 the Wesleys began to hold an annual conference with like-minded Anglican ministers who participated in the Methodist movement; in subsequent years the several lay preachers who assisted them were also included. In 1745, for example, the minutes recorded the names of John Hodges, Thomas Richards, Samuel Larwood, Thomas Meyrick, Richard Moss, John Slocombe, Herbert Jenkins, and Marmaduke Gwynne, all laymen working in connection with the Wesleys. The ever-changing list of lay preachers grew longer as the Methodist movement grew and more circuits were added. By 1753 the early Methodist preacher Thomas Mitchell reported that fourteen preachers attended the conference along with the Wesleys. The next year Peter Jacko, another Methodist lay preacher, reported, "I was appointed for the Manchester Circuit, which then took in Cheshire, Lancashire, Derbyshire, Staffordshire, and part of Yorkshire." The fact that Peter Jacko's circuit of ministerial responsibilities included more territory than four western counties gives some suggestion of the practical demands that were placed upon the early Methodist preachers.

Charles Wesley was a spiritual father to many of the Methodist lay preachers. Several of them, like John Valton, were converted under his preaching. In his autobiography Valton described the event: "I went to London to hear Mr. Charles Wesley on the ensuing Sabbath. His word was with power; and I thought my Saviour was at hand, never being so sensibly affected under a discourse before." Charles esteemed the vigor and dedication of these men, and many of them labored with him — to use John Wesley's phrase — as "sons in the gospel."

An early extant sermon, which Charles copied from John's manuscript during the first leg of his return trip from Georgia to England, in September 1736, evidences Charles's support for lay preachers. The sermon, which Charles also "owned" by preaching it on at least one occasion, was based on Proverbs 11:30: "He that winneth souls is wise." At one point the sermon raises a challenge against those who would stop soul-winning preachers on the grounds they are not of the priestly office: "Indeed, if Solomon had only said, 'the *priest* that winneth souls is wise,' they had some colour for saying to all who are not invested with this office, 'ye have neither part nor lot in this wisdom; even such sacrifices God is not pleased, when they are offered by unhallowed hands.' But Solomon's words are universal, 'He that winneth souls is wise!' Who is he that is wiser and inspired by a better spirit? Let him stand forth and make the restriction!" Bewailing what some American revivalists would call the dangers of an unconverted ministry, Wesley asked, "But is this a time for making restrictions? For binding the hands of any of our fellow-labourers? When the avowed opposers and blasphemers of our holy religion are so zealously labouring to destroy souls; when those who have themselves made shipwreck of faith so earnestly endeavour to plunge others in the same gulf; when even 'of ourselves have men arisen, speaking perverse things' [Acts 20:30], and not content 'to deny the Lord that bought them' [2 Peter 2:1] themselves, unless they drew disciples after them?"

But Charles was also very clear in his own mind about the proper role of the lay preachers: theirs was to be a ministry of the Word, but not of sacrament. His affirmation of the lay preachers' gifts and call, as well as his clear distinction between lay and ordained ministers, were evident in several hymns that Charles wrote in the mid-1740s. His hymn "For a Lay Preacher" was published in his *Hymns and Sacred Poems* of 1749. In it the lay preacher is acclaimed as an instrument of God's love but also clearly distinguished from those of the "sacred order." The lay preacher's proper role is to "speak" the words of God's love and grace but not to offer grace through the sacraments:

1. I thank Thee, Lord of earth and heaven,
    That Thou to me, e'en me, hast given
        The knowledge of Thy grace,
    (Which flesh and blood could ne'er reveal),
    And call'd a babe Thy love to tell,
        And stammer out Thy praise.

2. None of the *sacred* order I,
    Yet dare I not the grace deny
        Thou hast on me bestow'd,
    Constrain'd to *speak* in Jesu's name,
    And show poor souls th'atoning Lamb,
        And point them to His blood.

3. I now believe, and therefore speak,
    And found myself, go forth to seek
        The sheep that wander still;

For these I toil, for these I care,
And faithfully to all declare
    The peace which all may feel.

4. My God supply Thy servant's need,
    If Thou has sent me forth indeed
        To make Thy goodness known;
    Thy Son in sinners' hearts reveal,
    By gracious signs my mission seal,
        And prove the word Thine own.

5. O for Thy only Jesu's sake,
    Into those arms of mercy take
        Thy meanest messenger,
    And ever in Thy keeping have,
    And grant me, Lord, at last to save
        Myself with all that hear.

Wesley's modesty made him impatient about the pride and haughtiness of others. And his impatience was particularly acute when it came to the Methodist lay preachers. James Wheatley was a former cobbler turned lay preacher who had been an itinerant since 1742 and had been John Wesley's lay assistant in 1745-47. Beginning in 1749, Wheatley's pride and obstinacy came to Charles Wesley's attention. "I threw away some advice on an obstinate Preacher, (J. Wh.)," Charles wrote in his journal, "for I could make no impression on him, or in any degree bow his stiff neck." On July 10 of the same year, Charles had a second unfavorable encounter with Wheatley: "I dined with the Preachers," Charles recalled, "and was troubled at J. Wh's obstinacey. He is gone to the North, expressly contrary to my advice. Whither will his wilfulness lead him at last?"

Wheatley did indeed sow more trouble. By June 1751 he was facing charges of sexual misconduct from several women in the Bristol circuit. The Wesley brothers met with him in June 1751 and confronted him with the charges. When he confessed to the charges but continued to defend himself, the Wesleys decided he should not preach. The document that the Wesleys drew up on June 25, 1751, has been preserved in John Wesley's journal:

Because you have wrought folly in Israel, grieved the Holy Spirit of God, betrayed your own soul into temptation and sin, and the souls of many others, whom you ought, even at the peril of your own life, to have guarded against all sin; because you have given occasion to the enemies of God, whenever they shall know these things, to blaspheme the ways and truth of God:

We can in no wise receive you as a fellow-labourer till we see clear proofs of your real and deep repentance. Of this you have given us no proof yet. You have not so much as named one single person in all England or Ireland with whom you have behaved ill, except those we knew before.

The least and lowest proof of such repentance which we can receive is this, that till our next Conference (which we hope will be in October) you abstain both from preaching and from practicing physic. If you do not, we are clear; we cannot answer for the consequences.

John Wesley,
Charles Wesley

On June 28 James Wheatley stood before a group of nearly a dozen Methodist lay preachers, whom he had slandered by saying that they were acting just like him. Charles Wesley's journal records the event: "James Wheatley having, to screen himself, traduced all the Preachers, we had him face to face with about ten of them together. . . . The accuser of the brethren was silent in him, which convinced us of his wilful lying."

The fallout from the Wheatley affair was considerable. Not only had the Methodist ministry been called into question, but the Methodist preachers had also been defamed by Wheatley's actions and charges against them. Those who were inclined to use the fallen preacher's example as a charge against the gospel itself were numerous enough to make it difficult for Charles Wesley to even preach from some of the same Bible texts that Wheatley had used. In his journal, Wesley lamented, "I cannot yet preach from my favorite texts, because he has. He has, as much as lay in him, poisoned the fountain, debased the language of God, hardened the people's hearts, palled their spiritual appetite, and made them loathe religion, and all that belongs to it."

James Wheatley's actions and his accusations had to be addressed directly. The Methodist annual conference upheld and approved of his expulsion when it met in October that same year. And the Wesley brothers resolved to examine every preacher who worked in connection with them to be certain there were not more offenders in their midst. The Wheatley affair, as Charles Wesley later wrote, "put my brother and me upon a resolution of strictly examining into the life and moral behaviour of every Preacher in connexion with us; and the office fell upon me."

Charles had already been paying close attention to the relative abilities and ineptitudes of the lay preachers. In his unpublished journal entry for June 12, 1751, Charles reported, "Spoke kindly to Jo[seph] Hewish and got from him his *Book and licence*. I wish he were the only worthless, senseless, graceless man to whom my brother had given the same encouragement under his hand." Now, after the Wheatley affair, Charles Wesley had a formal mandate to examine the lay preachers. It was a task he undertook in earnest and with considerable energy. He believed lay preachers should be empowered to preach and included in more frequent Methodist conferences. But he also had a low threshold of patience when it came to hypocrisy and ineptitude on the part of the lay preachers, and he soon gained a reputation for dismissing them just about as rapidly as John Wesley appointed them. Charles apparently used the threat of dismissal as a tool to keep the preachers in line, and when he dismissed one, he wanted the event published everywhere, both to clear the Methodists of suspicion and to serve as an example to the other lay preachers who might be tempted to fall into sin or slacken their ministerial service.

On June 29, 1751, Charles began to formally examine the lay preachers, as he traveled and preached in various locations. On August 13th he met one "who thinks himself called to preach." The man had preached for some length of time in Scotland, and had not been instrumental in converting a single soul; "You might as well preach to the stones," he said of the Scots. Charles listened to his preaching "and liked him worse and worse. His false English and low vulgar, ridiculous expressions, I pass over, but with my strictest observation I could not perceive one word that was accompanied with the power of God." Charles must have certainly dissuaded the man by his opinion that "to leave his calling and set up for an itinerant, seems contrary to the design of God, as to his own and the Church's interest." A week later Charles was in Newcastle, talking an administrator from a coal mine into keeping his current position instead of becoming an itinerant Methodist lay preacher by confirming him "in his wise resolution not to reach himself beyond his measure."

John felt the need to remind Charles that they desperately depended upon a supply of lay preachers to hold the Methodist movement together. He urged Charles to be lenient with the lay preachers, at least when it was clear that they were inept but not immoral: "As to preachers, my counsel is not to check the young ones, without strong necessity. If we lay some aside, we *must* have a supply and of the two I prefer grace before gifts." This latter statement seemed to set Charles off, and he retorted by mail: "Are not both [gifts and grace] indispensably necessary? Has not the cause suffered, in Ireland especially, through the insufficiency of the preachers? Should we not first regulate, reform, and bring into discipline the preachers we have, before we look for more?"

In July 1751, during a stop at Leeds, Charles fell into a dangerous fever. Amidst "Shivering fits [that] shook me most violently for two hours" Charles Wesley dictated his thoughts on the state of the church and the Methodist movement. Thinking he might be dying, Charles wanted to leave an utterly frank report of what he thought was wrong with the movement and its ambiguous relationship with the Church of England. He sent the report to his friend Lady Huntingdon. He was clearly worried about the lay preachers: "Unless a sudden remedy be found, the preachers will destroy the work of God. What has wellnigh ruined many of them is their being taken from their trades. . . . The tinner, barber, thatcher, forgot himself and set up for a gentleman, and looked out for a fortune, having lost the only way of maintaining himself." Feeling that economic necessity was ruining the work of the lay preachers, Charles opined that the Methodists should embark upon a form of bi-vocational ministry that would guarantee financial support. He offered the following proposal:

> First, that every preacher that has a trade return to it (except a very few who cannot); that he labours with his hands . . . by day, and preach morning and etc., tarrying at his own place of abode and the neighbouring towns; that now and then he be permitted to

make an excursion, or perhaps take a journey to distant societies, and then return to his trade again.

Secondly, that no future preacher be ever taken from his business or once permitted to preach, till the point is set how he is to be [financially] maintained.

Thirdly, that no one be allowed to preach with us, till my brother and I have heard him with our own ears, and talked fully with him, and if need [be] to keep him with us some days.

Charles also confided to Lady Huntingdon his belief that his brother's insistence upon the lay preachers not working at their secular employments had the effect of unduly increasing John Wesley's authority over them, since it made them wholly dependent upon him for their livelihood. Charles rashly wrote:

The second reason which I have for insisting on the labourers keeping themselves (which I cannot mention to my brother lest it should be a reason with him against it) is, namely, it will break his power, their not depending on him for bread, and reduce his authority within due bounds, as well as guard against that rashness and credulity of his, which has kept me in continual awe and bondage for many years. Therefore I shall insist on their working as the one point, the single condition, of my acting in concert with him. . . .

Unfortunately for Charles, his letter miscarried and fell into his brother's hands. That John was furious over Charles's description of his unchecked authority over the lay preachers is apparent in John's letter of December 4, 1751. "On some points it is easier to write than to speak," John fumed, "especially where there is danger of warmth on either side. In what respect do you judge it needful to 'break my power,' and 'to reduce my authority within due bounds'? I am quite ready to part with the whole or any part of it. It is no pleasure to me, nor ever was."

Meanwhile the tension between the brothers continued over how stringent standards for the lay preachers should be. Charles wrote to John Bennet of one of them, "A friend of ours [John Wesley] (without God's counsel) made a preacher of a tailor. I, with God's help, shall make a tailor of him again." On August 8, John wrote to remind Charles, "We *must* have forty itinerant preachers, or drop some of our societies. . . . You cannot so well judge of this, without seeing the letters I receive from all parts." On August 24 John seemed to agree more with Charles: "Let us have but six [lay preachers], so we are all one. I have sent one more, J. Loveybond, home to his work. We may trust God to send forth more labourers." Still, he added in shorthand, "Only be not unwilling to receive them, when there is reasonable proof that [God] has sent them."

While preaching his way northward through the first weeks of September 1751, what Charles heard from the lay preachers in both doctrine and rumors against his brother convinced him it was time to call a conference of preachers. He had no clear single agenda. As he confided to his journal, "Had anyone asked me the end of our Conference, I could not have told him, only that I came to make observations, to get acquainted with the preachers, and [to] see if God had any thing to do with us, or by us." But it was clear he needed to talk about preaching. "I began without design to speak of the qualifications, work, and trials of a preacher," he later wrote, "and what I thought requisite of men, that acted in concert. As to preliminaries and disciplines we all agreed."

Then Wesley examined two preachers, "Brother Mortimer whom I admitted and [William] Darney, whom I rejected." Charles had several indictments against Darney, principally in terms of his attitude and conduct; Wesley particularly disliked his habit of begging material goods from those he was sent to serve: "His stiff neckedness I knew of old, and was now resolved to bend or break him. The preachers informed me of his obstinate behavior toward my patient (too patient) brother at the last conference; beside his scandalous begging wherever he comes, and railing at his brethren or whomsoever he is displeased with. At Epworth he got more clothes than his horse can carry. They were ashamed to see the bags and bundles which he carried." Darney seemed to confirm Wesley's rejection of him by losing his temper and "railing" at him: "I told him these things in few words," Charles wrote, "for he soon took fire and threw out, as I expected into such violence of behaviour, that I thought he would have beat me. I left him raging like a wild bull in a net." The next day he gave William Darney a public hearing. After giving him a public dressing-down that "turned him inside out," Wesley agreed to Darney's preaching among the Methodists as a probationer. He drew up the following note to be sent to be shared with the other Methodist preachers:

> I leave this word of notice with you for our sons in the Gospel, to Assistants or Preachers, in any degree. At the desire of a very dear and faithful brother, I have consented to let W[illiam] D[arney] preach among our children as *heretofore* altho[ugh] I believe his spirit is still whole and unbroken. But on these conditions, I consent:
>
> 1. That he does not rail or speak against any one, much less any labourers [in the gospel]
> 2. That he does not beg of our people
> 3. That he does not permit any more of his nonsense and
> 4. That he does not introduce the use of his doggerel hymns into our Societies.
>
> I cannot in conscience agree to his putting nonsense into their mouths. Indeed, they themselves would never consent to it. But he utterly refused to promise forbearance, therefore, I have promised him that in whatsoever Society of ours he uses his own verses, in that Society *he shall preach no more.* Witness my hand,
>
> C.W.

A letter Charles Wesley wrote to John Bennet during the process of his examining the lay preachers reveals Wesley's attitude throughout the process. "I know NO one of our preachers now," he wrote, "who can be *justly* charged with sin; if you or any man does, I shall thank you for informing me of the fact. Without *proof*, I ought not to receive any accusation against any of them."

By the end of 1751 John and Charles Wesley drew up the following agreement and issued it over both of their signatures. It was one of the most positive events to come out of Charles's examination of the preachers in that he and his brother took solemn counsel with respect to the ways they should work together for the furtherance of the movement. In several regards it represents a consensus formed out of the challenges of the previous year and their correspondence on the matter of the lay preachers.

With regard to the preachers, we agree —

1. That none shall be permitted to preach in any of our societies, till he be examined, both as to grace and gifts; at least, by the assistant who, sending word to us, may by our answer, admit him as a *local* preacher.

2. That such preacher be not immediately taken from his trade, but be exhorted to follow it with all diligence.

3. That no person shall be received as a travelling preacher, or be taken from his trade, by either of us alone, but by both of us conjointly giving him a note under both our hands.

4. That neither of us will re-admit a travelling preacher laid aside without the consent of the other.

5. That, if we should ever disagree in our judgment, we will refer the matter to Mr. Perronet.

6. That we will entirely be patterns of all we expect from every preacher; particularly of zeal, diligence, and punctuality in the work. . . .

It is clear that Charles's examination of preachers had increased a climate of gossip and backbiting in the Methodist movement, and this too had to be addressed in a formal agreement among the Wesleys and twelve lay preachers, issued on January 29, 1752. "It is agreed by us whose names are underwritten," the document read, "1. That we will not listen, or willingly inquire after any ill concerning each other. 2. That if we do hear any ill of each other, we will not be forward to believe it. . . ."

Ever the churchman, Charles Wesley recognized that the pragmatic employment of lay preachers in itself constituted a breach with the policy and practice of the Church of England. He admitted this in a letter he wrote to Samuel Walker, the Anglican rector of Turo, in 1756. "Lay preaching," Charles admitted, "it must be allowed is a partial separation [from the Church of England], and may but *need* not, end in a total one. The probability of it has made me tremble for years past, and kept me from leaving the Methodists. I stay not so much as to do good, as to prevent evil." Wesley depicted himself as staying with the Methodists in an attempt to counterbalance the separatist notions of the preachers; as he told Walker, "I stand in the way of my brother's violent counselors, the object both of their fear and hate." John Pawson, one of the Methodist lay preachers who went through struggles with Charles Wesley, evidenced some of the wounds of these skirmishes when he wrote: "It is well known that Mr. Charles Wesley was much prejudiced in favour of the clergy through the whole course of his life, and that it was nothing but hard necessity that obliged him, in any degree, to continue with the lay preachers."

The growing tension between Charles Wesley and the Methodist lay preachers was one of the constant irritations of the later years of Charles's ministry. Dr. Whitehead, Charles Wesley's personal physician and one of his earliest biographers, indicated that the ongoing strife with the lay preachers was one of the material reasons that Charles eventually withdrew from many of the public functions of Methodism, such as itinerant preaching and attending conferences. Given Charles's frank assessment of the Methodist preachers' ineptitudes and his willingness to dismiss them nearly as quickly as John Wesley appointed them, it is no wonder that the ministers who took on the leadership of Methodism after the Wesleys' demise honored and revered John Wesley as their founder and "father" — and studiously ignored the important work of Charles Wesley.

13 Father of a Family

The little three-story house at No. 4 Charles Street, with its tidy garden in back, was a bustling place. Here Charles and Sally Wesley brought eight children into the world, three of which survived infancy. In consequence of his marriage and these blessed events, Charles Wesley embarked upon a role that his more illustrious brother never knew: father of a family. While parenthood may have decreased Charles's significance as a traveling Methodist evangelist, it certainly increased his depth and experience as a human being. Clearly he struggled, as so many of us do, to find a balance between his professional life and the burgeoning demands of raising a family. On September 4, 1749, Charles wrote to his friend Ebenezer Blackwell and quoted part of his first family hymn. It evidences Wesley's desire to merge the private and professional aspects of his life into a whole fabric of Christian service:

> God of faithful Abraham, hear
>   His feeble son and Thine;
> In Thy glorious power appear,
>   And bless my just design.
> Lo! I come to serve Thy will,

And all Thy blessed will to prove,
Fired with patriarchal zeal,
And pure primeval love.

Me and mine I fain would give
A sacrifice to Thee,
By the ancient model live,
The true simplicity;
Walk as in my Maker's sight,
Free from worldly guile and care,
Praise my innocent delight,
And all my business prayer. . . .

Most of what we know about Wesley's family life is gleaned from the letters he wrote home to Sally and eventually to his children while he was traveling. Generally these letters begin by reporting the successes or trials that Charles was experiencing in his ministry. The only thing missing in these early successes was Sally: "I only wanted the 'desire of my eyes' to be there present. Such my God has made you and commanded me to love you next to himself." A few of these letters described scenes so lovely that Sally might want to join her husband on his ministerial rounds: "My very dear Sally," he wrote, "500 cows under my window offer you warm milk in bed; a new-laid egg also S. Butterfield can answer for; and all the same in her shop is at your service. I hope soon to get another horse for carrying double, so you may come as soon as you please, which will be as soon as you can." And if such worldly pleasures could not generally coax the family on the road with Charles, he might promise to bring some home with him: "Charles may have his choice of instruments; Sarah of kittens; you of soft pillows."

These early separations and the pain they brought Charles sometimes caused him to anticipate the ultimate separation — Sally's death — and wonder whether he was adequately prepared for it. In the throes of a lengthy separation, Charles wrote from London:

I often reflect on that hard saying, "Son of man, behold I take away the desire of your eyes with a stroke." And asking myself, could I bear Ezekiel's trial [Ezekiel 24:16]? Whether I shall ever be called to it, God knoweth; for known unto Him are all His works. But it is far more probable that my beloved Sally will see many good days in the vale, after my warfare is accomplished, and my weary soul at rest. Here indeed we have laid the foundation of an eternal friendship, and hasten to our consummation in bliss above. Till then we scarcely begin to know the end of our meeting upon earth. O that we may fully answer it, by helping each other onto heaven, and by bringing very many with us to glory!

Charles wrote home with birthday greetings: "Blessed be the day on which my dearest Sally was born! It has been continual sunshine — the fairest, calmest, brightest day, since I left you in Bristol. Such may all your succeeding ones be; at least may you enjoy that 'perpetual sunshine of the spotless mind.' The Lord lift you up in the light of his countenance upon you while you are reading this, and put gladness in your heart! May you taste the powers of the world to come and be a partaker of the Holy Ghost!" He also wrote at least one hymn, "On the Birthday of a Friend," that seemed to be for Sally:

9.   Come away to the skies
     My beloved arise.
   And rejoice on the day thou was born,
     On the festival day
     Come exalting away,
   To thy heavenly country return.

10.   We have laid up our love
      And treasure above,
   Though our bodies continue below;
      The redeem'd of the Lord
      We remember His word,
   And with singing to *Sion* go. . . .

Charles's letters home to Sally often betray how much he missed her and his family. A letter dated only February 15, from Seven Dials, reported, "My heart is with you all, yet my work is here. I trust the Lord sent me hither." Occasionally these sentiments were mixed with complaints about his not receiving any letters from them. "My dearest

Friend," he wrote on one March 17, "Grace and peace be multiplied upon you and yours, who are mine also. One letter in a week does not half satisfy me, under your absence. I count the days since we parted, and those still between us and our next meeting." Or: "Your letter this moment received has stopped my grumbling at your not sending me one in a week." He wanted her to reply sooner: "you *might* write, like me, without waiting for who wrote last!" One letter, dated only "Tuesday night," points out their mutual habit of praying for one another at five o'clock each day. "I have just been reading the letters and praying for you," he wrote. "Remember me at five." The next line shows his own reservations about the toll his work took on his wife: "I am weary of my own unprofitableness and ashamed that I have been of so little use to my dearest Sally. It is well you have one Friend who *may* be depended on. To Him I continually commend you."

As their first wedding anniversary approached, Charles was traveling and deeply immersed in ministry. On April 3, 1750, he scribbled off a few lines and enclosed a "Hymn for April 8" in anticipation of their anniversary:

1. Sweet day! so cool, so calm, so bright!
    The Bridal of the earth and sky!
  I see with joy thy cheering light
    And lift my heart to things on high.

2. My grateful heart to Him I lift
    Who did the guardian Angel send,
  Inrich'd [sic] me with an heavenly gift,
    And bless'd me with a bosom-friend.

3. The mountains at his presense flow'd,
    His Providence the Bars remov'd,
  His grace my Better Soul bestow'd,
    And join'd me to his Well-belov'd.

4. Twas God alone, who join'd our hands
    Who join'd us *first* in mind and heart,
  By love and indissoluble bands
    Which neither life nor death can part.

5. God of eternal power, and grace
    I bow my soul before thy throne;
  I only live to sing thy praise,
    I live and die to thee alone.

6. My more than life, to thee I give
    My more than friend to thee restore,
  (When summ'd with thyself to live)
    And fall, and silently adore.

7. Yet if thy welcome will consent
    To spare her yet another year
  With joy I take who thou has lent
    And clasp her to my bosom here.

8. Her in the arms of faith I bring,
    And place before thy gracious throne,
  Receive her, O thou heavenly king,
    And save whom thou hast called thine own! . . .

Charles wanted Sally to join him at various points in his travels, but he refused to order her to come, as many eighteenth-century husbands might have done. In a letter of 1760 he explained himself to her in this regard: "You will not mistake my tenderness for indifference. The greatest earthly blessing I could obtain were a sight of you and your children; but I should not buy it too dear; if you came unwillingly. Therefore do as you find best in your own heart. Come with Charley or without him, or not at all. Your will I shall receive as the will of Providence." Writing to Sally from Lakenham, Charles urged, "If your heart persuades you to leave father and mother, nurse, and sisters, for me, lose no time; but take two days for your journey to Bristol. . . . I can *almost promise* you more of my company here, than you could have anywhere else, as I have several useful books to read over, and defer it till you come." Again, Wesley left the travel plans up to his wife's decision: "Yet observe, I leave you to your free choice, because I mistrust whatever is *my doing*. Pray earnestly to God for direction, that *His* will, not mine may be done, in you and by you." On July 2, 1763, she wrote to him, "My ever dearest Friend and partner need not so lament to bring me up to him [in London], for I have had selfish motives sufficient especially since my late indisposition, which would have brought me to you, before now, were it possible." Charles even tried to induce Sally to visit him at the seashore to bathe away her rheumatism: "nothing but the *cure* of all evils [e.g. death] will prevent my bathing there next season. You will bear me company, if you was not afraid of losing your rheumatism. Multitudes wash away your complaint with the salt water."

As spouse and parent, Charles was concerned about the development and improvement of his family. Both he and Sally were capable keyboard musicians, so he frequently asked about her music. On one March 17 he wrote, "Not a word of your music! That is a bad sign; a sign of idleness, I fear. When you would have me look out after a harpsichord for you, you will tell me so." From London, on an Easter eve, he urged, "Do not neglect your short hand; do not neglect your music; but above all, do not neglect your prayers." On another occasion he asked, "How many of Lampe's tunes can you play? I am offered an exceedingly fine harpsichord for sixteen guineas! What encouragement do you give me to purchase it for you?" In 1758 he wrote Sally and urged, "Send for Jack Hamilton and tell him you must learn a new tune on the guitar every day." Like John Wesley, Charles was a firm believer in early rising — for his family as well as himself. "My Dearest Sally," he chided, "when you are quite in earnest for salvation, believe me, you will find no difficulty in rising at six." He also troubled himself about her physical care; her rheumatism in particular became a focal point of Charles's injunctions to exercise. "You are not to be cured of rheumatism," he wrote, "if you have no resolution to use the remedy of constant exercise."

Most often, however, he urged Sally's spiritual improvement. When he was away, he wondered, "Who is your chaplain? When none is near, *you* should read prayers yourself, as my mother and many besides have done. 'Be much in private prayer.'" Both he and she experienced periods of "heaviness" in which Christ's absence seemed acute, but this was a desirable sensation, Charles thought, because it set a person seeking after Christ. Hence Charles advised her on January 3, 1760: "Next to feeling Christ present, the most desirable state is to *feel Christ absent*. This we often do. O that we did it always!"

Because of his bedrock confidence in the love and fatherly care of God, Charles Wesley came to see physical and emotional suffering he endured during his life and ministry as a kind of discipline or chastening that God allowed (and sometimes caused) for his and Sally's improvement. He used this theology of suffering as a way of encouraging himself to bear up under trial, and he occasionally used it to encourage Sally during her frequent illnesses: "Yours of August 13th has just now brought me the mournful news of your increasing illness. Yet I would say, 'It is the Lord; let him do as seemeth him good.' Still my hope of you is stead fast, that hereby you shall be partaker of his holiness, who in tenderest love chastens you for your good. And you may be bold to say, 'when He has tried me, I shall come forth as gold.'" In another letter Charles described how this willingness to see illness and suffering as coming to his hand from God helped him make sense of these adversities: "My ever-dearest Sally —" he wrote, "Your illness would quite overwhelm me, were I not assured that it shall work together for your good, and enhance your happiness throughout all eternity. How does this assurance change the nature of things!" Charles explained this "assurance" further: "The slightest suffering (received from Him) is an inestimable blessing; another jewel added to our crown. Go on, then, my faithful partner, doing and suffering His blessed will, till, out of great tribulation, we both enter His Kingdom, and His joy, and His glory everlasting."

Charles Wesley was a doting father. His *Hymns for Children* (1763) and *Hymns for Families* (1767), for example, occasionally show the attention of a proud father. The following hymn, "For the Evening," sounds very much like a father's evening prayer for parent and child:

1. Saviour, Thou hast bestow'd on me
     The blessing of the light,
   And wilt my kind Preserver be
     Through this approaching night.

2. Evil from me far off remove,
     That, with Thy favour bless'd
   Beneath the shadow of Thy love
     I in Thine arms may rest.

3. Thy gracious eye which never sleeps
   Is always fix'd on man;
Thy love the slumbering children keeps
   From sorrow, fear, and pain.

4. Wherefore I safely lay me down,
   And trust myself to Thee,
The Father's well-beloved Son,
   Who ever pray'st for me.

In a similar way, his letters home are filled with requests for information about his children. "Can the boy walk? It is a question often asked me. You will tell me when his face is well, and how Sally continues. I presume you now begin seriously to think about weaning her."

Wesley expressed his concern for his children's growth and development often in terms of teeth and lessons: "I am looking towards Bristol and counting the hours till we meet. By your next I expect news of Sammy's teeth appearing; of Charles's and Sally's progress in their respective learning. He is a long time learning one solo and wants [needs] me to hear him *more diligently!*" "Tomorrow, three weeks," Charles wrote from London, "I hope to find you all well, and to see Sammy's first teeth, and hear Sally read, and Charles both read and play his new lesson, with all the old ones." "My dear Sally — what news of Sammy's invisible tormentors? All flesh is grass, you see in him. When his teeth break out, he may recover his strength, and looks and be the finest child in Bristol, till more teeth pull him down."

No family event, however mundane, seemed to escape Charles's poetical pen. Reflecting upon his child's teething pains, the poet-theologian concluded, in "For a Child Cutting His Teeth," that it must be due to original sin:

1. Suffering for another's sin,
   Why should innocence complain?
Sin by *Adam* enter'd in,
   Sin engendering grief and pain;
Sin entail'd on all our race,
   Forces harmless babes to cry,
Born to sorrow, and distress,
   Born to feel, lament, and die. . . .

The healing for this and every painful situation, however, is to be found in the blood of Christ, in the "double cure" of restored health and salvation by faith. This was the relief that Charles Wesley prayed for, for his child and his "house":

> 5. Help, the woman's heavenly Seed,
>   Thou that didst our sorrows take,
> Turn aside the dread decree,
>   Save him for Thy nature's sake!
> Pitying Son of man and God,
>   Still Thy creature's pains endure;
> Quench the fever with Thy blood,
>   Bless him with a perfect cure.
>
> 6. Thine it is to bless and heal,
>   Thine to rescue and repair;
> On our child the answer seal,
>   Thou who didst suggest the prayer;
> Send salvation to this house;
>   Then, to double health restored,
> I and mine will pay our vows,
>   I and mine will serve the Lord.

Even the family cats captured Charles Wesley's poetical imagination. The brave exploits of one "Grimalkin" claimed the interest of his poetical muse, as evidenced in a whimsical unpublished poem:

> 1. I sing Grimalkin brave and bold,
>   Who makes Intruders fly,
> His claws and whiskers they behold,
>   And squawl and scamper by.
>
> 2. The fiercest Cats before his power
>   Fly swifter than the wind,
> Over the walls and houses scour
>   But leave their Coat behind.
>
> 3. Their Coat I shall preserve from harm
>   As a Victorious Trophy:

> T'will keep Mamma so pure and warm
> Or make a Muff for Sophy.
>
> 4. A smile it will from Sister gain,
>   A Kiss from Hetty Farley
>   And rouse into a tuneful strain
>   The jealousy of Charley.

The children were often ill, and Charles was as often writing about their condition. "My Dearest Sally's letter did not reach me this morning," he wrote once. "I was in hopes the worst was over with Charles. The whooping cough does not always accompany the measles, and will not, I trust, in his case. The girl may not have them at all." They both worried that the same illness that had taken Jacky would also deprive them of little Sammy; "My dearest Sally," Charles wrote, "our preparation could not save the first Jacky, because God had prepared a better thing for him. The means may keep Samuel with us. Let us be thankful that he still holds up. If he should have the distemper soon, I believe it will only lessen his beauty." On another occasion, while one of his sons was in the midst of a serious illness, Charles wrote, "My Dear Sally's letter, this moment received has awakened all my love and concern for our dearest boy. But I hope you will have the comfort, while reading this, to see him as well as you wish. If not, (and the Lord is pleased to try us farther) let us remember we are not our own; neither are our children. The most likely way to keep them is, to give them up [to God] in the spirit of daily sacrifice."

Death was an all-too-frequent visitor to the Wesley home. On July 6, 1768, Charles received a laconic letter from Sally indicating that John James, aged four months, had died. "My dearest Mr. Wesley," she wrote, "This comes to acquaint you that our dear little babe is no more, his agony is over, but it was a hard struggle before he could depart. He was dying all yesterday from ten o'clock; about nine last night he departed. It seemed . . . about half an hour before he died that he could be heard from Nanse's parlour to the other side of the street, not through guilt (that is my comfort) but through extreme pain. Perhaps were I of Calvin's opinion I might have attributed it to a different cause, but glory be to a redeemer's love in declaring (for the consolation of the distressed parents) that 'of such is the Kingdom of

208

heaven.' O that I may land as safely in the harbour of Eternal Peace." In the next post Charles wrote back to Sally, "Father, not as I will, but as thou wilt. Thy will be done on earth as it is in heaven! Let my dearest companion in trouble offer up this prayer with as much of her heart as she can; and God, who knoweth whereof we are made, and considereth that we are but dust, will, for Christ's sake, accept our weakest, most imperfect, desires of resignation. I know, the surest way to preserve our children, is to trust them with Him who loves them infinitely better than we do."

Charles Wesley had his own ideas about child-rearing, and he freely passed them on to Sally, from a distance, while she was enmeshed in the actual business of raising their children. His prescription for young Jacky's health was "as much air and sunshine as you please, but not a grain of salt or a bit of meat." He apparently believed that to show the children his favor would spoil them; smarting under Sally's rebuke for that sort of behavior, Charles wrote, "I love them as well again as you do, only you make the most of a little love by showing it, and I make the least of a great deal by hiding it." He wanted her to be careful about their children's friendships: "It superfluous, yet I can not help cautioning you about Charles (and Sally too), to take care he contracts no acquaintance with other boys; children are corrupters of each other."

Charles Wesley Jr. was a musical prodigy. In a short "Account," his proud father described him: "Charles was born December 11, 1757. He was two years and three quarters old, when I first observed his strong inclination to music. He then surprised me by playing a tune readily, and in just time. Soon after, he played several, whatever his mother sung, or whatever he heard in the streets."

Many of the Methodists felt that the musical instruction and avocations of the Wesley boys were too "worldly" for a devout Christian family. A conscientious Quaker wrote to voice the criticism that many were making of Charles Sr. for allowing and even encouraging his son's musical gifts. In response to his letter, in February 1769, Wesley wrote: "My friend's mistake is owing to a prejudice of education. I can with a good conscience hold up my son a musician, not to please the giddy multitudes, but to earn his bread. Some trades which Quakers exercise without scruples, I think full as dangerous or more so than music. I do not blame them for calling a music room a prison-house, or a church a steeple house. But neither ought they to blame me for being of a different judgment."

When the Bristol Methodists raised a similar complaint, Charles Wesley answered them with an open letter, "to be read in the Society at Bristol," in February 1769. "I understand, my brethren," he wrote, "that some serious persons both in the Society and out of it, were troubled at my Son's lately playing at a concert. I shall give you my *reasons* for consenting to it, which lay me under a necessity of speaking of my private affairs." The Wesleys did not intend young Charles to be a musician; his father thought his namesake should follow him into the ministry and serve God as three generations of their family already had done. "But from his earliest infancy, the God of nature has marked him for a musician. My most judicious Christian friends have advised me NOT to force his inclination. Indeed, if I would, I could not. There is no way to hinder his being a musician but to cut off his fingers." Because of young Charles's God-given gifts and talents, his father was determined that he should have the best instruction he could find for him. "Whatever trade a boy is designed for, he must be taught that trade. If it be painting, he must be sent to the Zimmer; if navigator, to the sailors; if music, to the musicians. Some of the greatest in London would take my son 'prentice for nothing. Mr. Beard has offered me to get him admitted to the number of the King's Boys, of whose morals the strictest care is taken. One of the governors of the Charterhouse would have put him upon that Foundation. My brother knowing the wickedness of that school dissuaded me. I only mention these things to show you, my brothers, that I have some regard for his soul, as well as you." Perhaps these complainers had no love for music, or considered it "inseparable from sin." But Charles Wesley thought differently. "I was always a lover of music," he wrote; "so was my brother, and you ought to thank God for this very thing. He has been pleased to make good use of vocal music among us. Our hymns have helped to spread the Gospel. God himself has own'd and applied them to many of your hearts." Hence, because of the God-given gifts of his son, and because of the Divine usefulness of music, Charles concluded, "With a good conscience and a single eye I build up my son for a Musician. I make no secret of it. The world knows it; and let the world make their most of it. He goes to perform at the Concert, he goes not to his diversion, but to his business. He must learn his trade, and a fair and honest trade it is; and fairer than many others. Music is not sinful in itself. It may indeed be abused, and it may serve the noblest purposes. Witness Handel's 'Messiah.' If God gives my son grace, he will be preserved from the snares of his calling. He will be a Christian and a Musician too. . . . A Christian musician is much wanted. If my son becomes such, I shall esteem his music as a precious talent and together with him bless God and sing His praises through all eternity."

The life of faith mattered even more than music to Charles Wesley. His "Young Man's Hymn" reflects a father's hopes and prayers for the protection and faith development of his young son:

> 1. How shall a young unstable man
>   To evil prone like me,
>   His actions and his heart maintain
>   From all pollution free?
>   Thee, Lord, that I may not forsake,
>   Or ever turn aside,
>   Thy precepts for my rule I take,
>   Thy Spirit for my guide.
>
> 2. Governed by the engrafted word,
>   And principled with grace,
>   I shall not yield to sin abhorr'd,
>   Or give to passion place:
>   From youthful lusts I still shall flee,
>   From all the paths of vice,
>   My omnipresent Saviour see,
>   And walk before Thine eyes. . . .

Charles Wesley's daughter, Sally Jr., was also the object of his great affection. He frequently concerned himself about his daughter's spiritual state, and occasionally wrote her advice that eventually did find an echo in her own heart: "As soon as you are truly in earnest to save your soul," he wrote, "it will appear 1. By your early rising, 2. By your diligent use of the means of grace. 3. By the choice of your company and of your books. Commending you to Divine direction, and protection, I remain, Dear Sally's loving Father, and Friend. C.W."

On other occasions, Charles's concern for his daughter was more mundane. How seriously did she injure herself during that fall she received from wearing fashionable high heels? "My dearest Sally's letter, I have just received and am very uneasy to find you have met with such a fall, though I am thankful it pleased God to preserve you from greater hurt, and I hope the pain in your neck is owing only to the bruise and not to any bone being broken. Your Papa and Brother are equally anxious about you. . . . I wish you would not wear such heels to your shoes, which makes you more liable to fall. Let me hear again *soon* how you are."

Charles encouraged young Sally's poetical talents, as did her uncle John: "Your valuable God-father met us today at dinner. Sends his love and blessing to you, and learning you have a poetical genius, desired you would send him a hymn from the feelings of your heart." The following "Maiden's Hymn" was probably written with Sally in mind:

1. Holy Child of heavenly birth,
   God made man, and born on earth,
   Virgin's Son, impart to me
   Thy unsullied purity.

2. In my pilgrimage below
   Only Thee I pant to know,
   Every creature I resign,
   Thine, both soul and body, Thine.

3. Fairer than the sons of men,
   Over me Thy sway maintain:
   Perfect loveliness Thou art,
   Take my undivided heart.

4. All my heart to Thee I give,
   All Thy holiness receive,
   Live to make my Saviour known,
   Live to please my God alone.

5. Free from low, distracting care,
   For the happy day prepare,
   For the joys that never die,
   For my Bridegroom in the sky.

6. Here bethroth'd to Thee in love,
   I shall see my Lord above,
   Lean on my Redeemer's breast,
   In Thy arms for ever rest.

Most of the references to little Sammy Wesley in Charles Wesley's letters of the Bristol period have to do with his physical development: the arrival of new teeth, or his ability to walk. But he too was a musical prodigy, as his father described him in a brief account:

Samuel was born on St. Matthias's day, February 24th, 1766, the same day which gave birth to Handel, eighty-two years before. The seeds of harmony did not spring up in him quite so early as in his brother; for he was three years old before he aimed at a tune. His first were, "God save great George our King," Fischer's Minuet, and such like, mostly picked up from the street-organs. He did not put a true bass to them till he had learned his notes. While his brother was playing, he used to stand by, with his childish fiddle, scraping and beating time. . . .

Mr. Arnold was the first who, hearing him at the harpsichord, said, 'I set down Sam for one of my family.' But we did not much regard him, coming after Charles. The first thing that drew our attention was, the great delight he took in hearing his brother play. Whenever Mr. Kelway came to teach him, Sam constantly attended, and accompanied Charles *on the chair*. Undaunted by Mr. Kelway's frown, he went on; and when he did not *see* the harpsichord, he crossed his hands on the chair, as the other on the instrument, without ever missing a time.

He was so excessively fond of Scarlatti, that if Charles ever began playing his lesson before Sam was called, he would cry and roar as if he had been beat. Mr. Madan, his godfather, finding him one day so belabouring the chair, told him he should have a better instrument by and by. . . .

This unpublished "A Father's Prayer for His Son," which Charles wrote for young Samuel, voices his Christian concern for his youngest son:

1. God of all-sufficient grace,
      Hear an anxious Parent's cry,
   While my Intercessor prays,
      While I on his prayer rely,
   Deeply in his Spirit groan,
   Hear, and save my Son, my Son!

2. Whom incarnate fiends intice,
      Whom ten thousand baits allure,
   Save him from the snares of vice,
      From the world's pollution pure,
   Pure from every great offence
   Keep his thoughtless innocence.

3. From, or *in* the evils here,
      Father, Thou canst save thine own,
   Hold him back by legal fear,
      Till Thou make thy goodness known,
   All his unbelief remove,
   Manifest thy pardoning love.

4. Then redeem'd from all below,
      Conqueror of the world and sin,
   Let him after Jesus go,
      Wise immortal souls to win,
   Gain his calling's heavenly prize,
   Find his Saviour in the skies.

Charles Wesley was a happily married family man — in stark contrast to his brother. On the one hand he felt strongly the push to preach the gospel and to travel in circuits in cooperation with his brother; on the other hand he felt strongly the pull of wife and family. On June 15, 1758, Charles confided to Sally, "I believe I shall quite come over to you, and never stir from home — except to visit the sick or to preach. . . . My love of retirement increases with my business: and I should not be sorry, if all the religious world cast me off."

14 "The Old Ship"

Charles Wesley had an undying love for the Church of England. He ardently embraced the church from his youngest years, and here the influence of the two Samuels — his father and elder brother — must certainly be taken into account. Both men were staunch Church of England men, and their loyalty was compounded in young Charles with the kind of fervor that brings staunch devotion. Charles's parents, Samuel and Susanna, had been converted to the Church of England from non-conforming Puritan stock, and they embraced the Church of England with the zeal of converts.

Charles's early association with Methodism may seem contrary to his love for the Church of England, but he did not see it that way. The younger Wesley saw the Methodist movement as a renewal group located within the church, to revive, evangelize, and "leaven the whole lump" (Matthew 13:33). He considered support for the Church of England an implicit requirement for membership in the Methodist societies; in 1739, for example, he wrote in his journal of two Methodists: "We all consented [unanimously] that their names should be erased out of the Society-book because they disowned themselves [as] members of the Church of England."

The "Stillness Controversy" of 1739-40 had the effect of shaping and galvanizing the Methodist movement in its attachment to the Church of England and her spiritual disciplines. The "Moravianized" Methodists opted for a form of quietism and wanted to wait in stillness for the leading of the Holy Spirit, rather than attending church, prayers, or the Lord's Supper. This new teaching, which Charles Wesley considered to be of human invention (not grounded in Scripture and tradition), stood in clear opposition to the commands of God. "I tremble at the consequence," he wrote on June 11, 1740; "will they submit themselves to every ordinance of man, who refuse subjection to the ordinances of God? . . . I told them plainly, '*I should continue with them so long as they continue in the Church of England.*' My every word was grievous to them, I am a thorn in their sides and they cannot bear me."

Charles Wesley was not blind to the faults of the Church of England, but his criticisms were usually tinged with compassion and love. For example, he lamented her "desolate" state, as in this journal entry from December 2, 1740: "[God] opened my mouth again at the society, and I spoke in much grief and love of our desolate mother, the Church of England. My heart yearns towards her when I think upon her ruin and it pitieth me to see her in the dust." A long hymn Wesley wrote around this time and published in 1743 makes much the same point. It is entitled "Psalm LXXX — Adapted to the Church of England," and in twenty-seven verses he laments the strife in which the church finds herself and prays that God will vindicate and renew her:

> 7. A Strife we are to All around,
>   By vile intestine Vipers torn,
> Our bitter Household Foes abound,
>   And laugh our Fallen Church to scorn. . . .

> 26. Revive, O GOD of Power, revive
>   Thy Work in our degenerate Days,
> O let us by thy Mercy live,
>   And all our Lives shall speak thy Praise.

> 27. Turn us again, O Lord, and shew
>   The Brightness of thy lovely Face,
> So shall we all be Saints below,
>   And sav'd, and perfected in Grace.

In the mid-1750s, Charles Wesley's conflicts with the Methodist lay preachers took on the added dimension of raising the question of Methodism's relationship with the Church of England. The preachers, by preaching as laymen and by preaching in Anglican parishes without the permission of the priest assigned there, had already begun to violate the laws and statutes of the Church of England. Soon the movement towards separation began to become more explicit as many Methodist preachers clamored for sacramental authority; they lacked Anglican ordination and therefore also began to urge a formal separation so the Methodists could begin their own tradition of ordination. Some of the Methodist preachers had begun to take out licenses as Dissenting pastors under the 1689 Act of Toleration, which granted them legal protection from not following the rules and practices of the Church of England. In 1745, in his *Farther Appeal*, John Wesley explicitly forbade his followers from taking out licenses as Dissenters; he believed the Methodists should not license themselves under an act that was designed for pastors who were *not* members of the church. He saw licensing the preachers as Dissenters as a kind of separation from the Church of England, and he was opposed to it. This meant that the Methodist preachers had to either qualify for ordination in the Church of England or not administer the sacraments. The growing opposition to the Methodist movement within the leadership of the Church of England guaranteed that securing Anglican ordination for Methodist preachers (even for those who were properly qualified) would be no easy matter.

In the winter of 1754 and spring of 1755 events began developing that nearly brought the Methodist movement to the brink of schism with the Church of England. John Wesley's published journal is silent about this problem, no doubt to keep Methodism's "dirty laundry" out of the public eye. But Charles's manuscript journal indicates that two of the lay preachers, Charles Perronet and Thomas Walsh, had administered the Lord's Supper in London and in Reading. In his shorthand journal entry for October 19, 1754, the younger Wesley reported: "I was with my brother, who said nothing of Perronet except, 'We have in effect ordained already.' He urged me to sign the preachers' certificates; was inclined to lay on hands; and to let the preachers administer [the sacrament]." The act of giving the preachers certificates of authority allowing them to preach within the parish of Anglican priests, and the fact that some of them had already licensed themselves as Dissenters, may have been what John Wesley had in mind with "We have in effect ordained already." This line of thinking was not to Charles's liking, and he took pains to influence his brother to take a different direction. Five days later, Charles confided to his journal: "He is wavering, but willing to wait before he ordains or separates."

Charles was well aware that his relationship with his brother had become increasingly strained. Since the "Grace Murray affair" and John's subsequent marriage to Molly Vazeille, both brothers had lost confidence in the other. Charles's repeated refusals to carry what had formerly been his share of the itinerant ministry angered John as much as his younger brother's independent actions. John's apparent weakness and reserve in dealing with the ineptitudes of the Methodist lay preachers angered Charles and caused him to doubt his brother's resolve with respect to their regularity and with respect to the question of separation from the Church of England. Charles seemed to doubt that his influence with his brother would be substantial enough to sway him away from schism, so he began to marshal a more organized opposition. He solicited letters of support from Anglican evangelicals who were well respected by his brother John, including Walter Sellon (1715-92). Sellon had been Master of Classics at Wesley's Kingswood school in 1748, but had left that position by 1750. He was ordained to the Anglican priesthood through the intervention of Selina Hastings, the Countess of Huntingdon, and became curate at Smisby and Breeden in Leichestershire.

Charles first wrote Sellon about the Methodist preachers on November 29, 1754. He depicted his brother John as being strongly under the influence of the lay preachers who were leading him headlong into a separation from the Church of England. "They are continually urging him to separation," Charles wrote; "that is, to pull down all he has built, to put a sword in our enemies' hands, to destroy the work, scatter the flock, disgrace himself, and go out — like the snuff of a candle." John Wesley's journal for 1754 ends with the month of October, so there is no indication of him having received a letter from Sellon. But Sellon must have written because, on December 14, 1754, Charles Wesley was urging him to write *again:* "Dear Brother and Friend — write again and spare not, my brother took no notice to me of your letter." The "Melchisedechians," Charles's nickname for the lay preachers who wanted an order of priesthood without lineage or genealogy, were still pushing John Wesley towards schism. Charles believed his own influence with the Methodists was waning: "Since the Melchise-dechians have taken him in," he explained to Walter Sellon, "I have been excluded [from] his cabinet council. They know me too well to trust him with me." Even more alarming, from Charles's point of view, was an apparent shift in the attitude of the senior Wesley with respect to separation from the Church of England: "He is come so far as to believe a separation quite lawful, only not expedient. They are indefatigable in urging him to go so far, that he may not be able to retreat. He may *lay on hands,* say they, without separating." Charles was also aware that his current actions reflected badly on his relationship with his brother, so he swore Sellon to secrecy: "I charge you, keep it to yourself that I am in doubt of him; which I tell you, that you may pray for him the more earnestly and write to him the more plainly."

The next Methodist annual conference, slated for May 1755, promised to become a war over the issue of separation, so Charles specifically invited Sellon to the conference and urged him to attend: "Our Conference is in May," he wrote. "You must be there, if alive. The Methodist Preachers must quickly divide to the right or the left, the Church or [Independent] Meeting." Charles also had his own plan for handling the Methodists' problem of having a shortage of ordained preachers: "I know none fitter for training up the young men than yourself or J[ohn] Jones. We must, among us, get the sound preachers qualified for [Anglican] orders." But the solution of getting Methodists into Anglican orders was a solution that favored the needs of the Church of England more than it did those of the Methodist movement.

The correspondence between Sellon and Charles Wesley resumed again in February 1755. Sellon had, apparently, urged forcefulness on Charles's part as well. This was not a warning Charles needed, he thought; he was more likely to lose his temper and make the cause suffer for it. Charles was pleased to report that Sellon's letters had had their desired effect upon his brother: "Your letters, and some others wrote to him with the same honesty, have had the due effect on him. He has spoken as strongly of late, in behalf of the Church of England, as I could wish; and everywhere declares he never intends to leave her. This has made the Melchizedekians draw in their horns, and drop their design."

But the schismatics had not changed their minds regarding separation from the Church of England; they had only changed their tactics. To this end, Charles anticipated a thorough examination and sifting of the preachers at the next conference: "We must know the heart of every Preacher; and give them their choice of the Church or the meeting. The wound can no longer be healed slightly. Those who are disposed to separate had best do it while we are yet alive."

On their way to the 1755 Methodist conference, John and Charles together studied Micaiah Towgood's book *Dissent from the Church of England Fully Justified*. One of Charles Wesley's letters home to his wife Sally, from April 30, 1755, reports: "My time is chiefly spent with my brother at Bristol, in reading over the Dissenter's book. He found and showed me many flaws in his arguments against the Church, which he inter-weaves and answers in his excellent treatise on that question, whether it is expedient to separate from the Church of England." John Wesley's journal entry for April 28, 1755, describes the same instance and compares Towgood's book unfavorably to that of Richard Baxter: "Surely one page of that loving, serious Christian weighs more than the volume of this bitter, sarcastic jester."

Charles penned his poetical *Epistle to the Reverend Mr. John Wesley, by Charles Wesley, Presbyter of the Church of England,* prior to the conference and published it soon thereafter. Charles wasted no time in putting this open letter into circulation. The printer's bill indicates that the author received 3,000 copies of the *Epistle* on May 28, 1755, and ordered an additional 1,000 copies on the same day. The tone of the *Epistle* is consistent with the author's mission at the conference: he intended to force John Wesley into a more direct declaration of his fidelity to the Church of England. It is clear that the younger Wesley considered himself caught in the middle: "by Bigots [staunch Anglicans] branded for a Schismatick,/By real Schismaticks [the lay Preachers] disown'd, decry'd." That Charles included "Presbyter of the Church of England" in his byline emphasizes his stance throughout this controversy — primarily as an Anglican and secondarily as a Methodist.

The lengthy *Epistle* begins with Charles affirming both his undying loyalty to the Church of England and his friendship towards his brother:

My first and last unalienable Friend,
A Brother's Thoughts with due Regard attend
A *Brother,* still *as thy own Soul belov'd,*
Who speak to learn, and write to be reprov'd:
Far from the factitious undiscerning Crowd,
Distrest I fly to Thee, and *think aloud;*
I tell Thee, wise and faithful as Thou art,
The Fears and Sorrows of a burthen'd Heart,
The Workings of (a blind or heav'nly?) Zeal,
And all my Fondness for *The Church* I tell,
The Church whose Cause I serve, whose Faith approve,
Whose Altars reverence, and whose Name I love.

In essence, Charles attacked those who attacked the Church of England, and in defending the church he also tried to defend the Methodists while reproving the schismatics among them along the way. Proven by the quality of her doctrines and the purity of her practices and sealed by the blood of the martyrs, the Church of England is depicted as the *true* Church: "The Church of Christ (let all the Nations own),/The Church of Christ *and England* — is but One!" Charles saw the Methodist revival as a glorious proof that God was reviving and renewing the church. Charles Wesley described himself "As a blind Bigot on the Church's Side," and urged his brother to join him in the cause of renewing and defending the Church of England:

Partner of my Reproach, who justly claim
The larger Portion of the glorious Shame,
My Pattern in the Work and Cause divine,
Say is thy Heart as *biggotted* as mine?
Wilt Thou with me in the Old Church remain,
And share her Weal or Woe, her Loss or Gain.
Spend in her Service thy Last Drop of Blood,
And die — to build the Temple of our GOD?

Charles also suggested that recent developments threatened to derail the Wesleys (and the Methodists) from their original intent — renewing and reviving the Church of England. He pointedly reminded his brother, and other readers, that Methodism was not founded to "Raise a Party, or to found a Sect":

When first sent forth to minister the Word,
Say, did we preach ourselves, or Christ the Lord?
Was it our Aim Disciples to collect,
To raise a Party, or to found a Sect?
No; but to spread the Power of Jesus' Name,
Repair the Walls of our *Jerusalem*,
Revive the Piety of ancient Days,
And fill the Earth with our Redeemer's Praise.

The conference convened at Leeds on Tuesday, May 6, 1755. In his letter of April 23rd Charles Wesley confided to Lady Huntingdon his dread about participating in the event: "Tomorrow I proceed to the Conference with a heavy heart. Yet I must trust in the Lord, that He will look to His own cause." John Wesley, Charles Wesley, and William Grimshaw were present along with three Anglican priests and sixty lay preachers. The importance of the question at hand made it a required attendance for all the Methodist preachers in England. John Wesley read his (now lost) paper, "Ought We to Separate from the Church of England?" and that question was debated for the larger part of three days. John Wesley's journal summarized the events at Leeds in this terse fashion:

Our Conference began at Leeds. The point in which we desired all the preachers to speak their minds at large was, whether we ought to separate from the Church. Whatever was advanced on one side or the other was seriously and calmly considered. And on the third day we were all fully agreed in that general conclusion, that (whether it was *lawful* or not) it was in no way *expedient*.

Charles Wesley, who had apparently left the conference (perhaps in anger) on its third day, wrote to Sally that he was coming home with "good news": "All agreed not to separate. So the wound is healed — slightly. Yet some good news I may bring you from Leeds, if we live a month longer."

Lady Huntingdon was gradually becoming Charles Wesley's

closest friend and confidant as he expressed his opposition to the lay preachers and separation from the Church of England. She was his ally on both fronts, and he confided his inner thoughts and feelings more frankly to her than he did to his own brother. She was trying to keep Charles from taking these disputes with John and the lay preachers personally, as Charles was prone to do. He seemed to consider an attack upon the Church of England as an attack upon himself. On May 30, 1755, for example, he admitted to the Countess of Huntingdon: "You shame me out of the thought that my brother has injured me, but I have adopted your maxim, that ministers (like Kings) can do no wrong."

In this letter dated June 8, 1755, Charles told Lady Huntingdon the approach he had recommended at the Leeds conference regarding the separatist preachers: "I advised him to divide and scatter them. . . . I entreated him to try whether the most simple and unprejudiced preachers might not be set right. He took no thought about it." He had resolved to leave the administration of the Methodist societies to John — and therefore also the blame for direction that the Methodist movement was taking: "I have foreborn mentioning our Conference," Charles admitted, "either in public or in private, referring inquirers to him, leaving the government upon his shoulder. How far I am bound to declare this either to the preachers, to the public, or to him does not yet appear. But this is made plain to me, that *I must keep myself pure*, he is answerable for the consequences, not I."

On June 9, 1755, Charles reported to Lady Huntingdon some startling news that he had received from a lay preacher, John Jones, about his brother: "Mr. Jones assures me that others of our preachers are swiftly following the separatists through my brother's dissimulation — unless he sincerely meant what he said: 'We agree not to separate from the church *as yet*,' 'I allow, that presbyters have a right to ordain,' and that 'T. Walsh, and a *few more*, may be called in an extraordinary way to administer sacraments without any ordination at all.'" The same letter evidenced how deeply the current controversy was coloring Charles's relationship with his brother. It felt like an all-out struggle, with no quarter given and none taken: "I shall continue to honour him before the people," he wrote, "and to *do him all* the service in my power, for Christ and the work's sake. But no quarter do I expect from him, or his implicit followers."

The letters were flying fast and furious between the younger Wesley and the Countess of Huntingdon. Charles wrote again on June 11, indicating that he and John Wesley could not see the results of the Leeds conference in the same light. "He extolls 'the unity, nay and unanimity and the excellent spirit of the p[reacher]s,' at our late Conference. I am astonished at his art of putting out his own eyes and healing a wound slightly." Charles also intimated that he dared not communicate his own fullest thoughts on the matter to his brother: "I think it safest not to trust him with my thoughts lest he should put it quite out of my power to help him in any way." Charles's way of "helping" John was to strongly oppose any of the pragmatic steps that he might take towards separation from the Church of England. Charles thought, perhaps rightly, that if John knew how deeply opposed he was to this entire process, John would no longer take Charles into his confidence and Charles's influence with him would amount to nothing. His June 11 letter also indicates that Charles had begun to consider the course of his own future in the likely event that the Methodists should separate from the Church of England. He had already repeatedly announced that he would leave the Methodists if they left the Church of England, and he remained inclined to *"preach everywhere* as a supernumerary, if not independent."

On June 20, 1755, John Wesley wrote his brother in exasperated tones. Charles had gone ahead and published his *Epistle* despite the fact that, at least in John's view, the issue of separation had been settled at the recent conference. The elder brother asked incredulously, "Do you understand that they all promised by T. Walsh not to administer [the Lord's Supper] even among themselves! I think that an huge point given up — perhaps more than they could give up with a clear conscience." John, upon reflection, also indicated that as compared with the humility of the lay preachers, he was ashamed of the imperious attitude he had displayed at the conference, implying that Charles should reflect upon his own "spirit" as well. John felt caught between Charles Perronet and the lay preachers who wanted to administer the sacrament on the one hand, and his own brother on the other: "Here is C[harles] P[erronet] raving because his friends 'have given up *all*,' and C[harles] W[esley] [raving] because they 'have given up *nothing*.' And I in their midst staring and wondering both at one and the other." Meanwhile, the practical result of the conference was exactly what

Charles Wesley had worked for: "The practical conclusion was, not to separate from the Church. Did we not all agree in this? Surely either you or I must have been asleep; or we could not differ so widely in a matter of fact." John was satisfied and exhausted by this outcome, and hence he told his brother: "I do not want to do anything more unless I could bring them [the lay preachers] over to my opinion. And I am in no haste to do that."

John wrote Charles again three days later, in part to communicate the news that "the Good Bishop of London," Thomas Sherlock (1678-1761), "has excommunicated Mr. Gardiner for preaching without a licence." None of the Methodist lay preachers had Anglican licenses to preach, and under the current circumstances they too might be excommunicated. This certainly would resolve the question of the Methodists separating from the Church of England, hence John concluded: "It is probable the point will now speedily be determined concerning the Church. For if we must either *dissent* or *be silent, Actum est* ["it is all over"]. We have no time to trifle!" Charles paraphrased John's message and sent it along to his friend Lady Huntingdon, adding, "His preachers, I well know, would be overjoyed at a separation — and he would not be sorry."

John remained convinced that his brother was overreacting about the potential for schism. As he wrote to Charles later that June:

> Wherever I have been in England the societies are far more firmly and rationally attached to the Church than ever they were before. I have no fear about this matter. I only fear the preachers' or the people's leaving, not the Church, but the love of God, and inward or outward holiness. To this end I press them forward continually. I dare not, in conscience, spend my time and strength on externals. If (as my Lady [Huntingdon] says) all outward establishments are Babel, so is this establishment [the Church of England]. Let it stand for me. I neither set it up nor pull it down. But let you and I build up the city of God.

Tension between the brothers grew with the imminent arrival of another child for Charles. His wife Sally was expecting, and when the baby, Martha Maria, arrived at the end of June, John expected Charles to be ready to leave home again a month later to go to Cornwall and "see each of the country societies." Unfortunately, the child was seriously ill and lived only about a month. While Charles's journal for this period is missing, subsequent correspondence makes it clear that Charles refused to go to Cornwall as John had requested.

While he did not leave his family, Charles's mind remained on his work. On June 28, three days after the birth of his newest daughter, Charles wrote Lady Huntingdon again. It was already too late to stop the publication of his *Epistle,* and contrary to popular opinion, Charles intimated, he did not write the *Epistle* to embarrass his brother; instead, he wrote it to bear witness to his own testimony. Faced with the looming prospect of the Methodist/Anglican split, Charles was considering serving an Anglican parish, or perhaps some kind of retirement; it was unthinkable to him that he would leave the Church of England and follow the Methodists into separation. Doing so would mean joining with those he did not trust: the lay preachers, his brother, and perhaps worst of all, his sister-in-law Molly Wesley, who further complicated his relationship with his brother: "She stands betwixt [us] and forbids the bands of friendship." Charles's options, as he saw them, involved serving an Anglican parish or joining his old friend George Stonehouse in semi-retirement at rural Dornford, in Oxfordshire. Looking around would lead Charles to other possibilities — as he wrote two weeks later, he knew of "various retreats . . . against the time that my b[rother] casts me off" — but his choices still seemed limited.

John, for his part, believed Charles was acting and writing as if he did not understand the complexities of the issues at hand. Charles was so totally opposed to separation and so blindly committed to the Church of England that he could not see the validity of even scholarly views on the opposite side of the question. John also charged his brother with bigotry: "Your gross bigotry lies here, in putting a man on a level with an adulterer because he differs from you as to church government. . . . What miserable confounding the degrees of good and evil is this?"

To tip the balance against the separation of Methodism from the Church of England, Lady Huntingdon urged Charles to talk to George Whitefield. The Countess promised that Charles would meet a sympathetic ear and a loving heart in his old friend Whitefield; she also believed that the influence of Charles Wesley and George Whitefield, taken together, would more than counterbalance the influence the lay preachers seemed to have over John Wesley. Lady Huntingdon urged:

> I wish you would see Mr. Whitefield and talk matters over with him as he has done that already with your brother. His heart is honest, and he has a truly brotherly love for you and I think I know when he has proved it. I think if your brother found you [two] in friendship then it would keep him in order more than anything. I know he would not like you both to unite against those preachers he espouses, and could this end be obtained all might go on well again.

Charles Wesley continually marshaled support for the Anglican cause within Methodism, and in this mission Rev. Samuel Walker, an evangelical Anglican, became one of his frequent correspondents. On August 7, 1756, Charles wrote to Rev. Walker: "The Lord put it into your heart to speak a word in season to my brother who as you justly express it, was 'almost overcome by his preachers.'" Not only did Charles solicit Walker's help in influencing John to stand firm against the demands of the lay preachers; Charles also enclosed a copy of an agreement that he had drawn up on March 16, 1752. It was made up of two parts; the second part of the "agreement" included a resolution, "Never to leave the communion of the Church of England without the consent of all whose names are subjoined." The agreement was signed by Charles Wesley, John Wesley, and four of the principal lay preachers: William Shent, John Jones, John Downes, and John Nelson. Charles confided to Rev. Walker, "I should have broke off from the Methodists and my brother at that time [1752], but for the above agreement; which I think every preacher should sign or leave us." Charles also told Samuel Walker what he thought his brother should do with respect to the issue at hand:

> To this end, my brother, ought in my judgment, to declare and avow, in the strongest and most explicit manner, his resolution to live and die in the communion of the Church of England. 1. To take all proper pains to instruct and guard both his preachers and flock in the same: a treatise is much needed on this subject, which he

might write and spread through all his societies. 2. To wait with me
upon the Archbishop, who has desired to see him, and tell him our
whole design. 3. To advice, as far as they think proper, with such of
our brethren of the clergy as know the truth, and do nothing without their approbation. . . .

Samuel Walker replied that he and John Wesley had had "a short correspondence last winter, wherein I saw he was greatly pushed by his
preachers, unwilling to part with them, and yet not caring to part from
the Church of England." Once again, Walker pressed the point that "Lay
preachers, being contrary to the constitution of the Church of England,
are, as far as that point goes, a separation from it." So far as Samuel
Walker was concerned, lay preaching was a sticking point that could not
be easily passed. In fact, as long as the Methodists employed lay preachers, they had no right to ask the question whether they should separate
from the church; they had already begun to do so. The real question
then, as Walker saw it, was whether the Methodists would continue
down the path of separation — which they had already chosen — or
take steps to renew their union with the Church of England.

Finally, in 1758 John Wesley published his *Reasons against a Separation from the Church of England*. This was the written declaration of his
sentiments that Charles had been badgering John for. It was only
twenty-two pages long, and in it John sidestepped the question of
whether it was "lawful" for the Methodists to separate, but it satisfied
Charles, and he soon put it to work in his mission to keep the Methodists Anglican. Charles republished *Reasons* in 1760, and he appended
seven of his own poetical compositions. The seventh hymn in this
small collection is entitled "The Preacher's Prayer for the Flock." Comprised of ten verses, it takes on a strongly autobiographical character,
as the "preacher" prays particularly for "The lambs and sheep of *England's* fold":

3. Soon as their guides are taken home,
    We know the grievous wolves will come,
        Determined not to spare;
    The stragglers from Thy wounded side
    The wolves will into sects divide,
        And into parties tear.

4. Even of ourselves shall men arise,
   With words perverse and soothing lies,
      Our children to beset,
   Disciples for themselves to make,
   And draw, for filthy lucre's sake,
      The sheep into their net. . . .

The author's prayer itself actually begins in the seventh verse and continues through to the end:

7. When I, from all my burdens freed,
   Am number'd with the peaceful dead,
      In everlasting rest,
   Pity the sheep I leave behind,
   My God, unutterably kind,
      And lodge them in Thy breast.

8. Ah! never suffer them to leave
   The Church, where Thou art pleased to give
      Such tokens of Thy grace!
   Confirm them in their calling here,
   Till ripe by holiest love to appear
      Before Thy glorious face. . . .

Charles Wesley's love for the Church of England, "the old Ship," was profound. It was one of the fundamental constants of his life. Adam Clarke, one of the early Methodist preachers, recalled, "Mr. J. Wesley *mildly* recommended the people to go to the Church and Sacrament. Mr. C. Wesley threatened them with damnation if they did not."

In light of this, Charles's apparent willingness to put the government of the movement on John's shoulders resolved several questions. It allowed Charles to live a more settled life, caring for the needs of his family and frail health. It also allowed John to skillfully walk the tightrope between lay preaching and separation; this was a balancing act Charles was not emotionally equipped to handle, given his distaste for compromise. Charles's task, as he had come to see it, was less complicated. He intended to keep Methodism from separating from the Anglican communion so long as his brother and he both lived. He intended to "live and die in the Church of England."

15 Perfection

The paper trail for examining Charles Wesley's understanding of sanctification began to emerge during his Oxford years. In 1729 he and a few of his fellows earned themselves the "harmless name of a 'Methodist'" by attending the weekly Eucharist and following the "method of Study prescribed by the University." Also in 1729 Charles read Henry Scougal's devotional classic, *The Life of God in the Soul of Man;* he subsequently loaned the book to George Whitefield and it became the instrument of Whitefield's conversion. Scougal urged: "They who are acquainted with [religion] will . . . disdain all those shadows and fake imitations of it. They know by experience that true religion is an union of the soul with God, a real participation in the Divine nature, the image of God drawn upon the soul, or in the Apostle's phrase, *it is Christ formed within us.*" In describing this real, inward religion as "Divine Life" Scougal pointed both to both its source as well as its nature: "I come next to give an account of why I defined it by the name *Divine Life;* and so it may be called, not only in regard to its fountain and original [sic], having God for its author and being wrought in the souls of men by the power of his Holy Spirit, but also in regard of its nature, religion being a resemblance of the divine perfections, the image of the Almighty shining in the soul of man." In his emphasis upon real, inward religion as a recovery of the image of God, Scougal anticipated some of the central themes of the Wesleyan understanding of sanctification or Christian perfection.

John Wesley's *Plain Account of Christian Perfection* indicates that he (and the rest of the Oxford Methodists) read William Law's *A Practical Treatise On Christian Perfection* about this same time. John intimated that Law's devotional classics "convinced me more than ever, of the absolute impossibility of being half a Christian." In his treatise *On Christian Perfection*, William Law defined his subject in this manner:

> I call it *Perfection* for two reasons, first because I hope it contains a full representation of that height of holiness and purity, to which Christianity calls all its members; secondly, that the title may invite the reader to persue it with the more diligence, as expecting to find not only a discourse upon moral virtue, but a regular draught of those holy tempers which are the perfect measure and standard of Christian piety. . . .

That the Oxford Methodists imbibed the writings of William Law is clear, but we should not assume that the Wesleyan doctrine of Christian perfection came directly from him. Law had simply sharpened the Oxford Methodists' hunger for inner and outer holiness. But reading William Law also set them seeking Christian perfection through their own best efforts and intentions. This caused them some confusion, however, both with respect to their own understanding of salvation and whether they had in fact received it.

On October 21, 1735, aboard the *Simmonds* on his way to Georgia, Charles Wesley wrote and perhaps also preached a sermon based on Philippians 3:13-14. He described his aims in that exposition: "First to show that in this world Christians are never absolutely certain of their crown of reward. Secondly, that it is never to be attained by resting contented with any pitch of piety short of the highest. Thirdly, that a constant progress towards Christian perfection is therefore the indispensable duty of all Christians." In this pre-conversion sermon, Christian perfection is a goal or ideal to be striven for, albeit with one's highest efforts. While Wesley rightly saw Christian perfection as the pinnacle and goal of Christian life, he had a misapprehension as to how a person was to receive it. This was the legacy that William Law and the mystical divine had left him: they had given him a clear vision for the importance of Christian perfection but left him destitute of the actual means for reaching it. As Charles wrote again, later in the same sermon: "Christian perfection is the goal of our religious race; the stand whereon our crown of reward is placed. Hitherto therefore must all our desires be bent; hitherto must all our endeavours tend. To this are all the promises of the gospel made."

Charles's shorthand sermon on "Faith and Good Works," which was based on Titus 3:8, illustrates an important transition. He first preached this sermon on December 21, 1738, at St. Anthony's Church in the Islington section of London. Unlike his earlier sermons, "Faith and Good Works" begins by lauding the doctrine Wesley had learned in his "personal Pentecost," justification by faith alone. "Universal obedience" towards God, "godliness," and living a life that expresses "the whole mind that was in Christ Jesus" were pointed to as the fruit and evidence of justification. Justification preceded and prepared the way for sanctification: "First we are to insist that a man is justified, that is, forgiven and accounted righteous by grace only through faith, exclusive of all works and righteousness of his own; then, that he is to evidence this justification by universal obedience; by continually exercising himself unto godliness; by expressing the whole mind that was in Christ Jesus."

Two other extant Charles Wesley sermons figure materially in his description of sanctification or Christian perfection. The first of these is "The Single Eye," based on Matthew 6:22, 23 ("The light of the body is the eye; if therefore thine eye be single, thy whole body shall be full of light. But if thine eye be evil, thy whole body shall be full of darkness"). Charles preached it in America and in England, both before and after his "personal Pentecost." Purity of intention was to be found in not being "divided between two ends; if in all thy thoughts, words and works thou hast one only view, namely to serve and please God: 'thy whole body shall be full of light.'" This light shines upon the way of sanctification: "This single intention will be a light in all thy paths; all darkness and doubt will vanish before it. All will be plain before thy face. Thou will clearly see the way wherein thou shouldst go, and steadily walk in it." On the other hand, "if thou aimest at anything besides the one thing needful, namely a recovery of the image of God; 'thy whole body shall be full of darkness'; thou wilt see no light, which way soever thou turnest."

"The One Thing Needful" is another early Charles Wesley sermon that sheds light on his doctrine of sanctification. The sermon was based on Luke 10:42 and was copied (like the previous sermon) from John Wesley's manuscripts. Charles preached it both before and after his conversion experience, and hence he continued to find import in its description of sanctification.

Charles often considered sanctification or Christian perfection to be the recovery of the image of God, in which all humans had been created. This was an utterly unqualified conception of perfection which roughly paralleled the "original righteousness" in which humans were first created. Charles considered this recovery of the "image of God" to be the "one thing needful": "To recover our first estate, from which we are thus fallen, is the one thing now needful — to re-exchange the image of Satan for the image of God, bondage for freedom, sickness for health. Our one great business is to erase out of our souls the likeness of our destroyer, and to be born again, to be formed anew after the likeness of our Creator."

Since love is both the image and nature of God, an infusion of God's love is able to transform the human soul into its pristine state: "love is the health of the soul, the full exertion of all its power, the perfection of all its faculties. Therefore, since the enjoyment of these was the one end of our creation, the recovery of them is the one thing needful." This "renewal of our nature in this love" is the chief end of our creation and redemption, as well as "all the providences of God over us, and all the operations of his Spirit in us, must be, as the Eternal Wisdom of God hath declared, the one thing needful."

In sanctification, the "one thing needful" (the restoration of the image of God within) becomes the focus of our "single eye." Wesley urged, "On this then let us fix our single view, our pure unmixed intention; regarding nothing at all small or great, but as it stands referred to this. We must use any means; but let us ever remember we have but one end. For as while our eye is single our whole body will be full of light, so should it ever cease to be single, in that moment our whole body would be full of darkness."

The terminology surrounding the Wesleyan conception of sanctification as Christian perfection sounds extravagant and unguarded. This was due, in large part, to the Wesleys' penchant for using Bible words to describe Bible doctrines. The concept was based on scriptural passages like Matthew 5:48, "Be ye therefore perfect, even as your Father which is in heaven is perfect"; Hebrews 13:20-21, "Now the God of peace . . . make you perfect in every good work to do his will, working in you that which is well pleasing in his sight, through Jesus Christ"; and 1 John 4:18, "There is no fear in love; but perfect love casteth out fear; because fear hath torment. He that feareth is not made perfect in love." In these instances and many others the English word "perfect" stands for a New Testament Greek word from the *telos* family; these also carry the connotation of "whole, complete, or mature." So this kind of "perfection" was being made "whole" or "complete" by the renewing work of God within a person. It was not the perfection of moral effort or attainment, but rather the restoration of the image of God within through an invasion of the Holy Spirit and an infusion of divine love. Charles offered this description of Christian perfection in his journal entry for Monday, September 26, 1740: ". . . utter dominion over sin, constant peace, and love and joy in the Holy Ghost; the full assurance of faith, righteousness, and true holiness."

In his hymns and sacred poems Wesley wove a variety of images and metaphors together to describe a sanctification that was whole or complete (1 Thessalonians 5:23), and in that sense "perfect." His poetical commentary upon Jeremiah 4:14, "Wash thine heart, that thou mayest be saved," is an apt example of the parallelism Charles developed between Christian perfection and sanctification:

    1. FAIN would I wash my soul from sin,
        In Jesu's wounded side,
    From all the lusts that lodge within,
        The spawn of self and pride.
    I would be clean, Thou know'st I would,
        Before I hence depart,
    And feel the sprinkling of that blood
        Which purifies the heart.

    2. But what Thou didst for sinners shed,
        Thou only canst apply,
    And purge whom Thine own hands have made,
        From crimes of deepest dye.
    Thou wilt blot out th'engrafted stain,

My nature's filthiness;
   Nor let one evil thought remain,
     To violate my peace.

3. Enabled by Thy word, I rise
   And wash my sins away;
  Strong in the life Thy death supplies
   I for salvation pray.
 I pray, believing that Thy blood
   Its full effect may have,
 And bring me sanctified to God,
   And to perfection save.

4. Selfish and vain desires in me
   Shall never more reside,
  When Thou, with all Thy purity,
   Dost in my heart abide.
 Thy uttermost salvation then
   I in Thy presence prove:
 The crown of righteousness obtain,
   The heights and depths of love.

This prayer for perfection includes several typical Wesleyan emphases: the purification of the human heart by Jesus' saving blood, blotting out the stain of original sin, removing evil and selfish thoughts, the granting of inner peace, and filling with love. Charles stressed that the process of sanctification led to Christian perfection or "full salvation" because it was the completion of the saving work and purpose of God. It meant an undoing of the effects of the Edenic Fall and its ensuing corruption of human nature through an invasion of divine love that healed a divided mind and gave a "single eye." The Holy Spirit accomplished this transformation (which began with New Birth) by unifying one's inner life through a purifying infusion of God's love. This transformation and restoration was "the one thing needful," since it completed God's saving intention and brought wholeness to the Christian's life by casting out fear, selfishness, and sin as the Holy Spirit dwelt within the Christian's heart and the mind of Christ was formed within.

The following hymn, which was jointly published by the Wesley brothers in *Hymns and Sacred Poems* (1740), was written by Charles during this period. We know that this hymn was one of his early compositions because of various internal factors, most notably the use of the word "dear" in verse 3; this was a term that John Wesley studiously avoided in his hymns and often edited out of Charles's compositions. Based on Isaiah 45:22, "Look unto Me, and be saved, all ye ends of the earth," this hymn places the Scripture text upon the lips of Jesus Christ, and the risen Lord establishes a poetical dialogue between himself and the singer of the hymn. The hymn teaches justification by faith and grace, the "once for all" atonement of Christ, and lauds the cleansing power of his cross. "Justified, we ask for more," that is, for sanctification, which in verse 5 is described as the restoration of the divine image. Verses 6-7 seem to suggest that entire sanctification, salvation "to the utmost," occurs as a person enters Christ's heavenly presence.

1. Sinners, your Saviour see!
      O, look ye unto Me!
   Lift your eyes, ye fallen race!
      I, the gracious God and true,
   I am full of truth and grace,
      Full of truth and grace for you!

2. Look, and be saved from sin!
      Believe, and be ye clean!
   Guilty, labouring souls draw nigh;
      See the fountain open'd wide;
   To the wounds of Jesus fly,
      Bathe ye in My bleeding side.

3. Ah, dear, redeeming Lord,
      We take Thee at Thy word.
   Lo! to Thee we ever look,
      Freely saved by grace alone;
   Thou our sins and curse hast took;
      Thou for all didst once atone.

4. We now the writing see
    Nail'd to Thy cross with Thee!
With Thy mangled body torn,
    Blotted out by blood Divine;
Far away the bond is borne;
    Thou art ours, and we are Thine.

5. On Thee we fix our eyes,
    And wait for fresh supplies;
Justified, we ask for more,
    Give th'abiding Spirit, give;
Lord, Thine image here restore,
    Fully in Thy members live.

6. Author of Faith, appear!
    Be Thou its Finisher.
Upward still for This we gaze,
    Till we feel the stamp Divine,
Thee behold with open face,
    Bright in all Thy glory shine.

7. Leave not Thy work undone,
    But ever love Thine own.
Let us all Thy goodness prove,
    Let us to the end believe;
Show Thy everlasting love;
    Save us, to the utmost save. . . .

On Friday May 1, 1741, Charles's journal reports, "I visited a sister dying in the Lord; and then two others, one mourning after, then rejoicing in, God her Saviour. I found sister Hooper sick of love. Her body too, sunk under it." After visiting Mrs. Hooper several times, Wesley was at her side, on May 6, when she died, and he believed he had witnessed an example of Christian perfection: "My soul was tenderly affected for her sufferings, yet the joy swallowed up the sorrow. How much more then did *her* consolations abound! The servants of Christ suffer nothing. I asked her whether she was not in great pain. 'Yes,' she answered, 'but in greater joy. I would not be without either.'

'But do you not prefer life to death?' She replied, 'All is alike to me; let Christ choose; I have no will of my own.' This is that holiness, or absolute resignation, or Christian perfection!" Utter consecration, or resignation of the self to the will of God, was an aspect of the "single eye" that led to holiness. In "A Funeral Hymn for Mrs. Hooper," which was published in his *Hymns and Sacred Poems* (1742), Charles celebrated Mrs. Hooper's victorious death and Christian perfection:

> 4. In her no spot of sin remain'd,
>   To shake her confidence in God;
> The victory here she more than gain'd,
>   Triumphant through her Saviour's blood.

> 5. She now the fight of faith hath fought,
>   Finish'd and won the Christian race;
> She found on earth the Lord she sought,
>   And now beholds Him face to face.

> 6. She died in sure and steadfast hope,
>   By Jesus wholly sanctified;
> Her perfect spirit she gave up,
>   And sunk into His arms, and died.

> 7. Thus may we all our parting breath
>   Into the Saviour's hands resign:
> O Jesu, let me die her death,
>   And let her latter end be mine!

The Wesleyan hymns of the early 1740s were notable for their longing for sanctification. The original compositions, which are attributed to Charles (whereas the translations and adaptations are generally attributed to John), often used the language of pilgrimage and the imagery of a quest to describe their passion for holiness. This emphasis continued in *Hymns and Sacred Poems* (1742), which included several groups of hymns on sanctification: hymns on "Desiring to Love," "Groaning for Redemption," and "Waiting for the Promise." These hymns are full of expectancy and aspiration for perfect love, full salvation, Christian perfection, and a restoration of the image of God within

Christians by the work of the Holy Spirit. This same pattern was continued in the Wesleys' *Moral and Sacred Poems* (1744), which offered a similar series of hymns under the title "Desiring to Be Dissolved." *Hymns of Petition and Thanksgiving for the Promise of the Father,* which was published in 1746, is also about sanctification, because — drawing upon the description of Acts 2:33 — "the promise of the Father" meant the sending of the Holy Spirit into the hearts and lives of believers to utterly transform them. The fourth hymn is representative of many others. Based on Bible texts from John 14–16, it promises that the Holy Spirit comes to dwell in Christians, form Christ within, cleanse them, sanctify them, and prepare them for heaven:

1. Sinners, lift up your hearts.
       The PROMISE to receive!
   Jesus Himself imparts,
       He comes in man to live;
   The Holy Ghost to man is given;
   Rejoice in God sent down from heaven.

2. Jesus is glorified,
       And gives the Comforter
   His Spirit, to reside
       In all His members here:
   The Holy Ghost to man is given;
   Rejoice in God sent down from heaven.

3. To make an end of sin,
       And Satan's works destroy,
   He brings His kingdom in,
       Peace, righteousness, and joy
   The Holy Ghost to man is given;
   Rejoice in God sent down from heaven.

4. The cleansing blood to apply,
       The heavenly life display,
   And wholly sanctify,
       And seal us to that day,
   The Holy Ghost to man is given;
   Rejoice in God sent down from heaven. . . .

6. From heaven He shall once more
    Triumphantly descend,
And all His saints restore
    To joys that never end:
Then, then, when all our joys are given,
Rejoice in God, rejoice in heaven.

Hymns For Those That Seek and Those That Have Redemption in the Blood of Jesus Christ (1747) continued this line of development by extending the quest for holiness into the daily lives of many types of people. A collection of "occasional hymns," these compositions explore what sanctification looks like in everyday life; hence there are hymns "For a Believer, in Worldly Business," "On the Death of a Child," and "At Meeting of Friends." "For a Minister of Christ" is illustrative of many others as it sings of the saving power of God and the cleansing effects of Jesus' blood:

4. This is the saving power of God:
    Whoe'er this word receive,
Feel all th'effects of Jesu's blood,
    And *sensibly* believe:
Saved from the guilt and power of sin
    By instantaneous grace,
They trust to have Thy *life brought in,*
    And *always* see Thy face.

5. The pure in heart Thy face shall see
    Before they hence remove,
Redeemed from all iniquity,
    And perfected in love.
This is the great salvation! This
    The prize at which we aim,
The end of faith, the hidden bliss,
    The new mysterious name. . . .

This line of development reached its climax in Charles Wesley's two-volume *Hymns and Sacred Poems* of 1749. The hymnal was hastily built out of Charles's manuscripts and published without John Wesley's editorial approval or emendations as Charles rushed to earn some of the "bride price" he needed to marry Sally Gwynne that year. Many of the hymns in the 1749 edition were written years before. The second volume in the 1749 *Hymns and Sacred Poems* carried two series of hymns that evidenced Charles's own distinctive theological emphases (since they had escaped John's editorial pen) with respect to sanctification. The first series was entitled "The Trial of Faith." These fifteen hymns described the purifying effects of inward anguish and outward suffering. Typically, these hymns looked to Jesus Christ as a pattern for those who sought to understand the sanctifying effects of suffering:

1. Saviour of all, what hast Thou done,
    What hast Thou suffer'd on the tree?
   Why didst Thou groan Thy moral goran,
    Obedient unto death for me?
   The mystery of Thy passion show
   The end of all Thy griefs below.

2. Thy soul for sin an offering made
    Hath clear'd this guilty soul of mine;
   Thou hast for me a ransom paid,
    To change my human to Divine,
   To cleanse from all iniquity,
   And make the sinner all like Thee.

3. Pardon, and grace, and heaven to buy,
    My bleeding Sacrifice expired;
   But didst Thou not my pattern die,
    That by Thy glorious Spirit fired,
   Faithful I might to death endure,
   And make the crown by suffering sure? . . .

5. Thy every perfect servant, Lord,
    Shall as his patient Master be,
   To all Thine inward life restored,
    And outwardly conform'd to Thee,
   Out of Thy grave the saint shall rise,
   And grasp through death the glorious prize. . . .

Another hymn in this series raised John Wesley's editorial ire when he subsequently saw it. When Charles wrote

3. No, Thou gracious God and true,
    Thy promise cannot fail,
Thou at last shall bring me through
    The toils of sin and hell:
This from Thee even now I have —
    If Thou art not always nigh,
    If Thou canst not, wilt not save,*
Let me for ever die.

John penned an editorial "Too bold" into the manuscript at the point of the asterisk. While it is likely he did not like Charles setting a time-table for when and how God might save, it is also clear that he would not have liked the connection his brother drew between suffering the "toils of sin and hell" and the resultant salvation.

The second series, "Hymns For Those That Wait For Full Redemption," also prefigured a point at which John and Charles Wesley would differ regarding Christian perfection. "Full redemption" was another Wesleyan euphemism for entire sanctification or Christian perfection. These hymns were about salvation being a full liberation from all sin, both its guilt and its power. The first hymn in this series aptly illustrates the tone of many others:

7. Come, Jesus, and cleanse
    My Inbred offence,
O take the occasion of stumbling from hence,
    The infection within,
    The *possible sin*
Extirpate, by bringing Thy righteousness *in.*

8. By all Thou hast done
    For me to atone,
By all Thou hast suffer'd to make me Thine own,
    By all which Thou art,
    I beseech Thee, convert,
And renew, and eternally reign in my heart.

His 1749 collection of *Hymns and Sacred Poems* shows Charles Wesley dealing with the doctrine of full redemption or Christian perfection in his own way and on his own terms. He had begun to connect it with human suffering, and while he expected it primarily in the "article of death," he also saw the dangers of limiting God's work in a person's life by seeing only at the edge of life. In these hymns, Charles Wesley's singers are urged to press ardently on towards perfection, hoping — even expecting — to receive it *here*.

By late 1760 and early 1761 a major controversy was brewing in early Methodism. The issue this time was Christian perfection as entire sanctification. A few Methodist people in Otley, Yorkshire, professed entire sanctification — "being saved from all sin" — and this witness soon spread to London. On January 18, 1760, John Wesley reported in his journal, "I desired those who believed they were saved from sin (sixteen or seventeen in number) to meet me at noon, to whom I gave such cautions and instructions as I judged needful." These people believed that they had original sin, "the root of bitterness," removed from their inner life; they felt themselves to be sanctified in body, soul, and spirit. In Leeds, on March 12, John met with a number of people drawn from neighboring towns "who believed they were saved from sin." He reported their testimony in this manner: "(1) that they *feel* no inward sin and, to the best of their knowledge, *commit* no outward sin; (2) that they *see* and *love* God every moment and 'pray, rejoice and give thanks evermore'; and (3) that they have constantly as clear a *witness* from God of sanctification as they have of justification." John believed these testimonies were so "plain" that they were either true or were "wilful and deliberate lies." A year later, on March 6, 1761, John Wesley was back in London meeting with about forty people "who believe God has delivered them from the root of bitterness. Their number increases daily. I know not if fifteen or sixteen have not received the blessing this week."

Peter Jacko wrote to Charles Wesley on September 5, 1761, to report the results of the recent Methodist annual conference. Regrettably the minutes from this session are not extant, but it is clear Christian perfection figured largely in their conversations. Jacko wrote, "It is determined that there are no texts of Scripture which will absolutely support instantaneous Perfection; that there is no state in this world which will absolutely exempt the person in it from sin and that therefore they have need of caution and etc. These are some of the conclusions we came to. The rest, I suppose, your Brother will tell you soon." Jacko's note on this topic ended ominously: "Whether he and the rest of the contenders on the other side of the question will abide by these conclusions time will determine." Jacko's report implies that John Wesley was one of those who maintained that Christian perfection could be received in an instant. In fact John had written to the schismatic Thomas Maxfield, on November 25, 1762, "I like your doctrine of *perfection*, or pure love — love excluding sin. Your insisting that it is merely by *faith;* that consequently it is *instantaneous* (though preceded and followed by a gradual work), and that it may be *now,* at this instant."

John Wesley's letters and journal depict him trying to steer a middle course between an exuberant acceptance of these claims to Christian perfection, for fear of the growth of fanaticism (or "enthusiasm" in eighteenth-century religious parlance), and opposing them outright, for fear of losing the Methodist hope that God can deliver a person from willful sin in this life. He wrote a letter to the Methodists in Otley, dated July 7, 1761, in which he reminded them that "The perfection I teach, is perfect love; loving God with all the heart: receiving Christ as Prophet, Priest, and King, to reign alone over all our thoughts, words, and actions." In the same letter Wesley urged that it was a mistake to think that this sort of perfection could not occur in this life: "To say, that Christ will not reign alone in our hearts, *in this life,* will not enable us to give Him *all* our hearts. This, in my judgment, is making Him *half* a Saviour; He can be no more, if He does not *quite save* us from our sins." John did not sound overly distressed as he wrote his ailing brother Charles on December 26, 1761, "We are always in danger of enthusiasm; but I think no more now than any time in these twenty years. The word of God runs indeed, and loving faith spreads on every side."

Fanaticism did, however, soon rear its head in the London Methodist Society, due in part to the leadership of Thomas Maxfield and George Bell. The latter was especially given to extraordinary claims, including setting a date for the end of the world: February 28, 1763. By that time Thomas Maxfield had distanced himself from the extravagant claims of George Bell, but others would not. William Grimshaw had written John Wesley to warn him, on July 23, 1761, that some of the Methodist preachers taught that "He is a child of the devil, who disbelieves the doctrine of sinless perfection; and he is no true Christian, who has not attained it." Thomas Maxfield, George Bell, and others had preached and professed that by faith a person could be made "as perfect as an angel." On November 2, 1762, John Wesley wrote Maxfield an extensive epistle outlining what he liked and what he disliked about the latter's preaching on perfection. Wesley warned, "I dislike your supposing man may be perfect 'as an angel'; that he can be *absolutely* perfect; that he can be *infallible,* or above being *tempted;* or that the moment he is pure in heart he *cannot fall* from it."

Maxfield and the others had missed some of the subtlety of John Wesley's doctrine of Christian perfection. Wesley did not preach freedom from sin in an absolute sense; his was a *relative* perfection, a perfection in love that transformed the inner person to the degree that a person did not commit *intentional* sin. Hence, a person was delivered from the dominion of sin in heart and will but was not free from unintentional sin, or from human ignorance and error. Wesley's Christian perfection was a purity of heart that affected and improved a person's outward life but did not guarantee perfect performance or behavior.

Smarting under the criticism of George Whitefield, Martin Madan, and probably also his brother Charles, that he had dallied too long with the fanaticism of George Bell and the others, John Wesley published a letter in the January 8, 1763, edition of the *London Chronicle* in which he announced Bell and his followers were not part of the Methodist movement:

> One Bell, said to be a Lifeguardsman, holds forth to an assembly, near Hanover Square. He is supposed to belong to the Methodists; but he advances things which many Methodists abhor. Nevertheless his delusions spread. Many of his followers think themselves perfect, and declare they shall never die, "because," as they say, "our dear Lord, who certainly will come a second time, is at the door and we shall see him come."

But the damage had already been done. As John Wesley was forced to admit, "They made the very name of Perfection stink in the nostrils even of those who loved and honoured it before."

Charles Wesley's role in the controversy over Christian perfection is difficult to document, in large part because his journal from this period of time is not extant. It is likely that he believed his brother was being duped by the pretenders to perfection; it is certain that he was no friend to their views on perfection or to their religious fanaticism. The early Methodist preacher Joseph Clowney remembered that Charles, "from the beginning, had been in opposition to George Bell and his associates." On February 1, 1763, Charles wrote to Clowney to report: "Sad havock Satan has made of the flock, since you and I were first acquainted." Charles went on, "I had a warning four years ago of that flood of enthusiasm which has now overflowed us, and of the sect of ranters that should arise out of the Perfect witnesses. My late hymns are a farther standing testimony."

Indeed, Charles Wesley's hymns were his chief testimony during this debate, and they evidence the fact that he and his brother John had developed differing doctrines of Christian perfection. In 1762, in the midst of the controversy over Christian perfection, Charles Wesley published his *Short Hymns on Select Passages of Scripture*. In the "Preface" to this work Charles indicated that he intended to address the topic of Christian perfection in these hymns. "Several of the hymns," he wrote, "are intended to prove, and several to guard, the doctrines of Christian Perfection, I durst not publish the one without the other." Charles admitted that he was using strong language to chastise "Enthusiasts and Antinomians, who not living up to their profession, give abundant occasion to them that seek it, and cause the truth to be evil spoken of." In Charles's *Short Hymns* his distinctive emphases on Christian perfection came to the forefront. They are easily traced since John Wesley did not see the manuscript prior to publication and subsequently annotated it with comments about hymns he did not like. Three specific questions emerged between the Wesley brothers on the topic of Christian perfection: (1) Was Charles setting the doctrine of perfection too "high"? (2) Was Christian perfection an instantaneous blessing or was it received gradually over the course of an entire life? And (3) did perfection occur in the hour of death, or before? Charles's *Short Hymns* evidence that he took the opposite point of view from that of his brother on each of these three questions.

In a letter he wrote to Dorthy Furly, dated September 15, 1762, John Wesley stressed that Christian perfection is "an instantaneous deliverance from all sin," but that this was a qualified perfection not inconsistent "with living in a corruptible body; for this makes it impossible 'always to think right.' While we breathe we shall more or less mistake. If, therefore, Christian perfection implies this, we must not expect it till after death." Four years later John wrote his brother Charles to express his concern about Charles's approach: "One word more, concerning setting perfection too high. *That perfection* which I believe, I can boldly preach, because I think I see five hundred witnesses of it. Of *that perfection* which you preach, you do not even think you see any witnesses at all. . . . Therefore I still think to set perfection *so high* is effectually to renounce it." The same letter indicted Charles's hymns as culprits in the debacle surrounding Thomas Maxfield and the pretenders to Christian perfection: "When your hymns on one hand were added to his talking and acting on the other, what was likely to be the consequence?"

We have seen that, almost from the beginning of his ministry, Charles Wesley looked upon Christian perfection as the "one thing needful," a restoration of the image of God within a person. Seemingly reacting to the charge that this unqualified kind of perfection is impossible, Charles's "Short Hymn" on Matthew 5:48 ("Be Ye Perfect . . .") argues for its actual possibility:

1. Would'st Thou require what cannot be?
   The thing impossible to me
     Is possible with God:
   I trust Thy truth to make me just,
   Th'omnipotence of love I trust,
     The virtue of Thy blood.

2. Perfection is my calling's prize,
   To which on duty's scale I rise;
     And when my toils are pass'd
   And when I have the battle won,
   Thou in Thy precious Self alone,
     Shalt give the prize at last.

Where John Wesley was more apt to stress the instantaneous reception of Christian perfection in this life, Charles had come to emphasize the gradual work of Christian perfection that went on till a person laid down his or her life in death. Many of Charles's *Short Hymns* exemplified this emphasis. In Charles's hymn on Joshua 6:20, for example, Joshua's seven marches around the walls of Jericho became a metaphor for the lifelong quest for sanctification:

> Then let us urge our way,
>   And work, and suffer on,
>   Nor dream, the first, or second day
>   Will throw the bulwarks down:
>   We on the sacred morn
>   Our seventh toil repeat,
>   Expecting that the latest turn
>   Our labour shall complete.*

John Wesley editorialized "When God pleases!" at the point of the asterisk above; he reacted negatively to his brother implying that God would not give perfection in this life. Indeed, "gradual" was becoming one of Charles's favorite descriptions for Christian perfection:

> Shall we mistake the morning-ray
> Of grace for the full blaze of day?
> Or humbly walk in Jesu's sight,
> Glad to receive the *gradual* light*
> More of His grace and more to know,
> In faith and in experience grow,
> Till all the life of Christ we prove,
> And *lose ourselves* in perfect love!

John Wesley wrote: "And the Sudden!" at the asterisk in this hymn.

The six days of creation (Gen. 2:1) also reminded Charles Wesley of the gradual growth into Christian perfection:

> Who madest thus the earth and skies,
>   A world, a six days work of Thine,
>   Thou bidd'st the new creation rise,
>   Nobler effect of grace Divine!
>   We might spring up at Thy command,
>   For glory in an instant meet;
>   But by Thy will at last we stand
>   In *gradual holiness* complete.

Charles's poetical comment on Matthew 20:22 ("Ye know not what ye ask") was even more strident in its affirmation of a gradual perfection that was fully realized only in death:

1. ADVANCEMENT in Thy Kingdom here
   Whoe'er impatiently desire,
   They know not, Lord, the pangs severe,
   The trials which they *first* require:
   They all *must* first Thy sufferings share,
   Ambitious of their calling's prize,
   And every day Thy burden bear,
   And thus to *late* perfection rise.

2. Nature would fain evade, or flee
   That sad necessity of pain;
   But who refuse to die with Thee,
   With Thee shall never, never reign:
   The sorrow doth the joy ensure,
   The crown for conquerors prepared;
   And all who to the end endure,
   And grasp through death the full reward.*

At the asterisk, John Wesley wrote on this manuscript: "Not until Death?"

Charles left many of his *Short Hymns* in his manuscripts unpublished, perhaps because of their harsh and angry tone against the pretenders to Christian perfection. Their prideful claims combined with the utter inconsistency of their lives made these pretenders (such as Bell and Maxfield) odious to Wesley. In this verse the aged saint is characterized by humility that forbids him or her to claim Christian perfection, whereas a "youngling" is full of pride and conceit, and claims it too soon and too readily:

He will not speak a gracious word
   The aged follower of his Lord,
Ready for Jesus' sake to die,
   Declares "the chief of sinners!"
But now we hear a youngling say,

"Pardon'd and perfect'd in a day,
The chief of saints adore in me!"

Two published "Short Hymns" based on Hebrews 6:1, "Let us go onto perfection," illustrate Charles's frustration with those who mistakenly thought they could be made perfect in a brief period of time, with no effort on their own part. In the first of these, the "voice" of the hymn belongs to the pretender of Christian perfection, who gives expression to "our hasty nature":

"Go on? but how? from step to step?
No; let *us* to perfection *leap!*"
'Tis thus our hasty nature cries,
Leap o'er the cross, to snatch the prize,
Like *Jonah's* gourd, displays its bower,
And blooms, and withers, in an hour.

In the second hymn based on this verse, the "old apostles" are contrasted to "delusion's ranting sons" (like Bell and Maxfield) because of their willingness to claim perfection in this life:

Which of the *old* apostles taught
Perfection in an instant caught,
Show'd *our* compendious manner how,
"Believe, and ye are perfect *now*;
This moment wake, and seize the prize;
Reeds, into sudden pillars rise";
Believe delusion's ranting sons,
And all the work is done at once!

On July 1, 1764, Charles wrote to Joseph Clowney about his own role in putting out the flames of controversy over Christian perfection. Charles pointed Clowney to his hymns of this period as being illustrative of his "private judgment and mind" on this matter. He believed his side was winning the battle: "When I left London last year, the number of witnesses [to instantaneous perfection] was 500. Half of them have since recanted. Those who live another year may expect to see them all convinced of their own great imperfection."

John Wesley would continue to try to draw Charles closer to his own expressions and formulations of Christian perfection, most notably in his letter of January 27, 1767, in which the elder Wesley sought to build consensus between himself and his brother on "the thing, the manner, and the time" of Christian perfection. But by 1767 it must have been clear to John, as it was to most people in the Methodist movement, that he and his brother, while being in fundamental agreement about the nature of Christian perfection, preferred to emphasize opposite aspects of it. Where John had come to stress a qualified conception of perfection that could and should be expected *now*, instantaneously, Charles preferred to emphasize an unqualified perfection ("the one thing needful") that was gradually received over the course of a Christian's life and most fully experienced when he or she laid the mortal body down in death.

The controversies over the separation from the Church of England and Christian perfection shook Methodism throughout the 1760s. In the face of so much controversy, the fact that Charles seemed prone to take his own path did not help create unity and harmony within the movement. His single-minded loyalty to the Church of England and his willingness to sacrifice the lay preachers if necessary eroded some of Charles's influence with the Methodists — and some of his brother's confidence in him. This, coupled with Charles's virtual withdrawal from the itinerant aspects of his ministry, caused John to try to pull him into closer union and cooperation with him. In his letter of May 14, 1768, for example, John Wesley confided to his brother: "I am at my wits end with regard to two things — The Church, and Christian perfection." John's solution to this dilemma was for him and Charles to stand shoulder to shoulder, and work together: "Unless both you and I stand in the gap in good earnest, the Methodists will drop them both [the Church and Christian perfection]. Talking will not avail. We must *do*, or be borne away. Will you set shoulder to shoulder? If so think deeply upon the matter, and tell me what can be done." John's parting line in Latin, *age, vir esto! Nervos intendas as tuos* ["Come, be a man! Stretch your nerves"] — was a call to action. While Charles was always ready to join his brother in opposing the schismatics and moderating the perfectionists, by the end of the decade Charles's ministry was no longer his sole focus in life. Now his poetry and his burgeoning family claimed a larger portion of his time and attention.

16 Poet Laureate

Charles Wesley's hymns provided the soundtrack for the Wesleyan revival. He was a capable keyboard musician; a harpsichord stands in the "music room" of their little house in Bristol, where Sally taught the children to play. A small, single-rank pipe organ that belonged to Charles is nestled in the corner of the "Foundery Room" at Wesley's Chapel on City Road, London. But so far as we know, Charles composed no original music, though he might have adapted contemporary music to fit the meter of his hymns. Known chiefly as a lyricist, Wesley is well described as the poet laureate of Methodism.

Charles Wesley's hymns gave creative expression to the central themes of the Methodist movement. In many instances the hymns amount to poetical commentaries on specific Bible verses. In other instances they give voice to Wesleyan doctrines, often as seen through specific instances in Charles Wesley's life. In this way, the Wesleyan hymns are much more than background music for the Wesleyan revival; they are a central part of the event itself. A cursory examination of their many uses bears this out. Not only were Wesley's hymns an autobiographic window into Charles's spiritual pilgrimage; they were aids to Wesleyan worship, tools of Christian education, and weapons of Wesleyan evangelism. Often the sermon text that Wesley contemplated for the next day's engagement became, in his meditative preparation, the point of departure for a hymn. He subsequently sang the hymn before the congregation or multitude (if they gathered outdoors), to announce the beginning of the evangelistic service. It was "given out" to the people by singing it in a dialogue format, as Wesley "lined it out" for them and they sang it back to him. Sometimes Charles's hymns were used as an "invitation" whereby seekers were enjoined to make a profession of faith and "receive the atonement" of Christ. They were also the means for teaching unlettered people basic Christian theology.

Generally speaking, Charles Wesley has been overlooked as the cofounder of Methodism and a creative formulator of Wesleyan theology. John Earnest Rattenbury, who gave Charles Wesley's theology its first sustained and original treatment in 1941, readily admitted that "in the conventional use of the term, he was not a formal theologian. He cannot be classed as of the same calabre as Augustine, Anselm, Aquinas, Calvin, or Schleiermacher." But Rattenbury rightly argued that to diminish Charles Wesley's role as a theologian on that account was to understand the term "theologian" too narrowly. He concluded that Charles Wesley was indeed a theologian, one who created, crafted, and communicated theological doctrines in a more creative and original medium than more "formal" theologians do — "an experimental theologian." More recent research, such as that by Teresa Berger, in her *Theology in Hymns?* has demonstrated that Charles's hymns are theological statements in the form of first-order language. In Berger's view, Charles Wesley's theology and his role as a theologian are best understood in terms of theology as doxology. This means, in part, that theological affirmations (shaped in the form of acts of praise) directed *to* God are every bit as important as vehicles of theology as more studied statements *about* God. This form of theology — one that speaks *to* and not simply *about* God — is, as we shall see, a particularly apt approach for understanding and doing Wesleyan theology.

Religious experience was an important part of the process that Charles Wesley used in his sermons and songs. The language of poetry is not the same as the language of philosophical syllogism or theological diatribe; it is the language of experience, imagination, and adoration, but it is theological language nonetheless. By uniting heart and mind in an act of praise and adoration, Wesley's hymns cause the singer to participate in and to experience the gospel's truths in a way that sterile theological definitions do not. Indeed, Charles Wesley wrote his hymns, as T. S. Gregory pointed out, "not only to express but to induce the experience they reveal." In sermon and in song, Charles Wesley intended to communicate biblical teaching in a way that causes singers to replicate the Bible's Christian experiences. This "experimental" or experiential religion played an important role in the function of Charles's hymns and his theology. This function was signaled in John Wesley's famous preface to the 1780 *Collection of Hymns for the Use of the People Called Methodists*, in which Wesley described the hymnal as a "a little body of experimental and practical divinity":

> It is large enough to contain all the important truths of our most holy religion, whether speculative or practical; yea, to illustrate them all, and to prove them both by Scripture and reason. And this is done in regular order. The hymns are not carelessly jumbled together, but carefully arranged under proper heads, according to the experience of real Christians. So that this book is, in effect, a little body of experimental and practical divinity.

That religious reformers of the stature of John and Charles Wesley would encapsulate their reform in something as mundane as a hymnbook is one surprise; that they would be willing to call a collection of hymns "a body of experimental and practical divinity" is quite another. This tells us something quite explicit about Wesleyan theology; it is "practical divinity"; something that is formed and shaped according "to the experience of real Christians." Their emphasis upon the experimental dimension of Christian theology demanded that Wesleyan theology be formed in the crucible of Christian living, and Charles Wesley's hymns were among the main tools in this process. These hymns were formed and tested by lived Christian experience, and they were constructed in such a way as to actually induce the experiences they described.

The Wesleys were a family of poets. Charles's father, Samuel Wesley Sr., wrote religious poems, several of which his son John turned into hymns. At least one of these, "Behold the Savior of Mankind," which John published as "The Crucifixion," continues in modern hymnals. Samuel Wesley Jr. established a significant reputation as a poet and epigramist. At least one Wesley female, Mehethable — who was called "Hetty" — also wrote poems.

We have seen in an earlier chapter how Charles Wesley responded to the event of his evangelical conversion by writing several hymns to commemorate the day and communicate that experience. This microcosm can safely stand for the macrocosm of the Wesleyan hymnological corpus. Charles began writing hymns and sacred poems as expressions of his ability to see God at work in his life and the lives of those around him. These doxological hymns poured forth with surprising rapidity and in significant volume. It is difficult to say exactly how many hymns Charles Wesley wrote. Not only is the question complicated by the question of which Wesley brother wrote which hymn; it is further complicated by the question of what exactly constitutes a "hymn." For example, does a religious poem count as a "hymn" even though it was never intended to be sung? If we phrase the question more broadly, however, it seems safe to say that Charles Wesley composed more than 9,000 hymns and sacred poems. That amounts to, on average, a hymn a day, every day, for twenty-five years of his adult life. This effort came while he was enmeshed in the harried tasks of an itinerant ministry and a growing family. The greater miracle, however, was not that Charles's pen was so ready to write, but that from this voluminous production so much would have an enduring value. More than 400 different Charles Wesley hymns continue in modern Christian hymnals.

Charles Wesley's published journal gives some hints as to how he wrote hymns. One commentator has wryly called him an "evangelical centaur"; half-man and half horse, who probably composed many of his hymns while riding from one preaching post to another. For example, Charles once wrote, "I crept on, singing or making hymns, till I got unawares to Canterbury." On at least one occasion, Charles surprised his Christian friends by riding his horse through their garden and directly to the front door, through which he burst shouting: "Pen and ink! Pen and ink!" After having writing implements produced for him, he sat down and rapidly wrote down the hymn he had been composing in his head while he rode. After entrusting his composition to paper, Charles somewhat sheepishly greeted his hosts, and politely apologized for bursting in on them in such a manner. Making hymns became so much a part of Charles's daily regimen that he was able to gauge the severity of an injury by its ability to interrupt that process, however slightly. "Near Ripley," he wrote, "my horse threw and fell upon me. My [traveling] companion thought I had broken my neck; but my leg was only bruised, my hand sprained, and my head stunned; *which spoiled my making of hymns,* or thinking at all, till the next day, when the Lord brought us to New Castle." Charles was so "stunned" that he could not write a hymn for a whole day! Clearly, missing a day's composition must not have happened very often for a man who wrote the equivalent of a hymn a day, every day for most of his adult life.

An examination of the hymnbooks the Wesley brothers produced brings us to what Frank Baker termed "the vexed problem of joint authorship." In seeking to determine whether John or Charles authored the various Wesleyan hymns of that decade, there are three kinds of evidence to which we can turn our attention when trying to make an authorial determination. The first kind of evidence is in the form of manuscripts. Many of these hymns are extant in handwritten copies, and John's handwriting is easily distinguished from Charles's, and vice versa. But finding a composition in the handwriting of one brother or the other is not utterly foolproof evidence, because as we have seen in both sermons and hymns that the brothers copied each other's works and "improved" them. Still, we may generally conclude that those hymns that exist in manuscripts written or edited in Charles's hand were his own compositions.

A second kind of evidence, which we might call "historical evidence," stems from our ability to locate some of the Wesleyan hymns in the immediate life situation that gave them birth. This is generally done through a close study of their journals, letters, and other written materials. We have seen, for example, how it is possible to trace several conversion hymns to Charles Wesley's pen, and a long poetical lament on the loss of Grace Murray is easily attributed to John.

The third kind of evidence, which might be called "internal evidence," or "prosodic evidence," is by far the most difficult. By a close study of the ascertained compositions of John and Charles Wesley, experts have developed a series of poetical characteristics which are thought to distinguish the poems of one brother from the other. Henry Bett, in his *Hymns of Methodism* (1913), was the first scholar to follow this approach rigorously, and he developed thirteen "canons" of comparison which he used to work his way through the compositions included in the 1780 *Collection*. Based on matters like rhyme pattern (Charles preferred alternative rhyme patterns, while John had a predilection for consecutive rhyme patterns) and phraseology, Bett determined that more than nine-tenths of the original compositions in the 1780 "big hymn book" were written by Charles Wesley. This "prosodic" approach to the identification of the Wesleyan hymns was also examined by Frank Baker in his *Representative Verse of Charles Wesley* (1962). Baker added several refinements to Bett's earlier work, but with the proviso that much more work needed to be done on these criteria before they could be used with anything that approached complete certainty.

Based upon the research of Henry Bett, Frank Baker, and others, the general approach to the "vexed problem of joint authorship" has been to assume that all of the translations from foreign languages and adaptations from the writings of other poets are the work of John Wesley. This generalization is true, by and large. But it is also clear that Charles created several of the Wesleyan hymns that are translations from German, and it is possible that he made some of the adaptations. It has also been largely assumed that all or most of the original compositions in the Wesleyan hymnbooks can safely be attributed to Charles Wesley. This too is an overgeneralization. It is true in large part, since it seems that after their evangelical conversions Charles Wesley became the "poet laureate" of Methodism — the designated person who gave the movement its chief expression in poem and song — and John Wesley became the editor-in-chief. But it is also clear that John Wesley continued to write verse after 1738; his long lament upon losing Grace Murray is the most obvious example of this continued production. Hence, Henry Bett argued that sixteen of the original compositions in the 1780 *Collection* can be traced to John Wesley's pen on the basis of internal or "prosodic" evidence. So while one might be safe to conclude that Charles made *most* of the original compositions after 1738, one cannot rest secure in that generalization without checking it against other indications, such as the three types of evidence described above.

It is hard to imagine anyone who has been as saturated with the Bible as John and Charles Wesley were; biblical phrases seeped from them, not only in sermon and song, but also in the course of their casual speech and private writings. John Wesley famously described himself as *homo unius libri* — "a man of one book" — meaning he read only the Bible. But even more than his brother, Charles was "a man of one book"; his chief theological reference and poetical resource was the Bible. Hence, John Rattenbury wryly observed, "a skillful man, if the Bible were lost, might extract it from Wesley's hymns. They contain the Bile in solution." Charles's hymns have rightly been called "mosaics" of biblical allusions; he selected, shaped, and polished Bible words, phrases, and allusions, and cemented them together to form his own image-laden works of art.

Charles Wesley was also a talented biblical exegete. Well schooled in the biblical texts and original languages, he edited ("corrected") brother John's expansive *Notes Upon the Old and New Testaments*. His study and application of the Bible in his poems was not limited to the renderings of the Authorized (King James) Version, Book of Common Prayer, or recent commentaries (like those of Matthew Henry) — even though he used each of those resources. Charles's dexterity in the Greek New Testament is often evidenced in his poetical treatment of difficult Bible passages such as Philippians 2:7. The Greek words, *heauton ekenose*, say — literally — "he emptied himself," when referring to the condescension of Christ in assuming human form. The translators of the King James Version (the standard translation of Wesley's day) avoided the bold simplicity of the Pauline phrasing and translated the *kenosis* ("emptying") with the words "he made himself of no reputation, and took the form of a servant." While the King James reading avoids the (apparently) scandalous phrasing of the Greek words, Wesley would have none of this type of evasion. Instead he wrote:

> He left His throne above,
>   *Emptied of all but love,*
> Whom the heavens cannot contain,
>   God, vouchsafed a worm to appear,
> Lord of Glory, *Son of Man,*
>   Poor, and vile, and abject here.

Charles Wesley's bold and direct translation of "emptied" pushed beyond the renditions of his own day and returned to the plain meaning of the Greek New Testament in a way that prefigured more modern translations.

Charles Wesley's approach to the Bible was essentially Christ-centered. It mattered not where the biblical passage began; Charles's exposition of it found a Christ-centered focus and managed to preach full salvation (justification and sanctification) through it. Hence, he tended to "evangelize the Old Testament," and treat it as though it were contemporary with Christ and the New Testament church. Instead of paraphrasing the Old Testament, like his poetical predecessor Isaac Watts did by reporting the gist of a biblical passage, Charles Wesley poetically restructured the passage according to his own theological agenda. Thus "The Taking of Jericho," which is based on Joshua 6, turns the biblical narrative into a text of full salvation. The pagan citadel becomes a stronghold "within," "the strength of inbred sin." Playing off his knowledge that "Joshua" and "Jesus" stem from the same Hebrew root words — meaning "God saves" — the Joshua of the biblical passage reminded Wesley of the Jesus of human redemption. Hence a new "Captain" like Joshua leads an assault against the citadel of sin, the unregenerate human heart:

1.   Arise, ye men of war,
       Prevent the morning ray,
   Prepare, Your Captain cries, prepare,
       Your Captain leads the way:
       He calls you forth to fight,
       Where yonder ramparts rise,
   Ramparts of a stupendous height,
       Ramparts that touch the skies.

2.   Who dares approach those towers?
       Who can those walls o'erturn?
   The city braves all human powers,
       And laughs a siege to scorn,
       Who shall the city take,
       The *Jericho* within?
   Not all the powers of earth can shake,
       The strength of inbred sin.

3.   Impregnable it stands,
       Strong, and wall'd up to heaven;

But God into our *Joshua's* hands
   The citadel hath given;
   The fortress and its kind,
   And all its valiant men,
Our Captain to the ground shall bring,
   And on their ruins reign.

For Charles, the victory at Jericho signified a characteristically Wesleyan theme: freedom from the guilt and power of sin. Freed from "actual and inbred sin," the city — the human heart — is wholly devoted to God, and sin is "forever" slain:

13.   Its proud aspiring brow
     Lies level with the ground;
It lies, and not one stone is now
     Upon another found.
     The walls are flat, the deep
     Foundations are o'erthrown;
The lofty fortress is a heap,
     And sin is trodden down.

14.   The strength of sin is lost,
     And *Babylon* the great
Is fallen, fallen to the dust,
     Has found its final fate.
     Partakers of our hope,
     We seize what God hath given,
And trampling down all sin go up,
     And straight ascend to heaven.

15.   But shall not sin remain,
     And in its ruins live?
No, Lord, we trust, and not in vain,
     Thy fullness to receive;
     Thy strength and saving grace
     Thou shalt for us employ,
The being of all sin erase,
     And utterly destroy.

16.   Actual and inbred sin
       Shall feel Thy two-edged sword:
  The city is, with all therein,
      Devoted to the Lord:
     Thy word cannot be broke,
     Thou will Thine arm display,
  Thou wilt with one continual stroke
     Our sin for ever slay. . . .

This hymn, a full eighteen verses in its original form, was published in Charles Wesley's *Hymns and Sacred Poems* (1749). The victory at Jericho, in Wesley's hands, became a song of sanctification and Christian perfection; it even included the destruction of inbred sin.

Isaac Watts, who wrote evangelical hymns in the generation prior to Charles Wesley, was a pioneer in the art of paraphrasing the Psalms and other Bible passages into poetical compositions. Watts's ideal was to follow the biblical text as closely as possible and to restate its message in the best poetical diction he could muster. In contrast to the work of Dr. Watts, Wesley wove together biblical words, phrases, and images from all across Scripture. Thus, where Isaac Watts paraphrased the Bible in his hymns, Wesley actually commented, and created theology while he versified.

Wesley had a poetical penchant for looking beneath the literal text in order to grapple with the text theologically and artistically. His hymn based on Luke 9:33 (the Transfiguration account) gives a clue to Wesley's recognition that he was looking beneath the primary meaning of Scripture as he "transfigured" biblical passages into Christ-centered poems about full salvation. He wrote:

Who tastes the Truth and Jesus sees
   In all the Scripture-mysteries
The Law and the Prophets' End,
   Delights to meditate and pray,
Would gladly on the mountain stay,
   And never more descend.

The first three lines are especially significant because they point to Charles's willingness to find Jesus in "all the Scripture mysteries" as well as in the Old Testament's "Law and the Prophets." Commenting on Luke 16:31 ("If they hear not Moses and the Prophets, neither will they be persuaded, though one rose from the dead"), Wesley acknowledged that one should seek to find Christ in all the Scriptures, and he looked to the New Testament's redemptive message to find that "sufficient proof of reconciling grace" of which the Old Testament speaks:

> Taught by their incredulity
> The standing meaning vouchsafe by thee
>   We thankfully embrace,
> The Scriptures search to find our Lord
>   And listen to the joyful Word
> Of reconciling grace.
>
> The sinner poor Thy Word believes,
> As full sufficient proof receives,
>   What Thou are pleased to impart;
> But love alone can change the will,
>   But only Gilead's balm can heal
> The blindness of my heart.

These sentiments closely parallel those registered above. The "standing meaning" of the biblical text prods the singer to "search the Scriptures to find our Lord." But Wesley's commentary on this text did not stop with Christology. He connected Christology with redemption from sin and sanctification; indeed, he generally found the full gospel message in virtually any biblical passage that came under his consideration.

Charles Wesley was conscious of his theological tendency for looking beneath the literal surface of the Bible's texts to find "the precious mine below." The following hymn, based on Isaiah 29:11, is a good example of Wesley's awareness of the interpretive process he was developing. In his verse he criticized the proud and superficial learning which is unable to discern even the foundational themes of the Bible:

> Proud learning boasts, its skill in vain
> The sacred oracles to explain,
>   It may the literal surface show,

But not the precious mine below;
The saving sense remains conceal'd,
Till by the Spirit of faith reveal'd,
The Book is still unread, unknown,
And open'd by the Lamb alone.

This verse is full of powerful images for describing Wesley's poetical approach to the Bible. It shows his clear interest in the "precious mine below" the "literal surface" of Scripture. The hidden deposit is described as "the saving sense" of the text, which is revealed by "the Spirit of faith" and "the Lamb [of God] alone." Wesley's Christ-centered approach emerges again, since the Lamb opens "the Book," poetically as its central theme and redemptively as "the saving sense" of the Bible is applied to the life of reader or singer.

Typology is an interpretive tool that seeks to find a deeper meaning hidden beneath the literal sense of the biblical text. It was popular among more mystical ancient Christian writers like Origen (ca. 185-254) and Clement of Alexandria (ca. 150-215). Not surprisingly it provided Wesley with a favorite device for plumbing the depths of "the precious mine below." Wesley's application of typology followed the general pattern of finding a New Testament or Christological "type" lurking behind an Old Testament person, event, or institution. Hence, as we saw above, Jesus was often found typified in Joshua and other heroes of old. Charles's typologies were very direct and clear: "Moses the meek man of God,/A type of Christ was seen. . . ." Virtually any Old Testament hero could, in Charles Wesley's poetical imagination, become an instrument for teaching about Christ and full salvation; Moses, Joshua, Samson, and David were among his favorite figures for typological identification. But Charles utilized typology all across the Old Testament; the ark of the covenant, to which the Israelites fled for mercy, typified the wounds of Christ. Jacob's ladder (Genesis 28:12-13), upon which angels ascended and descended from heaven, became a powerful image for describing the work of Christ, in his incarnation, death, and resurrection. Isaac carrying the wood of his own sacrificial death (Genesis 22:6) became, in Charles Wesley's hands, a vehicle for describing the saving effects of the cross of Jesus Christ.

Wesley used typology extensively. He understood it as a valid poetical device for developing thematic theological connections across the landscape of Scripture. Generally, his typologies do not seem grotesque or artificial, like so many others of the same age do. Charles took literary pains to make the connection between the Old Testament type and the New Testament reality to which it pointed transparent in his exposition of the text. Often he used the life situation or the emotional reality of the biblical passage to bridge the gap between the type and its point of reference. In his hymns, typology formed an obvious corollary to Wesley's Christ-centered approach to Scripture. It fit well with the practical situation of a poet who was also an evangelist who deemed it his task to proclaim the whole gospel message in every hymn and through any Bible passage.

Allegory was another tool in Charles Wesley's interpretive approach to Scripture. Like typology, allegory is a "deeper identification" that makes a connection between two characters or incidents which on the surface of things seem quite separate. But where typology rests on a strong thematic or symbolic identification between two seemingly separate elements, allegory specializes in finding a spiritual identification for virtually every aspect of the passage under consideration. In this sense allegory can be considered to be an extended typology. Allegory, also like typology, has a long and respected history of application in the church, yet it always brings the inherent danger of the text being extended at the whim of the biblical expositor. This danger becomes especially acute in allegory as opposed to typology, since both biblical and contemporary history is held in abeyance. But for this same reason allegory becomes a particularly versatile interpretive tool in the hands of a poetical commentator who wishes to mine the depths of meaning beneath the Bible's texts.

Charles Wesley generally used allegory to expound and expand New Testament passages. In Wesley's lengthy hymn, the reader or singer becomes the wounded traveler of the biblical narrative of the Good Samaritan; robbed of true religion, he or she has been left to die. The mortal wound which has been inflicted is Adam's sin: "Dead in Adam, dead, within/My soul is wholly dead." The traveler is stripped naked, "Naked, helpless stripped of God." She or he is bloodied with his or her own guilt. The priest who "Comes down in vain" symbolizes the "patriarchs and prophets of old." The Levite of the biblical account becomes one of the contemporary false teachers of religion, who "offers no relief/All my wounds he open tears." Jesus, who is the Good Samaritan in Wesley's exposition of the passage, is full of grace and compassion; he "heals my spirit's every wound." The recovery of the traveler is a recovery from mortal sin, through the "wine and oil of grace," at the hand of Christ, "The Good Physician." The result of that healing prescription is not only health, but also "cleansing" and "wholeness" — which are Wesleyan euphemisms for sanctification or Christian perfection: "Perfect then the work begun/ And make the sinner whole." Similar allegorical exposition can be found in hymns that were based on Charles Wesley's favorite sermon texts, including "Blind Bartimaeus," "The Pool of Bethesda," "The Woman of Canaan," and "Wrestling Jacob." His use of allegory was not limited to the New Testament; Old Testament events like "The Taking of Jericho," "Jonah's Gourd," "The Children in the Fiery Furnace," and "Daniel in the Den of Lions" were also allegorized into stories of Christian salvation.

Seen in his historical and literary context, once again Charles Wesley broke with the literary style of important literary precursors. Unlike John Bunyan's *Pilgrim's Progress* (1684) and allegories of an earlier era, Charles Wesley never narrated the allegorized account to the reader. The reader or singer is not a spectator to the redemptive events; rather, we become one of the actors in the unfolding drama. We are the wounded traveler robbed of vital piety, or Jacob wrestling for "the blessing"; Blind Bartimaeus's affliction becomes our own sinful blindness; and we are the woman taken in adultery — guilty, but by God's grace no longer accused. Where the Puritans narrated the account to us as spectators, Wesley made the singer participate in the biblical action. Where earlier allegorists used the device to communicate ideals or principles, Charles Wesley used allegory to take the reader or singer to the redemptive core of a biblical passage by recreating the event afresh in the reader's imagination. Wesley took an old tool and reshaped it to fit the needs of a new age.

There was a dramatic, image-building process at work in Charles Wesley's poetical approach to Scripture. He wove, blended, and allegorized Scripture into a poetic form that communicated the gospel message in a dramatic and participatory form. His poetical reconstructions were full of the Bible, and they communicated a sense of life experience that drew the singer into the text. Wesley had a talent for taking a familiar passage and changing its context or blending it with another passage or image to make it fresh and alive in the imagination of the reader. For example, the mournful call of Matthew 27:25, "His blood be upon us and upon our children," which in its biblical context was the shout of the crowd rejecting Jesus Christ before Pilate's judgment seat, became in Charles's poetical imagination "the best of prayers, if rightly understood." The shout of dereliction was transformed into a prayer for redemption through the saving "blood" of Christ.

Charles's process of recasting biblical allusions or imagery into something new or startling had as its goal creating a sense of the drama and emotion around the text to draw people into its saving message. Thus these biblical hymns, like Charles's sermons, were weapons of Wesleyan evangelism; they had the not-so-subtle agenda of inviting people to come to vital Christian faith. Charles often undertook this task by making the hearer of the sermon or the singer of the hymn into a contemporary of the crucifixion of Christ:

> My stony heart Thy wrath defies,
> And dares against Thy judgments rise,
>   Self-hardened from Thy fear;
> What can'nst Thou with Thy rebel do?
>   Try me by love, and in my view
> With all Thy wounds appear.
>
> Ah! Who that piteous sight can bear!
> Behold the Lamb hangs bleeding there!
>   There, there! On yonder tree!
> Pierced are His feet, His hands, His side!
>   My Lamb, My love is crucified!
> O God! He died for me!

The hymn vibrates with emotion and is cast in imagery and tense that demands participation in a new religious event orchestrated by the poet. Time and space are not boundaries to poetic imagination and religious experience; Wesley's hymns use poetical drama to bridge the distance between the biblical past and the contemporary reader by involving readers in the events and experiences described in the text.

Charles Wesley used many literary devices to create this dramatic dialogue between the past and present in his hymns. One method was to paint the picture of the crucified Christ on the canvas of the reader's mind and heart. Charles's verses are full of graphic images and language. His phrases are short and well chosen — full of color and action — and they communicate in vivid word pictures the author's excitement and emotion.

Second, the sense of spiritual need or culpability on the part of reader or singer is often heightened by the spokesperson in Wesley's hymns accepting blame or guilt for the death of Christ: "The covenant-blood/Underfoot I have trod/And again I have murdered the meek Son of God." In this example, formed on the pattern of Hebrews 6:6, Wesley personified the seriousness of rejecting the reconciliation offered in Christ's death. The present rejection of this redemption is equated with the guilt of those who murdered Jesus in the historical past; by this dramatic interpretation those who reject Christ now also "crucify" him. The poetic transition from the past to the present place a sense of responsibility and onus for decision upon the singer of this hymn. And as we saw in the application of allegory, Charles Wesley's spokespersons often transform the reader into one of the actors in the biblical drama.

A third literary device Wesley employed to create a sense of contemporaneity in his hymns was dialogue. In a few of his expositions of the atonement, for example in this hymn based on John 6:67, Charles's poetical spokespersons enter into dialogue with Jesus as he hangs before them upon the ever-present cross:

13. Saviour, I with guilty shame,
    Own that I, alas, am he!
  Weak, and wavering still I am,
    Ready still to fly from Thee:
  Stop me by Thy look, and say,
    "Will you also go away?"

14. You, whom I have brought to God,
    Will you turn from God again?
  You, for whom I spilt my blood,
    Will you let it flow in vain?
  You, who felt it once applied,
  Can you leave My bleeding side?

12. No, my Lamb, my Saviour, no,
      (Every soul with me reply,)
    From Thy wounds we will not go,
      Will not from our Master fly:
    Thine is the life-giving word;
    Thou art our eternal Lord. . . .

This dialogue between Jesus Christ and the singer of Wesley's hymn reaches its climax in verse thirteen of this poem, where the poetic voice implores: "Speak Thyself into our heart."

On a few rare occasions, Charles Wesley explained his intention in writing his hymns. One such occasion was Wesley's composition "On the True Use of Musick." Methodist tradition connects the composition of his hymn with Charles's confrontation by a drunken mob of sailors while he was preaching on the docks at Portsmouth. The rabble successfully interrupted Wesley's preaching by half-singing, half-shouting one of the dance hall ditties of the period, which immortalized the scandalous deeds of one "Nancy Dawson." Wesley remarked that he liked their melody (which must have been quite similar to "Pop Goes the Weasel" played on a sailor's horn-pipe) but not their lewd lyrics. Like Elijah of old, Charles devised a contest for the competing gods of music. He challenged the sailors to return later in the day, promising to have a song they could all sing together; expecting to make further sport of the Methodist evangelist, they agreed to come, only to be won to the Christian faith by Wesley's apology for the proper use of music. "On the True Use of Musick" is extant in manuscript form and was published in Charles's *Hymns and Sacred Poems* (1749). The first five (of the original seven) verses are given here in their manuscript form. In the hymn Charles asks in effect, "Why should the Devil have all the good music?"

1. Listed into the Cause of Sin,
     Why should a Good be Evil?
   Musick, alas! too long has been
     Prest to obey the Devil;
   Drunken, or lewd, or light the Lay
     Flow'd to the Soul's Undoing,
   Widen'd, and strew'd with Flowers the Way
     Down to Eternal Ruin.

2. Who on the Part of GOD will rise,
   Innocent Sound recover,
   Fly on the Prey, and take the Prize,
   Plunder the Carnal Lover,
   Strip him of every moving Strain,
   Every melting Measure,
   Musick in Virtue's Cause retain,
   Rescue the Holy Pleasure?

3. Come let us try if JESU's Love
   Will not as well inspire us:
   This is the Theme of Those above,
   This upon Earth shall fire us.
   Say, if your Hearts are tun'd to sing,
   Is there a Subject greater?
   Harmony all its Strains may bring,
   JESUS'S Name is sweeter.

4. JESUS the Soul of Musick is;
   His is the Noblest Passion:
   JESUS's Name is Joy and Peace,
   Happiness and Salvation:
   JESUS's Name the Dead can rise,
   Shew us our Sins forgiven,
   Fill us with all the Life of Grace,
   Carry us up to Heaven.

5. Who hath a Right like Us to sing,
   Us whom his Mercy raises?
   Merry our Hearts, for CHRIST is King,
   Cheerful are all our Faces:
   Who of his Love doth once partake
   He evermore rejoices:
   Melody in our Hearts we make,
   Echoing to our Voices. . . .

A second hymn, also entitled "On the True Use of Musick," was published in *Hymns and Sacred Poems* (1749). It was based on the Bible text of 1 Corinthians 14:15, "I will sing with the Spirit, and I will sing with the understanding also."

> 1. JESUS, Thou soul of all our joys,
>   For whom we now lift up our voice,
>   And all our strength exert.
>   Vouchsafe the grace we humbly claim,
>   Compose into a thankful frame,
>   And tune Thy people's heart.
>
> 2. While in the heavenly work we join,
>   Thy glory be our sole design,
>   *Thy* glory, not our own:
>   Still let us keep our end in view,
>   And still the pleasing task pursue,
>   To please our God alone. . . .

As early as 1751, Charles recognized that his deteriorating health was beginning to seriously impede his itinerant ministry. In his journal entry for August 9 of that year he wrote: "Preaching, I perceive, is not my principal business. God knoweth my heart, and all its burdens. O that He would take the matter into His hands, though He lay me aside like a broken vessel!" As family responsibilities, illness, and alienation caused by struggles with the lay preachers gradually took their toll on Wesley, they conspired to keep him from the incessant itinerant travel of his early ministry. As a result, he turned his attention more directly to the task of making hymns. This was reflected in the composition of his *magnum opus, Short Hymns on Select Passages of Scripture.* Charles's preface to that work reports, "God, having graciously laid His hand upon my body, and disabled me for the principal work of the ministry, has thereby given me an unexpected occasion of writing the following hymns." Two volumes of these poetic reflections on specific Bible verses, comprised of 2,030 hymns, were published in 1762. Hundreds more of them remained in manuscript and have only recently been published by S. T. Kimbrough and Oliver Beckerlegge in their *Unpublished Poetry of Charles Wesley.* Meditating upon passages from Genesis through Revelation, these poems are no less a Methodist commentary upon Holy Scripture than John Wesley's more famous *Notes.* These

Short Hymns show that the younger Wesley was both a talented linguist and biblical scholar, as well as a very productive poet. This massive project and many more like it also remind us that Charles Wesley was not unproductive as a Methodist minister and theologian, even though he gradually restricted his traveling and focused his efforts on his home, family, and the Methodist societies in Bristol and London.

Charles Wesley was the "poet laureate" of early Methodism because he gave poetical expression to the hopes, aspirations, and experiences of the movement. But Wesley's hymns were more than the background music of early Methodism; they were themselves vehicles of Wesleyan evangelism and expressions of Wesleyan theology. Viewed in this larger context, it is clear that Charles Wesley was a theologian — a poetical craftsman of "practical divinity." He considered music to be a gift from God, and he tirelessly made the most of it.

17 "To the Brink of Separation"

The tensions between Charles Wesley and the lay preachers escalated considerably in the late spring of 1760, when several of the Methodist preachers in the Norwich circuit began to administer the Lord's Supper without the Wesleys' knowledge or permission. This was a blatant breach of Anglican church law, and as such it represented a further step towards separation — on the part of the Methodist preachers. Upon hearing about the Norwich administrations, Charles Wesley wrote several Methodist preachers in the area in an attempt to galvanize them against the practice of lay administration. A letter to his brother, dated March 2, 1760, was encapsulated in an epistle to Sally. John had urged Charles to go to Norwich to quell the controversy, and Charles agreed to go but only with clear and decisive support from his brother. Charles chided his brother for his weakness in dealing with the preachers:

> Dear Brother, I have thought and prayed about going to Norwich and am ready to go; but not on a fool's errand. Your [lack] of resolution yesterday saved you the reading of a long letter. Did you give Murlin and his fellows the least check? Did you blame them in the slightest word? What must be the consequence? The rest, se-

cure in your weakness, will do what they list; will, sooner than you are aware, follow the example of those three, and draw as many disciples after them as they can, into a formal separation.

If your weak conscience will not let you touch them, what signifies my going to N[orwich]? You will not stand by me. Your fear and dissimulation will throw the blame upon me; and perhaps disown me. Write a letter by me to the Preachers, what you would have them and me do. Blame them as strongly as your conscience will let you. Otherwise you betray them and all the Preachers, you betray your authority, and our children, and our Church; and are the author of the separation.

I see my first step, which is to secure this people. The Lord, I doubt not, will direct and help me. You might answer this from the first place you stop at. Can you find in your heart to speak a word tonight of continuing in the Church of England? . . .

Charles stressed that he and John Wesley, and the other preachers, did not have prior knowledge of their plans to administer the Lord's Supper, and this lack of prior knowledge was to be taken as a shield from complicity in the events that transpired at Norwich. On two previous occasions, at Methodist conferences, the preachers had signed documents in which they promised to act in concert with one another and keep others informed of their actions. Wesley viewed this as a momentous event, because if the example of the Norwich lay preachers were followed it would lead immediately to a separation from the Church of England. Hence, he told Nicholas Gilbert, "They never acquainted their fellow-labourers, no not even my brother, of their design. They did it without any ordination by Bishops or Elders; upon the sold authority of a six-penney licence; nay, all had not that. Do you think they acted right? If the other preachers follow their example, not only separation but general confusion must follow."

Not only did the Norwich administrations seem to bring the Methodist movement to the brink of separation with the Church of England; Charles saw the event as bringing the lay preachers to the point of having to decide whether they would license themselves as Dissenting clergy or seek ordination within the Church of England. With separation from the Anglicans, the ambiguous status of the Methodist lay preachers would come to an end. Charles wrote Nicholas Gilbert

273

and several others, "Indeed you must become at last in the Church ministers, or Dissenting. . . . God will make a way for their regular ordination in the Church. With this I desire to live and die."

To all those lay preachers who desired ordination in the Church of England, Charles held out hope that they would receive it; additionally he promised them his help and friendship in that process. Wesley reminded Nicholas Gilbert that he would be a faithful friend to him if Gilbert was a friend to the Church of England: "I never professed a friendship and proved false to my profession," he wrote. "I never (that I know) forgot a kindness done me. Your fidelity to the Church of England, although your duty, I shall accept as the greatest kindness you can possibly show me; beyond my personal benefit whatsoever." On the other hand, if the lay preachers became impatient and pursued another route to ministerial status by "breaking with their brethren and each set up for himself then will every man's sword be turned against his brother and the flock [will] be torn into a hundred pieces or sects."

Charles warned all of his correspondents that he would leave the Methodists, and indeed he would leave his brother, if the Methodists separated from the Church of England. To Nicholas Gilbert, for example, he wrote: "My soul abhors the thought of separating from the Church of England. You and all the preachers know, if my brother should ever leave it, *I should leave him*, or *rather he* [would leave] *me*. While they have any grace remaining they can never desire to part *us*, whom God hath joined."

Charles's letter to Sally of April 13, 1760, reported a meeting he had with the Methodist leaders about the lay preachers, the Norwich incident, and the fact that the preachers were threatening to license themselves as Dissenters. Charles confronted them with letters from Rev. Grimshaw, his brother John, and with the force of his own personality. Charles took the opportunity to both reprove and defend the preachers, but he also made it clear that his most foundational loyalties lay with the Church of England:

> At three I met all the Leaders; read them my brother's and Mr. Grimshaw's letters. The latter put them in flame. All cried out against the Licensed Preachers; many demanded, that they should be silenced; many that they should give up their licenses; some

protested against ever hearing them more. . . . I took occasion to moderate, the others, to defend the Preachers or at least protect them; and desired the Leaders to have patience till we had our Conference, promising then to let them know all that should pass at it. They could trust me, I added, that I would not deny the cause of our Church or deceive them. . . . My chief concern upon earth, I said was the prosperity of the Church of England, my next, that of the Methodists. My third that of the Preachers. That if their interest should ever come in competition, I would give up the Preachers, for the good of the Methodists, and the Methodists for the good of the whole body of the Church of England. That nothing could ever force me to leave the Methodists, but their leaving the Church. You cannot conceive what a Spirit rose in all that heard me. They all cried out. They would answer for 99 out of 100 in London, that they would live and die in the Church. . . .

In July 1760, Charles wrote to his brother John about issues and events surrounding the Norwich incident, using a metaphor from classical antiquity. In Roman history, no legion of the army was allowed to cross the river Rubicon; if it did, that legion was considered traitorous because it was marching on Rome to overthrow the government. Hence, when Julius Caesar's legions crossed the Rubicon, he passed the point of no return. He would become Roman Emperor or die trying. For Charles Wesley the events at Norwich symbolized the Methodists' "Rubicon." Would they separate from the Church of England or not? Had they already reached the point of no return? "In the fear of GOD (which we both have) and in the Name of Jesus Christ," Charles wrote, "let us ask, Lord what would *Thou* have us do?" In the event that John had not been apprised of the situation, Charles filled him in. "The case stands thus," he wrote; "three preachers whom we thought we could have *most* depended upon have taken upon them to administer the sacrament without any ordination and without acquainting us (or even yourself) of it before hand; why may not all the other preachers do the same, if each is judge of his own right to do it? And every one is left to act as he pleases, if we take no notice of them that have despised their brethren."

Charles's ire at the lay administrations found its way into his poetical commentary on the Bible, *Short Hymns on Select Passages of*

275

Holy Scripture (1762), which he was writing at this time. The Scripture passage in Numbers 16:10, "And seek ye the priesthood also?" fit, in Wesley's poetic imagination, with this dilemma over the lay administrations:

> Raised from the people's lowest lees,
> Guard, Lord, Thy preaching witnesses,
> Nor let their pride the honour claim
> Or sealing covenants in Thy name:
> Rather than suffer them to dare
> Usurp the priestly character,
> Save them from the arrogant offense,
> And snatch them uncorrupted hence.

So angry was Charles about the actions of the Norwich three that he would rather see the Methodist lay preachers dead and in heaven than have them alive on earth usurping "the priestly character." In a similar way, the Old Testament verses about Uzzah — "an upstart priest," who as a king improperly claimed priestly authority, made him Wesley's poster-child for those among the Methodists who undertook a similar offense:

> "But now (the warm Enthusiast cries)
>   The office to myself I take,
> Offering the Christian sacrifice,
>   Myself a lawful priest I make,
> To me the honour appertains;
>   No need of man, when God ordains." . . .

Since the "upstart priests" mimicked Uzzah's offense, Wesley also hoped that they would follow him in receiving divine judgment. The warning in 2 Chronicles 26:21, "Uzzah was a leper unto the day of his death," reminded Charles that the lay preachers also awaited God's judgment upon their sinful pride:

> Ye upstart priests, your sentence know,
>   The marks you can no longer hide,
> Your daring deeds too plainly show

The loathsome leprosy of pride;
And if ye still your crime deny,
Who lepers live, shall lepers die.

Charles had dire predictions of the outcome of the lay preachers' actions if the Wesley brothers did not take a concerted stand against them. As he told John in his manuscript letter of July 1760:

That the rest will soon follow their example, I believe because 1. They think they may do it with impunity. 2. Because a large majority imagine they have a right as Preachers to administer the sacraments. So long ago as the Conference at Leeds, I took down their names. 3. Because they have betrayed an impatience to Separate. The Preachers in Cornwall and others would find it had not been mentioned at our last Conference. Jacob Rowel's honesty I commend, Christopher Hooper, Jos. Cowley, J. Hampson, and several more are ripe for a Separation. Even Mr. Cross says, he would give the Sacrament if *you* bid him. The young Preachers, you know, are now unprincipled men and truly at the mercy of the old. *You* could persuade them to any thing, and not you only. Charles Perronet could do the same, or any of the Preachers who have left us or any of them at Norwich.

The Norwich affair gave Charles greater grievances against the lay preachers than he had already had, and it exacerbated his fears about the Methodists separating from the Church of England. "Upon the whole," he confided to his brother John, "I am fully persuaded *almost* all of our preachers are corrupted already; more and more will give the sacrament and set up for themselves even before we die, and all except the few that get Orders [in the Church of England] will turn Dissenters before or after our death." The younger Wesley also had some harsh words for his brother's complicity in these events: "You must wink very hard not to see all this. You have connived at it too long. But I now call upon you in the name of God to consider with me what is to be done? First to prevent a separation 2. To save a few uncorrupted preachers. 3. To make the best of those that are corrupted."

John Wesley was evangelizing Ireland during the summer of 1760, so he was unavailable to meet with the Methodist lay preachers.

Nor do we have any letters from John to Charles written during these challenging days. John's published journal is strangely silent about the Norwich administrations and what was done about them; certainly these events did not fit well with Wesley's carefully crafted public depiction of the Methodist movement. One of Charles's letters to Sally reports that John had resolved to handle the Norwich affair at the next Methodist annual conference five months away:

> My brother's final resolution (or irresolution) is not to meddle with the Sacred Gentlemen at Norwich *till* the Conference, i.e. *till* they are confirmed in their own evil and pride and practice, and till they have poisoned all the Preachers and half the flock. At the Conference, I presume, he will put to the vote whether they have a right to administer. Then by a large majority they [will] consent to a Separation.
>
> Five months interval, we have to do . . . whatever the Lord directs by way of prevention. If I am to stand in the gap now as formerly, I shall have the strength of body given me, and strength of grace. If I cannot act in the Spirit of Love and Meekness, I will go aside into my corner, for my few remaining days. . . .

Soon several of the Methodist lay preachers began taking out licenses as Dissenters so that they could baptize and administer the Lord's Supper. In a letter of March 27, 1760, Charles Wesley wrote John Nelson to criticize the duplicity of these actions: "My dear Brother," he wrote, "I think you are no weathercock. What think *you* then of licensing yourself as a *Protestant Dissenter,* and baptizing and administering the Lord's Supper — and all the while calling yourself a *Church of England* man? Is this honest? Consistent? Just? Yet this is the practice of several of our sons in the Gospel, even some whom I most loved, and most depended upon. . . . John, I love thee from my heart; yet rather than see thee a Dissenting Minister, I wish to see thee smiling in thy coffin." A letter, which Charles wrote to Sally, dated March 26, 1768, further illustrates Charles's frustration over the ambiguous status and actions of the Methodist lay preachers. "My dear Sally," he wrote satirically, "You are not acute enough to understand our policy. We have allowed our lay preachers to take out licences as *Dissenting Protestants.* To the Government they therefore say, 'we are Dissenting Ministers'; to the Methodists they say 'we are not Dissenters, but members of the Church of England.' To Press Warrant or Persecuting Justice, they say again: 'we are Dissenters,' to me at our next Conference, they will unsay it again. This is their sincerity, and my brother applauds their skillfulness — and his own."

Charles had deep personal regard for many of the Methodist lay preachers, some of whom were his "sons in the gospel." In March 1760 he wrote a series of letters to the Methodist preachers for whom he had the most respect and affection. It is clear that these letters had the intention of trying to dissuade the lay preachers from taking out licenses as Dissenters, administering the Lord's Supper, and separating from the Church of England. He stressed reason, honesty, and filial bonds as he sought to persuade the preachers to follow the course of action which he favored. He opined that the preachers would not want to be the reason of a separation between the Wesley brothers: "You and they know," he wrote John Johnson, "if my brother left the Church, I should leave him; and this alone would be sufficient to hold you back [from separation], that you would not part whom God hath joined." He closed that letter by pleading, "if, I say, you can discern the signs of the times, and your heart is as my heart, then give me your hand, and let us both give our lives to the service of God and his Church." Reflecting upon the Norwich administrations of the Lord's Supper, Charles asked Christopher Hooper: "Is not administering the sacraments formally separating from the Church? And have they not laid me, for one, under a necessity of either owning or disowning them? At least, their proceedings? God grant their rashness may not prove fatal to themselves." During this same month Charles resumed his correspondence with his fellow Anglican evangelical, William Grimshaw. He wrote Grimshaw, in ominous terms, about the Norwich administrations and the licensing of the preachers: "To have them and things as they are, is to betray our charge; to undermine the Church; and, as far as in us lies, to destroy the work of God."

Charles dreaded the impending Methodist conference; he felt that it could devolve into a final showdown over separation from the Church of England. But it seems that his publicity campaign had worked its magic. Nearly a year after the event his brother John wrote him describing the situation as he saw it: "Our conference ended, as it began, in peace and love. . . . I do not think, to tell you a secret, that the work will ever be destroyed. Church or no Church. What has been done to prevent the Methodists leaving the Church you will see in the Minutes of the Conference." Howell Harris, who was present at this conference, reported in his diary: "Surely the Lord has made a stand against a breach to be made in the work by introducing licensing and even ordination, and so a total separation from the Church. Charles and I were the rough workers, and John more meekly, and said he could not ordain, and said if he was not ordained he would look upon it as murder if he gave the ordinances. He struck dumb the reasoners by saying he would renounce them in a quarter of an hour, that they were most foolish and ignorant in the whole Conference." The "Large Minutes," which contain a section that may well date from this period, asks the question: "Are we not unawares, by little and little, sliding into a separation from the Church?" The answer, which is presented as a consensus of the movement, replied:

> O use every means to prevent this! (1). Exhort all our people to keep close to the Church and sacrament. (2). Warn them all against niceness in hearing, — a prevailing evil. (3). Warn them also against despising the Prayers of the Church. (4). Against calling our society, "the church." (5). Against calling our Preachers "ministers"; our Houses, "Meeting-houses": Call them plain preaching-houses or chapels. (6). Do not license them as Dissenters. . . . (7). Do not license yourself till you are constrained; and then not as a Dissenter, but a Methodist. . . .

Hence, John Wesley concluded to Charles: "I have done at the last conference all I can do. Allow me liberty of conscience, as I allow you."

Whether or not John Wesley was done with the issue of the separation, the issue, it seemed, was not done with him. In 1764 it reared its head again, this time over the issue of the Methodists conducting worship, during church hours, in parishes that were served by effective evangelical Anglican clergy. The Wesleys had been building a network of Anglican clergy supportive of the Methodist movement; now these men came to Bristol to ask for support from the Wesleys. The Methodist lay preacher John Pawson remembered the meeting: "In the year 1764 twelve of those gentlemen attended our conference in Bristol, in order to prevail upon Mr. Wesley to withdraw the preachers from every parish where there was an awakened minister; and Mr. Charles Wesley honestly told us, that if he was a settled minister in any particular place, we should not preach there. Mr. Hampson replied, 'I would preach there, and never ask your leave, and should have as good a right to do so as you would have.'" Pawson editorialized on Charles's comment: "Mr. Charles Wesley's answer was in a strain of high church eloquence indeed! But I leave it." At this same conference Samuel Walker, rector of Turo, presented a plan whereby the Methodist lay preachers would become leaders over local societies (instead of itinerant preachers) who would work in cooperation with Anglican priests. This plan also came to naught.

That the Wesley brothers were on a collision course over separating from the Church of England was probably clear to both of them. In a remarkable letter to Mark Davis, an itinerant preacher who worked with Charles in Bristol in the summer of 1772, the poet explained his own understanding of the differing approaches that he and his brother took to the matter: "All the difference betwixt my brother and me (I told him) was that my brother's first object was the Methodists, and then the church; mine was first the church, and then the Methodists. That our different judgment of persons was owing to our different temper: his all hope, and mine all fear." This difference between the brothers was becoming clear to all, as was Charles's pessimism about the movement staying within the Church of England. Charles rightly recognized that the fear of separation seriously affected his judgment of the preachers, just as John's more optimistic hopes for the future of the movement affected his.

The tension between the location of the Methodists as a renewal movement within the Church of England and their need for sacramental worship and ordained leadership was an ongoing problem. In 1776 the controversy had spread to the Methodist societies in Ireland. John Wesley's journal entry from Dublin on July 7 reports, "Our little Conference began, at which about twenty preachers were present. On Wednesday we heard one of our friends [speak] at large upon the duty of leaving the church; but after a full discussion of the point we all remained firm in our judgment that it is our duty not to leave the church wherein God has blessed us, and does bless us still."

Thomas Maxfield (d. 1784) was one of the preachers who raised the specter of schism within the Methodist movement. Maxfield had been converted under the ministry of George Whitefield and served as a pastoral assistant to the Wesleys. In 1741 — with the urging and support of Susanna Wesley — he become the first Methodist lay preacher when neither of the Wesley brothers were available to preach in London. He was subsequently ordained in the Church of England, to the end that he could assist the Wesleys in the burgeoning work in London. His alienation from the Wesleys began in the controversy over Christian perfection (1761-63), when he sided with the extremism of George Bell. Smarting under their rebuke, Maxfield subsequently published a poisonous pamphlet against the Wesleyans. In April 1779, Charles Wesley still held out hope that Maxfield might return to the Wesleyan flock. He urged John to meet with him and give him another chance: "I still love T.M.," Charles wrote. "I can see some advantages to us, as well as him, from his return to us, *provided* he is first convinced [of his errors]. Receive him *unconvinced* and you will have to put [him] away again when perhaps it will scarce be in your power. One more trial, if you please, we will make upon him, in a conference between us three. Possibly we may gain our brother." The "trial" amounted to naught, and the Wesleys separated from Maxfield in 1779.

Alexander McNab (1745-97) was another of the preachers that stirred schism within the Methodist movement. A Mr. Smyth, "a clergyman whose labours God had greatly blessed in the north of Ireland," relocated to Bath — presumably so that the waters of the spa could have a healing effect upon the ill health of his wife. John Wesley installed him as the regular preacher in the Methodist chapel at Bath with instructions to preach every Sunday morning and evening while he was there. As soon as John Wesley moved on with his itinerancy, McNab began to "vehemently oppose" Smyth's monopoly on the pulpit. John's journal describes McNab as "affirming it was the common cause of all the lay preachers; that they were appointed by the Conference, not by *me*, and would not suffer the clergy to ride over their heads — Mr. Symth in particular, of whom he said all manner of evil." Hence, John wrote, "the society was torn in pieces and thrown into the utmost confusion." Others in the Bath society defended Smyth's work, while McNab and his party attacked him. By December 1779, Charles was on the scene in Bath managing the conflict with McNab. He urged his brother to have nothing to do with the maverick lay preacher, and urged that he be removed from his post. "If you have even read all my journals," Charles lamented, "you see that M[cNab] is far enough from repentance yet he might own his fault in words other than lose £50 a year. . . . I have told him not words would prove his sincerity. We *want* to see which he will follow. To support your authority, I have laid upon him the mark of dissuasion removing him from the house; but no other. Yet he is still owned by you as a son and a preacher."

John Wesley's plan for investing authority in the Methodist conference was bearing republican fruit, as McNab and others used the authority of the conference to challenge Wesley's own prerogatives. Charles's fearful mentality had him imagining that an entire party of share-the-authority republicans had arisen among the Methodist lay preachers. He saw McNab's push for power as the tip of a proverbial iceberg. While John considered this affront to his authority to be "a blow at the very root of Methodism," McNab was preaching for him again within three months. Charles, who had applauded his brother's firm resolve in dealing with the maverick McNab, soon found himself chiding John yet again for his weakness in dealing with the preachers. John's leniency and apparent vacillation made Charles hesitate to attend the next Methodist annual conference. He did not want to be a witness to the ordinations of Methodist lay preachers — which he foresaw might be coming in the near future. "I am not sure they will not prevail upon you to ordain them," Charles wrote.

On December 8, 1779, Charles reported to John what he knew, or thought he knew, about the lay preachers' strategy: "*Divide et impera* [divide and conquer] was the means by which they gained their ascendancy over you. *Divide et impera* — and you will receive your authority." Charles seemed to imagine the lay preachers were like a flock of vultures circling overhead as John Wesley crept nearer and nearer to the grave. "Supposing you as good as dead, they began to divide the spoils. . . . Having this power in their own hands they never suspected you to *rebel* or act with such vigour against them." The poet sought to rouse his brother to decisive action at the next annual conference. He urged strong and concerted action against the schismatics: "You cannot in *this matter* [leave] . . . any preacher unreproved. . . . Establishing your authority for the rest of your days. You still are no match for near 200 smooth tongued men. Rouse yourself, for they nag for your skin. Begin proving your sons one by one. Pray for resolution and love." As if trying to fulfill his brother's wish that he would stand by and work with him in equal strides, as he had in former days, Charles Wesley promised: "I would give up my wife and children to cleave to you, if you stand firm and faithful to yourself, the cause of God and the Church of E[ngland]."In a letter of June 8, 1780, John told his brother, "I verily believe I have as good a right to ordain [like a bishop], as to administer the Lord's Supper [like an elder]. But I see [an] abundance of reasons why I should not use that right, unless I am turned out of the Church. At present, we are just in our place." This admission, and his brother's timidity, caused Charles to write John the following month stating his reluctance in going to the Bristol conference: "My reasons against accepting your invitation to the Conference are: 1. I can do no good; 2. I can prevent no evil; 3. I am afraid of being a partaker of other men's sins, or countenancing them by my presence. 4. I am afraid of myself; you know I cannot command my temper, and you have not the courage to stand by me. 5. I cannot trust your resolution; unless you act with a vigour that is not in you *conculmatum est* our affairs are past hope."

But Charles relented and attended the conference in August. He kept his temper by keeping his silence. He had resolved not to contradict his brother in the presence of the preachers, and it seems that he was able to stand by that resolve even when McNab appeared at the conference — uninvited — and was permitted to address the assembly. Afterward, Charles later wrote his brother a letter. He reiterated his reluctance to attend the conference, "yet I accepted your invitation, only because you desired it. And as I came merely to please you, I resolved not to contradict your *will* in anything. Your *will*, I perceived was to receive Mr. M[cNab] unhumbled, unconvinced, into your confidence, and into your bosom." Still, despite McNab's appearance at the conference, the Methodists resolved to remain in the Church of England, "the Old Ship."

Charles Wesley's fullest report of the impact of the 1780 conference is encapsulated in a poem entitled "Written After the Conference of 1780, the Last At Which the Writer Was Present." The poem is dipped deep in sadness and disappointment. Its singer is weary of contending against impossible odds, he is tired of being a "prophet of ills" who continually brings bad news and predicts evil outcomes. Weary of his "useless ministry," Charles resigns himself and his friends to the hand of God and looks expectantly to his release from these earthly trials:

1. Why should I longer, Lord, contend,
   My last important moments spend
      In buffeting the air?
   In warning those who will not see,
   But rest in blind security,
      And rush into the snare?

2. Prophet of ills why should I live,
   Or by my sad forebodings grieve
      Whom I can serve no more?
   I only can their loss bewail
   Till life's exhausted sorrows fail,
      And the last pang is o'er.

3. Here then I quietly resign
   Into those gracious hands Divine,
      Whom I received from Thee,
   My brethren and companions dear,
   And finish with a parting tear
      My useless ministry.

4. Detach'd from every creature now,
   I humbly at Thy footstool bow,
      Accepting my release;
   If Thou the promised grace bestow,
   Salvation to Thy servant show
      And bid me die in peace.

Charles had several "last conferences," and he would continue to attend them intermittently as his health and resolve permitted. But his days of struggling against the lay preachers were over. They were gradually gaining the upper hand, and John Wesley seemed to realize that — for better or worse — the future of the Methodist movement lay with them.

Charles would continue to lobby and pray for the Anglican church, and soon after the 1780 conference he wrote this "Prayer for the Church of England." It was subsequently published in his brother's *Arminian Magazine* in 1781:

1.   Head of Thy church, attend
   Our long-continued prayer,
And our *Jerusalem* defend,
   And in Thy bosom bear
   The sheep of *England's* fold,
   Mark'd with their Shepherd's sign,
Bought with a price, redeem'd of old,
   And wash'd in blood Divine.

2.   Call'd out of *Babylon*
   At Thy command they came;
Our ancestors their lives laid down,
   And triumph'd in the flame:
   The Church's seed arose
   Out of the martyrs's blood,
And saw their anti-Christian foes
   Before Thy cross subdued.

3.   Again Thy Spirit of grace
   Doth with our *Israel* strive.
And even in our degenerate days
   His ancient work revive.
   Ten thousand witnesses
   Stand forth on every side,
And, bold in life and death, confess
   Jehovah crucified.

4.   O that the faithful seed
   May never, never fail,
Victorious through their conquering Head
   O'er all the powers of hell!
   Still with Thy people stay,
   By *England's* Church adored,
Till every island flee away
   Before our glorious Lord.

The two decades between the Norwich administrations (1760) and the 1780 conference were filled with conflict for Charles Wesley.

He still resolved to live and die in the Church of England, but he had begun to doubt his own ability to stem the tide of the growing power and demands of the lay preachers. Charles had also begun to lose confidence in his brother's resolution and his willingness to withstand the preachers' constant push towards separation. He feared that separation from the Church of England was inevitable. His evolving strategy was to continue to love and support his brother and stand by him publicly even as he sought to strengthen John's resolve against the preachers' incursions upon his leadership and authority. Charles continued to "preach up the Church" at every opportunity, and to lobby like-minded Methodists for their support, but his days of passionately opposing the preachers were now well past. Watching Methodism's gradual slide towards separation must have been nearly unbearable for him. But he bore it nonetheless, and made what gestures he could against the lay preachers' efforts. He also channeled his most passionate energies in a more productive direction — one that led to a more stable and satisfying life with his growing family.

18 The London Years

The last phase of Charles Wesley's life and ministry seemed to be his most satisfying. This was due in large part to the fact that he gradually relocated to London and undertook as his chief ministerial function the care of the Methodist chapels at West Street and the Foundery. This gave the poet a more regular family life than was possible in earlier years. The long evangelistic journeys of his early life were well past him; Charles's hymns now did most of the traveling for him. He still made regular journeys to Bristol, generally during the month of August, but Charles and his family learned to enjoy a more settled and more socially stimulating family life in London. The settled life of the London years also created a situation in which Wesley wrote fewer and fewer letters home to Sally and his family; hence the paper trail we have been following sometimes dwindles down to almost nothing. John Wesley was still trying to dislodge his brother from the comfortable bosom of his family; Charles was still trying to comply with his brother's demands — but more and more on his own terms.

As early as 1760, Charles had begun to see the logic of relocating to London. In April of that year he wrote to his wife Sarah from London: "As I shall take much more public care upon me than I have ever done here-to-fore, my office will require me to spend more time in town, *perhaps to settle* here. But this we shall never do, unless it is manifested to us that this is the will of God concerning us." The same topic was on his mind six days later, when Charles expressed what he assumed was his wife's point of view: "You would rather sit still in Charles-street [Bristol], I believe, than come to the best house in London." One month later his correspondence returned to the same topic, this time taking a more negative tone because the hustle and bustle of the metropolis had robbed Charles of several nights' sleep: "I cannot live in London," he wrote, "because I cannot live without sleep."

With this sort of personal ambivalence and with his wife's clear preference for Bristol, Charles made no immediate plans to relocate his family to London. It is clear, however, that relocation became a repeated topic of conversation. Eventually, their friend Mrs. Gumley heard of it and offered Wesley the use of her London townhouse. It was an attractive four-story Georgian house, on Chesterfield Street, in the Mary-le-bone section of London. Her lease on the house had an additional twenty years to run, and Mrs. Gumley made it available to Charles free of charge save for the ground rent on the lot, which was owed annually to the Duke of Portland. The house was furnished after a fashion that would suit a person of Mrs. Gumley's elevated tastes and station.

The location of the house, far from the city's center, irritated John Wesley, who used the geographic distance between them as an excuse for not consulting more constantly with his brother about the direction of the Methodist movement. On May 3, 1786, while John and Charles were feuding over John's ordinations for North America, he told his brother: "Commonly, when I am in London, I am so taken up [with work], that I cannot spare time to go three miles backward and forward. That was [in Greek] *the first and grand mistake;* the getting you a house so far from me, as well as far from both the chapels." As to Charles's commute, Methodist tradition has left us a memorable picture of Charles Wesley dressed for winter, even in summer, riding several miles across London on his small mare, whose hair was as gray as that of her rider, composing hymns in his head as he went to speaking engagements at the Methodist chapels.

Although Charles Wesley took possession of the house in Mary-le-bone at the end of 1770, it seems he also maintained the little house in Bristol till 1778 (though this is disputed by his biographers). A letter written on September 10 of that year depicts him closing up their house in Stokes-Croft and looking for a place to store those possessions that he could not bring with him to London. It was with a tinge of nostalgia that he wrote Sally, "We shall never more keep house in Bristol." Charles and his eldest son, Charles Jr., visited London in the spring of 1771, while Sally and the other children continued on in Bristol. On May 1 he wrote to her from London in a teasing tone: "It is hardly fair to blame *me* for not *permitting* you to come with us. Once only you mentioned coming and staying a month to settle us at Marybone and then to leave us. A likely story that we should so easily part with you!" Charles was putting a brave front on their family separation; "to bring up my whole family, our income would not *permit*. But to blame *that* is to blame Providence. I clearly saw it my duty to bring Charles up although I was sure to drop my old bones in the ground adjoining."

The elder Charles saw it as his duty to bring his namesake to London so that the young musician could study under more talented masters, as we saw in Chapter Thirteen. Soon, young Charles was taking lessons from Mr. Joseph Kelway (d. 1782), one of the most famous organists in London, who performed at St. Martin-in-the-Fields. As his young prodigy blossomed, Kelway introduced Charles Jr. to other musical associates. "On Tuesday evening," the proud father wrote his wife, "at Mr. Kelway's, we met Mr. Smith and Mr. Tate. They stared, and looked at each other, as if they did not believe their own ears, while Charles played like his master. It was hard to say which of the three was most delighted. The first masters count it an honour to assist him." In case Sally was worried about the care of her son, her husband assured her: "I have taken the best care of him I could, and am still waiting on him as his loving servant."

John Wesley's City Road Chapel opened in London in 1778, and this development is what probably forced (and perhaps facilitated) the complete relocation of the Charles Wesley family to the metropolis. Since it was a new congregation, the Wesley brothers agreed that one of them would fill the pulpit there until the congregation became large and stable. With Charles moving to the city, it became his task to preach and lead worship there, with lay pastors assisting or filling in as necessary because of his weakening health. Ironically, Charles did not seem to view his work at City Road as being a kind of separation from the Church of England; yet it was. He conducted Anglican-style worship during church hours, and even offered the Lord's Supper in a Methodist building. Calling the place a "chapel" instead of a "church" did nothing to mask the growing distance between the Methodists and the Church of England. These developments had the further impact of giving London (and Bristol) Methodism the appearance and experience of being more of a separate church than a society within the Church of England.

Whether or not he intended it in that way, Charles Wesley's constancy in the City Road pulpit was seen as a slight by the Methodist lay preachers. His presence there blocked their opportunities to preach at the grand new edifice. In June 1779 Charles wrote John to tell him that the lay preachers were complaining among themselves and stirring up trouble in London: "Dear Brother," Charles wrote, "Mr. B. has been lately with the committee and was there informed that our preachers (the three principal) [John Pawson, Thomas Rankin, and Peter Jacko] have written to the country preachers heavy complaints of their ill usage by the clergy here." After going through the list of the clergy serving at City Road Chapel and absolving each of them one by one, the poet concluded, "The persecuting clergy, therefore, are neither more nor less than your own brother Charles, and the whole ground of their complaint against me is, 'My serving the chapel on Sunday afternoon, as well as in the morning.'"

This conflict between Charles Wesley and the lay preachers was more or less the continuation of old grievances. Charles wanted ordained Anglicans to take leadership in the Methodist movement, so he favored using clergymen over lay preachers. John Pawson recalled that Charles Wesley "had always a very warm side towards the clergy. . . ." The lay preachers felt that their enthusiasm and vigor in the pulpit more than made up for their lack of formal training, and they resented Charles Wesley's attempts to keep them in what he considered to be their proper place and role. This conflict also raises an interesting question about Charles's continuing effectiveness as a preacher during his declining years. Pawson, one of the preachers offended at Charles Wesley's preeminence in London, reported that "the congregation fell off exceedingly and that the society was brought into great disorder." John Wesley's biographer, the Methodist preacher Luke Tyerman, suggests that Pawson and Rankin were probably more effective preachers than the elderly Charles Wesley; he further opined that they had as much right to preach at City Road as Charles Wesley did. But this assessment may reflect too much the bitterness of controversy and the later opinion of the Methodist establishment. Thus, it was with faint praise that Pawson reported, "when he was favoured with freedom of mind, which was but seldom, then his preaching was truly profitable; but in general, it was exceedingly dry and lifeless."

Charles Wesley's London years were no retirement from the active work of ministry. In addition to preaching several times a week, and meeting the Methodist societies on a biweekly basis, he renewed his work with the poor and the outcasts. Even in the last years of his life, he went regularly to London's Newgate Prison, where he preached "the condemned sermon," a final opportunity to save the soul of a condemned felon. Charles seemed to have come full circle, ministering in prison just as he had nearly a half-century earlier. Henry Moore accompanied Charles on at least one such occasion. "I witnessed with feelings which I cannot describe the gracious tenderness of his heart," he wrote. "I saw the advantage of proclaiming the Gospel to those who knew they were soon to die, and felt that they had greatly sinned."

Charles's last published collection of hymns was *Prayers for Condemned Malefactors* (1778). It was a twelve-page pamphlet written for these hopeful evangelistic visits to London's prison. In one copy of this hymnbook, published in 1785, someone — perhaps Wesley himself — scrawled: "these prayers were answered, Thursday, April 28, 1785, as nineteen malefactors, who all died penitent. Not unto me, O Lord, not unto me." The first poetical prayer in this collection represents well the soteriological intention and compassionate tone of the rest:

Friend of all the sinful race,
Jesus, full of truth and grace,
Sent the wandering sheep to find,
Save these outcasts of mankind.

Earnestly remember them,
That they may themselves condemn:
Them for whom we life request,
On the brink of hell arrest.

O reverse their sorest doom,
Snatch them from the wrath to come,
Touching whom we now agree
Mercy to implore from Thee.

Mercy they can ne'er receive,
Till Thou dost repentance give;
Giver of the grief unknown,
Look — and break their hearts of stone.

Let them hear Thy dying cries,
Then the dead in sin arise;
Stubborn guilt doth then relent,
Rocks are by Thy passion rent.

With severest anguish torn,
Felons look on Thee, and mourn,
Poor repenting thieves confess
Christ their Lord — and die in peace!

He continued to offer a Christian witness as he traveled the city's streets. In letter to his son, Charles remarked, "A woman in the streets cursed me heartily for having endeavoured to save her — against her will." On one occasion, as he traveled around town, Charles was nearly run over by a delivery wagon. His anger at the driver nearly got the better of Wesley: "Had I beat him down, he knew he deserved it, and worse; for he plainly designed to run over me." In a more reflective mood, Charles wrote "Thanksgiving for an Escape From being Crushed to Death. November 8th, 1782":

1.   Thee Father, I praise,
      Almighty in grace,
      Through Jesus my Lord
   Thy power be acknowledged, Thy mercy adored!
      In dangers and snares
      Thou number'st my hairs,
      Thy wings are outspread,
   My soul to defend, and to cover my head.

2.   When destruction was nigh,
       I was under Thine eye;
       When the ruin came down,
Unconscious of harm, and unhurt, I went on:
       Without Thy decree
       No evil could be,
       And, restrain'd by Thy will,
Death himself had no power, or commission to kill.

3.   Reserved by the love
       Of my Saviour above,
       Thy servant I am,
Thy kingdom to spread, and to hallow Thy name:
       Thee in Jesus to know,
       And publish below
       Thy unspeakable grace,
Which abolishes death, and redeems our whole race.

4.   For this at Thy feet
       Expecting I sit,
       Till Thy counsel Thou show,
And discover the work Thou wouldst have me to do;
       Whatsoever it be,
       Let me do it to Thee,
       And Thy blessing receive,
And an heir of Thy kingdom eternally live.

The Wesleys' relocation to London allowed Charles to reconnect with old friends, like Lord Mansfield — who had been his friend when they were schoolboys at Westminster School. Now he lived sufficiently close for the two elderly men to go walking in a nearby park, and for the Chief Justice of England to bring his violin to the Mary-le-bone residence to play music with the Wesley boys. Charles's friendship with General Oglethorpe, whom he had known since the Georgia mission, was rekindled during these London years, as was Wesley's friendship with Lord Dartmouth (whom he met through Lady Huntingdon) and the Moravian James Hutton, in whose home Charles had lived more than thirty before. To Hutton, Charles wrote in 1771, "Take it for granted that I am *fixed, resolved, determined, sworn,* to stand by the Methodists, and my Brother, right or wrong, through thick and thin. . . . Not-withstanding my incurable bigotry, can and will you love me? If so, I am your man, your first and latest of friends, your faithful old, C.W."

The London years also saw Charles Wesley make many new friends and acquaintances. Many of these, including famous musicians like Kelway and Dr. William Boyce (1710-79), came into his orbit through the musical talent of his sons. Sir Edward Walpole, for example, came to hear the young Wesleys play, and later wrote, "The young gentlemen, who are the most extraordinary geniuses I have met with, have done great honour to my little attempts in musick by their approbation and if the anthem, or any other piece would be acceptable to them, they shall have a copy." Charles's sister, Martha — Mrs. Hall — was involved in London's literary circles, and through her Charles came to know the famous poet, essayist, and lexicographer Dr. Samuel Johnson, as well as playwright and producer David Garrick (1717-79) and essayist Hannah Moore (1745-1833). Dr. Johnson took a literary interest in young Sally Wesley, and she sometimes accompanied her aunt Martha to his home to discuss literature and writing. At the home of Hannah Moore, Charles met the rising young politician William Wilberforce (1759-1833), who in his journal recalled their encounter. "I went," he wrote, "I think in 1785 to see [Hannah Moore], and when I came into the room Charles Wesley arose from the table, around which a numerous party sat at tea, and coming forwards to me, gave me solemnly his blessing. I was scarcely ever more affected. Such was the effect of his manner and appearance that it altogether over set me, and I burst into tears, unable to restrain myself." Wilberforce remembered Charles so fondly that, in 1792, he saw to it that his widow received an annual pension, valued at £60 per year, for the next thirty years. Wilberforce was concerned that, with the passing of John Wesley, the Methodists might forget the widow of their less popular cofounder.

The rank and file among the Methodists did not appreciate the fact that one of the founders of their movement moved so easily in the circles of the rich and famous. Indeed, many seemed to resent it. As early as 1775, John Fletcher wrote to Charles warning him that people were complaining about his fine house, love for music, and aristocratic friends. "You have your enemies," Fletcher confided. "They complain of your love for music, company, fine people, great folks, and the want of your former zeal and frugality. I need not put you in mind to cut off all sinful appearances." But it is also true that the people who resented Wesley's love for music and keeping "company" with great people had no appreciation for his sons' musical careers. In fact, the Methodists had no opportunities to offer the Wesley boys. Their preaching houses had no organs; they had no prestigious venues in which they might play and no paying positions to which they might aspire. Charles Wesley's desire to see his sons well placed in musical careers, as much as his own love for music and fine company, caused him to begin to move among the wealthy and influential people who could help young Charles and Samuel advance their careers. But to many Methodists this was betrayal, and they held it against him.

If Wesley appeared to the Methodists to betray his spiritual calling through association with the powerful and well-to-do, he did bring religious zeal and guidance to his new friends. In 1776, when Kelway was more than seventy years old, he contracted a serious illness, and Wesley wrote his son's tutor a letter of spiritual counsel that expressed deep concern over the health and spiritual state of their friend and benefactor. The poet-evangelist told Kelway: "The true repentance is better felt than described. It surely implies a troubled and wounded spirit, a broken and contrite heart. It is what the publican felt when he could only cry, 'God be merciful unto me a sinner'; what Peter felt when Jesus turned and *looked* at him; and what the trembling jailer felt when he asked, 'what must I do to be saved.'" By way of repentance, Wesley urged his reader to come to peace with God through Jesus Christ: "By this brokenness of heart our Saviour prepares for divine faith and present pardon, sealed upon the heart, in peace which passes all understanding, in joy unspeakable and full of glory, and in love which casts out the love of sin, especially our bosom sin, our ruling passion, whether the love of pleasure, of praise, or of money." In this mosaic of biblical phrases and themes Charles Wesley showed himself to be, as he described himself to Joseph Kelway, "the faithful servant and friend of your soul."

During Kelway's illness, young Charles took instruction from Dr. William Boyce. In his narrative of his son's musical development, Charles Wesley wrote: "Charles has now been some years under Dr. Boyces's tuition, learning composition, and hopes to continue learning as long as the Doctor lives. At the same time he retains the most grateful veneration for his old master, Mr. Kelway, and played to him, while he was able to hear him, every week. He believes he has the greatest masters in Christendom." Charles Wesley had considerable respect for William Boyce, both as a man and as musician. "I hope he [Charles] has caught a little of his master's temper, as well as his skill. A more modest man than Dr. Boyce I have never known. I never heard him speak a vain or ill-natured word, either to exalt himself, or to depreciate another." In 1777 Wesley penned a poem that celebrated the talents and character of Boyce. When the doctor died in 1779 it became his eulogy, and the younger Charles Wesley set it to music:

> Father of harmony, farewell!
>   Farewell for a few fleeting years!
> Translated from the mournful vale;
>   Jehovah's flaming ministers
> Have borne thee to thy place above,
> Where all is harmony and love. . . .

Of Charles Wesley Jr.'s musical skill and development we know quite a lot. Not only did his father leave us lengthy accounts of the musical training of both sons, but Daines Barrington was so amazed to find so much musical talent in one family that he published an extraordinary account of Charlie's and Sam's abilities in *The Philosophical Transactions of the Year 1781*. But precious little is known about young Charles's thoughts and personality. Biographers have found him to be "a withdrawn and mildly unsociable character," and in this he seemed to show some of the same proclivities as his more famous father. Music was his entire world — so much so that he ignored the more basic facts of life, like dressing neatly. As soon as 1777, his father was comparing Charles's academic skills unfavorably to those of his younger brother: "If Charles does not make more haste, Sam will over take him in Latin." He seemed to lack the typical Wesleyan drive for education and self improvement, and was content to bury himself in music. He has been described, by his uncle John, as kind, good-humored, and affable. His morals were correct and he was conventionally religious, but he was not the passionate religious practitioner that his parents were. He was a kind and supportive son to his parents, and got along well with his sister Sally; indeed in later years, he came to depend upon her significantly. He seemed free from ambition, but also in a negative sense — in that he was not highly motivated. Often indolent, it took him many years to find suitable employment for his considerable musical talents.

The temperament of Charles Wesley's two sons is a study in contrasts. Where Charles was dreamy and absentminded, Samuel had the quick and sharp mind of his father and uncle. Samuel absorbed much more of the lessons from the classics that his father tried to instill in his boys. Where Charles seemed to withdraw from the world, Samuel was fatefully drawn to it. He was not as easily amendable to his parents' wishes or the weight or the Wesley legacy as Charles was. Samuel chafed repeatedly, for example, over his father's prohibition of the theater. Where Charles seemed out of touch with the world, Samuel seemed overly interested in it and was readily corrupted by it. Both of Charles Wesley's sons seemed to have been inoculated against Methodism at an early age, perhaps because of their own father's struggles within the movement. But where Charles was conventionally religious, Samuel was not. Indeed, he seemed to react deeply and destructively against the religious tradition of his parents.

Joseph Kelway had intended to introduce young Charles Wesley to the royal court at St. James, in hope of pleasing King George III and perhaps securing royal preferment for the boy. In 1775 the eighteen-year-old musician was summoned to a command performance before King George III. Although he went with fear and trembling, Charles made a tremendous impression upon his majesty, and was invited back on an annual basis throughout his reign. When the king heard that young Charles was met with the report "We want no Wesleys here!" upon applying for an organist position at St. Paul's Cathedral, and then also failed in a position at Westminster Abbey, his majesty told him: "The name of Wesley is always welcome to me," and he gave Charles a gift of £100. King George IV engaged Charles Jr. as the musical tutor for his daughter, Princess Charlotte, so he was well known at court. Charles Sr. was more worried than enthusiastic about his son's employment at the Court of St. James: "I am not sanguine in my expectation of good from Windsor," he wrote in 1786. "If Charles has received no evil by it, it is a miracle, and I am satisfied." His parents' ambivalence toward royal preferment stopped Charles Jr. from applying for the post of organist at the Chapel Royal, a position he might well have achieved, and which would have provided him with a suitable venue for his skill.

The old man — and Charles Wesley was an old man when his children began to reach adulthood — was deeply concerned about their education and their religious upbringing. A letter to Charles, dated September 7, 1779, evidences this. "What do you understand by that Scripture phrase, 'God gave him favor in the sight of . . .' such an one?" he wrote. "Does it not teach you to refer *all* good to God? He raises us up friends, and expects our thankful acknowledgement of it. Such is Lady Gatehouse, Mr. Barrington, and others. — And if God is for us, who can be against us? Acquaint thyself now with Him, and be at peace, i.e. know God and be happy."

When Charles Jr. turned twenty-five, he became interested in a young woman, and his thoughts turned towards marriage. His parents did not know the girl, so Sally inquired about her to her brother-in-law. John Wesley reported: "I hear the girl is good, but of no family." "No fortune either," Sally retorted. On August 30, 1782, his father wrote young Charles, intertwining the topics of matrimony and vital piety: "Dear Charles, if any man would learn to pray (the proverb says) let him go to sea. I say, if any man would learn to pray, let him think of marrying; for if he thinks aright, he will expect the blessing and success from God alone; and ask it in frequent and earnest prayer." Charles Wesley was not sufficiently satisfied with his son's spiritual development to recommend marriage to him: "Hither to," he wrote, "my dear Charles, your thoughts of marriage have not made you more serious, but more light, more unadvisable, and more distracted; this slackened my desire to see you settled, before I leave you. You do not yet take the way to be happy in a married state: you do not sufficiently take God into your council." John Wesley was more supportive of Charlie's courtship than was his own father. Perhaps remembering the lost love of Grace Murray, his uncle encouraged him and sent him £50 in support of the wedding. But the wedding did not transpire, and young Charles never married — he lived out his days first in the company of his widowed mother, and then with his sister Sally.

Charles Jr. was an extremely talented musician, but the social climate and religious tradition in which he was born, as well as his family name, made it difficult for him to find suitable employment as an organist. He was sixty years old before he was able to hold a permanent paying position. This may have been due in part to his own idiosyncratic nature, but it was also part of the liability of being a Wesley. In 1796, for example, he applied for the position of organist at St. Paul's Cathedral, a position for which he was eminently well suited, and was rebuffed with the jibe: "We want no Wesleys here!" Ironically, the church that Charles Wesley had so long sought to defend and serve wanted little of the service of his sons; in the Church of England the name "Wesley" had come to stand for "enthusiast" and "schismatic."

Sarah Wesley Jr. was Charles's only surviving daughter. Like her mother, she went by the nickname "Sally"; also like her mother, she was an attractive child who had her good looks marred by smallpox. Her father theorized that it saved her from many temptations. She was three years younger than her brother Charles, and six years older than Samuel. Her brothers were both musical prodigies and hence garnered more public and published notice than she did. She was a bright, and lively girl, and in this she probably took after her mother. In her interest and talent for literary matters she probably took after her father.

Charles's letters to his daughter were full of the same sort of mixture of practical and pious advice that we saw in his communications with his eldest son. He wrote to Sarah to insist upon her following the famous Wesleyan "early to bed, early to rise" regimen: "Dear Sally — Go to bed at nine, and you may rise at six with ease. It is good for soul, body, and estate to rise early." He often wrote to encourage her reading. But most of his advice and inquiries revolved around religion and spiritual life: "Can you begin the day better than with prayer and the Scripture? What benefit have you from [meeting with] your Band? The knowledge of yourself; or to know Jesus Christ? . . . How go you in arithmetic? God teach you so to number your days, that you may apply your heart unto wisdom!"

His concern for Sally's spiritual health persisted. On November 17, 1779, Charles Wesley wrote his daughter — again — about the state of her soul. She seems to have been having doubts. Her father wrote to reassure her: "God, I trust will lead you into his whole design in leaving you, as it were, to yourself. You are very near discovering it if you can always say from your heart: 'I have no hope that fixes upon earth.' Go on and say with David, 'And now, Lord, what is my hope? Truly my hope is ever in Thee.'" He recalled her pious youth: "In your earlier days He *was* your Hope. You began to seek true happiness in Him. You felt His drawings. At times you faintly sighed for His love. . . . Nothing can ever make you happy but the favor and approbation of God in Christ. The seal of that favour is the Peace of God which surpasses all conception. Probably you again wish while reading this, to experience that divine power and conscious love of your Saviour. What would I give you might experience it? My life is a mere trifle. God laid down His own to purchase the blessing for you and charges you by the late Providences to ask till you receive, to seek till you find it and Him in your heart!" Sally gradually did become serious about her Christianity, and worked closely with her father during his final years. She was his chief copyist and scribe in his declining years.

Samuel Wesley, like his brother Charles, was a musical prodigy. He demonstrated considerable skill on the violin when he was still a child. He took lessons from two separate teachers in Bristol; and in 1772, took lessons from the famous Wilhelm Cramer. Samuel also showed considerable interest in keyboard instruments, and his skill on the organ — second only to his brother — became apparent when he was so young that his feet did not yet reach the instrument's pedals. He also excelled at improvisation on the organ and at composition. Samuel's *Eight Lessons for the Harpsichord* was published when he was only eleven years of age. Wesleyan tradition has passed on an account of Charles Wesley taking young Samuel to watch a regimental band perform in parade. After their performance, the director asked the little boy whether he liked the piece they played. "Yes, I did," he replied. "I wrote it."

In terms of his personality and talents, Samuel was quite different from his brother Charles. Where both boys seemed thoroughly inoculated against passionate Methodism, Charles was conventional in his religious beliefs and practices, but Samuel was not. Where music was Charles Jr.'s whole world, it was not so with Samuel. He was well studied in the classical languages and literature, and would have probably been a success in various other professions — had he not been so exceptionally talented in music. Where Charles was dreamy, quiet, compliant and withdrawn, Samuel was a witty conversationalist, gregarious and sometimes quite stubborn. Like his father, Sam had a quick mind. He also had a strong streak of independent thinking, and was occasionally prone to unpredictable and unconventional actions.

While Charles Wesley concerned himself in the Christian nurture of all his children, he seemed particularly concerned about his youngest son's spirituality. In 1773, when Samuel was but eight years old, his father wrote him:

> Come now, my good friend Samuel, and let us reason together, God made you for Himself, that is to be ever happy in Him. Ought you not, therefore, to serve and love Him? But you can do neither unless He gives you the power. "Ask," He says Himself, "and it shall be given you"; that is, pray for it every night and morning in your own words, as well as in the words which have been taught you. You have been used to say your prayers in the sight of others. Henceforth, go into a corner by yourself, where no eye but God's may see you. There pray to your heavenly Father who seeth in secret; and be sure He hears every word you speak, and see everything you do, at all times and in all places.

He added, "You should begin to live by reason and religion. There should be sense even in your play and diversions, therefore, I have furnished you with maps and books, and harpsichord. Every day get something by heart, whatever your mother recommends. Every day read one or more chapters in the Bible. I suppose you mother will take you now, in the place of your brother, to be her chaplain, to read the Psalms and lessons, when your sister does not." One of God's most tangible gifts to the young boy lay in the area of music. "You have a natural inclination to it [music]," his father wrote, "but God gave you that therefore God should be thanked and praised for it. Your brother has the same love of music, and much more than you; yet he is not proud or vain of it. Neither, I trust, will you be."

Some years later, Charles wrote his wife with concern about the spiritual state of their youngest child: "Sam [needs] more care taken with him. If I should not live to help him, it will lie upon you. Make him a living Christian, he will never wish to be a dead Papist." Samuel's religious state continued to be a concern to his father, and yet he stubbornly resisted Charles's religious advice. In 1786 the elder Wesley confided to his namesake: "I hope he [Samuel] continues to ride daily; but one thing he still lacks, to make him happy, or tolerably easy. He cannot believe *me,* so he must find it out as he can."

The tension and occasional conflict between Charles Wesley and his younger son may have been, in part, an accident of temperament: it is likely that they were too much alike to get along amicably. It is also true that they lived in different worlds; Charles Wesley was in his seventies when his son Samuel was a teenager. The father's circle of acquaintance, while growing somewhat larger during the London years, was rooted in Methodism, and beyond that in the Church of England; Samuel's circle of acquaintance was swelled enormously by his musical talent, and it was through him and his brother that their father met aristocrats and entered into the fashionable social life of London. Where Charles's youth had been spent in study, devotion, and poverty, Samuel had many more economic and social advantages. Where the father was often tempted to think less of himself and his abilities than he should have, the son had the opposite proclivity. As a Methodist, even a traveling one, Charles felt strongly inclined to exercise firm, fatherly control over Samuel's development and pastimes; Samuel seemed to chafe under his father's restrictions, and since these were frequently rooted in Methodist convictions, he probably resented his father's religion as well. Where Sally was forbidden to attend fashionable balls, Samuel was forbidden the theatre, but the latter needed more reminding than the former because of his ardor for "worldly" events.

Perhaps nothing epitomizes the London years of Charles Wesley's life better than the concerts he hosted in his Mary-le-bone home in order to showcase the musical talent of his extraordinary sons. A manuscript letter Charles wrote to the famous artist William Russell on December 21, 1778, described the plan for the first of these events. "It is proposed by messrs. Cha. and Sam. W[esley] — to have every other Thursday at their own house an entertainment of their own music chiefly, consisting of overtures, concerto's, quartetott's, duets for 2 organs, solo's, extempore voluntaries, and etc." The concerts were supported by subscription: three guineas for all six nights of concerts. The plan for the first concert in the first series was also preserved in the proud father's letter to Russell.

Plan of the First Night:
1. Overture. C.W.
2. Organ Concerto. C.W.
3. Extempore on harpschord. S.W.

4. Overture on Handel
5. Organ extempore. C.W.
6. Overture: Lord Mornington

Second Act.
1. Overture. C.W.
2. Organ extempore. S.W.
3. Lesson on Handel. C.W.
4. Violin Solo. Composed and performed by S.W.
5. Duet for 2 organs. Composed by C.W. Performed by C. & S.W.
6. Organ extempore. C.W.

This was an ambitious evening for the Wesley boys; Charles was twenty-two years old when this first series of concerts was arranged, and Samuel was only thirteen. The Wesleys' in-house concert series ran for nine seasons from 1779-87. The people who attended these concerts were, typically, genteel lovers of music, monied aristocrats — not profoundly religious people, and not Methodists. The reaction of the Methodist leadership was fairly predictable. Thomas Coke, the future apostle of American Methodism, recalled his initial reaction: "I looked upon the Concerts which he allows his sons to have in his own house, to be highly dishonorable to God; and himself to be criminal, by reason of his situation in the Church of Christ; but," Coke added, "on mature consideration of all the circumstances appertaining to them, I cannot blame him."

Within two days of the first concert, January 14, 1779, Charles Wesley penned an apologia for his sons' concerts. He listed his reasons for holding such events:

I. To keep them out of harm's way: the way (I mean) of bad music and bad musicians, who by free communication with them might corrupt both their taste and their morals.
II. That my sons may have a safe and honourable opportunity of availing themselves of their musical abilities, which have cost me several hundred pounds.
III. That they may enjoy their full right of private judgment, and likewise their independency: both of which must be given up if they swim with the stream and follow the multitude.

IV. To improve their play and their skill in composing: as they must themselves furnish the principal music of every concert. Although they do not call their musical entertainment a concert. It is too great a word. . . .

In a personal letter to his brother John, Charles added, "I am clear, without a doubt, that my sons' concert is after the will and order of Providence. It has established them as musicians, and in a safe and honourable way."

When John Wesley subsequently published this letter from his brother in his *Methodist Magazine* in 1789, he inserted an asterisk and added his doubts to his brother's claim that the concerts were according to "the will and order of Providence." In 1781, however, John Wesley accepted his nephews' invitation and attended their concert on February 25 of that year. John's journal reported: "I spent an agreeable hour at a concert at my nephews', but I was a little out of my element among Lords and Ladies. I love plain music and plain company best." Subsequent journal entries indicate that John Wesley attended his nephews' concerts on at least three additional occasions.

These concerts epitomize the London years, not only because they stress the musical prowess of Charles Wesley's sons but also because they demonstrate how he was moving into a world caught between the Methodist establishment and the fashionable circles of famous people in the metropolis. In 1783 the famous musician William Jackson advised Charles to "plant out his sons" so that they might more readily succeed as musicians. Charles refused. Ever the Methodist, he wanted to be able to continue to shape the moral and spiritual life of his young musicians. Ever the family man, Charles feared the influence of rich and worldly people upon his sons even as he courted their attention in order to launch their musical careers. Still, rank-and-file Methodists were beginning to look upon him with growing suspicion. And darker clouds were looming on the horizon.

19 "Ordination Is Separation"

The year 1784 was a climactic one in the life of Charles Wesley. In several ways it signaled the beginning of the end of his life. It was filled with heartache, disappointment, and struggle. His health was frail and failing, but this was nothing new; his health had been an ongoing battle for decades. Charles's continued disappointment over his brother's apparent drift towards separation from the Church of England weighed heavily upon him. Since the 1760s he had been nagging and scolding John and the lay preachers about the steps they seemed to be taking towards schism. Now, as the brothers were well into old age, the issue of what would happen to the Methodists after their deaths became a more pressing matter.

John Wesley, under the prompting of his brother and the lay preachers, had been casting about for a solution to the problem of succession. Charles had repeatedly declined to take over for his brother. Finally in 1784 John decided upon a plan. On February 28 he issued his famous "Deed of Declaration," which had the effect of leaving the governance of the Methodist movement in the hands of the "legal one hundred" Wesleyan preachers who would constitute the future governing body of Methodism. In some respects, this plan seemed to be a capitulation to the lay preachers and the democratic sentiments that

306

had been hatched in Bristol decades before. But as John Wesley consistently outlived one designated successor after another, this approach seemed to be the only one left to him.

Charles could have not looked upon the "Deed of Declaration" with favor. It was precisely the predicament that he had long predicted: the lay preachers would take control of the movement after the Wesleys' death and force a separation from the Church of England. One can only guess what might have happened had Charles Wesley lived longer than his brother. It is clear that the relations between Charles Wesley and the lay preachers, which had been extremely strained over the years, would not have allowed the younger Wesley to work harmoniously with them in John's absence.

John Wesley continued to maintain that this and the subsequent steps he took in 1784 did not constitute a separation from the Church of England, but Charles was becoming deaf to his denials. As late as 1786, John Wesley would write, "Indeed, I love the Church as sincerely as ever I did; and I tell my societies everywhere, 'the Methodists will not leave the Church, at least while I live.'" But the "while I live" clause must have rung rather hollow to Charles, and with the publication of the "Deed of Declaration" it must have been clear to everyone, including John himself, that the Methodists would break with the Church of England following the Wesleys' deaths.

John was caught. Throughout his ministry, and at the strong insistence of his brother, he had maintained that lay preachers should not administer the sacraments. This meant that either the Methodist preachers had to secure Anglican ordination or the Methodists would have to get used to having the sacraments (particularly the Lord's Supper) infrequently. But both Wesleys believed in — to borrow one of John's sermon titles — "The Duty of Constant Communion," so the option of infrequent communion was distasteful to them. But they were also notoriously unsuccessful in securing Anglican ordination for their preachers. The dilemma of the Methodists in North America was particularly acute because there was only one ordained Methodist (Francis Asbury) to serve the entire continent. Four years earlier, in 1780, John had requested the ordination of a "pious man" for service in America. The bishop refused on the flimsy grounds that there were already threescore Anglican clergymen in America. Enraged, Wesley retorted that threescore would not suffice if they knew no more about saving souls than catching whales.

Caught between his own fundamental commitments to frequent communion and against lay administration, John Wesley endeavored to develop a way forward. It was guided by John's reading of the early church writers as well as more recent works such as *The Irenicum* (1659) by Bishop Stillingfleet, and Lord Peter King's *Enquiry into the Consitution, Discipline, Unity, and Worship of the Primitive Church* (1691). His reading of this material in the 1740s had convinced Wesley that the hallowed tradition that ordination was based upon apostolic succession was a myth, and that the New Testament office of presbyter was really the same as that of bishop. The latter belief bore fruit in John Wesley's mind, and under the necessity of the needs of Methodists in America and the intense pressure from the lay preachers, he hatched a plan.

On September 1, 1784, John Wesley "appointed" Dr. Coke as Superintendent for America, and then subsequently "appointed" lay preachers Richard Whatcoat and Thomas Vassey as elders for the same ministry. Apparently Wesley had proposed the idea of setting apart missionaries for America to a group of senior men he met at his Leeds conference for that purpose. James Creighton, who was among them, recalled, "They did not approve the scheme because it seemed inconsistent with Mr. Wesley's former professions respecting the Church. Upon this, the meeting was abruptly broken up by Mr. Wesley's going out." After this meeting, Coke (who held a law degree as well as elder's orders in the Church of England), Whatcoat, and Vassey offered themselves for service in America. They were told to meet Wesley in Bristol seven weeks later for a briefing prior to their departure. While the senior preachers had disapproved of Wesley's plan for ordaining these men prior to sending them to America, John's mind was made up.

Wesley was convinced that he had the scriptural authority as a presbyter to set apart these three men for ministerial service; he seemed to care little that it was a complete breach of Anglican ecclesiastical authority. Charles Wesley, who was serving in Bristol at the time the ordinations occurred, could have been invited to join his brother in laying hands on the Methodists, but he was neither invited to participate nor informed of the event till long after it occurred. In the public record, Wesley used the word "appointed" to describe the event, but John's shorthand record is more honest: "ordained Rd. Whatcoat, and T. Vassey." Anglican elders Wesley and Coke joined one other presbyter in forming the presbytery that laid hands on them at five o'clock in the morning at the house of Dr. John Castleman in Bristol. The odd hour and location of the event may have been a matter of necessity, but they gave Wesley's ordinations a clandestine feel.

Certainly, John Wesley intended to keep his brother out of the picture so that he could not intervene; the ordinations for America were presented to Charles as an accomplished fact, and he had to find out about them from Henry Durbin, a Bristol druggist, two months later. Charles's reply to Durbin described him as being utterly shocked: "I am thunderstruck," he wrote. "I cannot believe it." Henry Durbin wrote back the same day, "If you were thunderstruck before, I think your brother printed the declaration of ordination in a louder clap; I must give you advice now, not to be *angry* with him. You pity poor Atlay's insanity, you ought to pity your brother's; while you were in Bristol, your brother, Dr. Coke and Mr. Creighton ordained the two preachers for America at five in the morning at Mr. Castleman's, and Dr. Coke was reordained. This I had from a person to whom Dr. Coke owned t'was done. Your brother as head of the Methodists is now a Presbyterian, contrary to all his declarations, but like Saul, he forced himself *to the sacrifice*. I think he should not preach in the Churches or read the Prayers, as he has renounced it."

No letters between the Wesley brothers are extant from the fall of 1784. Charles busied himself in writing poems and epigrams, as well as letters to others about the ordinations. His "Manuscript Ordinations" from this period was headed with a quotation from William Chillingworth's *Religion of Protestants* (1638): "That a Pretense of Reformation will acquit no man from Schism, we grant very willingly, and therefore say that It concerns every man who separated from any Church-Communion *even as his Salvation is worth* to look most carefully to it, that cause of his separation be just and necessary." The biting sarcasm and disappointment of these hymns well illustrate Charles Wesley's reaction to his brother's ordinations for America. The hymns also suggest that Charles was looking for a reason for his brother's action. The first hymn in the collection seems to blame the action on his brother's weakness, age, and (implied) senility:

309

W[esley] himself and friends betrays
  By his own good sense forsook,
While suddenly his hands he lays
  On the hot head of C[oke]:

Yet *we* at least should spare the weak,
  His weak Co-equals *We,*
Nor blame an hoary Schismatic,
  A Saint of Eighty — three!

A second poem from the same collection was called *"Occidit, occidit,"* which is Latin for "It happened! It happened!" It echoes Charles's frustration and sense of utter betrayal at his brother's ordinations for America:

1. And is it come to this? And has the Man
    On whose Integrity our Church relied,
  Betray'd his trust, render'd our boastings vain,
    And fallen a Victim to ambitious Pride?

2. Whose zeal so long her Hierarchy maintain'd,
    Her humble Presbyter, her duteous Son
  Call'd an High Priest, & by Himself Ordain'd,
    He glorifies himself, & mounts a Throne.

3. Ah! Where are all his Promises and Vows
    To spend, & to be spent for Sion's Good,
  To gather the lost sheep of Israel's house,
    The Outcasts bought by his Redeemer's blood?

4. Who won for God the wandering Souls of men,
    Subjecting multitudes to Christ's command,
  He shuts his eyes, & scatters them again,
    And spreads a thou[san]d Sects throughout the land. . . .

The closing stanzas of this lengthy poem lament John's public humiliation and shame. They urge the reader not to repeat the tragic news lest the opposition have cause to triumph:

9. How is the Mighty fallen from his height,
   His weapons scatter'd, & his buckler lost!
   Ah! tell it not in Gath, nor cause delight
   And triumph in the proud Philistine Host.

10. Publish it not in Askelon, to make
    The world exult in his disastrous End!
    Rather let every soul my Grief partake,
    And ah! My Brother, cry, & ah my Friend!

11. The pious Mantle o'er his Dotage spread,
    With silent tears his shameful Fall deplore,
    And let him sink, forgot, among the dead
    And mention his unhappy name no more.

Another epigram shows that Charles vacillated between anger and sarcasm on the one hand and disappointment and betrayal on the other. In this poem Charles imagines that Methodists will no longer have to argue with Presbyterians over the issue of ordination, simply because the Methodists now have a presbytery of their own:

1. So easily are Bishops made
   By man's, or woman's whim?
   W[esley] his hands on C[oke] hath laid,
   But who laid hands on him?

2. Hands on himself he laid, and *took*
   An Apostolic Chair:
   And then ordain'd his Creature C[oke]
   His Heir and Successor.

3. Episcopalians, now no more
   With Presbyterians fight,
   But give your needless Contest o'er,
   "Whose Ordination's right?"

4. It matters not, if Both are One,
   Or different in degrees,

> For Lo! Ye see contain'd in John
> The whole Presbytery!

On November 25, 1784, Charles Wesley received a second letter from Henry Durbin containing a rambling litany of charges and fears relating to John Wesley's ordinations. But he assured Charles that his brother's actions did not reflect badly upon the younger Wesley: "D. Complin is much concerned at your Brother's rash act, which *will leave a blot* on his character, that will never wipe off with all his logic. Your character is not harmed in the least by it, your verses are some excuse for him. Therefore I pity him, though I am like the man who fell among thieves, I was covered with bruises, wounds and troubles on every side." Durbin had some unflattering things to say about Dr. Coke, and these certainly echoed Charles's own sentiments about the man: "the Doctor is *base enough* to do anything in his Zeal for another *Presbyterian* Church, he is *intoxicated* with power." The next day, Charles Wesley received a letter from the Bristol printer William Pine. Charles seemed to have urged him to reread John Wesley's earlier edition of *Reasons Against Separation,* and Pine responded, "I have read over *The Reasons Against Separation.* Your brother's adversaries will too soon avail themselves of them. He must now give up *consistency* for ever. I think it will be best for us who have his real welfare at heart to *be as quiet* as possible, and pray and believe that God will bring good out of this evil."

On April 28, 1785, Charles Wesley wrote a lengthy, autobiographical letter to one Dr. Chandler, who was just about to embark for America. The letter is an overview of Charles's life and ministry, and it offers five important paragraphs about the issue of separation from the Church of England:

> I never lost my Dread of Separation, or ceased to guard our societies against it. I frequently told them, "I am your servant as long as you remain in the Church of England; but no longer. Should you forsake her, you would renounce me."
>
> Some of our Lay-Preachers very early discovered an inclination to separate, which induced my brother to print his *Reasons Against Separation.* As soon as it appeared, we beat down the schismatical spirit. If any one did leave the Church, at the same time he left our

society. For nearly fifty years we kept the sheep in the fold; and having filled the number of our days, only waited to depart in peace.

After our having continued friends for above seventy years, and fellow labourers for above fifty, can anything but death part us? I can scarcely yet believe it, that, in his eighty-second year, my Brother, my old, intimate friend and companion, *should have assumed* the Episcopal Character, ordained Elders, Consecrated a Bishop, and sent him to ordain our lay Preachers in America! I was then in Bristol, at his Elbow; yet he never gave me the least hint of his Intention. How was he surprised into so rash an action? He certainly persuaded himself that it was right.

Lord Mansfield told me last year, that "ordination was separation." This my Brother does not and will not see; or that he has renounced the Principles and Practice of his whole life; that he has acted contrary to all his Declarations, Protestations, and Writings, robbed his friends of their boast, realized the Nag's head ordination, and left an indelible blot on his name, as long as it shall be remembered!

But this same letter also indicated that Charles was not done with his brother. Using the language and metaphor of marriage, he asserted that they were joined for life — whether or not Charles joined John in his plans for the new Methodist Church: "Thus our Partnership here is dissolved, but not our Friendship. I have taken him for better or worse, till death do us part; or rather, re-unite us in love inseparable. I have lived on earth a little too long — who have lived to see this evil day. But I shall very soon be taken from it, in steadfast faith, that the Lord will maintain his own cause, and carry on his own work, and fulfill his promise to his church, 'Lo, I am with you always, even to the end!'" At the end of the letter, Charles opined in a lamenting postscript: "But what are your Methodists now? Only a new sect of Presbyterians! And after my brother's death, which is now so near, what will be their End? They will lose all their influence and importance; they will turn aside to vain janglings; they will settle again upon their lees; and like other Sects of Dissenters, come to nothing!"

In the middle of 1785 Charles penned another volume of manuscript poems, later entitled "Ms. Brothers." It was written into a blank copy book, but most of the pages were subsequently cut out of the book. One lengthy poem, called "True Yokefellows," remains in the manuscript book. This poem is a prayerful recounting of the long relationship Charles Wesley enjoyed with his brother John. It begins, "Happy the days, when Charles and John/By nature and by grace were One." It is a prayerful reminiscence of the years they spent together. Between the lines of the poem, one can hear Charles Wesley trying to come to terms with his brother's ordinations for America and the tension they caused. Charles lays most of the blame at the feet of the Methodist lay preachers. They had been "rais'd out of the people's lees,/Raw, inexperience'd Novices,/They soon their low Estate forgot."

> 6. They urged the Elder Presbyter
>   Himself a Bishop to declare,
>   And then to answer their demands,
>   By laying on his hasty hands;
>   The mighty Babel to erect,
>   And found a new Dissenting Sect,
>   His Mother-Church to rend, disclaim,
>   And break the Party with his Name
>   But for a length of years he stood,
>   By a whole Army unsubdued,
>   By friendship kept, refus'd to yield,
>   And all their fiery Darts repel'd,
>   And check'd the Madness for a space
>   Of Corah's bold, rebellious race,
>   Who heard, like Eli's sons unmov'd,
>   His words, too tenderly reprov'd,
>   "In vain you tempt me to do till
>   For separate I never will
>   Will never with my Brother break,
>   Will never die a Schismatick!"

In this poem Charles raised the wistful wish that he and John had died peacefully before John could cause schism with the Anglicans and separation between the brothers. He even imagined that John should dread meeting his father's ghost in heaven:

7. O had he died *before* that day,
   When W[esley] did himself betray
   Did boldly on himself confer
   The Apostolic Character!
   O that we both had took our flight
   Together to the realms of light,
   Together yielded up our breath
   In life united, and in death!
   Leaving an honest Name behind,
   We then assur'd that Rest to find
   Had past the valley undismay'd,
   Nor fear'd to meet a Father's shade [ghost]
   A Cloud of Witnesses inroll'd
   In heaven, the sheep of England's fold,
   A noble host of Martyrs too
   Who faithful unto death, and true,
   Spent their last breath for Sion's good,
   And strove resisting unto blood. . . .

Charles ascribed John's part in the defection and the ordinations to ignorance: "In ignorance he did the Deed,/The Deed which endless mischiefs fraught,/Alas, he did he knew not what." Charles prayed that God would pity John in his mistake, and turn his heart back to the Mother Church: "Incline him humbly to revoke/The fatal Step his haste hath took,/And his true heart again shall be,/Turn'd back to England's Church and Thee."

The last verse of Charles's poem invokes a prayer upon John Wesley, the Methodist lay preachers, and the people. He asks God to guide and protect them, and form them into one glorious crown of glory for Wesley to wear in the life to come:

9. . . .With glory crown his reverend head
   Found in the way of righteousness
   There let him stay, and die in peace:
   Let all the children of his prayers,
   Seals of his Ministerial care,
   To Him by his Redeemer given,
   Compose his Crown of joy in Heaven!

On August 14, 1785, Charles wrote what may have been his first letter to his brother since the ordinations of eleven months before. At any rate, it is the first extant letter between them, and it begins (as do many of Charles's letters from the period) with the younger brother urging his correspondent to read his *Reasons Against a Separation from the Church of England,* which had been published in 1758. Charles was concerned about their respective places in history:

> Alas! What trouble are you preparing for yourself, as well as for me, and for your oldest, truest, and best friends! Before you have quite broken down the bridge, stop, and consider! If your sons have no regard for you, have some regard for yourself. Go to your grave in peace; at least suffer me to go first, before the ruin is under your hand. So much I think, you owe to my father, my brother and to me, as to stay till I am taken from this Evil. I am on the brink of the grave. Do not push me in, or embitter my last moments. Let us not leave an indelible blotch on our memory, but let us leave behind us the name and character of honest men.

This letter may have been the first attempt at a reconciliation between them, because Charles concluded, "This letter is a debt to our parents, and to our brother [Samuel], as well as to you, and to your faithful friend."

The next day, Charles wrote a letter to his wife, Sally. The restraint he had shown in his letter to brother John was thrown off. Sally's observation that the ordinations had turned the Methodists into a sect of Dissenters seemed to rekindle Charles's ire and fears about the future of the movement. "You think right," he wrote. "'What has been done already, has fixt [sic] the Preachers Dissenters.' Who would not live fourscore years for so glorious an end — to turn 7,000 Church of England people, Dissenters! My B[rother] cannot undo what has been done. *His* Bishop [Coke] may now ordain all the Preachers without his leave; or the 3 Scottish Preachers may do it (and will) without either of them." Charles saw the ordinations for America as a "Pandora's Box" out of which would come all sorts of evil that could not be restored to its proper place. His incredulity mixed with sarcasm as Charles imagined his brother following in the footsteps of his grandfather and namesake, who (as a Puritan) rebelled against the monarchy and was among those who brought about the death of King Charles I. "Surely I am in a dream!" he wrote. "Is it possible that J.W. should be turned Presbyterian? J.W. the schismatic grandson to J.W. the regicide! How would this disturb (if they were capable of being disturbed) my Father and Brother [Samuel] in paradise!"

On August 19, John Wesley responded to Charles. "Dear Brother," John wrote, "I will tell you my thoughts with all simplicity, and wait for better information. If you agree with me, well; if not, we can, as Mr. Whitefield used to say, agree to disagree." In a lengthy, rambling reply, John defended his views to his brother. What obedience, he asked — quoting a line from one of Charles's poems — was due to "Heathenish Priests and mitred infidels?" He gave the bishops obedience, out of respect to the laws of the land, but John had come to the conclusion: "I firmly believe I am a scriptural *episkopos* [bishop or overseer], as much as any man in England, or in Europe; for the uninterrupted succession I know to be a fable, which no man ever did or can prove." John protested that this belief of his did not interfere with his loyalty to the Church of England, "from which I have no more desire to separate than I had fifty years ago. I still attend all the ordinances of the Church, at all opportunities; and I constantly and earnestly advise all that are connected with me so to do." After a lengthy examination as to what truly constitutes adherence to the Church of England, John seemed to decide that it was a matter of embracing the church's doctrine and discipline. Although many in the church had forsaken its discipline, the Wesleys had not. He concluded:

> All those reasons against a separation from the Church, in this sense, I subscribe to still. What then are you frightened at? I no more separate from it now than I did in the year 1758 [when he wrote his *Reasons Against Separation*]. I submit still (though sometimes with a doubting conscience) to 'mitred infidels.' . . . I walk still by the same rule I have done for between forty and fifty years. I do nothing rashly. It is not likely I should. The high day of my blood is over. If you will go on hand in hand with me, do. But do not hinder me, if you will not help. Perhaps if you had kept close to me, I might have done better. However, with or without help, I creep on: as I have been hitherto, so I trust I shall always be, Your affectionate friend and brother, John Wesley.

Nearly three weeks later, Charles answered his brother's letter. Charles's anger had cooled, and his tone was conciliatory once again. "Dear Brother — I will tell you my thoughts with the same simplicity. There is no danger of our quarrelling, for the second blow makes the quarrel; and you are the last man upon earth whom I would wish to quarrel with." Charles seemed offended that his brother had quoted a line from one of his own poems back at him, and he took this opportunity to deny the sentiments about unconverted Anglican clergy expressed in it: "That juvenile line of mine, 'Heathenish Priests, and mitred infidels,' I disown, renounce and with shame recant. I never knew of more than one 'mitred infidel,' and for him I took Mr. Law's word." Charles further protested that he did not understand what obedience to the Anglican bishops his brother feared: "They have let us alone, and let us act just as we pleased, for these fifty years. At present some of these are quite friendly towards us, particularly toward you. The Churches are all open to you, and never could there be less pretense for a separation." Nor was Charles willing to argue about the issue of John's episcopal status and the arguments against the apostolic succession of the Church of England: "That you are a scriptural *episkopos* or overseer, I do not dispute. . . . Neither *need we* dispute whether the uninterrupted succession be fabulous, as you believe, or real as I believe." Charles also seemed unwilling to contend any longer that ordination meant separation: "If I *could* prove your actual separation [from the Church of England], I would not, neither wish to see it proved by any other." Now Coke would bear the brunt of Charles's ire, though John still had blame by association:

> But do you allow that the Doctor [Coke] has separated? Do you not know and approve of his avowed design and resolution to get all the Methodists in the three Kingdoms into a distinct, compact body? A new episcopal church of his own? Have you seen his ordination sermon? Is the high-day of his blood over? Does he do nothing rashly? Have you not made yourself the author of all his actions?

Charles responded to his brother's question "What then are you frightened at?" in a similar vein: "At the Doctor's rashness and your supporting him in his ambitious pursuits; at an approaching schism, as causeless and unprovoked as the American rebellion; at your own eternal disgrace, and all those frightening evils which your *Reasons [Against Separation]* describe." The poet repeated back to John his own offer to "go on hand in hand" and to "creep on in the old way in which we set out together." But he smarted under John's rebuke, "Perhaps if you had kept close to me, I might have done better." Charles retorted pointedly: "When you took that fatal step at Bristol, I kept as close to you as close could be; for I was all the time at your elbow. You might certainly have done better, if you had taken me into your council." But Charles's epistle ended on a conciliatory note, and a resolution to be firmly united to his brother:

> I thank you for your intention to remain my friend. Here in my heart is as your heart. Whom God hath joined let not man put asunder. We have taken each other for better, for worse, till death do us — part? No: but unite eternally. Therefore in the love which never faileth, I am "Your affectionate friend, and brother." CW.

John Wesley replied to Charles's conciliatory closing in his letter of September 13, 1785. "Dear Brother," John wrote, "I see no use of you and me disputing together; for neither of us is likely to convince the other. You say, I separate from the Church. I say I do not. Then let it stand." While agreeing to disagree, John continued the argument by responding to two of Charles's points. First, he stood by his earlier quotation, borrowed from Charles's hymn, against the unconverted clergy, even though the poet disowned it: "Your verse is a sad truth," John wrote. "I see fifty times more of England than you do; and I find few exceptions to it." Secondly, the elder brother defended the character of Coke against Charles's insinuations and attacks: "I believe Dr. Coke is as free from ambition as from covetousness. He has done nothing rashly, that I know. But he has spoken rashly, which he retracted the moment I spoke to him of it." John closed with a sense of urgency about the present situation: "If you will not or cannot help me yourself," he wrote, "do not hinder those that can and will. I must and will save as many souls as I can while I live, without being careful about what may *possibly be* when I die." The elder Wesley also warned his brother against stirring up dissension among the Methodists he served in London: "I pray, do not confound the intellects of the people in Lon-

319

don. You may thereby a little weaken my hands, but you will greatly weaken your own."

John's letter was combative enough to draw another reply from his brother six days later. "Dear Brother," Charles began, "I did not say you separate from the Church; but I did say, 'if I could prove it, I would not." Returning to the topic of the unconverted clergy, Charles lamented his brother's callous attitude: "That 'sad truth' is not a new truth. You saw [it] when you expressed in your *Reasons* such tenderness of love for the unconverted clergy." Charles resented his brother's warning about spreading dissension. "'How confound their intellect?' 'How weaken your hands?'" he asked. Then he added, perhaps with a sense of disappointment as well as resignation: "I know nothing which I could do to prevent the *possible* separation, but pray, God forbid I should sin against him by ceasing to pray for the Church of England and for you, while any breath remains in me!"

Even though this letter signaled the end of Charles's correspondence with his brother over the issue of the ordinations for America, Charles continued to lobby his point of view to the Methodists, and to his brother, throughout the last years of his life. On April 18, 1786, John tried to convince Charles that he had not "opened the flood-gates" of ordination and schism: "They will ordain no one without my full and free consent. It is not true that they have done it already." Charles had apparently written John about what he thought would be a showdown over separation at the 1786 Methodist conference. John admitted: "Eight or ten Preachers, it is possible (but I have not met with one yet), will say something about leaving the Church, before the Conference." But John continued to support the church by word and example: "The last time I was at Scarbough I earnestly exhorted our people to go to Church; and I went myself. But the wretched minister preached such a sermon, that I could not in conscience advise them to hear him any more."

Charles attended the 1786 conference, along with eighty Methodist preachers. Everyone expected a heated debate about separation, but apparently the question of further ordinations was raised and then quickly laid aside. Charles's letter home to Sally, dated July 29, 1786, showed his encouragement upon hearing several among the preachers speak against separation from the church and hearing all agree to "remain in the Old Ship":

My dearest Partner will be pleased to hear the result of our Conference. The Dissenting Party made a bold push for a separation, strongly urging my Brother to ordain a preacher for a desolate place in Yorkship. John Atlay made a noble stand against them, and fairly conquered them all, with the Dr. [Coke] at their head. . . . All agree to let my Brother and me remain in the Old Ship, till we get safe to land. He will (I am to think) be no more solicited to make a separation. . . .

Apparently Charles sat by and made no disturbance at the meeting, other than shouting "No!" during a debate about holding Methodist services during the stated hours of Anglican worship.

John's pragmatic ordinations for missionary churches in America continued, and he expanded his efforts to Canada, Scotland, and the West Indies, a few at a time. Charles felt betrayed by these concessions to practicality, and they saddened him deeply. Yet he continued to plead, nag, and scold his brother against ordinations for England, and against formal separation from the Anglican Church. With the preachers lined up on one wing of the movement, and his brother staunchly holding down the opposite position, it seemed that Charles hoped that the Methodist movement would be able to maintain its balance and move forward as a reform movement within the Church of England. In one of the last letters Charles wrote his brother, dated April 9, 1787, he addressed the issue of ordinations again. "Stand to your own proposal," he wrote. "I leave America and Scotland to your latest thoughts and recognitions. . . . Keep your authority while you live. . . . You cannot settle the succession; you cannot divine how God will settle it. Have the people of —— given you leave to die, *E.A. P. J.?*" (The abbreviation "E.A.P.J." is Latin for "Church of England Presbyter John.")

All told, John Wesley ordained at least twenty-seven of his preachers into the order of presbyter, and one (Thomas Coke) to the level of superintendent. Significant debate later emerged within the Methodist movement as to whether Wesley regretted his extraordinary ordinations. It is likely that he did regret them because of his own love for the Church of England and because of the strife they caused with his beloved brother and oldest friends. While he was elderly and enfeebled by the time his illegal ordinations became an annual event,

John Wesley certainly knew what he was doing in this regard. He saw that the future of Methodism lay outside the familiar confines of the mother church, and as much as it might have pained him, John felt obligated to prepare the Methodists for the transition that lay immediately ahead of them.

Charles Wesley, for his part in all this, adhered to the original plan. He continued to view Methodism as a renewal movement that functioned best within the bounds of the Anglican communion. He clung valiantly, and stubbornly, to that original vision. At times keeping the movement within the church became Charles's chief ministry among the Methodists. But for all his efforts, the Methodists *would* separate from the Church of England and set up their own church and order of ministry. And it should be no surprise that the lay preachers he battled so long over issues of authority and separation were not prone to sing his praises or canonize his memory. But in the end, Charles got what he wanted most: he lived — and died — in the Church of England.

20 Last Battles

If 1784 was a disappointing and frustrating year in Charles Wesley's public life because of his brother's ordinations for America, his family life was no easier. Charles was not satisfied with the religious development of his three children, particularly his sons. Charles Jr. was conventionally and compliantly religious. Sally attended Methodist meetings and was willing to openly identify herself with the tradition of her famous father and uncle. But Samuel Wesley, even more so than his brother and sister, was still a work in progress. He lacked his older brother's compliant nature, and he rebelled against the public strictures and private practices associated with Methodism.

His father was well aware of Samuel's religious rebellion. Charles's letter home to Sally, dated September 7, 1779, sounds ominously prophetic: "Sam [needs] more pains to be taken with him. If I should not live to help him, it will be all upon you. Make him a living Christian, and he will never wish to be a dead Papist." It is clear, however, that by 1783 Samuel was attending Roman Catholic worship, and later that year or early the next he made an affiliation with Catholicism.

Exactly how this came about is a rather complicated matter. It certainly seemed to have more to do with the attractiveness of the music played at Roman Catholic worship than it had to do with theological doctrine or outright rebellion against the religion of his father. As Sam would subsequently write to Benjamin Jacob in November 1808, "If Roman doctrines were like the Roman *music,* we should have heaven on earth." Methodist music was non-existent in the eighteenth century, as were professional, musical positions associated with Methodism, so from a musical standpoint Methodism had nothing to offer Samuel Wesley. In fact, there was a decided prejudice against organs and performance music among Methodists at this time; they tended to prefer congregational song (as did John Wesley himself). Good church music was being played in the Anglican churches and cathedrals, but it was chiefly William Boyce's *Cathedral Music.* The Wesley boys had studied with Dr. Boyce and could play his music as well as he could himself. Hence there were very few public places where Samuel Wesley could go to hear new and interesting religious music. The Roman Catholic chapel attached to the Portuguese Embassy on South Street in the West End of London was one such place. It was the first place in London to set the popular Christmas carol "O Come All Ye Faithful" to the soaring tune used today *(Adeste Fideles);* it was one of the few venues in London where the organ music of Frederick Handel could be heard on a regular basis. Soon Samuel Wesley was a frequent attendant at worship services held at the Portuguese Embassy. He found that he shared musical tastes with Vincent Novello, the young organist and director of music at the chapel, and they became lifelong friends.

Mary Freeman Shepherd, a London socialite, seems to have also played a role in Samuel's involvement in Roman Catholicism. She was Catholic, and she frequented services at the Portuguese Embassy. She was also a person to whom young Samuel wrote, on at least one occasion, about the dilemma posed by his conversion to Catholicism. In a letter dated December 28, 1783, Samuel told her that he dared not to declare himself openly to be a Roman Catholic because of his respect for his father. "This [announcement] I know, would give him extreme uneasiness," Samuel reported. "I know his rooted prejudice against the Roman Church, and therefore should not wish to occasion a moments pain on that account. . . . I cannot act in opposition to my conscience, but I will not distress the author of my being by taking such a step as I know would rob him of his comfort." But gossip will make the most of this sort of situation, and soon the report had spread rather widely around London that Samuel Wesley, the son of the famous

Methodist evangelist and poet, had joined the Roman Catholic Church.

Circumstantial evidence suggests that Samuel's brother and sister had heard about this development long before his father, but no one wanted to break the news to the elderly Charles Wesley. Finally the Duchess of Norfolk, a Roman Catholic and friend of the family, paid the Wesleys a visit. She bore the sad tidings in part because her own son had recently turned against Catholicism and become a Protestant; she had, no doubt, a particular empathy for the Wesleys' feelings. As she endeavored in vain to convince Charles that Samuel's conversion stemmed from a genuine sense of religious awakening and devotion, Wesley could only reply, "Say, the loaves and fishes, Madam, the loaves and fishes." He attributed Samuel's conversion to matters of wealth and opportunity, as well as the evil influence of people who should have known better.

While there is no extant prose describing what Charles Wesley thought of his son's "perversion to Popery," the poetical record is ample. Charles wrote at least eleven lengthy poems lamenting his son's conversion. The first extant example is full of disappointment and despair over the "loss" of his child: "Farewell, my all of earthly hope," he wrote. One might think that Samuel had died, so constant is Charles's lament of his loss throughout the poem. Verse 5 of the hymn describes the event as "unconscious parricide," which suggests that Samuel's conversion was hastening Charles into his grave. Sally Wesley deciphered verses 4 and 5, which were crossed out in the manuscript, and preserved them on a separate piece of paper. "Made out through the blots," she wrote, suggesting the manuscript may have been smudged by the poet's tears. While the poem seems to suggest Charles had disowned Samuel and intended not to see him again in this life, it was a fleeting feeling. The poem concludes with a prayer for Samuel's eternal salvation, so that he can meet Charles again "in the skies":

1. Farewell, my all of earthly hope,
   My nature's stay, my age's prop,
       Irrevocably gone!
   Submissive to the will divine
   I acquiesce, and make it mine;
       I offer up my Son.

2. But give I God a sacrifice
    That costs me nought? My gushing eyes
        The answer sad express,
    My gushing eyes and troubled heart
    Which bleeds with its belov'd to part,
        Which breaks thro' fond excess.

3. Yet since he from my heart is torn,
    Patient, resign'd, I calmly mourn
        The darling snatch'd away:
    Father, with Thee thy own I leave;
    Into thy mercy's arms receive,
        And keep him to that day.

4. Keep (for I nothing else desire)
    The bush unburnt amidst the fire,
        And freely I resign
    My Child for a few moments lent
    (My Child no longer!) I consent
        To see his face no more.

5. Receive me! and accept my pain!
    Nor let him view my parting scene
        Or catch my parting breath!
    Nor let the hast'ner of my end,
    Th'unconscious Parricide, attend
        To trouble me in death!

6. But hear my agonizing prayer
    And O, preserve him, and prepare
        To meet me in the skies
    When thron'd in Bliss the Lamb appears,
    Repairs my loss and wipes the tears
        For ever from my eyes!

The fifth hymn in this collection depicts Samuel as one who, like Daniel, has fallen into a lions' den; he is with the young men in the fiery furnace, and then falls into Sodom, and Babylon. Laying aside biblical metaphors, Charles expressed his concerns more directly as he prayed:

4. From drunken, riotous excesses,
   From vice, and open wickedness
       His giddy youth restrain,
   While flattery soothes, and pleasure smiles,
   And harlots spread their slighted toils,
       And glory courts in vain.

A later poem, in the same unpublished manuscript, begs God to preserve Samuel from the doctrinal and practical errors Wesley associated with Roman Catholicism ("Those doctrine of the hellish foe/ Which contradict Thy word"). He asks God to help his son find "the true, unerring Way" of "His heavenly Teacher." Charles was convinced that God would convict Samuel of his lack of holiness of heart, that Samuel would receive Christ as Savior, and that in due time God would receive him unto himself:

6. Pierc'd with his want of purity,
   Convinc'd, thy face he cannot see,
       Or know Thee as Thou art,
   Without an inward change intire;
   O may he after this aspire
       This holiness of heart.

7. Till wash'd and thro' thy blood applied,
   Of wrath, concupiscence & pride,
       His soul is emptied here,
   He cannot in the judgment stand,
   Mixt with the sheep at thy right-hand,
       Or in thy sight appear.

8. But if Thou here his Saviour art,
   Possest of Mary's better part,
       Attentive at thy feet,
   If humbly he thro' life remain,
   Thou wilt receive him up to reign,
       The partner of thy seat.

In English Catholic circles the conversion of a Wesley was celebrated like the landing of a very large fish. As a convert Samuel Wesley achieved a degree of celebrity and was treated quite well in his new faith by his new friends. No doubt he reveled in such treatment. Soon he put his musical talents to the service of Catholicism by writing music for the mass — which he dedicated to Pope Pius VI. The 464-page manuscript was signed, "S. Wesley, May 22, 1784," and shipped to Rome in the safety of a tin box. Samuel received a grateful letter of thanks for his work from the pope.

Where Charles Wesley was heartbroken and almost inconsolable over Samuel's conversion, John Wesley was more measured. Uncle John wrote "Dear Sammy" a remarkable letter on August 19, 1784, in which he professed his undying love as well as his concern for his nephew. John was not overly concerned that Sammy had become a member of the Roman Catholic Church; he was, he said, more deeply concerned that his nephew was not "born again." "I have often been pained for you," John wrote, "fearing you did not set out the right way: I do not mean with regard to this or that set of [religious] opinions, Protestant or Romish (all of these I trample under foot); but with regard to those weightier matters, wherein, if they go wrong, either Protestants or Papists will perish everlastingly. I feared you were not born again." This was an extremely important matter, John opined, because a person "cannot see the kingdom of heaven, except he experience that inward change of the earthly, sensual mind for the mind which was in Christ Jesus." Uncle John suggested that Samuel might well be on his way to Christian maturity if he had concerned himself as much about religion as he did music. He pressed the issue: "Whether of this Church or that I care not; you may be saved in either, or damned in either; but I fear you are not born again, and except you are born again you cannot see the kingdom of God. You believe the Church of Rome is right. What then? If you are not born of God *you* are of *no Church*." There is no record of whether or what Samuel wrote back to his uncle, but there was no mistaking the love and poignancy of his uncle John's appeal: "O Sammy, you are out of your way! You are out of God's way! You have not given Him your heart."

By 1786 Samuel's father was taking a similar tack. His letter to his son Charles, dated May 2nd of that year, indicated that Samuel's father and siblings remained troubled because Samuel had — as Charles Jr.

put it — "changed his religion." Charles Sr. disputed the fact that his youngest son had any real religion at all: "Nay, he has changed his opinions and mode of worship: but that is not religion; it is quite another thing." Young Charles must have asked his father, "Has he then sustained no loss by the change?" The senior Wesley answered emphatically: "Yes, unspeakable loss; because his new opinion and mode of worship are so unfavorable to religion that they make it, if not impossible to one who once knew better, yet extremely difficult."

At this point Charles Wesley launched into a full definition of religion. "What then is religion?" he wrote, "It is happiness in God, or in the knowledge or love of God. It is faith working by love; producing 'righteousness, peace, and joy in the Holy Ghost.' In other words, it is a heart and life devoted to God; or communion with God the Father, and the Son; or the mind which was in Christ Jesus, enabling us to walk as He walked." The fundamental question, then, for the poet was not what church his son frequented, but whether Samuel "has this religion" or not. "[I]f he has [it]," Charles wrote, "he will not finally perish, notwithstanding the absurd, unscriptural opinions he has embraced and the superstitious and idolatrous modes of worship. . . . If he has not this religion, if he has not given God his heart, the case is unspeakably worse: I doubt if he ever will; for his new friends will continually endeavour to hinder him, by putting something else in its place, by encouraging him to rest in the form, notions, or externals, without being born again, without having Christ in him, the hope of glory, without being renewed in the image of Him that created him. This is deadly evil."

By August of 1786, Charles Wesley was sending his love to his Catholic son — through his elder brother: "My love to Sam," he wrote, "and tell him whenever he sells his organ, I expect to have the refusal on first offer. I will give him as much or more for it than any other bidder. So he needs not sell it for an old song."

Samuel's flirtation with Roman Catholicism was certainly at an end by 1793, when he was married in the Church of England. But Samuel continued to be a great concern and a worry to his aged father. Not only was his spiritual state in question, which was a crucial matter to Charles Wesley; in 1787 he had absentmindedly stepped into a deep excavation in the London streets and suffered a serious head injury. It is reported that he lay unconscious for hours prior to being found and treated. While Samuel lay in a coma, his concerned father apparently refused medical permission for brain surgery — which may well have been the proper response, given the primitive state of surgical procedures in those days. Samuel recovered from his injuries, but it remains an open question among his biographers whether the bouts of depression and instability that plagued him in later life were attributable to the aftereffects of this accident and the care he received.

Charles's health had been frail, intermittently, for many years. But he often found himself revived in the process of preaching and serving the Methodist societies. In an undated letter to Sally, for example, he wrote, "My work, I very well know keeps me alive more than it wears me out. That and my life will probably end together." In the fall of 1778, however, the contrast between his brother's continued vigor and his own rapid physical decline had become obvious to him. He wrote of himself: "I creep along the streets, tottering over the edge of the grave. My strength seems to abate daily, perhaps through my long walks." In the same letter Charles quoted from a poem to reinforce his point:

> This course of vanity almost complete,
> Tired in the field of life, I hope retreat
> In the still shades of death: for dread and pain,
> And grief shall find their shafts lanced in vain,
> And their points broke, retorted from the head,
> Safe in the grave, and free among the dead.

During this period Charles gradually made peace with the fact of his brother's ordinations. He continued to serve the London chapels (chiefly the Foundery, then City Road and West Street). It may be that, as his health began to wane, Charles Wesley was, as his antagonist John Pawson described him, "like Samson shorn of his strength." It also seems likely that Charles's extemporaneous preaching method, which served him so well when his lively mind surged with poetical imagination, began to fail him as he grew old and feeble. John Telford offers recollections of Charles Wesley opening the Bible, in order to preach upon "the first words presented," only to find that his thoughts and words did not flow as freely as they had in former years; during long pauses, he looked to heaven, as if waiting for divine help. Sometimes Wesley was so exhausted by the task of preaching that he had to ask the congregation to sing a few hymns while he regained the strength to continue. But there are also testimonies to Charles Wesley's continued effectiveness as a preacher. On June 27, 1781, his brother John wrote to him, "From several I have lately heard that God has blessed your preaching. See your calling!" Henry Moore, another early Methodist preacher, remembered that even a few months before his death the elderly Charles Wesley was sufficiently animated in the City Road pulpit to have swept the hymnal off the pulpit in front of him; it fell whizzing past the head of Thomas Coke, who as lector was seated directly in front of Wesley. In a second grand gesture the sleeve of Wesley's pulpit robe caught the corner of his Bible. It too took off on a trajectory aimed at the doctor's head; this time anticipating the arrival, Dr. Coke rose to receive the Bible with open arms. Moore heard the elderly Charles Wesley preach many times, and he considered his extemporaneous presentations to be superior to Charles's published Oxford sermon, "Awake Thou That Sleepest." Moore opined that, even in his later years, Charles had "the remarkable talent for uttering the most striking truth with simplicity, force and brevity."

Wesley also continued to write hymns during this final period of his life. One of his collections, which was left in manuscript, was penned in 1786. Entitled "Hymns for the Methodist Preachers," it contains sixteen long poems which celebrate and pray for the Methodist evangelists; several of them have a strongly autobiographic tone. "An OLD Methodist Preacher's Prayer," for example, concludes,

> 10. Thy Face I shortly hope to see,
> And partner of thy victory
> To tread the tempter down,
> And more than conquerer thro' thy blood
> By the mere Mercy of my God
> To gain the glorious crown.

Asides mentioned in Charles Wesley's correspondence during this final period of his life help us chronicle his physical decline. In a sorrowful letter to John William Fletcher, dated June 21, 1785, Charles seemed to be making an excuse for not visiting his old fiend during his final months. "I *need* no invitation to [visit] Madeley," he wrote. "While I had strength, I [lacked] opportunity. Now I have neither." In the same note, Wesley described his own state: "If you are weary of writing, I am much more, who have almost lost the use of my hand and my eyes." In the fall of 1786, in a letter to his wife, it became clear that the old man no longer trusted his health sufficiently to ride around England alone: "I want one of my sons to ride with me, that in case of necessity, he might pick me up, and deliver me to the worms."

Correspondence from the autumn of 1787 located Charles in Bristol, for what would prove to be his final visit there. Living in a rented room, he forlornly suggested that perhaps his absence to his family was more comfortable than his presence. His family had not the funds to make the trip to Bristol, and he had not the money to give them to make it possible: "Your mother is inconsiderable. Charles has not £10 to spare for a journey to Bristol, and back again. Silver and gold have I none. But I want none, neither do I run in debt for want of it." His eyes continued to trouble the poet: "My eyes fail me, for writing and reading. Perhaps they may not be quite darkened, till they are closed." He told his wife he was too weak to finish packing to return home: "On Saturday night I thought myself near my [death] through an intense pain in my side. I had small hope of officiating yesterday, yet the Lord gave me back and increased my strength. Probably, I shall depart without taking leave [of Bristol]." The next day, August 14, he wrote Sally again: "Last night my troublesome old companion, lumbago, paid me a visit before the time. Tis well if he does not lay an embargo upon me; or possibly hasten my return home to be nursed." He urged his wife to visit him in Bristol, thinking they may never return: "I am the more willing to stay here as long as I can because I do not flatter myself in the hope of seeing my Bristol friends again in the flesh." Charles's wife Sally may have been too ill to visit Bristol, leaving the increasingly infirm Charles to comfort his wife. On September 2, 1787, he wrote her again: "I am a prophet, you know, and the son of a prophet. As such I tell you, you will live to bring up Charles's children, possibly Sally's and almost probably the monk's [Sam's]."

By October 30, Wesley was back in London, in the house in Maryle-bone. On that day he wrote to his friend Betsy Briggs — or rather, he dictated it to his daughter, Sally — declining an invitation to meet her for a visit: "I am a prisoner here by an inflammation in my eyes or I would meet you more than half way. Probably for the last time we should meet on earth. Send me a line of information concerning your dear mother's health, and all your family." Three months later, on January 13, 1788, Wesley was writing to Samuel Bradford, a Methodist lay preacher who assisted him in London. Charles's health continued to decline, but not his willingness to serve: "I am become as a dead man out of mind and am content. Send me the history of your covenant night [service]. I would gladly join you, in renewing the covenant at West-Street [chapel]."

By February 1788 Charles was reduced to a general state of great weakness and only occasionally able to leave his bed. John was aware of his brother's continued illness, and urged upon him his own favorite cures — fresh air and exercise. Charles should ride, even if he needed to hire a coach. "Dear Brother," he wrote on February 18, "you must go out every day, or die. Do not die to save the charges. You certainly need not want anything as long as I live." One week later, John Wesley left London for an itinerant swing through the west and north country. It is assumed that he visited his brother prior to departing, but there is no record of that meeting. A few days later, on March 2, John Wesley addressed his brother from Bath: "Many inquire after you, and express much affection, and desire seeing you. In good time! You are first suffering the will of God. Afterwards he has a little more for you to do: that is, provided you now take up your cross (for that it frequently must be), and go out at least an hour a day. I would not blame you, if it were two or three. Never mind the expense. I can make that up. You shall not die to save charges. I shall shortly have a word to say to Charles [Jr.], or his brother, or both. Peace be with all your spirits!" Three days later, John wrote again from Bristol: "Dear Brother, I hope you keep to your rule, of going out every day, although it may sometimes be a cross. Keep to this but one month, and I am persuaded you will be as well as you were this time twelve-month."

John's niece, Charles's daughter Sally, must have written John Wesley to apprise him of the serious state of her father's health. He was not able to take food, and this was hastening Charles's decline. John Wesley wrote back, almost immediately, once again recommending one of his favorite folk remedies, but also his favorite physician:

> My Dear Sally — when my appetite was entirely gone, so that all I could take at dinner was a roasted turnip, it was restored in a few days by riding out daily, after taking ten drops of elixir of vitriol in

a glass of water. It is highly probable this would have the same effect in my brother's case. But in the meantime I wish he would see Dr. Whitehead. I am persuaded there is not such another physician in England. . . .

John sent advice on how Charles's children should be treating him at this time. "Now Sally," he wrote, "tell your brothers from me that their tenderly respectful behavior to their father (even asking his pardon if in anything they have offended him) will be the best cordial for him under heaven. I know not but they may save his life thereby. To *know* nothing will be wanting on your part gives [me] great satisfaction." John also wrote Sam, urging him to become "a *real spiritual* Christian." He also warned the prodigal son, "Your father is on the wing. You are not likely to see him long; and you know not that you will see me any more."

Charles Wesley's last days were spent in a state of gradual physical decline. His daughter, in an account she wrote to her uncle John, recalled, "He took solemn leave of all his friends. I once asked if he had any presages that he should die. He said, 'No'; but his weakness was such, that he thought it impossible he 'should live through March.' He kindly bade me remember him, and seemed to have no doubt but I should meet him in heaven."

Two weeks before his death, Charles made a point to have prayed for those he considered his enemies — "with many tears," Sally recalled. Among these he named in particular Mary Freeman Shepherd, whom he blamed for luring his son Samuel into the Roman Catholic Church. "I beseech thee, O Lord, by thine agony and blood sweat," he said, "that she may never feel the pangs of eternal death!"

About a week before Charles's death, his son Samuel visited him. Though it was difficult for the dying man to speak, Sally recalled, upon seeing Samuel he took hold of his hand and said, "I shall bless God to all eternity, that ever you were born. I am persuaded I shall."

Charles Wesley did not fear death. Indeed, soon after he had been converted he evidenced what modern readers might consider a strange fascination with death. On June 11, 1738, for example, he wrote in his journal, "While Mr. Piers was preaching on death, I found great joy in feeling myself willing, or rather, desireous, to die." And he wrote these rather morbid-sounding lines in 1746:

1. Ah! lovely Appearance of Death!
       No Sight upon Earth is so fair:
   Not all the gay Pageants that breathe
       Can with a dead Body compare.
   With solemn Delight I survey
       The Corpse, when the Spirit is fled,
   In love with the beautiful Clay,
       And longing to lie in its stead.

2. How blest is our Brother, bereft
       Of all that could burthen his Mind!
   How easy the Soul, that hath left
       This wearisom Body behind!
   Of Evil incapable thou,
       Whose Relicks with Envy I see;
   No longer in Misery now,
       No longer a Sinner like me. . . .

He carried a peace about death into advancing age and final illness. While his wife Sarah was nursing him, she would ask whether Charles wanted anything. Young Sally remembered, "He told my mother, the week before he departed, that no fiend was permitted to approach him; and said to us all, 'I have a *good hope!*' When we asked if he wanted anything, he frequently answered, 'Nothing but Christ!'" Three days before he died, Sally recalled, "He slept much, without refreshment, and had the restlessness of death for, I think, the whole week. He was eager to depart; and if we moved him, or spoke to him, he answered, 'Let me die! Let me die!' His frequent prayer during these trying days was: Patience, and an easy death!'"

One of the last poems that Charles Wesley wrote with his own hand preserves the same death-defying attitude that was seen in his early hymns and hopes. Using Hosea 14:2, "Take away all iniquity and give good," Wesley described his attitude about the prospect of his translation from this life to the next. For him, death meant the final arrival of true holiness and a wonderful homecoming for God's "ready servant," with the saints departed and "the heavenly Lamb":

How long, how often shall I pray,
Take all my iniquity away;

And give the plentitude of good,
The blessing bought by Jesu's blood;
Concupiscence and pride remove,
And fill me, Lord, with humble love.

Again I take the words to me
Prescribed, and offer them to Thee:
Thy kingdom come, to root out sin,
And perfect holiness bring in;
And swallow up my will in Thine,
And human change into divine.

So shall I render Thee Thine own,
And tell the wonders Thou has done,
The power and faithfulness declare
Of God, who hears and answers prayer,
Extol the riches of Thy grace,
And spend my latest breath in praise.

O that the joyful hour was come,
Which calls Thy ready servant home,
Unites me to the Church above,
Where angels chant the song of love,
And saints eternally proclaim
The glories of the heavenly Lamb.

Dr. Whitehead, who on John Wesley's advice had become his attending physician during Charles Wesley's final illness, also became his earliest biographer. The doctor left the following account of Wesley's last days:

Mr. Charles Wesley had a weak body, and a poor state of health, during the greatest part of his life. I believe he laid the foundation of both, at Oxford, by too close application to study, and abstinence from food. He rode much on horseback, which probably contributed to lengthen out life to a good old age. I visited him several times in his last sickness, and his body was indeed reduced to the most extreme state of weakness. He possessed that state of mind which he had been always pleased to see in others — unaffected humility and holy resignation to the will of God. He had no transports of joy, but solid hope and unshaken confidence in Christ, which kept his mind in perfect peace. . . .

A few days before he died, Whitehead recalled, Charles Wesley called for his wife to take down the following lines at his dictation. These, his last lines, express well the triumphant faith by which Wesley lived:

In age and feebleness extreme,
Who shall a sinful worm redeem?
Jesus, my only hope Thou art,
Strength of my failing flesh and heart;
O could I catch a smile from Thee,
And drop into eternity!

In his last moments, Charles's family gathered around him and watched him "drop into eternity." His daughter described it in the account she sent her uncle John. "Last morning," she wrote, "which was the 29th of March, being unable to speak, my mother entreated him to press her hand, if he knew her; which he feebly did. His last words which I could hear were, 'Lord, my heart — my God!' He then drew his breath short, and the last so gently, that we knew not exactly the moment in which his happy spirit fled. His dear hand was in mine for five minutes before, and at the awful period of, his dissolution."

Charles had one last request of the "Old Ship," the Church of England. The Anglican parish priest of Mary-le-bone had visited him at his request while he was on his deathbed. Charles told him, "Sir, whatever the world may have thought of me, I have lived, and I die, in the communion of the Church of England, and I will be buried in the yard of my parish church." John Wesley, who had prepared a crypt for his brother and himself behind the New Chapel on City Road, was stung by Charles's refusal to be buried there. His family must have told John that Charles preferred to be buried in consecrated ground, because in a letter he wrote to Rev. Peard Dickenson, John lamented, "It is a pity but the remains of my brother had been deposited with mine. Certainly that ground is as holy as any in England, and it contains a large quantity of 'bony dead.'" On May 17, 1788, John wrote, and subsequently published, a treatise entitled: "Thoughts on the Consecration of Churches and Burial-grounds." These thoughts were ably summarized in the last paragraph: "I take the whole of this practice to be a mere relic of Romish superstition. . . . Surely it is high time now that we should be guided not by custom, but by Scripture and reason." While John Wesley was quick to turn his personal disappointment into a public teaching moment, he had certainly missed the point of his brother's choice. Charles was not buried in consecrated Anglican ground because of custom or "Romish superstition." It was an acted parable of his lifelong resolve to live in the Church of England.

The Methodist preacher Samuel Bradburn, with whom Charles Wesley worked during his London years, preached at Wesley's funeral "to an inconceivable concourse of people, of every description from 2 Sam. 3:28: 'A Prince and great man is fallen this day in Israel.'" John Wesley, who only heard of his brother's death through Sally's letter, was not able to be present for the funeral. Charles, fittingly, was carried to his rest in the Mary-le-bone parish churchyard by six clergymen of the Church of England. The words carved on his tombstone were his own; they had been written for the death of his friend, the Moravian bishop Latrobe, but they fit their author's character equally well:

> With poverty of spirit blest,
> Rest, happy saint, in Jesus rest;
> A sinner saved, through grace forgiven,
> Redeemed from earth to reign in heaven.
>
> Thy labours of unwearied love,
> By thee forgot, are crowned above;
> Crowned, through the mercy of thy Lord,
> With a free, full, immense reward.

The Methodist conference of 1788 took terse notice of Charles Wesley's passing, under the question "What Preachers have died this year?" Amidst a list of seven others, it was reported, "Mr. Charles Wesley, who after spending fourscore years with much sorrow and pain, quietly retired into Abraham's bosom. He had no disease; but after a gradual decay of some months, 'The weary wheels of life stood still at last.' His least praise was his talent for poetry; although Dr. Watts did not scruple to say, 'that single poem, *Wrestling Jacob,* is worth all the verses which I have ever written.'" But such words only hinted at Charles Wesley's true poetic legacy. His verse, which carried so much Methodist theology and life experience, would spread far beyond the movement, throughout his beloved Church of England, and on into churches around the world.

A Note on the Sources

The earliest and perhaps most interesting biography of Charles Wesley is by his physician, Dr. John Whitehead, *The Life of Wesley* (1793). It contains significant amounts of primary source material, including many early Wesley family letters. Adam Clark's *Memoirs of the Wesley Family* (1848) is a similar work. Taken together, these two seem to supply much of the material used in many of the earlier Charles Wesley biographies. Thomas Jackson's two-volume *The Life of Charles Wesley, A.M.* (1841) is certainly the most complete early biography. It makes extensive use of Charles's journal, which was subsequently edited and published by Thomas Jackson in 1848.

I have also utilized additional manuscript sources, some of which have been published in my *Charles Wesley: A Reader* (Oxford and New York, 1989), and some of which remain unpublished. Most of the manuscripts of Charles Wesley's letters and papers are housed in The Methodist Archives of the John Rylands Library and Research Centre, Deansgate, Manchester. I am grateful to Mr. David Riley and his colleague Mr. John Tuck, as well as Dr. Peter Nockles and his colleague Dr. Gareth Lloyd, for their diligence in locating and copying manuscript materials for me. Additional Charles Wesley materials are housed in the Methodist Church, Overseas Division (Methodist Missionary Society), England, and the Cheshunt Foundation, Westminster College, Cambridge University, U.K. I am grateful to Mrs. M. J. Fox and Dr. S. H. Mayor for supplying me with copies of rare material from their holdings. I was also fortunate to use the ample Wesleyan manuscript and microfiche holdings in the Frank Baker Collection at Duke University Divinity School. My thanks to Dr. Dick Heitzenrater and Dr. Randy Maddox for their help and hospitality during the Summer Seminar on Wesleyan Studies in June 2006.

The most useful contemporary biographies of Charles Wesley are Charles Wesley Flint's *Charles Wesley and His Colleagues* (1957), because of its accuracy and comprehensive scope, and Mabel Bailsford's *Tale of Two Brothers* (1954), because she writes her biography more critically than most. My *Charles Wesley on Sanctification: A Biographical and Theological Study* (Grand Rapids, 1986) examines Charles's life and thought in the context of his most important theological construct. S. T. Kimbrough, ed., *Charles Wesley: Poet and Theologian* (Nashville, 1992), carries a series of essays that offer useful interpretive perspectives on Charles Wesley. See Kenneth G. C. Newport, "Charles Wesley and the Articulation of Faith," *Methodist History* 42:1 (October 2003): 33-48, and Gareth Lloyd, "Charles Wesley and His Biographers: An Exercise in Methodist Hagiography," *Bulletin of John Rylands Library* 82:1 (Spring 2000): 81-99, for important surveys of how Charles Wesley expressed himself and how he has been presented by his biographers.

Most of the direct information about Charles Wesley from the earliest period comes from his correspondence, since his journal for these years is not extant. In addition to the aforementioned sources, Frank Baker's *Charles Wesley as Revealed by His Letters* (London, 1948) should be consulted. The new critical edition of John Wesley's *Letters*, edited by Frank Baker, in *The Works of John Wesley* (Nashville, 1982), offers some previously unpublished correspondence between Charles and his brother. Charles Wallace's *Susanna Wesley: The Complete Writings* (Oxford, 1997) should also be consulted for correspondence between Mrs. Wesley and her sons. Richard Heitzenrater's *The Elusive Mr. Wesley*, 2 vols. (Nashville, 1984), contains some very interesting material from the period, including the documents surrounding the published controversy about the Oxford Methodists stirred up by the death of William Morgan.

For more detailed information about the Oxford Methodists, see

Luke Tyerman's *The Oxford Methodists* (1873), as well as Richard Heitzenrater's unpublished Ph.D. dissertation, "John Wesley and the Oxford Methodists, 1725-1735" (Duke University, 1972). *The Diary of an Oxford Methodist, Benjamin Ingham, 1733-34*, transcribed by Richard Heitzenrater (Durham, N.C., 1985), is another very useful source on this period. The best readable survey of the general historical period is Roy Porter's *English Society in the Eighteenth Century* (New York, 1982). Maldwyn Edwards, *The Family Circle* (London, 1949) remains a useful study on the inner workings of the Wesley family.

Charles Wesley's published journal begins with his arrival in the New World, March 9, 1736. It is available in two versions. The extensive two-volume edition edited by Thomas Jackson, *The Journal of Charles Wesley, M.A.* (London: John Mason, 1848), is riddled with omissions. It seems that Jackson did not read John Byrom's shorthand, which was used extensively throughout the journal. He also glossed over controversial sections with no indication of his omissions. A fuller and more accurate text was produced by Nehemiah Curnock and John Telford and published under the title *The Journal of the Rev. Charles Wesley, M.A. 1736-1739* (1909). While the newer edition gives the full manuscript text, it was never completed and covers only the first three years of Wesley's life. The forthcoming *Manuscript Journal of the Rev. Charles Wesley, M.A.*, edited by S. T. Kimbrough Jr. and Kenneth G. C. Newport (Nashville, 2007), promises to overcome the difficulties presented by the earlier versions of Charles's journal and present all available material. It will be an indispensable resource for understanding Charles Wesley's life. *The Works of John Wesley: Letters*, 2 vols. (Nashville, 1980), edited by Frank Baker, contain many materials pertinent to the study of Charles Wesley's life. W. Reginald Ward and Richard P. Heitzenrater, *The Works of John Wesley: Journal and Diaries*, 7 vols. (Nashville, 1988-), are extremely helpful in this same regard.

The best contemporary biographies of John Wesley are Henry Rack, *Reasonable Enthusiast: John Wesley and the Rise of Methodism* (Philadelphia, 1989), and Richard Heitzenrater, *Wesley and the People Called Methodists* (Nashville, 1995). These works are particularly helpful in understanding the context of Charles Wesley's ministry and his relationship with his brother John. The older work by Luke Tyerman, *The Life and Times of the Rev. John Wesley*, 3 vols. (London: Hodder and

Stoughton, 1890), preserves some manuscript materials that are not readily available elsewhere.

The most complete source for Charles Wesley's hymns is the *Poetical Works of John and Charles Wesley* (London, 1968) in 13 volumes, edited by George Osborn. Frank Baker's *Representative Verse of Charles Wesley* (Nashville, 1962) could be consulted in lieu of the hard-to-find *Poetical Works*, as should *The Works of John Wesley*, vol. 7: *A Collection of Hymns for the Use of the People Called Methodists* (Nashville, 1983), edited by Franz Hildebrandt and Oliver Beckerlegge. S. T. Kimbrough and Oliver Beckerlegge's *The Unpublished Poetry of Charles Wesley*, 3 vols. (Nashville, 1992), offers an excellent opportunity to study those hymns and poems of Charles Wesley that remained unpublished in his own lifetime. The contents of two earlier editions of Charles Wesley's sermons, along with Thomas Albin and Oliver Beckerlegge, eds., *Charles Wesley's Earliest Sermons: Six Manuscript Shorthand Sermons Now for the First Time Transcribed from the Original* (Illford, 1987), and Charles Wesley, *Sermons by the Late Rev. Charles Wesley* (1816), have been put together in and superseded by Kenneth G. C. Newport, ed., *The Sermons of Charles Wesley: A Critical Edition with Introduction and Notes* (Oxford, 2001).

For information on George Whitefield see *George Whitefield's Journals* (London, 1960), and *The Letters of George Whitefield* (Carlisle, Penn., 1976). Harry Stout, *The Divine Dramatist* (Grand Rapids, 1991), is an interesting contemporary biography. On Lady Huntingdon see Boyd Schlenther, *Queen of the Methodists* (Durham, 1997), and Edwin Welch, *Spiritual Pilgrim* (Wales, 1995). For a short overview see my "Lady Huntingdon's Reformation," *Church History* 64 (Dec. 1995): 580-94. For a sympathetic presentation of the English Moravians and their role at the inception of the Methodist movement, see Frederick Dreyer, *The Genesis of Methodism* (Bethlehem, Penn., 1999).

For information about Charles Wesley's marriage and family life, I have used many manuscript sources, some of which are also found in Frank Baker's *Charles Wesley as Revealed by His Letters*, Dr. Whitehead's *The Life of Wesley*, and Thomas Jackson, *The Life of Charles Wesley, M.A.* 2 vols. (1849). I have also consulted Osborn's *Poetical Works*, manuscript hymns, and Kimbrough and Beckerlegge's *The Unpublished Poetry of Charles Wesley*.

The relationship between John and Charles Wesley is made more intelligible by Bailsford's *Tale of Two Brothers* and Luke Tyerman's *The Life and Times of the Rev. John Wesley.* Augustin Ledger, *Wesley's Last Love* (London, 1903), is essential for unraveling the difficult events surrounding the Grace Murray affair. Manuscript sources as well as Baker's *Charles Wesley as Revealed by His Letters* were also indispensable in this regard. Baker's *Works of John Wesley: Letters,* vol. 2, has some important materials from this period, as does Luke Tyerman's *Life and Times of John Wesley,* vol. 3.

Chronicling Charles Wesley's work with the lay preachers depends upon the fine work of Frank Baker in *The Works of John Wesley: Letters,* vol. 2 (Nashville, 1980) as well as that of Reginald Ward and Dick Heitzenrater, *The Works of John Wesley: Journal and Diaries,* vol. 3 (Nashville, 1991). Unpublished manuscript letters were used, as well as Baker's *Charles Wesley as Revealed by His Letters.* Hymns were drawn from Osborn's *Poetical Works,* and from manuscript sources. A few extracts of letters from John Whitehead's *Life of the Rev. John Wesley, M.A. . . . With the Life of Rev. Charles Wesley, M.A.* (Boston: J. McLeish, 1844) were used and were checked against the correspondence supplied in Baker's *John Wesley's Letters,* vol. 2. I am grateful to Richard Heitzenrater for an opportunity to see an advanced copy of his "Purge the Preachers," published in *Charles Wesley: Life, Literature, Legacy,* edited by Ted Campbell and Kenneth G. C. Newport (London, 2007). Once again, important materials remain in manuscript form, some of which are also available in Tyerman, *Life and Times,* vol. 3; Baker, *Charles Wesley as Revealed by His Letters,* and Jackson, *The Life of Charles Wesley,* vol. 2.

Untangling the Wesleyan doctrine of Christian perfection and Charles Wesley's development of that doctrine is a complicated matter. The fourth volume of Ward and Heitzenrater, *Journal and Diaries,* is indispensable — particularly for the chronology of the events. My *Charles Wesley on Sanctification* (Grand Rapids, 1986) offers a fuller account of Charles's views on Christian perfection and his role in this controversy. Newport, *Sermons of Charles Wesley,* should be consulted to trace the early development of Wesley's preaching on sanctification. Osborn, *Poetical Works,* as well as Kimbrough and Beckerlegge, *Unpublished Poetry of Charles Wesley,* vol. 2, evidence a similar development in Charles Wesley's poetical verse. See Kenneth Newport, "George Bell, Prophet and Enthusiast," *Methodist History* 35 (1997): 95-105, on

George Bell; and Charles Goodwin, "Setting Perfection Too High: John Wesley's Changing Attitudes Toward the 'London Blessing,'" *Methodist History* 36 (January 1998): 86-96, for an examination of the controversy over Christian perfection that racked the London Methodist society. Tyerman's *Life and Times*, vol. 2, offers some letters and documents, first published in Wesley's *Arminian Magazine*, that are not readily found elsewhere. The full text of most of the Wesleyan "Minutes of Conference" is found in John Telford, *The Works of John Wesley*, 14 vols. (London, 1872), vol. 8, 275-339.

Frank Baker's *Representative Verse of Charles Wesley* is essential for understanding Charles Wesley's work as a poet. Henry Bett's classic *The Hymns of Methodism in Their Literary Relations* (London, 1912) is equally indispensable. T. S. Gregory, "Charles Wesley's Hymns and Poems," *London Quarterly and Holborn Review* (Oct. 1957): 253-62, offers a useful study of Charles's poetical method. Carlton Young, "John Wesley's 1737 Charlestown Collection of Psalms and Hymns," *The Hymn* 41, no. 4: 19-27, is a good introduction to Methodism's first hymnal. John Ernest Rattenbury, *The Evangelical Doctrines of Charles Wesley's Hymns* (London, 1941), and Teresa Berger, *Theology in Hymns?* (Nashville, 1995), are excellent sources on Charles Wesley's role as a poetical theologian. Thousands of examples of Charles Wesley's hymns and sacred poems are found in Osborn's *Poetical Works*, as well as Kimbrough and Beckerlegge, *Unpublished Poetry of Charles Wesley*.

For examining the Wesleys' relationship with the Church of England, Frank Baker's *John Wesley and the Church of England* (London, 1970), is still essential reading. Once again a significant amount of unpublished manuscript material has been consulted. Some of this material is also available in Baker, *Charles Wesley as Revealed by His Letters*; Jackson, *Life of Charles Wesley*, vol. 2; Whitehead, *The Life of Wesley*; and Tyerman, *Life and Times*, vol. 3. "Psalm LXXX — Adapted to the Church of England," can be found in "Ms. Cheshunt," "Ms. Clark," and Baker's *Representative Verse* and Osborn's *Poetical Works*. Baker's *John Wesley's Works: Letters*, vol. 2, has some important correspondence between the brothers. Heitzenrater and Ward's *Works of John Wesley: Journal and Diaries*, vols. 3-6, should be consulted as well. Charles Wesley's irritated poems about his brother's ordinations for America (1784) can be found in "Ms. Ordinations" and in Kimbrough and Beckerlegge, *Unpublished Poetry of Charles Wesley*.

Looking at the London years of Charles Wesley's later life requires quite a collection of resources. Unpublished and published correspondence from Charles Wesley has been consulted; published correspondence can be appended to Thomas Jackson's edition of *The Journal of Charles Wesley*. While Charles Wesley's journal is silent on this period, Jackson has also included "The Rev. Charles Wesley's Account of His Two Sons," and an "Account of Charles and Samuel Wesley, Communicated to the *Philosophical Transactions*," by Daines Barrington, in his edition of the published *Journal of Charles Wesley*, vol. 2, 140-66. Tyerman's *Life of John Wesley*, vol. 3, has some useful material on this period, as do the biographies of Charles Wesley by Thomas Jackson, Charles Flint, and Frederick Gill. Philip Olleson's recent article "The Wesleys at Home: Charles Wesley and His Children," *Methodist History* 36, no. 3 (April 1998): 139-52, should be consulted. Eric Routley's *The Musical Wesleys* (London, 1968), is very helpful on the musical sons of Charles Wesley. James Lightwood, *Samuel Wesley, Musician: The Story of His Life* (New York, 1972), is also very helpful in unraveling the life of Charles's youngest son. Alyson McLamore offers the definitive study on the London concerts in her "'By the Will and Order of Providence': The Wesley Family Concerts, 1779-1787," *Royal Musical Association Research Chronicle* 37 (2004): 71-219. The journal of John Wesley for this period was consulted through Ward and Heitzenrater, *The Works of John Wesley: Journal and Diaries*, vols. 5-6. John Wesley's letters were consulted through the Jackson (Wesleyan Conference) edition of *The Works of John Wesley*, vol. 12, since the new critical edition of his letters has not yet been published.

The Methodists' steady march towards separation from the Church of England is ably chronicled in Frank Baker's *John Wesley and the Church of England*. The unpublished source "Ms. Ordinations" is particularly important for tracing Charles Wesley's reaction to the ordinations of 1784. In addition to manuscript sources for Charles Wesley's correspondence for this period, Baker's *Charles Wesley as Revealed by His Letters* should be consulted, along with Tyerman, *The Life and Times of John Wesley*, vol. 3, and Thomas Jackson, *The Life of Charles Wesley*, vol. 2. John Wesley's correspondence can be found in *The Works of John Wesley, A.M.* (London: Wesleyan Conference, 1782), as well as in John Telford's *The Letters of the Rev. John Wesley, A.M.*, 8 vols. (London, 1931), vol. 8. Charles Wesley's epigrams and hymns written on his brother's ordinations can be found in my *Charles Wesley: A Reader.* Charles's unpublished hymn, "True Yokefellows," can be found in Baker's *Representative Verse of Charles Wesley.*

Charles Wesley's "Last Battles" are ably illustrated through his unpublished correspondence. Additionally, Dr. Whitehead's *Life of Wesley* and Thomas Jackson's *Life of Charles Wesley,* vol. 2, offer important collections of materials from this period of his life. Baker's *Representative Verse* can be consulted for the full text of "The Lovely Appearance of Death." Kimbrough and Beckerlegge's *Unpublished Poetry of Charles Wesley,* vol. 1, offers a large collection of poems on Charles's son Samuel and his conversion to Catholicism. Several of these are also published in Osborn's *Poetical Works,* vol. 8. The mention of Charles Wesley's passing in the Methodist Minutes of Conference, as well as John Wesley's treatise "Thoughts on the Consecration of Churches and Burial Grounds," can be found in the Wesleyan Conference edition of *The Works of John Wesley.*

Index

"For the Persecuted," 147-48; "Friend of all the sinful race," 292; "A Funeral Hymn for Mrs. Hooper," 238; "God of all-sufficient grace," 214; "God of faithful Abraham, hear," 199-200; "Head of Thy church, attend," 286; "He left His throne above," 258; "Holy Child of heavenly birth," 212-13; "The Horrible Decree," 111-12; "How long, how often shall I pray," 335-36; "How shall a young unstable man," 211; "Hymn for April 8," 202-3; "An Hymn for Seriousness," 33-34; *Hymns and Sacred Poems* (1749), 33, 117, 142, 161-62, 189, 240, 241, 243, 261, 268, 269; *Hymns for Children* (1763), 205; "Hymns for Christian Friends," 117; *Hymns for Families* (1767), 205; "Hymns for the Methodist Preachers" (1786), 331; "Hymns for the Persecuted," 142; *Hymns For Those That Seek and Those That Have Redemption in the Blood of Jesus Christ,* 240; "Hymns For Those That Wait For Full Redemption," 242; *Hymns of Petition and Thanksgiving for the Promise of the Father* (1746), 239; *Hymns on God's Everlasting Love,* 108-14, 127; "In age and feebleness extreme," 337; "In a Storm," 122; "In Body remov'd from a Friend," 168; "The Invitation," 69-70; "I sing Grimalkin brave and bold," 207-8; "I thank Thee, Lord of earth and heaven," 189-90; "It happened! It happened!", 310-11; "JESUS, Thou soul of all our joys," 270; "The Just Shall Live by Faith," 66-68; "Listed into the Cause of Sin," 268-69; "Lord, if Thou know'st it good for me," 156; "The Maiden's Hymn," 212-13; "A Man of Fashion," 74;

"The Means of Grace," 87-90; "Ms." Brothers, 313-14; "My stony heart Thy wrath defies," 266; "O for a Thousand Tongues to Sing," 51-52; "On the Birthday of a Friend," 201; "On the Death of a Child," 169-70; "On the True Use of Musick," 268; "O Thou, who didst an Help ordain," 166-67; "Prayer for the Church of England," 285-86; *Prayers for Condemned Malefactors* (1778), 292; "The Preacher's Prayer for the Flock," 228-29; "Psalm LXXX — Adapted to the Church of England," 216; "Saviour of all, what hast Thou done," 241; "Saviour, Thou hast bestow'd on me," 205-6; *Short Hymns on Select Passages of Scripture* (1762), 246, 247-50, 270, 271, 275-77; "Sinners, lift up your hearts," 239-40; "Sinners, your Saviour see!", 236-37; "So easily are Bishops made," 311-12; "A Strife we are to All around," 216; "Suffering for another's sin," 206; "Sweet day! so cool, so calm, so bright!", 202-3; "Thanksgiving for an Escape From Being Crushed to Death," 293-94; "Thee Father, I praise," 293-94; "Thou GOD of Truth and Love," 164-65; "To the Rev. Mr. Whitefield," 121; "To the Same [Whitefield], Before His Voyage," 121-22; "To the Son," 53-54; "The Trial of Faith," 142-44, 241; "True Yokefellows," 314-15; "Two are Better far than one," 159-60; "Universal Redemption," 102-4, 127; "Wedding Song," 166-67; "Wesley himself and friends betrays," 310; "When first sent forth to minister the Word," 222; "Where Shall My Wondering Soul Begin?" 48-49; "Why should I longer, Lord, con-